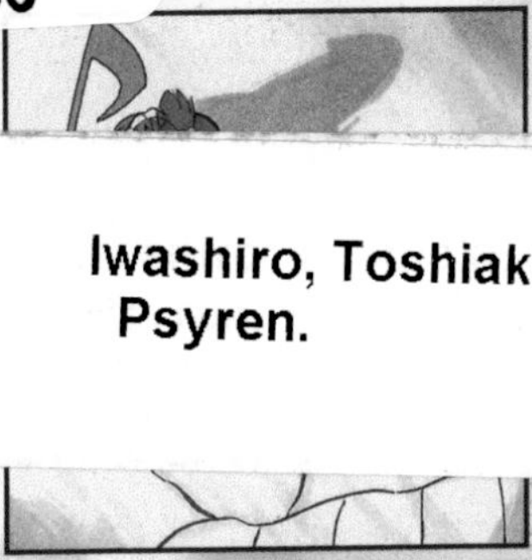

## Toshiaki Iwashiro

I've been given the opportunity to undertake a new challenge.
I look forward to spending many drowsy hours slaving over
my manuscripts.

I hope you like Ageha Yoshina and Sakurako Amamiya!

Toshiaki Iwashiro was born December 11, 1977, in Tokyo and
has the blood type of A. His debut manga was the popular
*Mieru Hito*, which ran from 2005 to 2007 in Japan in
*Weekly Shonen Jump*, where *Psyren* is currently serialized.

## PSYREN VOL. 1
## SHONEN JUMP Manga Edition

This graphic novel contains material that was originally published in
English in SHONEN JUMP #97–100. Artwork in the magazine may
have been slightly altered from that presented here.

### STORY AND ART BY TOSHIAKI IWASHIRO

Translation/Camellia Nieh
Lettering/Annaliese Christman
Design/Sam Elzway
Editors/John Bae, Joel Enos, Carrie Shepherd

PSYREN © 2007 by Toshiaki Iwashiro
All rights reserved.
First published in Japan in 2007 by SHUEISHA Inc., Tokyo.
English translation rights arranged by SHUEISHA Inc.

Printed in the U.S.A.

Published by VIZ Media, LLC
P.O. Box 77010
San Francisco, CA 94107

10 9 8 7 6 5 4 3 2 1
First printing, October 2011

www.viz.com

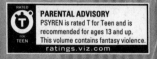

**PARENTAL ADVISORY**
PSYREN is rated T for Teen and is
recommended for ages 13 and up.
This volume contains fantasy violence.
ratings.viz.com

THE WORLD'S
MOST POPULAR MANGA

SHONEN JUMP

www.shonenjump.com

SHONEN JUMP MANGA EDITION

# PSYREN

## 1

### URBAN LEGEND

Story and Art by
**Toshiaki Iwashiro**

# PSYREN

## VOL. 1
## URBAN LEGEND

### CONTENTS

Call.1: Urban Legend .................................... 005

Call.2: Paradise .......................................... 073

Call.3: Danger Zone ................................... 099

Call.4: Alfred the Taboo ............................. 123

Call.5: Scenery .......................................... 143

Call.6: The Will to Survive ......................... 163

Call.7: The Return ...................................... 183

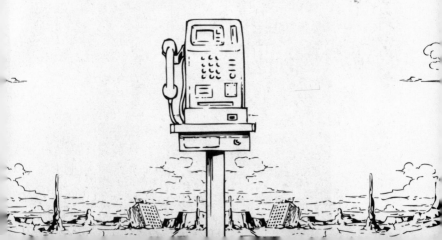

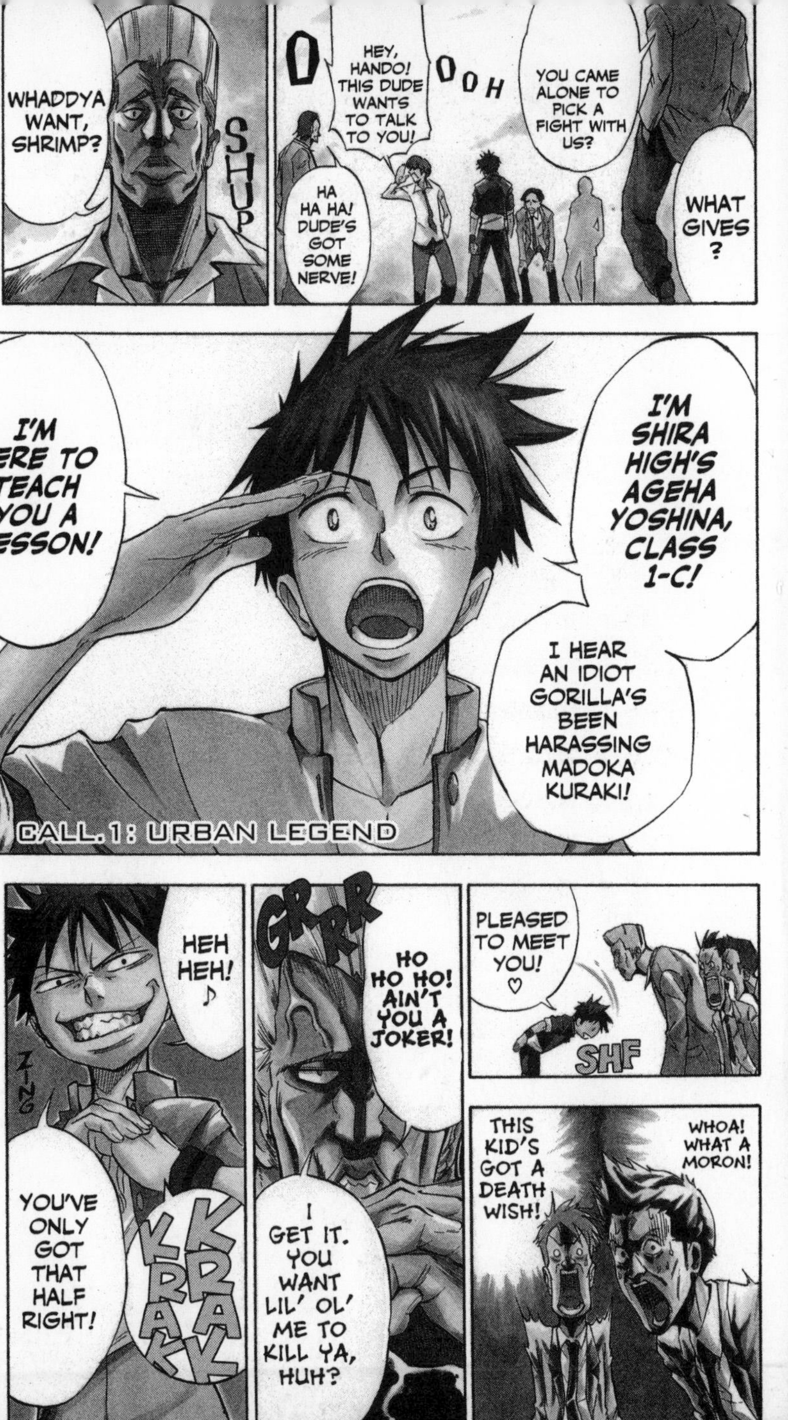
YOU CAME ALONE TO PICK A FIGHT WITH US?
WHAT GIVES?
OOOH
HEY, HANDO! THIS DUDE WANTS TO TALK TO YOU!
HA HA HA! DUDE'S GOT SOME NERVE!
WHADDYA WANT, SHRIMP?
SHUP
I'M SHIRA HIGH'S AGEHA YOSHINA, CLASS 1-C!
I HEAR AN IDIOT GORILLA'S BEEN HARASSING MADOKA KURAKI!
I'M HERE TO TEACH YOU A LESSON!
CALL. 1: URBAN LEGEND
PLEASED TO MEET YOU! ♡
SHF
WHOA! WHAT A MORON!
THIS KID'S GOT A DEATH WISH!
GRRR
HO HO HO! AIN'T YOU A JOKER!
I GET IT. YOU WANT LIL' OL' ME TO KILL YA, HUH?
HEH HEH! ♪
ZING
KRAK KRAK
YOU'VE ONLY GOT THAT HALF RIGHT!

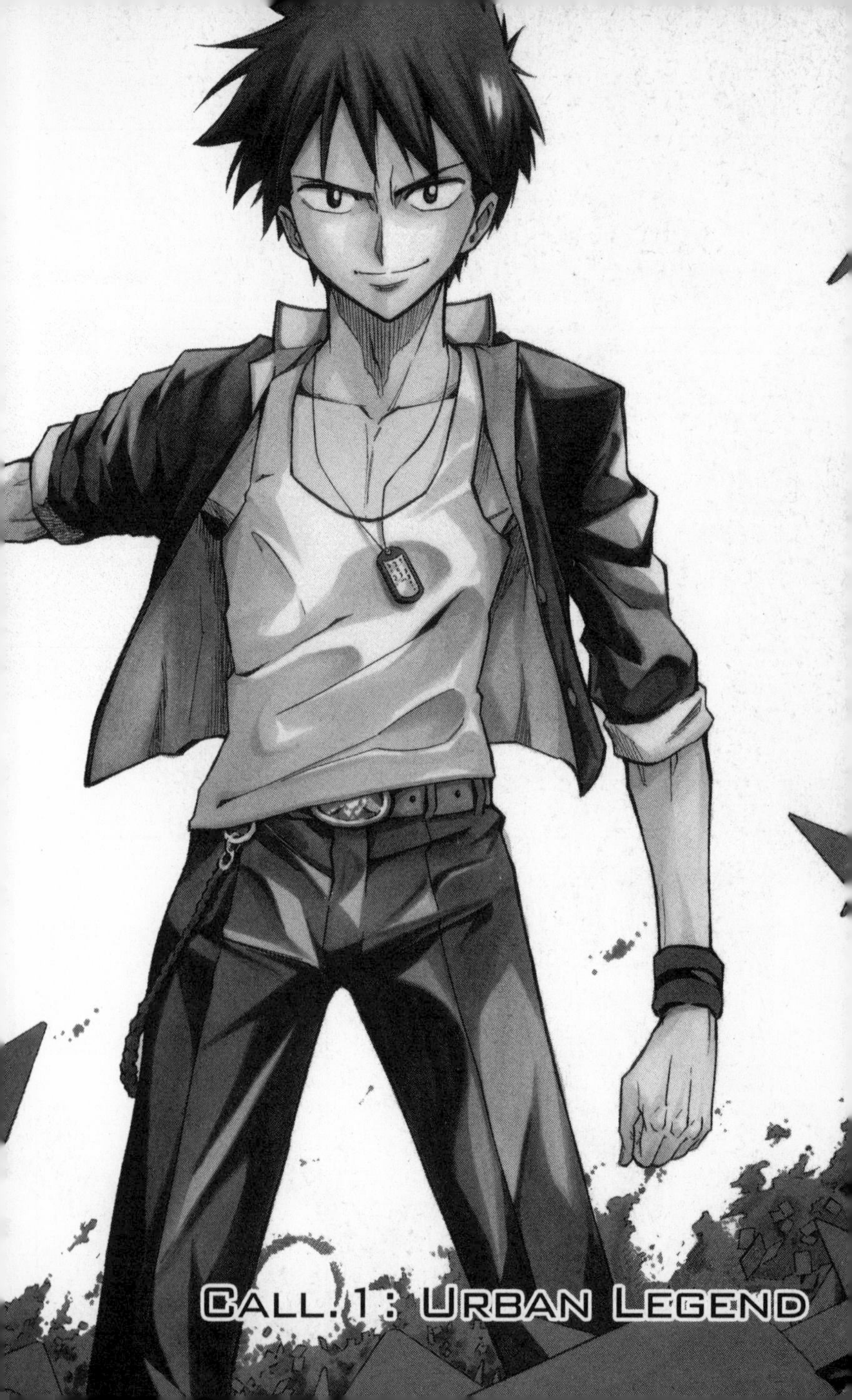
Call. 1: Urban Legend

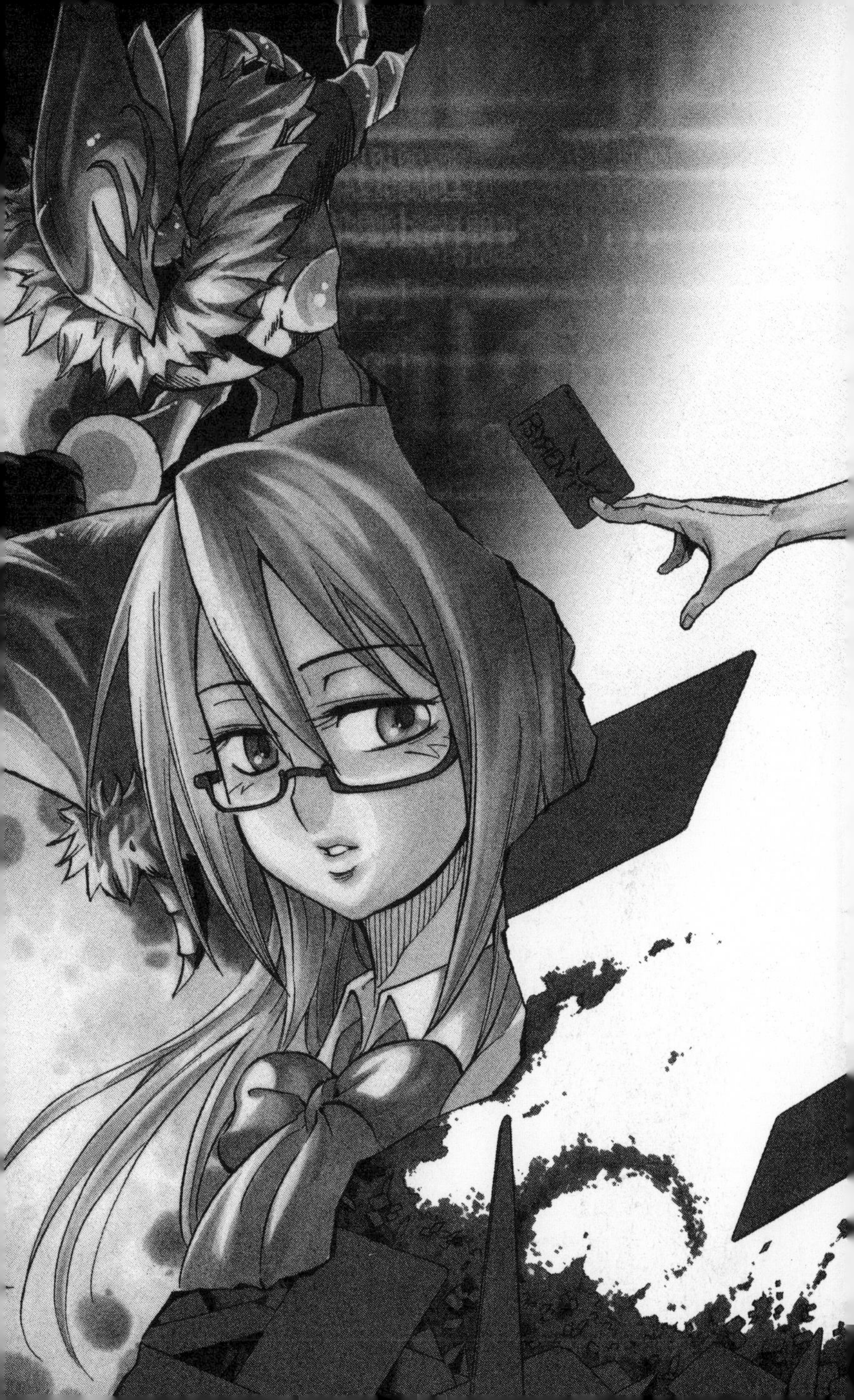

PSYREN

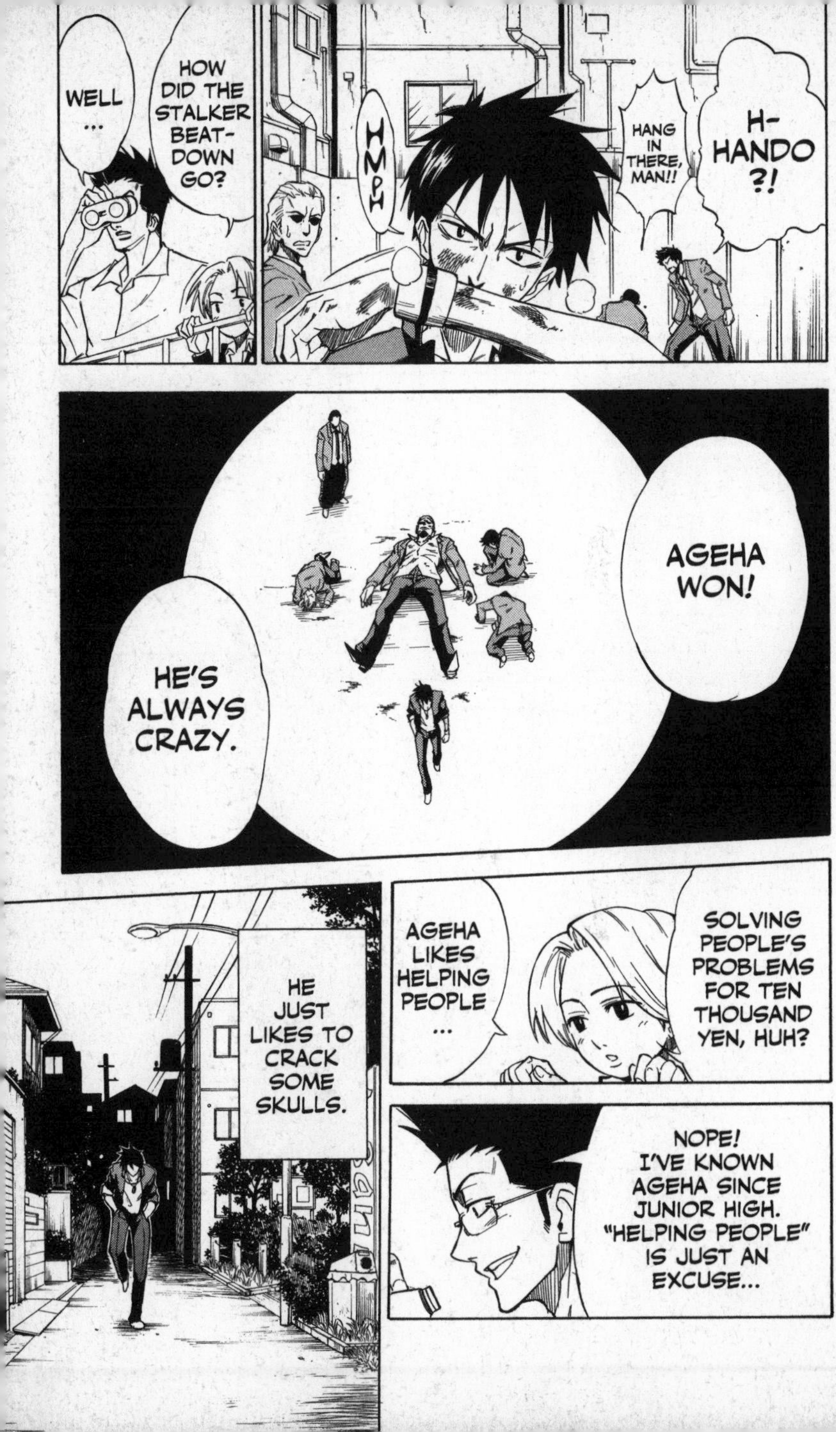
H-HANDO?!
HANG IN THERE, MAN!!
HMPH
HOW DID THE STALKER BEAT-DOWN GO?
WELL...
AGEHA WON!
HE'S ALWAYS CRAZY.
SOLVING PEOPLE'S PROBLEMS FOR TEN THOUSAND YEN, HUH?
AGEHA LIKES HELPING PEOPLE...
NOPE! I'VE KNOWN AGEHA SINCE JUNIOR HIGH. "HELPING PEOPLE" IS JUST AN EXCUSE...
HE JUST LIKES TO CRACK SOME SKULLS.

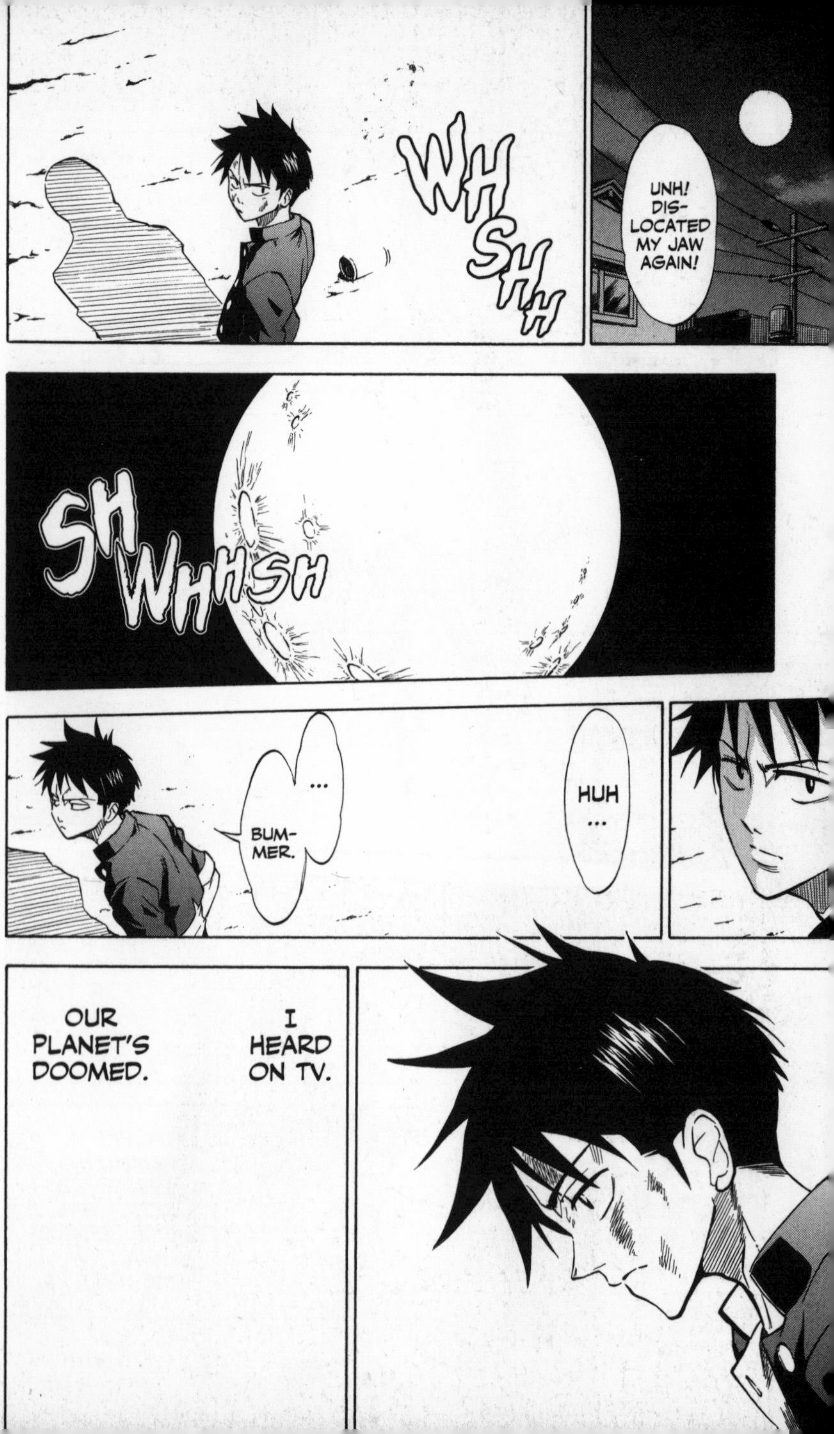
UNH! DIS-LOCATED MY JAW AGAIN!
WHSHH
SH WHHSH
HUH ...
... BUMMER.
I HEARD ON TV.
OUR PLANET'S DOOMED.

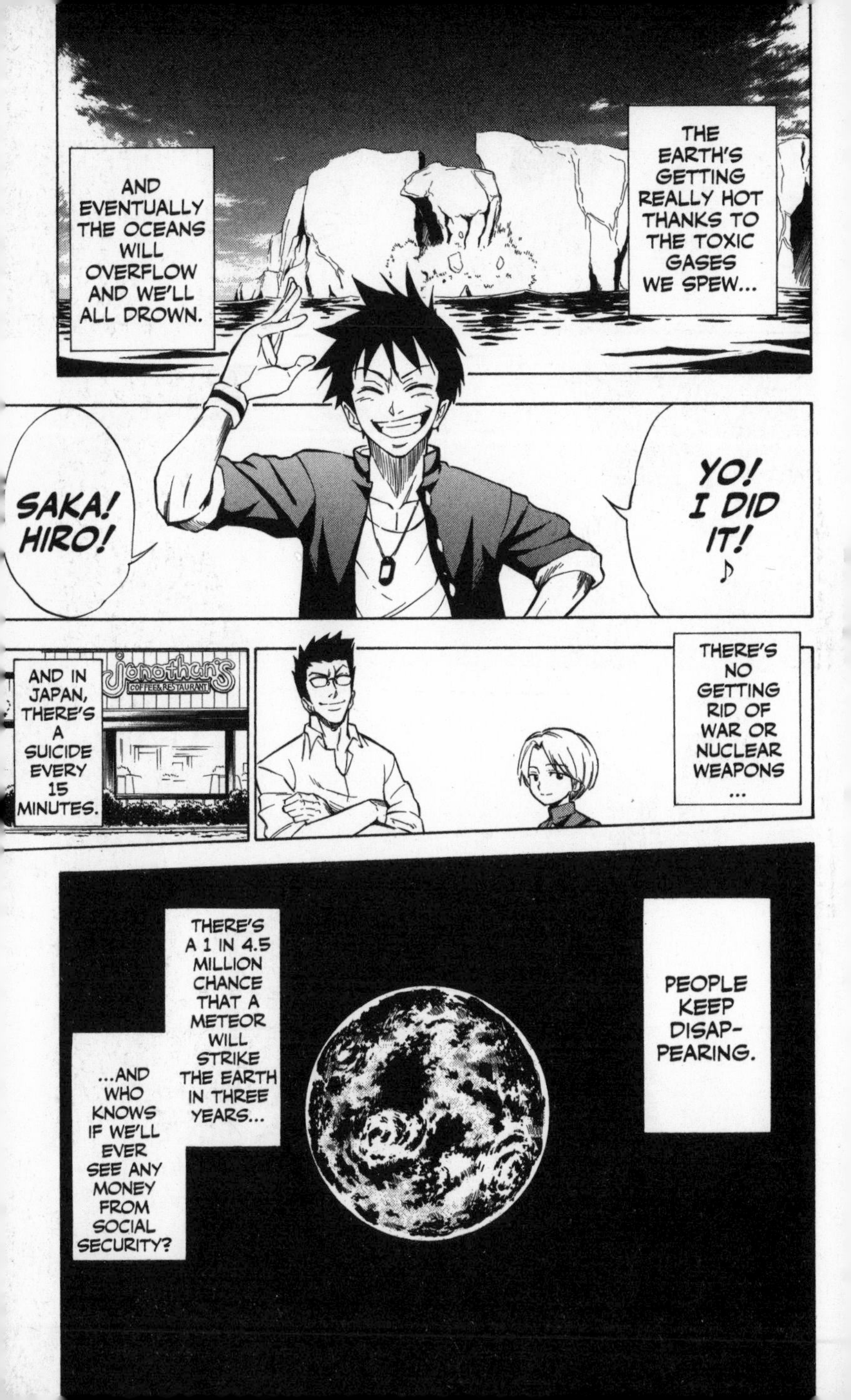
THE EARTH'S GETTING REALLY HOT THANKS TO THE TOXIC GASES WE SPEW...
AND EVENTUALLY THE OCEANS WILL OVERFLOW AND WE'LL ALL DROWN.
YO! I DID IT! ♪
SAKA! HIRO!
THERE'S NO GETTING RID OF WAR OR NUCLEAR WEAPONS ...
jonathan's
COFFEE & RESTAURANT
AND IN JAPAN, THERE'S A SUICIDE EVERY 15 MINUTES.
PEOPLE KEEP DISAP-PEARING.
THERE'S A 1 IN 4.5 MILLION CHANCE THAT A METEOR WILL STRIKE THE EARTH IN THREE YEARS...
...AND WHO KNOWS IF WE'LL EVER SEE ANY MONEY FROM SOCIAL SECURITY?

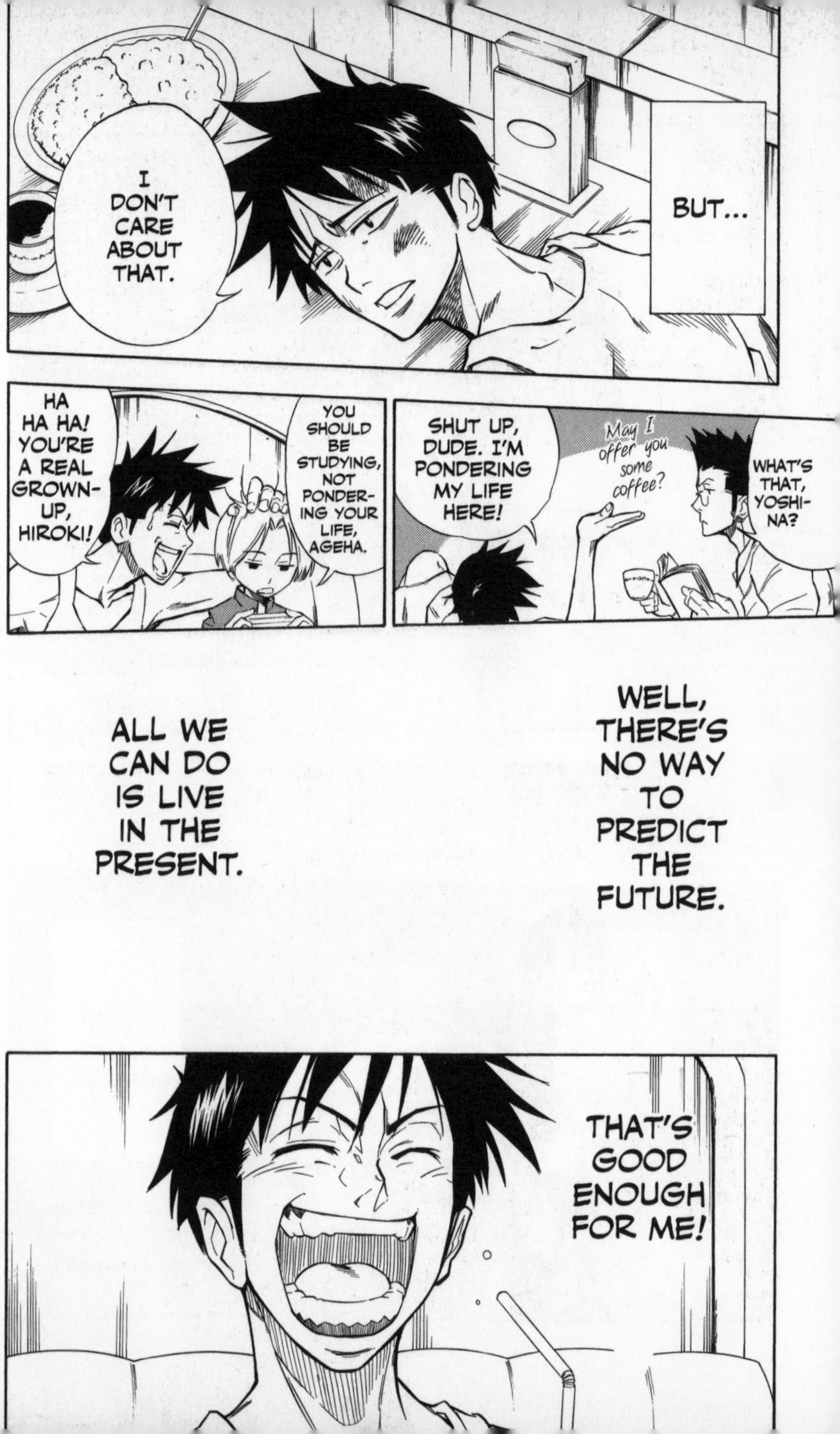
BUT...
I DON'T CARE ABOUT THAT.
WHAT'S THAT, YOSHINA?
May I offer you some coffee?
SHUT UP, DUDE. I'M PONDERING MY LIFE HERE!
YOU SHOULD BE STUDYING, NOT PONDERING YOUR LIFE, AGEHA.
HA HA HA! YOU'RE A REAL GROWN-UP, HIROKI!
WELL, THERE'S NO WAY TO PREDICT THE FUTURE.
ALL WE CAN DO IS LIVE IN THE PRESENT.
THAT'S GOOD ENOUGH FOR ME!

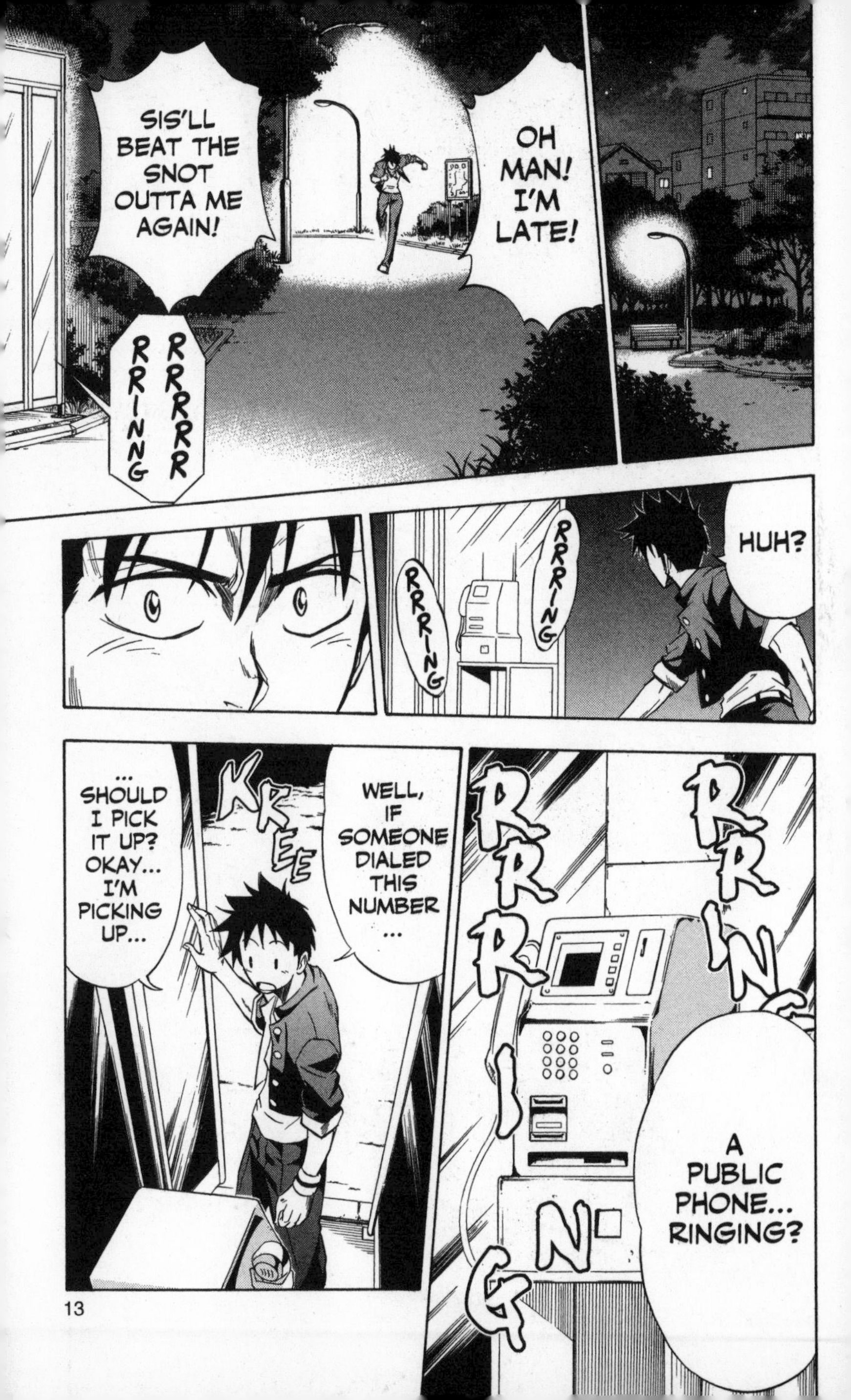
OH MAN! I'M LATE!
SIS'LL BEAT THE SNOT OUTTA ME AGAIN!
RRRRRR
RRINNG
HUH?
RRRING
RRRING
RRING
A PUBLIC PHONE... RINGING?
RRRING
WELL, IF SOMEONE DIALED THIS NUMBER ...
KREE
... SHOULD I PICK IT UP? OKAY... I'M PICKING UP...

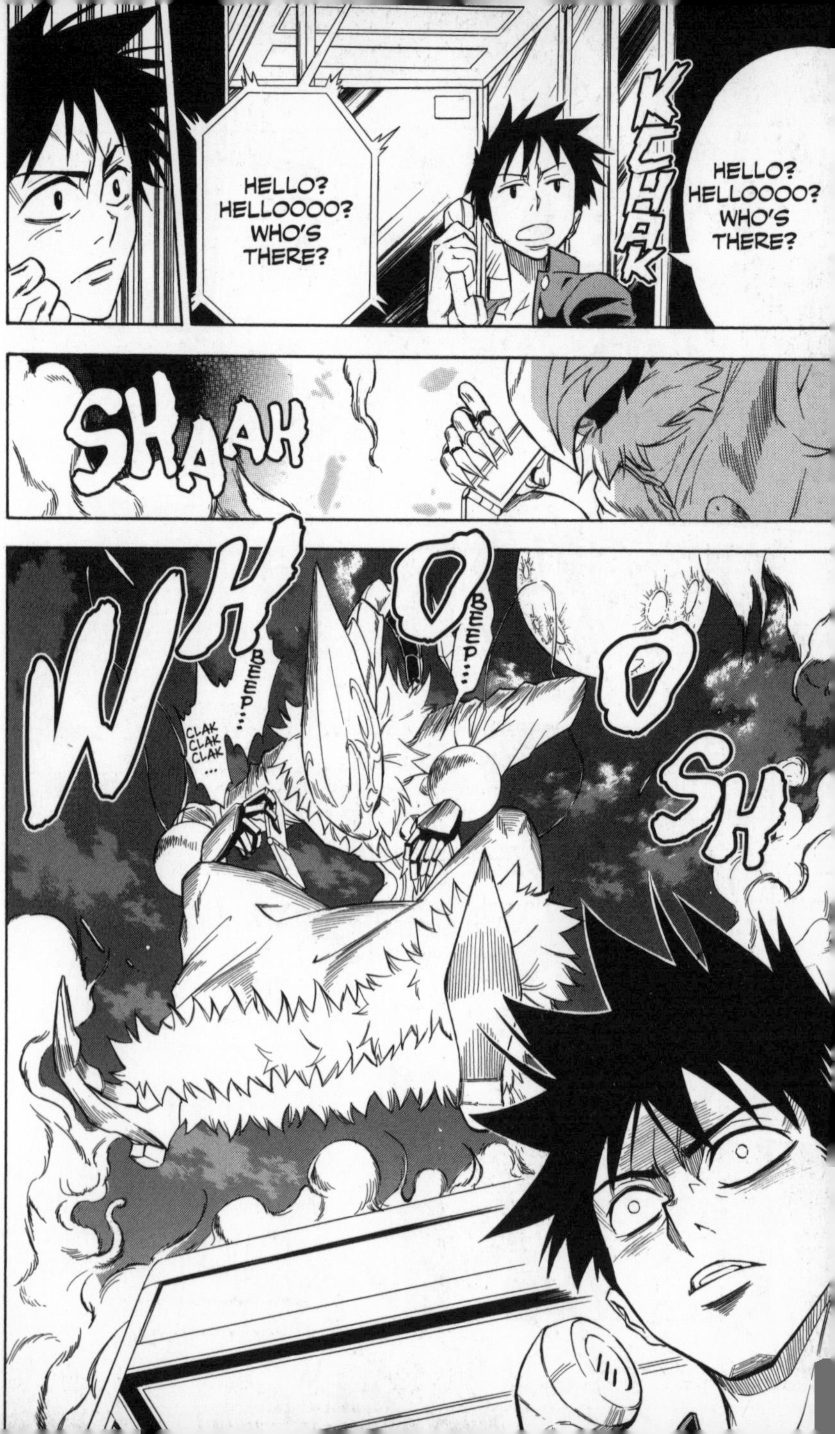

KCHAK
HELLO? HELLOOOO? WHO'S THERE?
HELLO? HELLOOOO? WHO'S THERE?
SHAAH
WHOOOSH
BEEP...
BEEP...
CLAK CLAK CLAK...

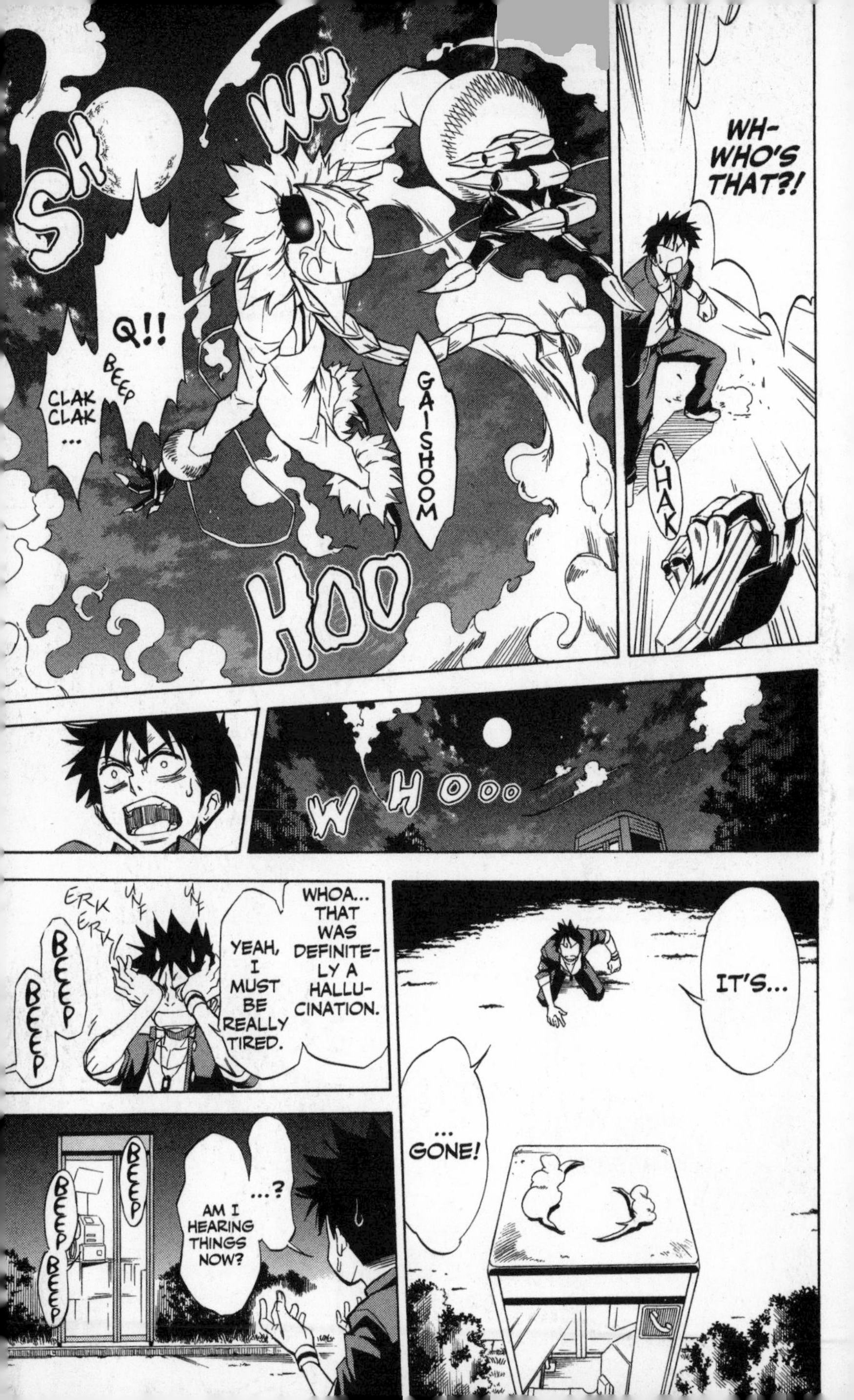
WH-
WHO'S
THAT?!
CHAK
SHWHHOO
Q!!
BEEP
CLAK CLAK ...
GAISHOOM
WHOOO
IT'S...
... GONE!
WHOA... THAT WAS DEFINITE-LY A HALLU-CINATION.
YEAH, I MUST BE REALLY TIRED.
ERK ERK
UNF UNF
BEEP BEEP BEEP
...?
AM I HEARING THINGS NOW?
BEEP BEEP BEEP BEEP

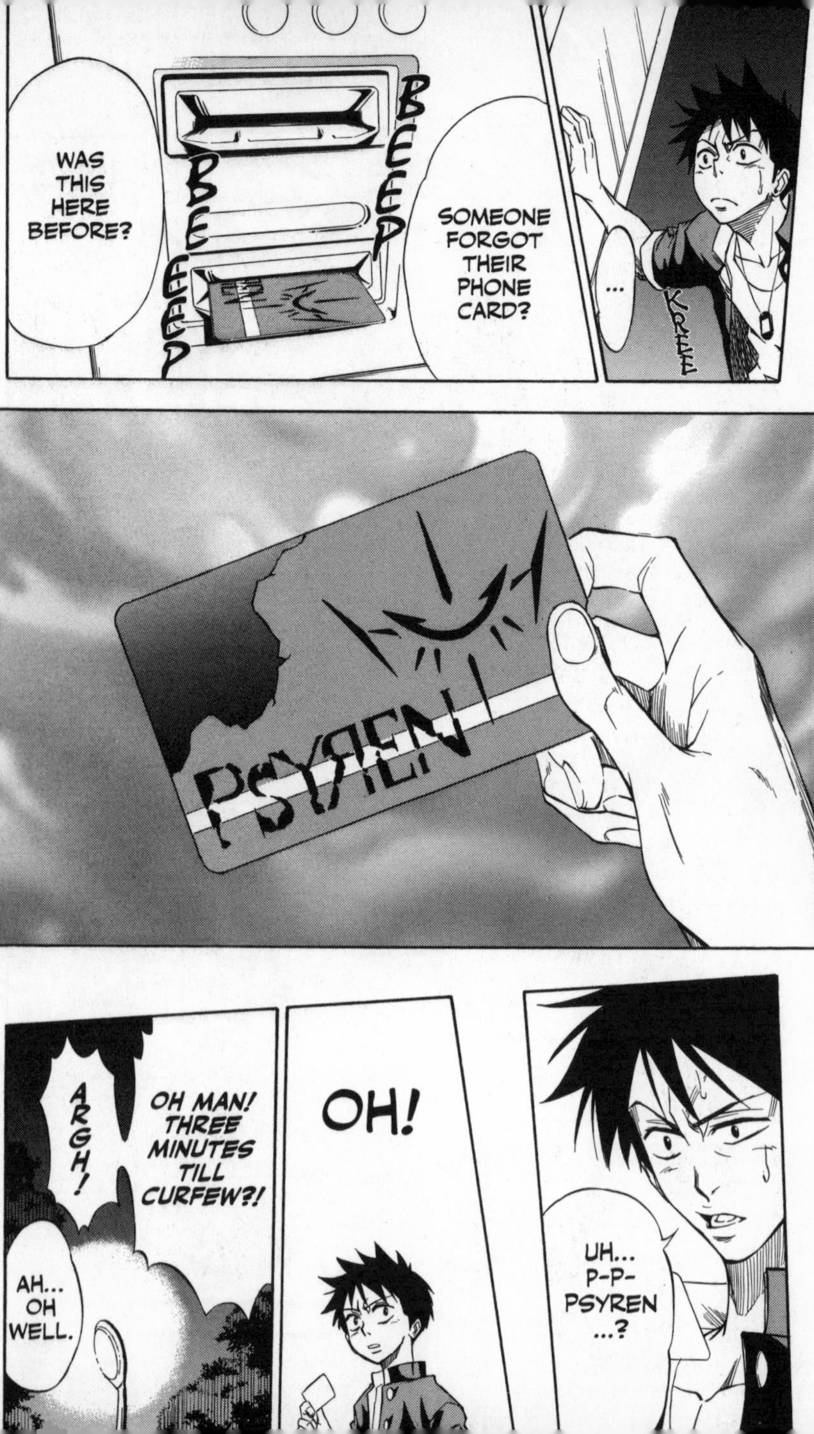
...
KREEE
BEEP
SOMEONE FORGOT THEIR PHONE CARD?
WAS THIS HERE BEFORE?
BEEEEP
PSYREN
UH... P-P-PSYREN ...?
OH!
ARGH!
OH MAN! THREE MINUTES TILL CURFEW?!
AH... OH WELL.

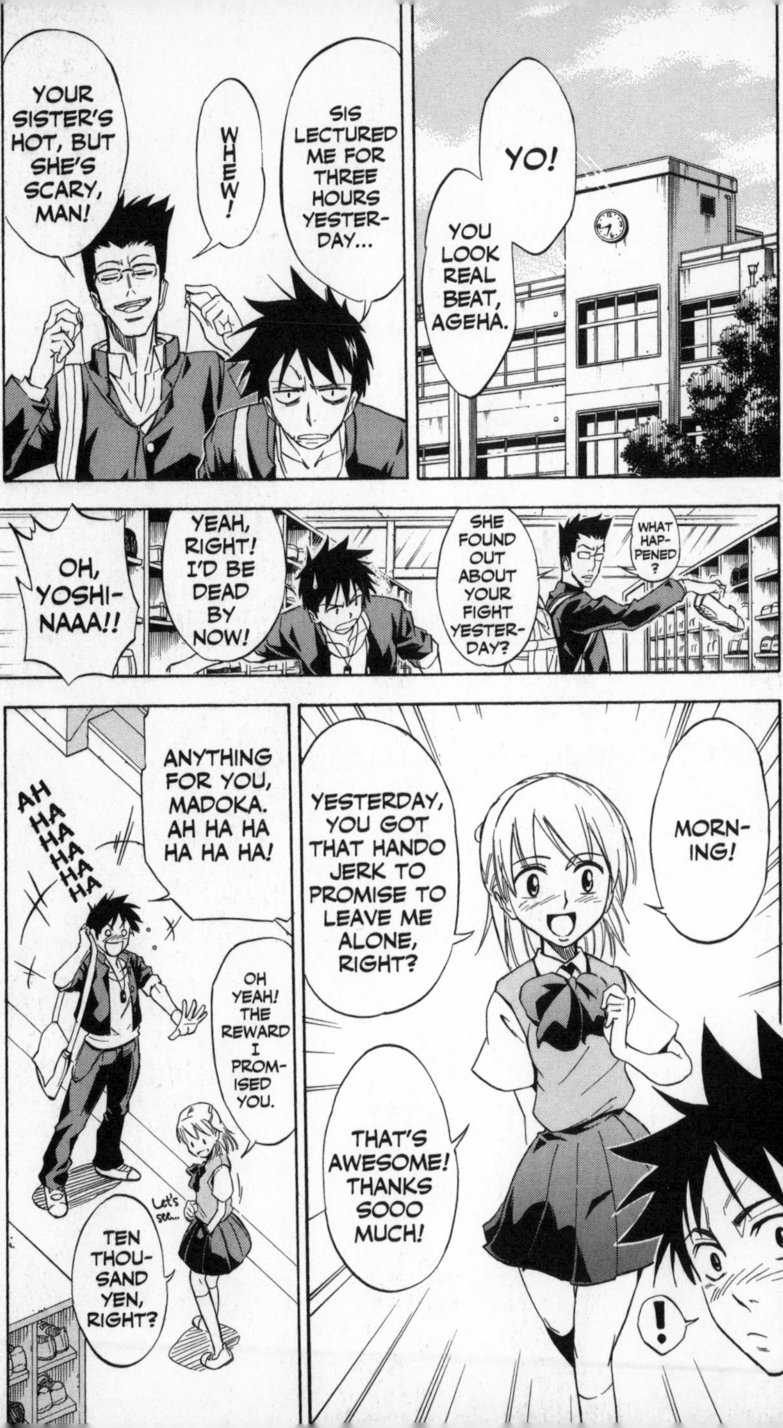
YO!
YOU LOOK REAL BEAT, AGEHA.
SIS LECTURED ME FOR THREE HOURS YESTERDAY...
WHEW!
YOUR SISTER'S HOT, BUT SHE'S SCARY, MAN!
WHAT HAPPENED?
SHE FOUND OUT ABOUT YOUR FIGHT YESTERDAY?
YEAH, RIGHT! I'D BE DEAD BY NOW!
OH, YOSHINAAA!!
MORNING!
YESTERDAY, YOU GOT THAT HANDO JERK TO PROMISE TO LEAVE ME ALONE, RIGHT?
THAT'S AWESOME! THANKS SOOO MUCH!
!
ANYTHING FOR YOU, MADOKA. AH HA HA HA HA HA!
AH HA HA HA HA HA HA
OH YEAH! THE REWARD I PROMISED YOU.
Let's see...
TEN THOUSAND YEN, RIGHT?

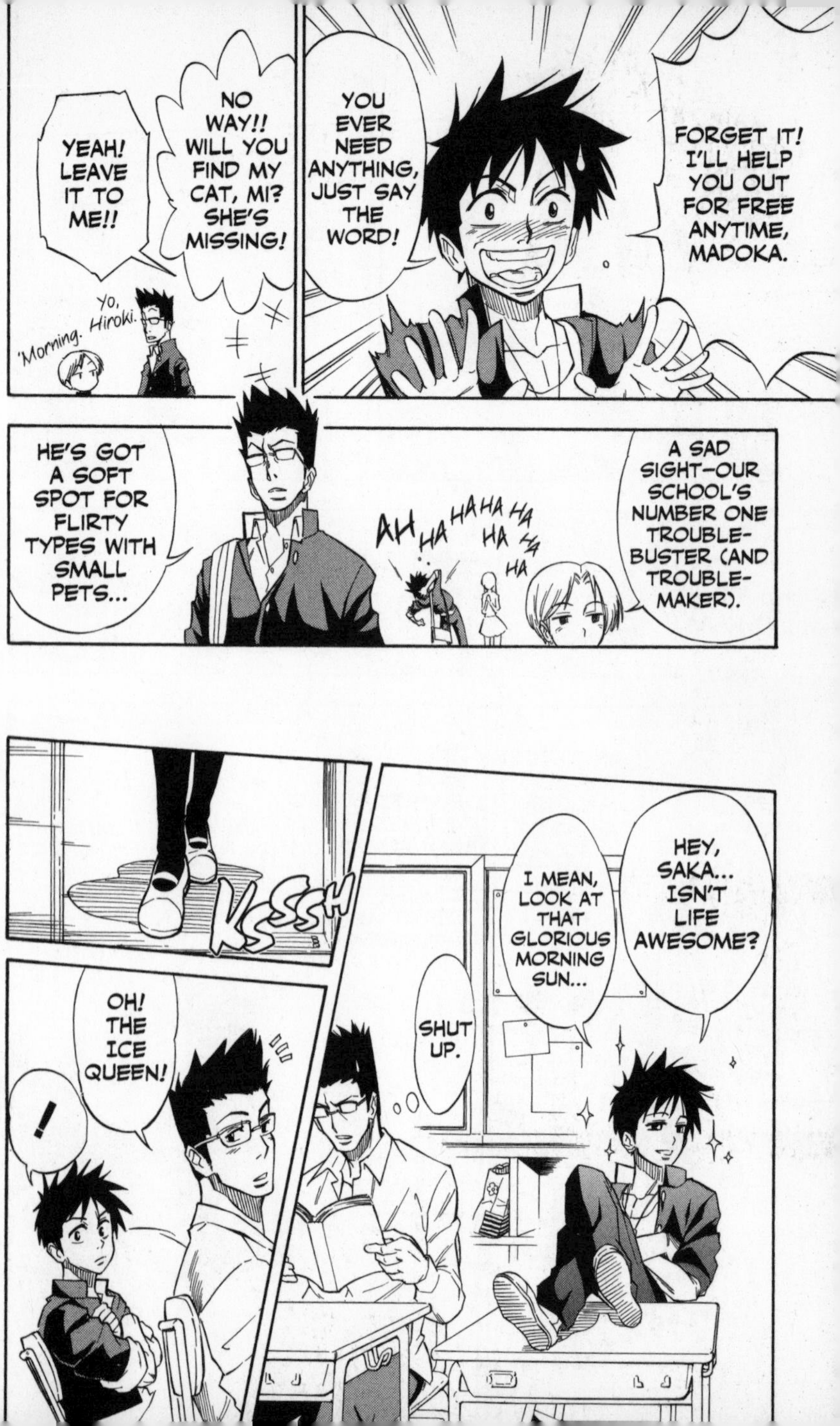
FORGET IT! I'LL HELP YOU OUT FOR FREE ANYTIME, MADOKA.
YOU EVER NEED ANYTHING, JUST SAY THE WORD!
NO WAY!! WILL YOU FIND MY CAT, MI? SHE'S MISSING!
YEAH! LEAVE IT TO ME!!
Yo, Hiroki.
'Morning.
A SAD SIGHT—OUR SCHOOL'S NUMBER ONE TROUBLE-BUSTER (AND TROUBLE-MAKER).
AH HA HA HA HA HA HA HA HA
HE'S GOT A SOFT SPOT FOR FLIRTY TYPES WITH SMALL PETS...
HEY, SAKA... ISN'T LIFE AWESOME?
I MEAN, LOOK AT THAT GLORIOUS MORNING SUN...
SHUT UP.
KSSSH
OH! THE ICE QUEEN!
!

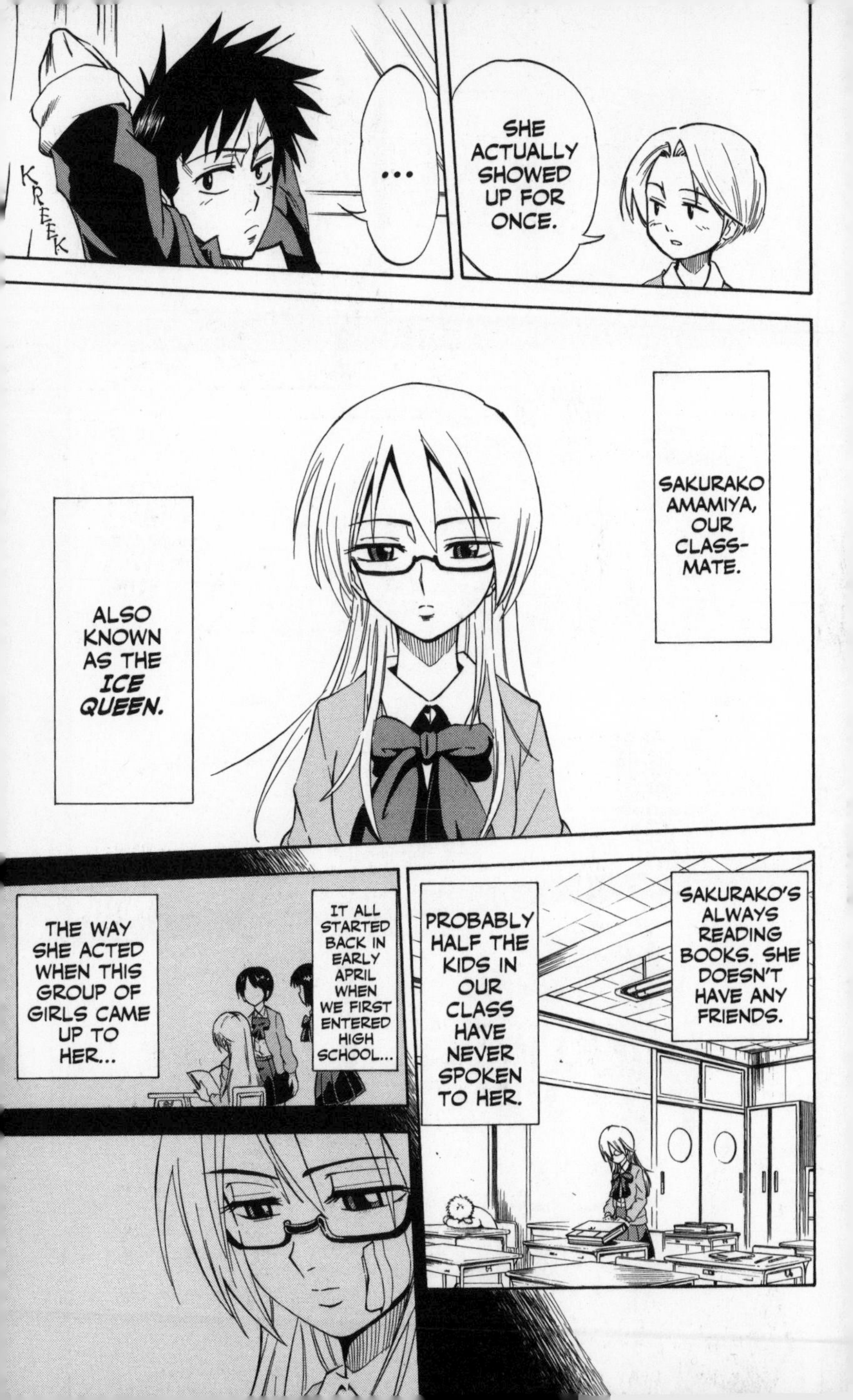
SHE ACTUALLY SHOWED UP FOR ONCE.
...
KREEK
SAKURAKO AMAMIYA, OUR CLASS-MATE.
ALSO KNOWN AS THE *ICE QUEEN.*
SAKURAKO'S ALWAYS READING BOOKS. SHE DOESN'T HAVE ANY FRIENDS.
PROBABLY HALF THE KIDS IN OUR CLASS HAVE NEVER SPOKEN TO HER.
IT ALL STARTED BACK IN EARLY APRIL WHEN WE FIRST ENTERED HIGH SCHOOL...
THE WAY SHE ACTED WHEN THIS GROUP OF GIRLS CAME UP TO HER...

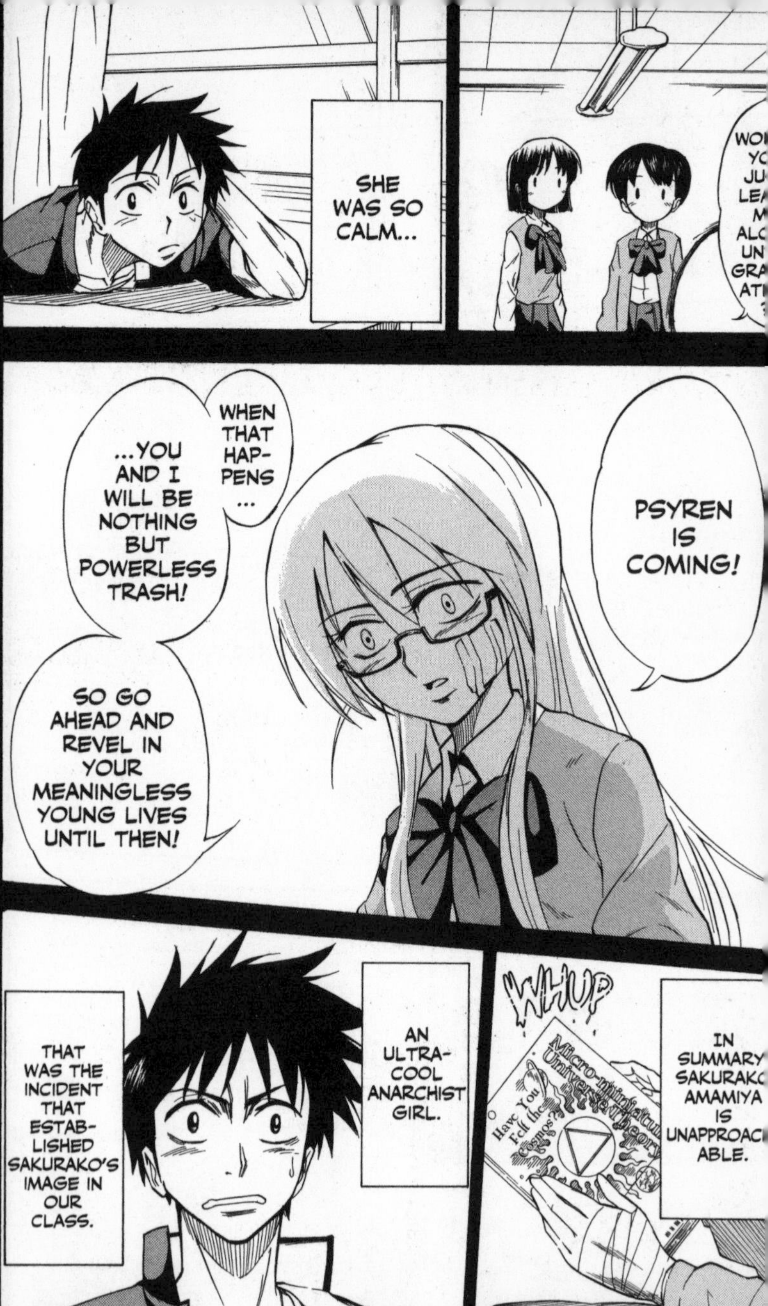
SHE WAS SO CALM...
PSYREN IS COMING!
WHEN THAT HAP- PENS ...
...YOU AND I WILL BE NOTHING BUT POWERLESS TRASH!
SO GO AHEAD AND REVEL IN YOUR MEANINGLESS YOUNG LIVES UNTIL THEN!
WHUP
IN SUMMARY SAKURAKO AMAMIYA IS UNAPPROAC ABLE.
Have You Felt the Cosmos?
AN ULTRA- COOL ANARCHIST GIRL.
THAT WAS THE INCIDENT THAT ESTAB- LISHED SAKURAKO'S IMAGE IN OUR CLASS.

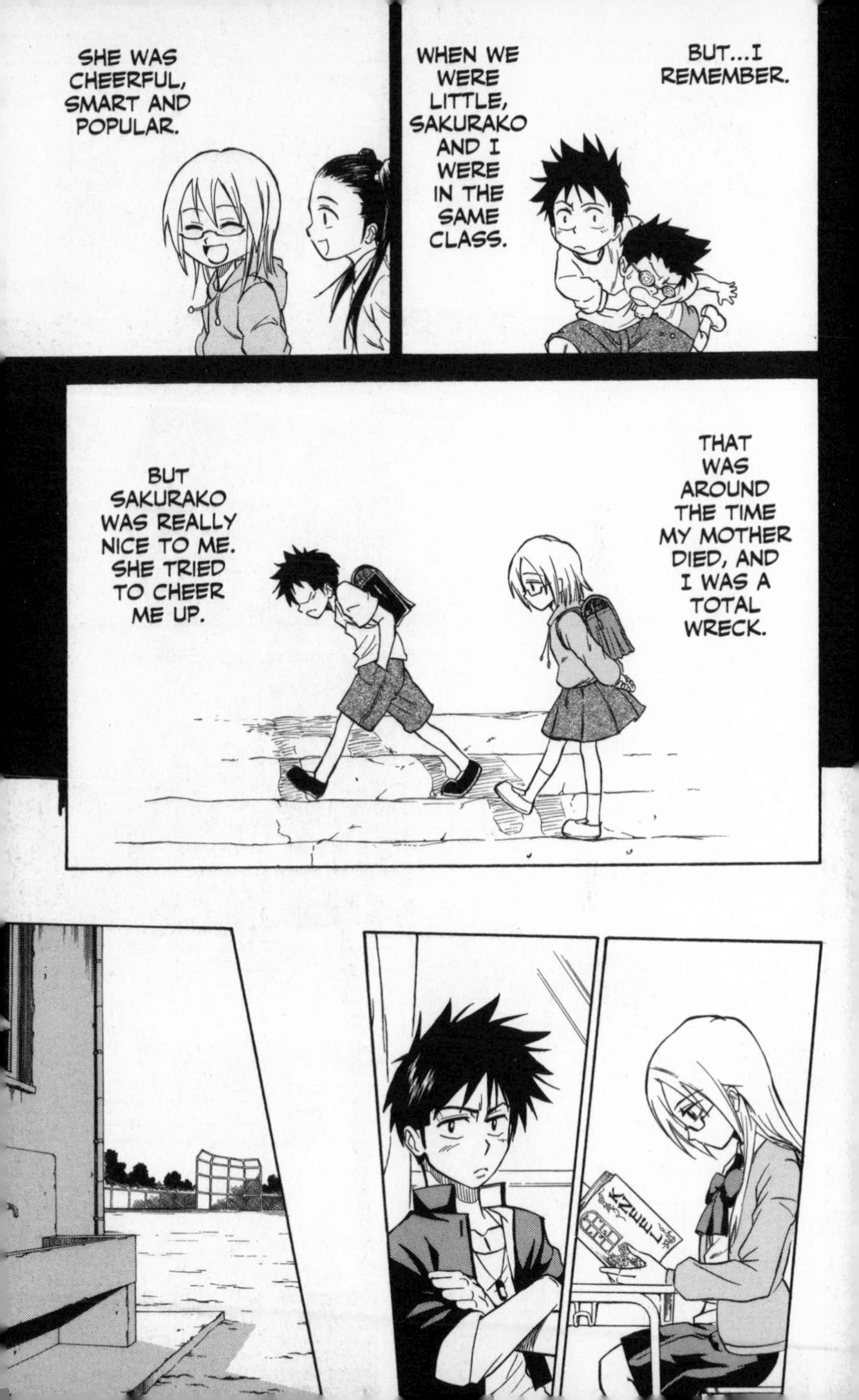
BUT...I REMEMBER.
WHEN WE WERE LITTLE, SAKURAKO AND I WERE IN THE SAME CLASS.
SHE WAS CHEERFUL, SMART AND POPULAR.
THAT WAS AROUND THE TIME MY MOTHER DIED, AND I WAS A TOTAL WRECK.
BUT SAKURAKO WAS REALLY NICE TO ME. SHE TRIED TO CHEER ME UP.

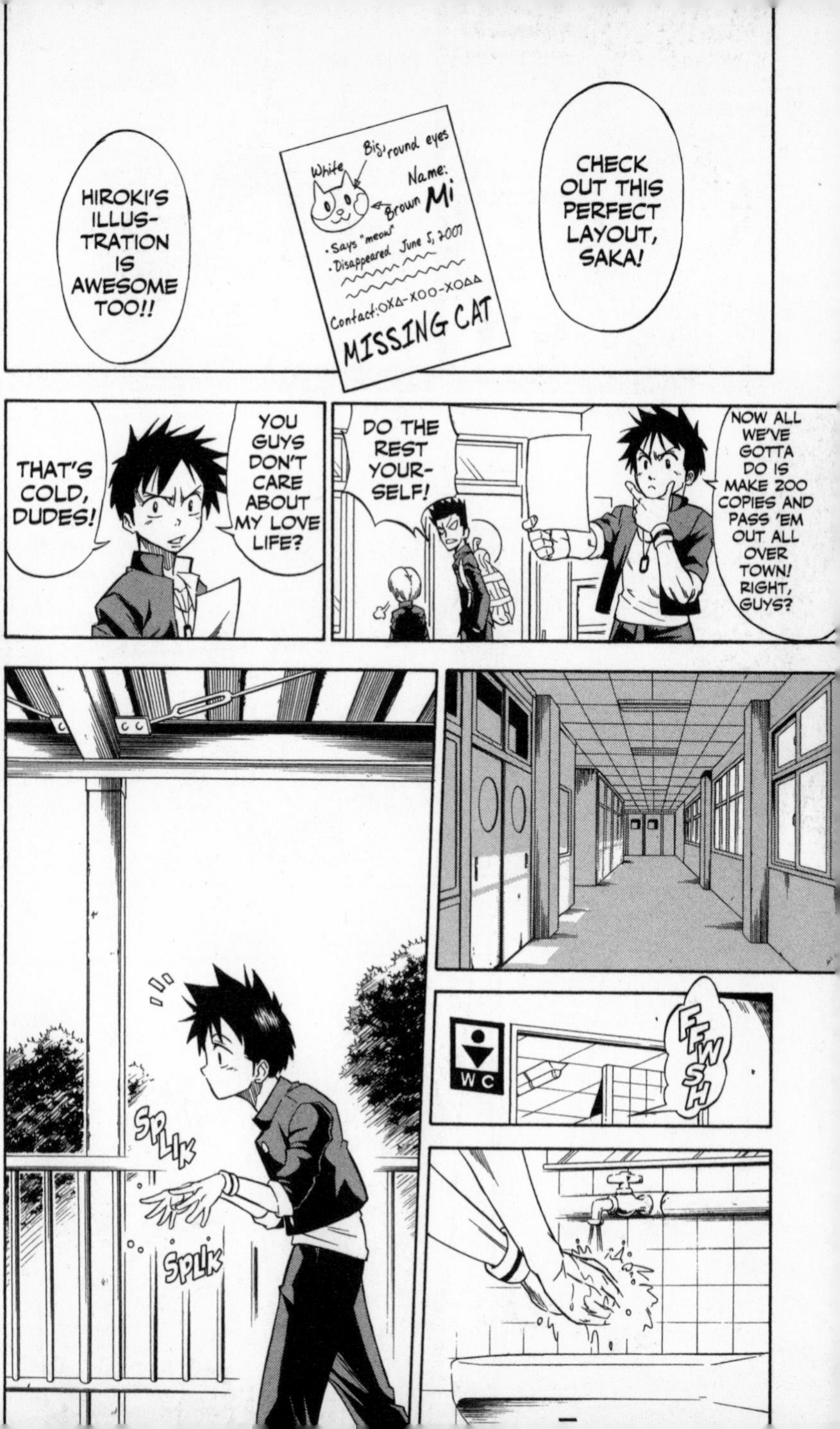
CHECK OUT THIS PERFECT LAYOUT, SAKA!
Big, round eyes
White
Name: Mi
Brown
• Says "meow"
• Disappeared June 5, 2007
Contact: OXΔ-XOO-XOΔΔ
MISSING CAT
HIROKI'S ILLUS-TRATION IS AWESOME TOO!!
NOW ALL WE'VE GOTTA DO IS MAKE 200 COPIES AND PASS 'EM OUT ALL OVER TOWN! RIGHT, GUYS?
DO THE REST YOUR-SELF!
YOU GUYS DON'T CARE ABOUT MY LOVE LIFE?
THAT'S COLD, DUDES!
WC
FFWSH
SPLIK
SPLIK

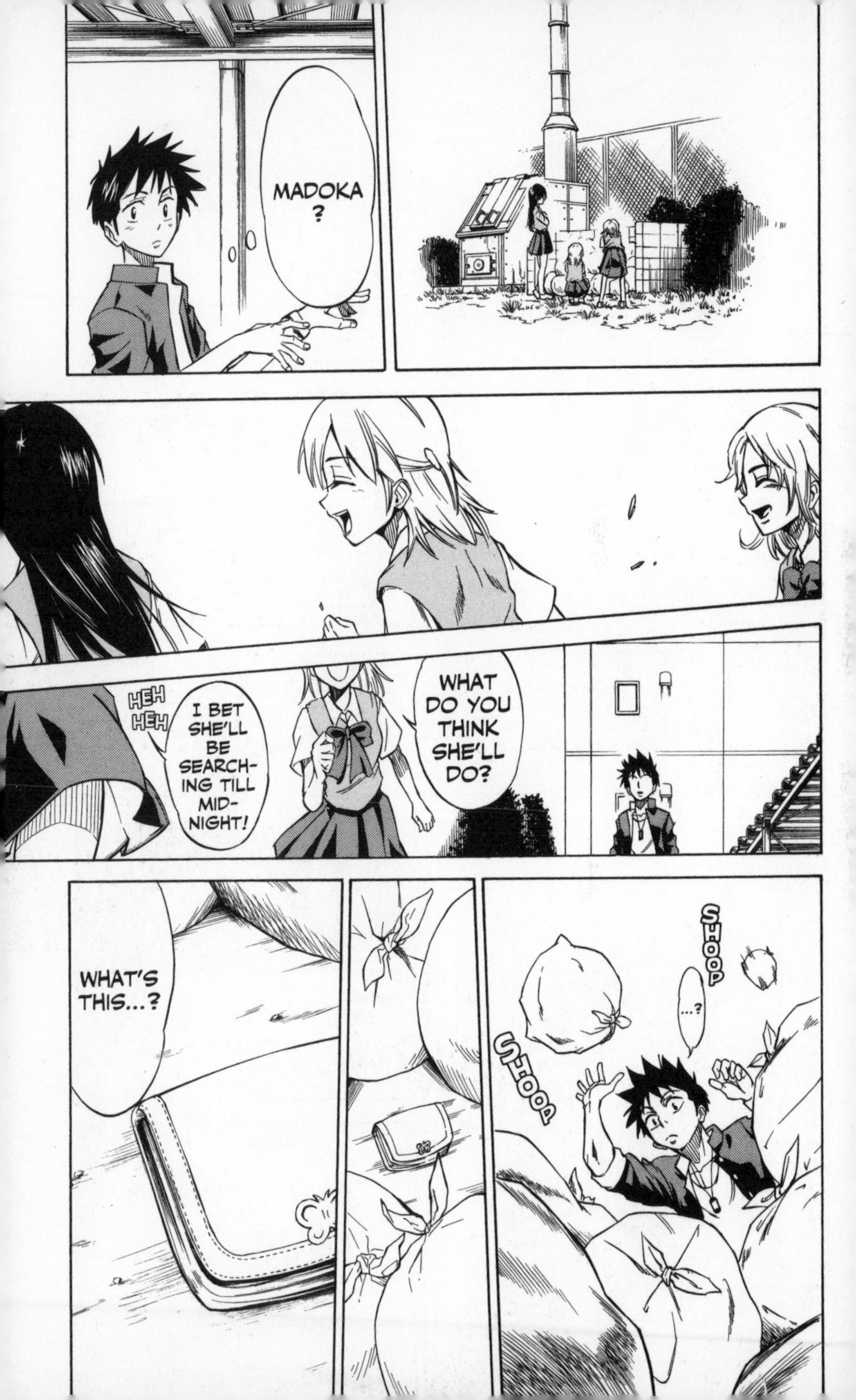
MADOKA ?
WHAT DO YOU THINK SHE'LL DO?
I BET SHE'LL BE SEARCHING TILL MIDNIGHT!
HEH HEH
SHOOP
...?
SHOOP
WHAT'S THIS...?

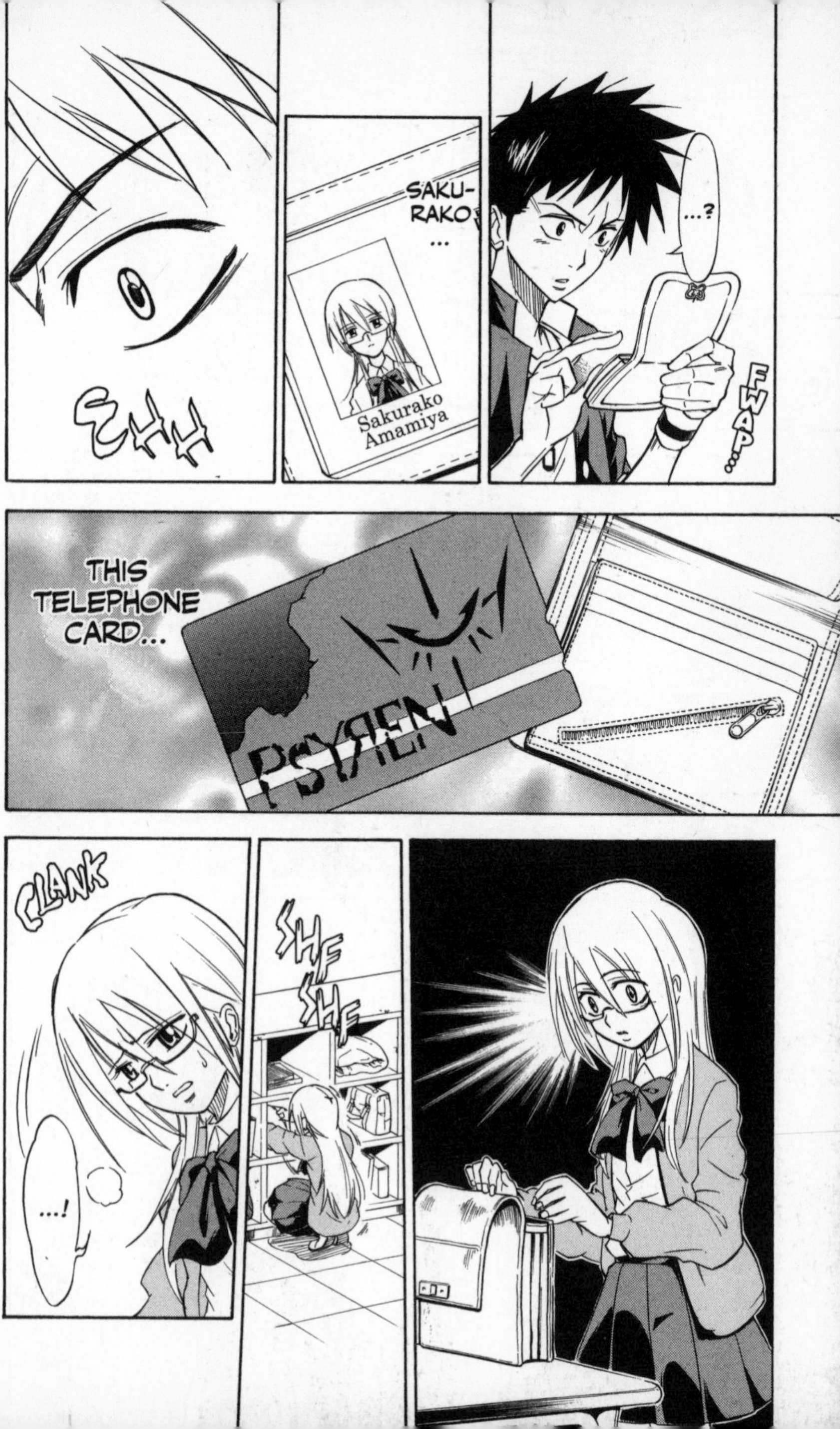
...?
FWAP...
SAKU-RAKO...
Sakurako Amamiya
EHH
THIS TELEPHONE CARD...
PSYREN
SHF SHF
CLANK
...!

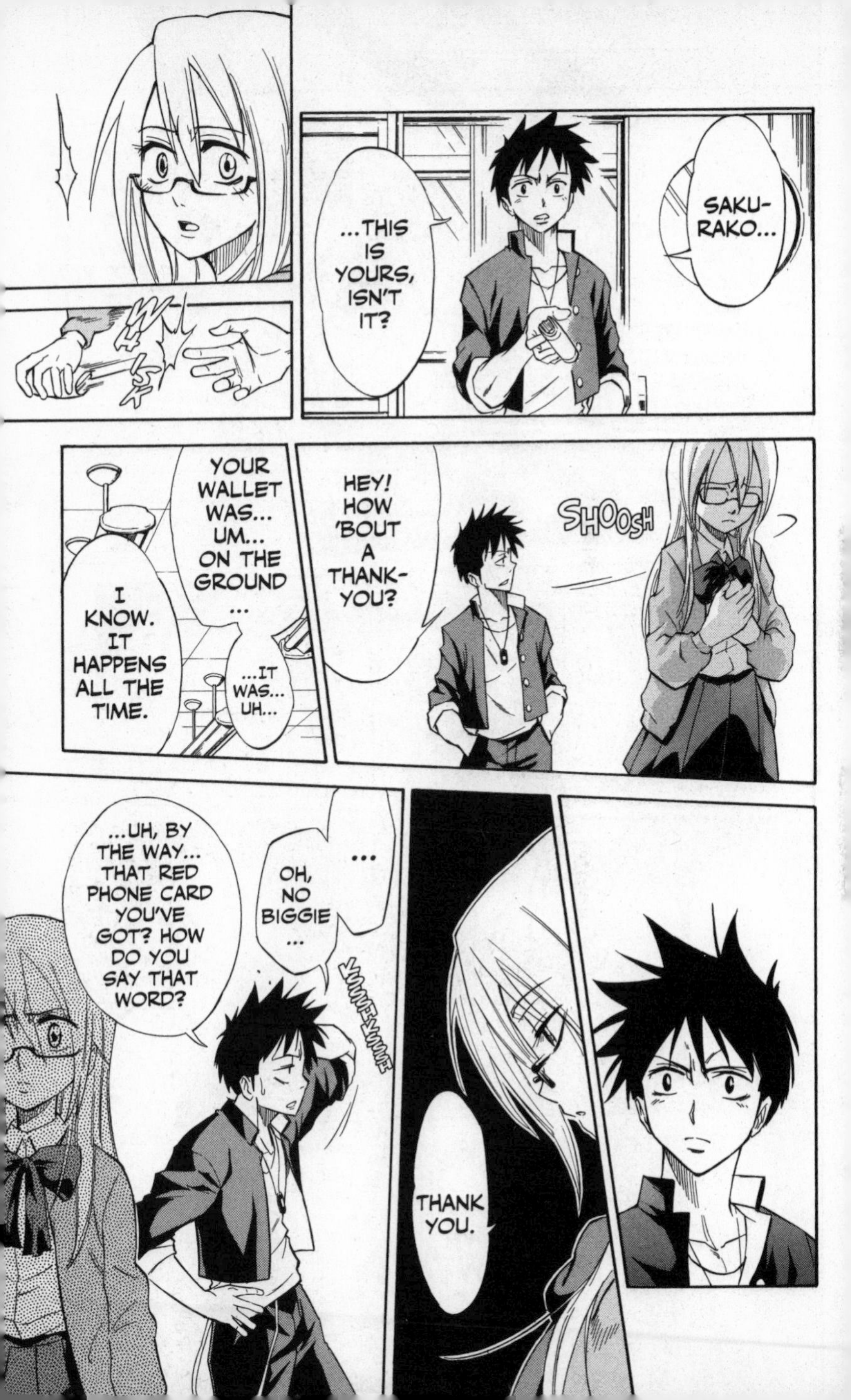
SAKU-RAKO...
...THIS IS YOURS, ISN'T IT?
WHISK
SHOOSH
HEY! HOW 'BOUT A THANK-YOU?
YOUR WALLET WAS... UM... ON THE GROUND...
...IT WAS... UH...
I KNOW. IT HAPPENS ALL THE TIME.
THANK YOU.
...
OH, NO BIGGIE...
...UH, BY THE WAY... THAT RED PHONE CARD YOU'VE GOT? HOW DO YOU SAY THAT WORD?

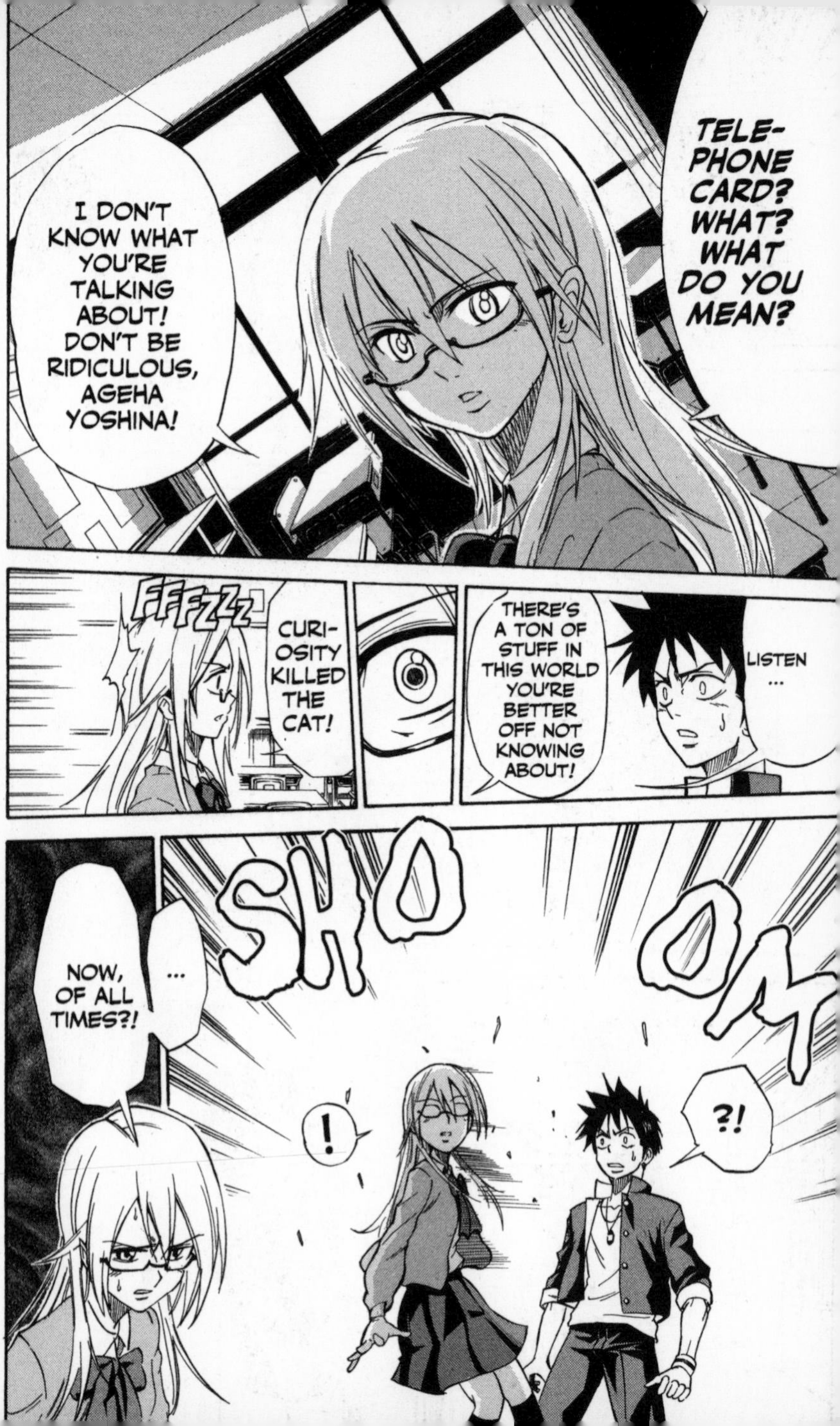
TELE-PHONE CARD? WHAT? WHAT DO YOU MEAN?
I DON'T KNOW WHAT YOU'RE TALKING ABOUT! DON'T BE RIDICULOUS, AGEHA YOSHINA!
LISTEN ...
THERE'S A TON OF STUFF IN THIS WORLD YOU'RE BETTER OFF NOT KNOWING ABOUT!
CURI-OSITY KILLED THE CAT!
FFFZZZ
SHO OM
?!
!
...
NOW, OF ALL TIMES?!

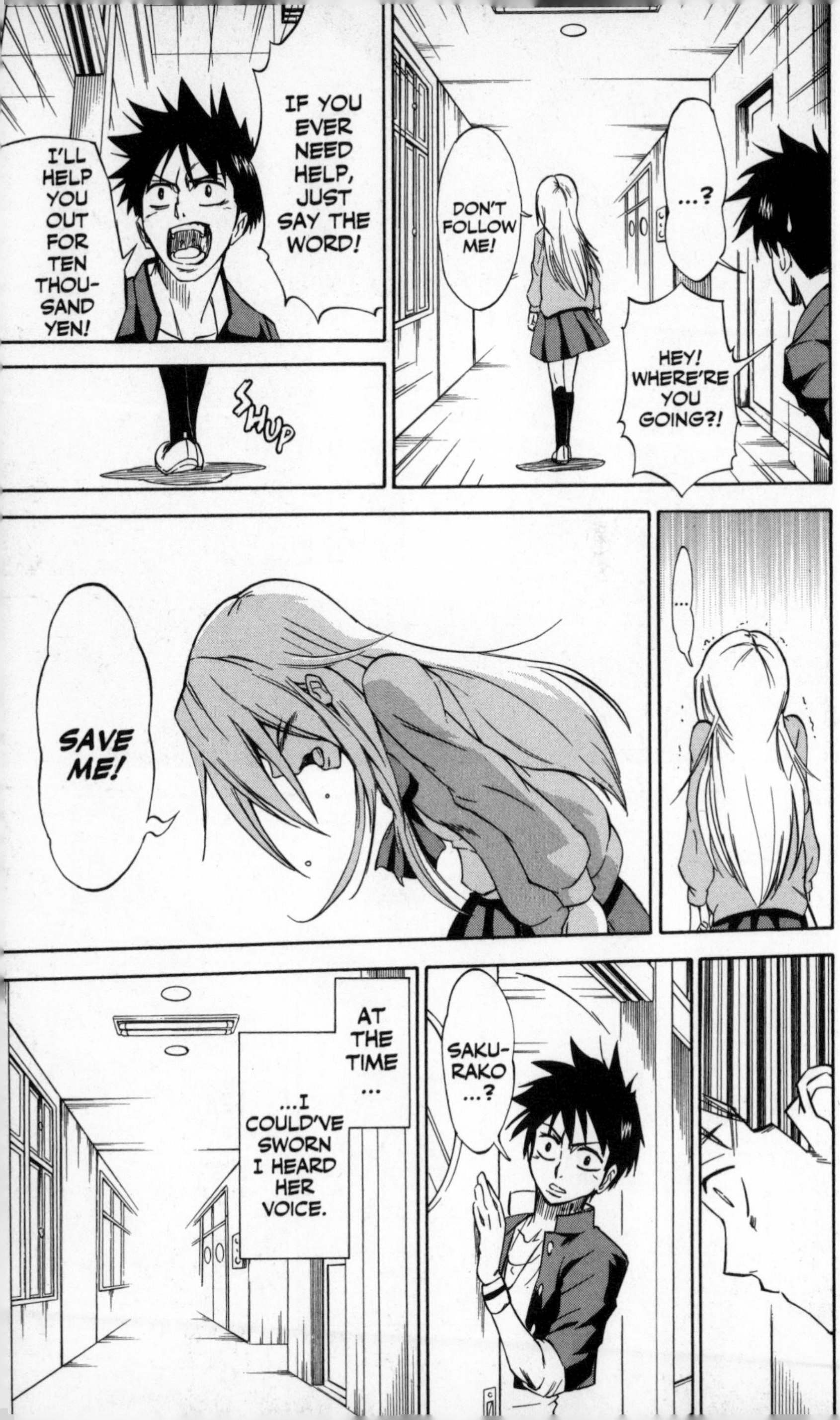
...?
DON'T FOLLOW ME!
HEY! WHERE'RE YOU GOING?!
IF YOU EVER NEED HELP, JUST SAY THE WORD!
I'LL HELP YOU OUT FOR TEN THOU-SAND YEN!
SHUP
...
SAVE ME!
SAKU-RAKO ...?
AT THE TIME ...
...I COULD'VE SWORN I HEARD HER VOICE.

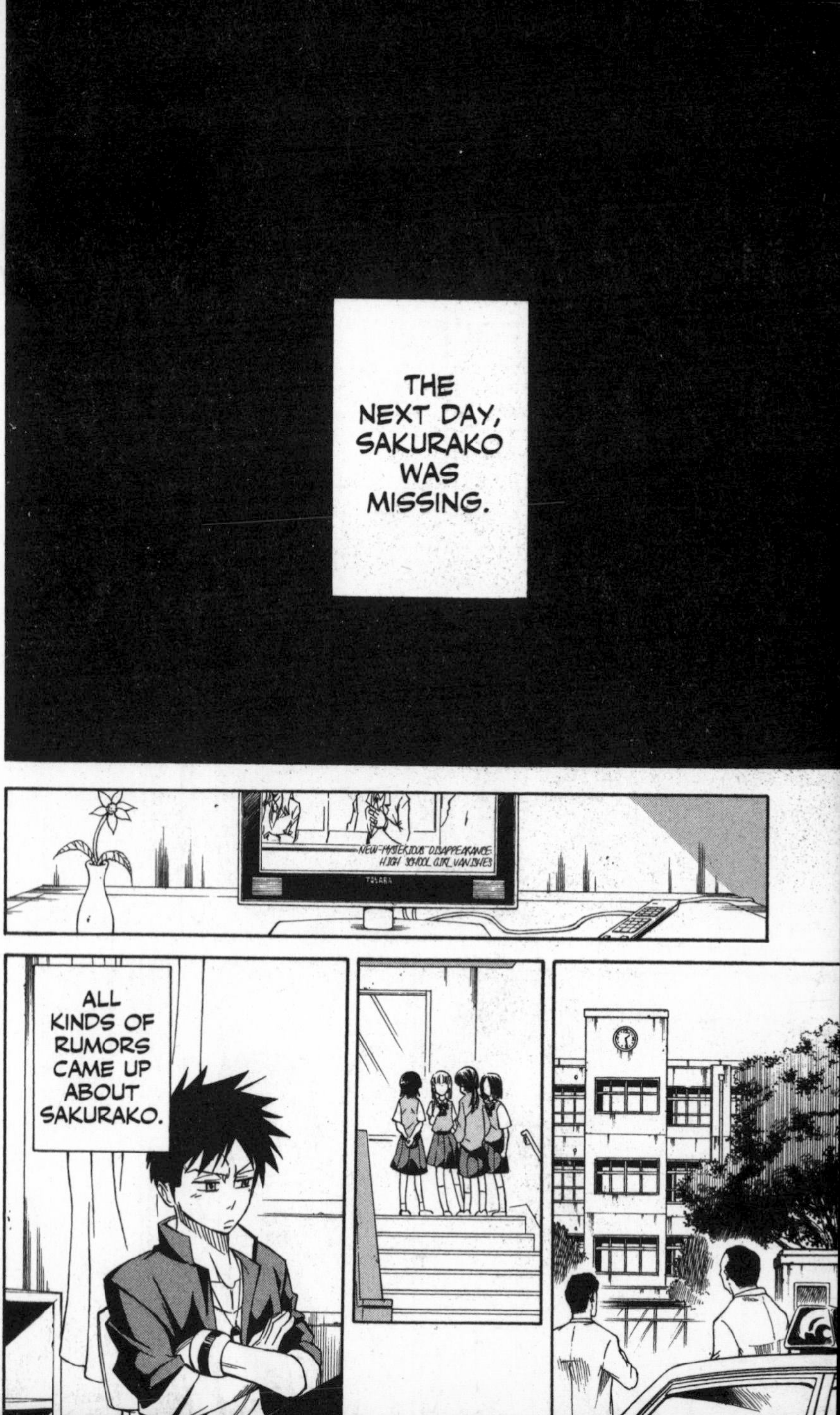
THE NEXT DAY, SAKURAKO WAS MISSING.
NEW-MYSTERIOUS DISAPPEARANCE
HIGH SCHOOL GIRL VANISHES
ALL KINDS OF RUMORS CAME UP ABOUT SAKURAKO.

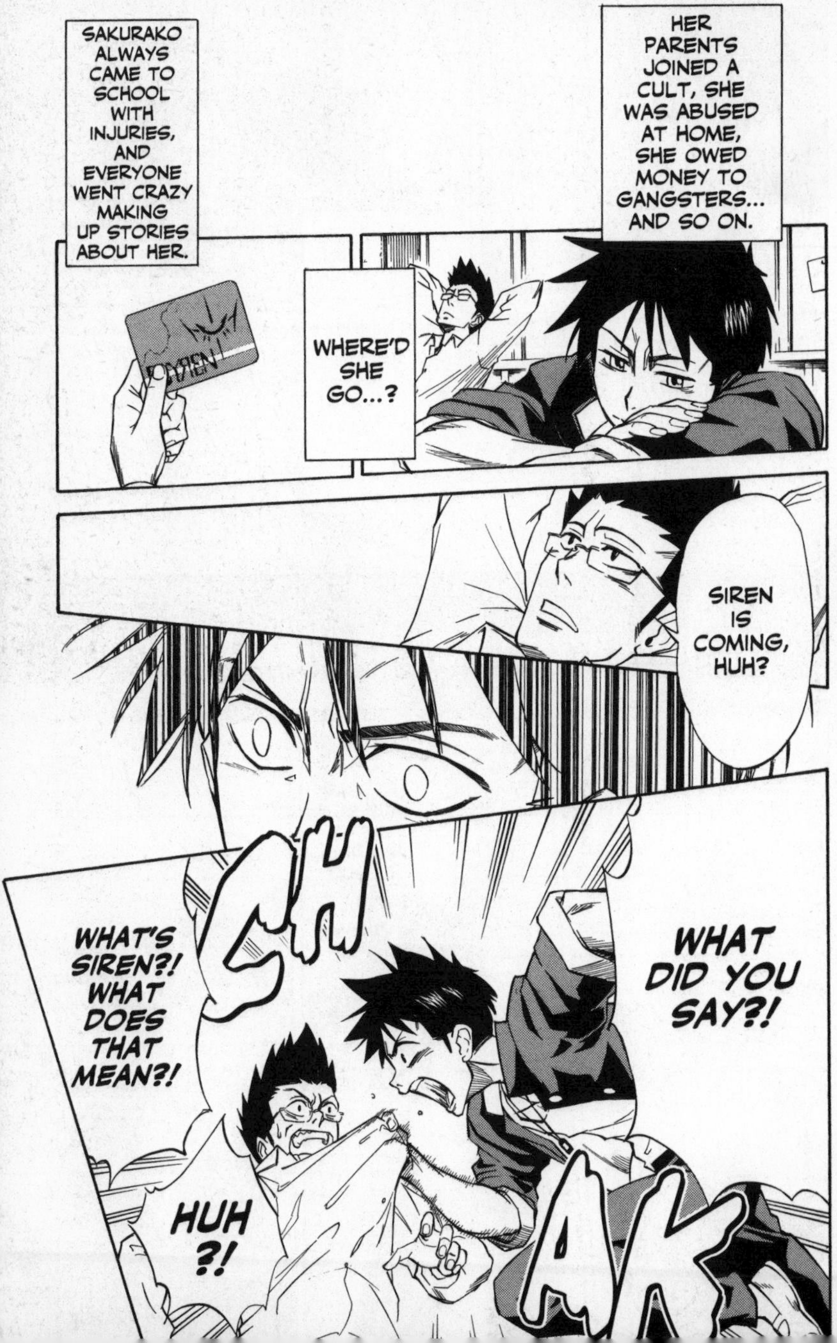
HER PARENTS JOINED A CULT, SHE WAS ABUSED AT HOME, SHE OWED MONEY TO GANGSTERS... AND SO ON.
SAKURAKO ALWAYS CAME TO SCHOOL WITH INJURIES, AND EVERYONE WENT CRAZY MAKING UP STORIES ABOUT HER.
WHERE'D SHE GO...?
SIREN IS COMING, HUH?
WHAT DID YOU SAY?!
WHAT'S SIREN?! WHAT DOES THAT MEAN?!
HUH ?!
CHAK

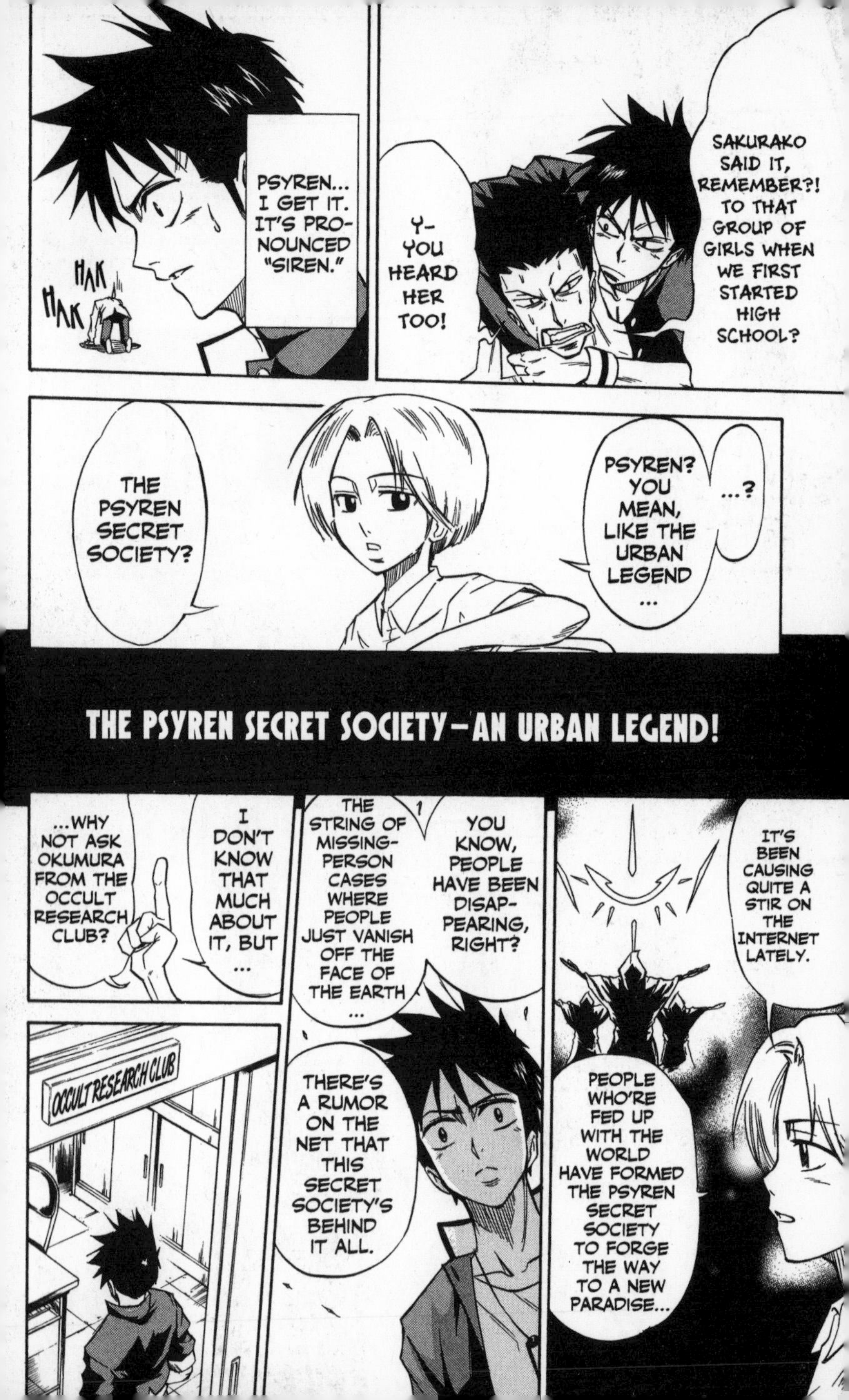
SAKURAKO SAID IT, REMEMBER?! TO THAT GROUP OF GIRLS WHEN WE FIRST STARTED HIGH SCHOOL?
Y-YOU HEARD HER TOO!
HAK HAK
PSYREN... I GET IT. IT'S PRO-NOUNCED "SIREN."
...?
PSYREN? YOU MEAN, LIKE THE URBAN LEGEND...
THE PSYREN SECRET SOCIETY?
THE PSYREN SECRET SOCIETY—AN URBAN LEGEND!
IT'S BEEN CAUSING QUITE A STIR ON THE INTERNET LATELY.
YOU KNOW, PEOPLE HAVE BEEN DISAP-PEARING, RIGHT?
THE STRING OF MISSING-PERSON CASES WHERE PEOPLE JUST VANISH OFF THE FACE OF THE EARTH...
I DON'T KNOW THAT MUCH ABOUT IT, BUT...
...WHY NOT ASK OKUMURA FROM THE OCCULT RESEARCH CLUB?
PEOPLE WHO'RE FED UP WITH THE WORLD HAVE FORMED THE PSYREN SECRET SOCIETY TO FORGE THE WAY TO A NEW PARADISE...
THERE'S A RUMOR ON THE NET THAT THIS SECRET SOCIETY'S BEHIND IT ALL.
OCCULT RESEARCH CLUB

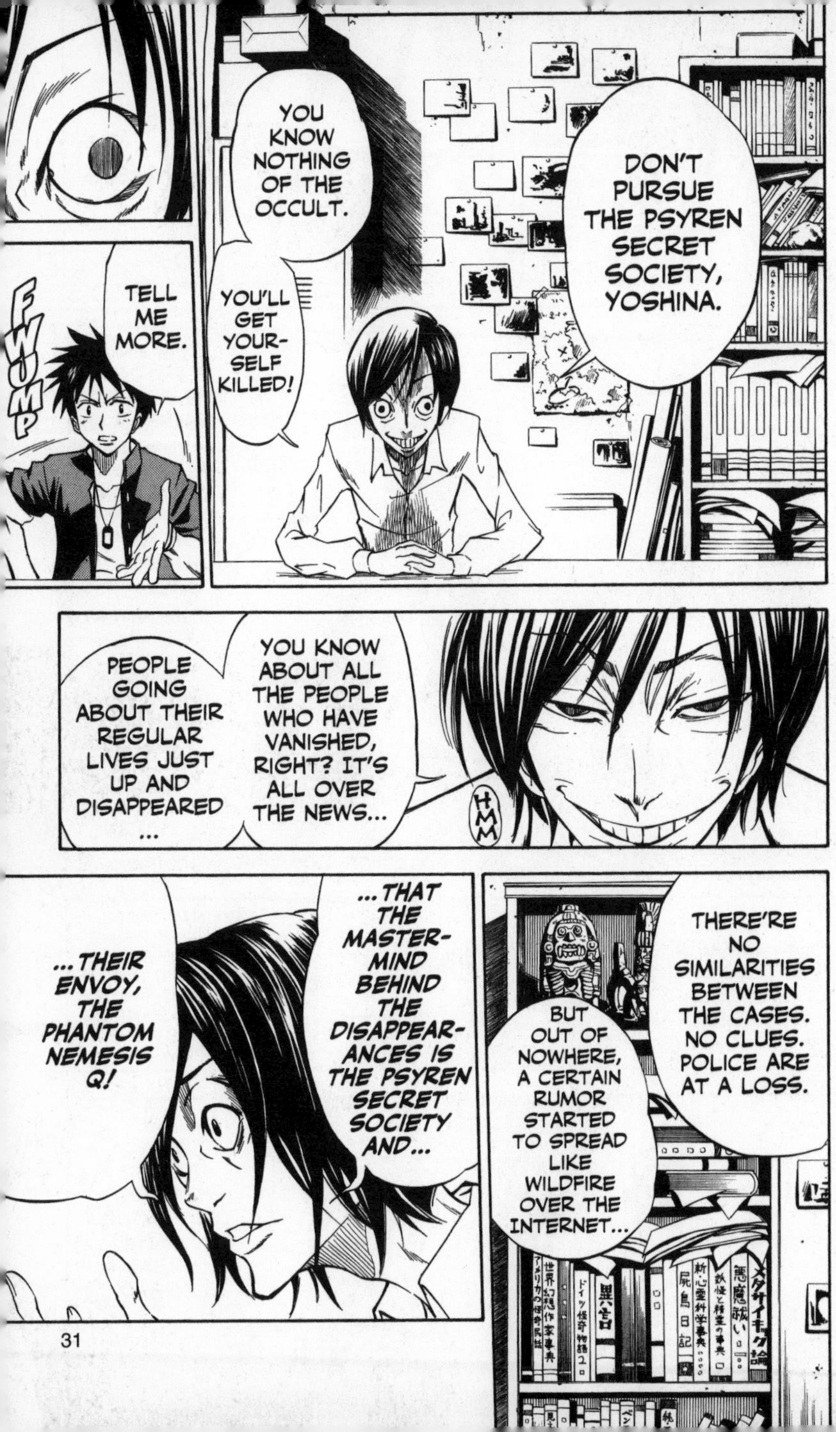
DON'T PURSUE THE PSYREN SECRET SOCIETY, YOSHINA.
YOU KNOW NOTHING OF THE OCCULT.
YOU'LL GET YOUR-SELF KILLED!
FWUMP
TELL ME MORE.
HMM
YOU KNOW ABOUT ALL THE PEOPLE WHO HAVE VANISHED, RIGHT? IT'S ALL OVER THE NEWS...
PEOPLE GOING ABOUT THEIR REGULAR LIVES JUST UP AND DISAPPEARED...
THERE'RE NO SIMILARITIES BETWEEN THE CASES. NO CLUES. POLICE ARE AT A LOSS.
BUT OUT OF NOWHERE, A CERTAIN RUMOR STARTED TO SPREAD LIKE WILDFIRE OVER THE INTERNET...
...THAT THE MASTER-MIND BEHIND THE DISAPPEAR-ANCES IS THE PSYREN SECRET SOCIETY AND...
...THEIR ENVOY, THE PHANTOM NEMESIS Q!

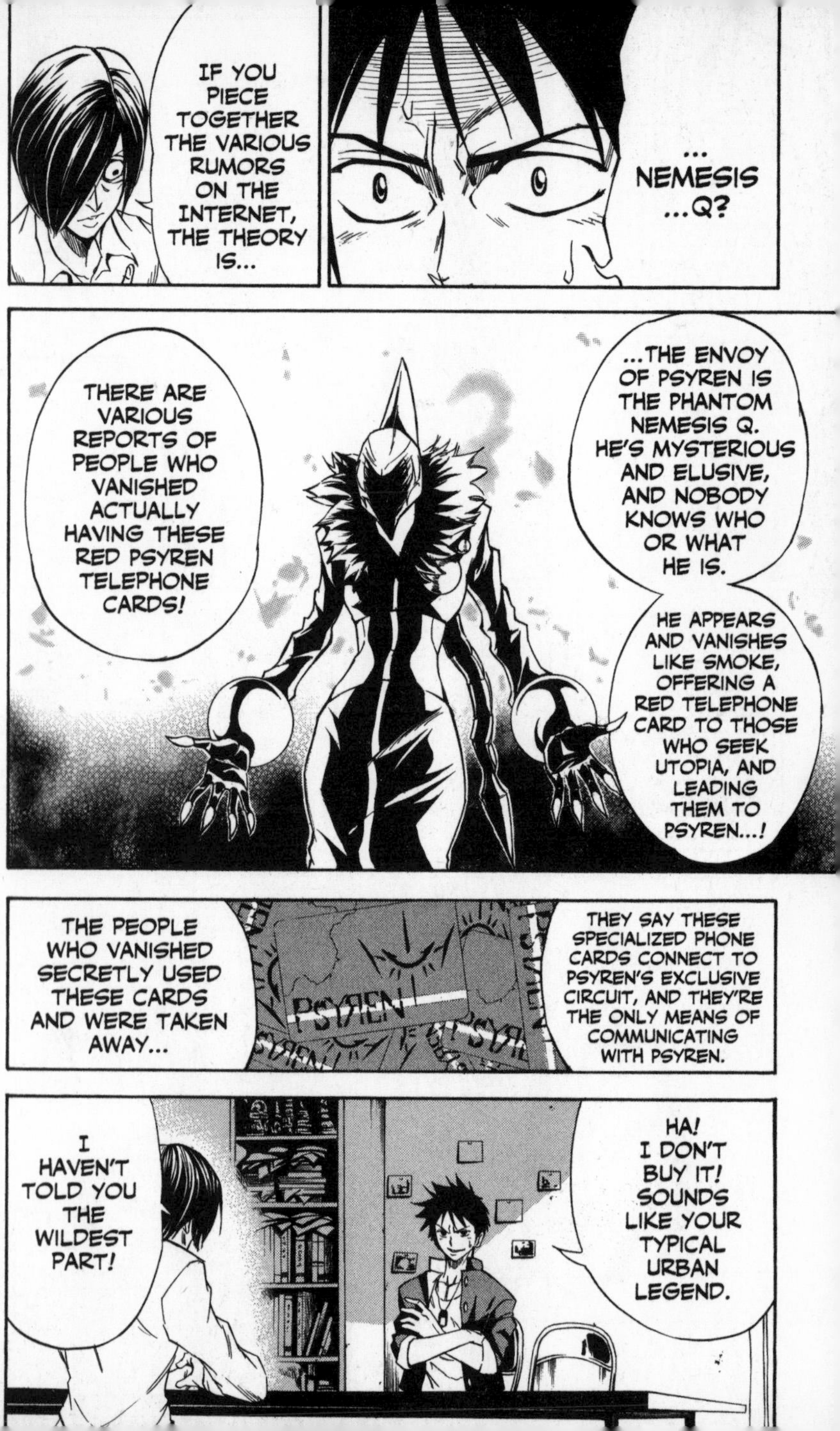
...NEMESIS ...Q?
IF YOU PIECE TOGETHER THE VARIOUS RUMORS ON THE INTERNET, THE THEORY IS...
...THE ENVOY OF PSYREN IS THE PHANTOM NEMESIS Q. HE'S MYSTERIOUS AND ELUSIVE, AND NOBODY KNOWS WHO OR WHAT HE IS.
HE APPEARS AND VANISHES LIKE SMOKE, OFFERING A RED TELEPHONE CARD TO THOSE WHO SEEK UTOPIA, AND LEADING THEM TO PSYREN...!
THERE ARE VARIOUS REPORTS OF PEOPLE WHO VANISHED ACTUALLY HAVING THESE RED PSYREN TELEPHONE CARDS!
THEY SAY THESE SPECIALIZED PHONE CARDS CONNECT TO PSYREN'S EXCLUSIVE CIRCUIT, AND THEY'RE THE ONLY MEANS OF COMMUNICATING WITH PSYREN.
PSYREN
THE PEOPLE WHO VANISHED SECRETLY USED THESE CARDS AND WERE TAKEN AWAY...
HA! I DON'T BUY IT! SOUNDS LIKE YOUR TYPICAL URBAN LEGEND.
I HAVEN'T TOLD YOU THE WILDEST PART!

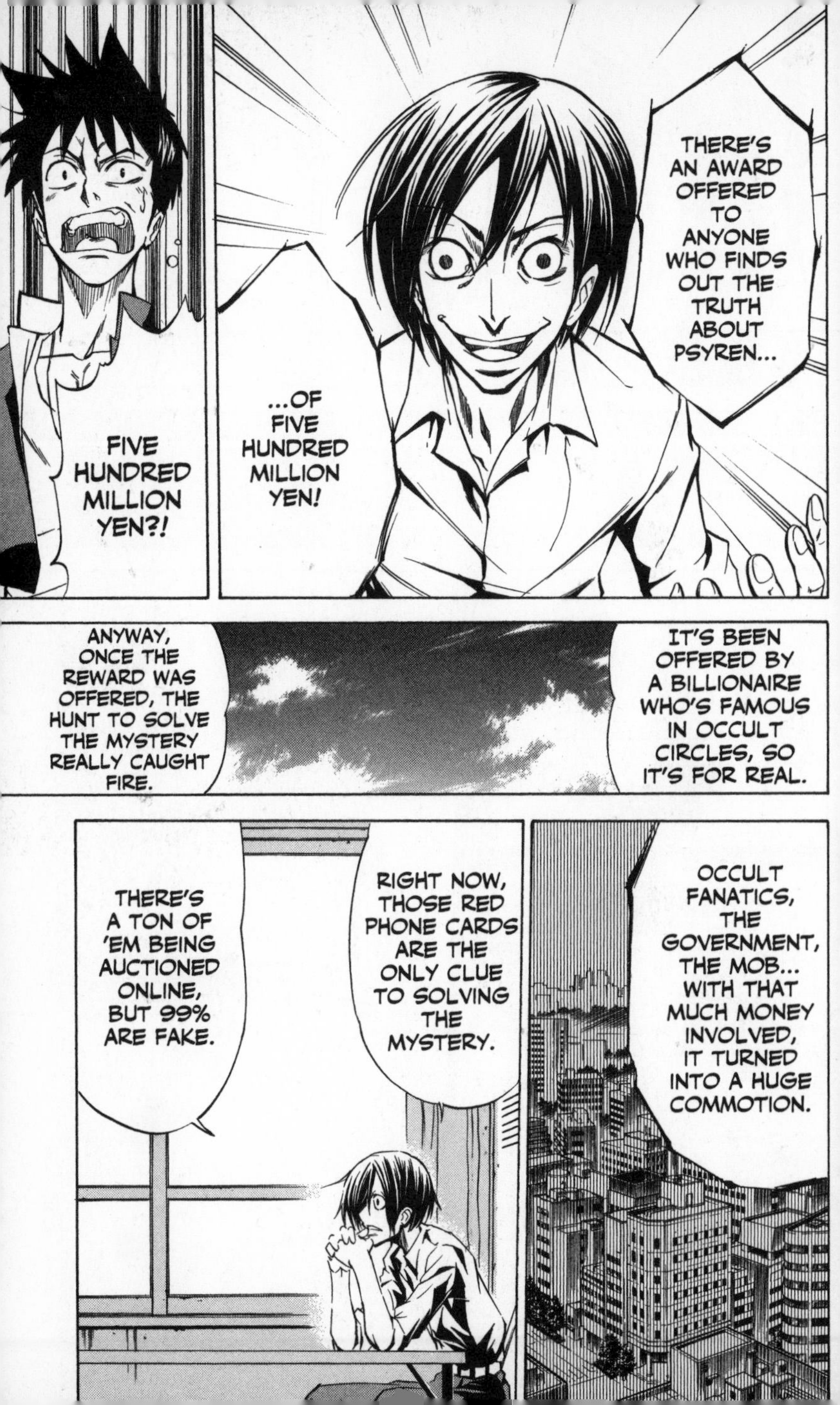
THERE'S AN AWARD OFFERED TO ANYONE WHO FINDS OUT THE TRUTH ABOUT PSYREN...
...OF FIVE HUNDRED MILLION YEN!
FIVE HUNDRED MILLION YEN?!
IT'S BEEN OFFERED BY A BILLIONAIRE WHO'S FAMOUS IN OCCULT CIRCLES, SO IT'S FOR REAL.
ANYWAY, ONCE THE REWARD WAS OFFERED, THE HUNT TO SOLVE THE MYSTERY REALLY CAUGHT FIRE.
OCCULT FANATICS, THE GOVERNMENT, THE MOB... WITH THAT MUCH MONEY INVOLVED, IT TURNED INTO A HUGE COMMOTION.
RIGHT NOW, THOSE RED PHONE CARDS ARE THE ONLY CLUE TO SOLVING THE MYSTERY.
THERE'S A TON OF 'EM BEING AUCTIONED ONLINE, BUT 99% ARE FAKE.

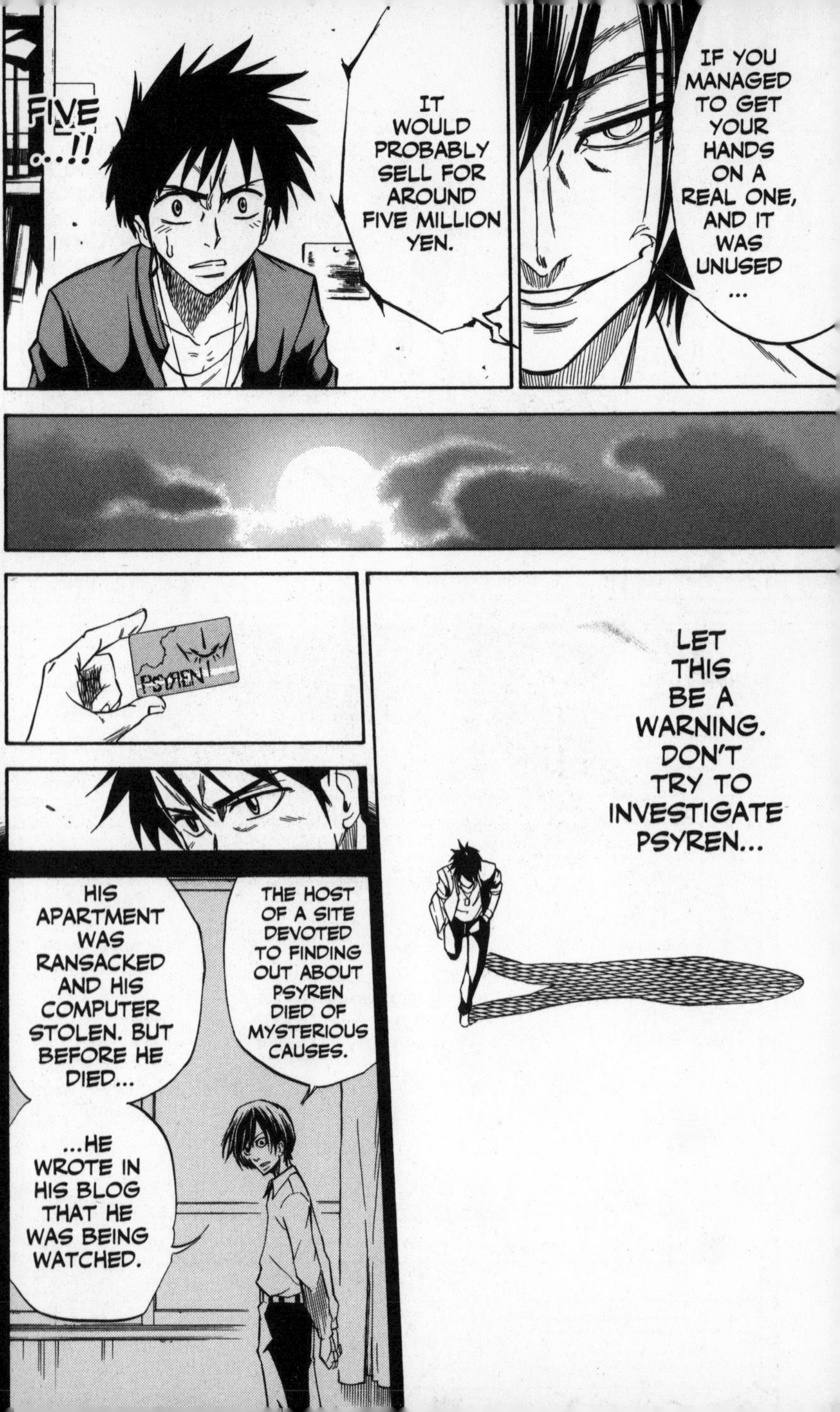
IF YOU MANAGED TO GET YOUR HANDS ON A REAL ONE, AND IT WAS UNUSED ...
IT WOULD PROBABLY SELL FOR AROUND FIVE MILLION YEN.
FIVE ...!!
LET THIS BE A WARNING. DON'T TRY TO INVESTIGATE PSYREN...
PSYREN
THE HOST OF A SITE DEVOTED TO FINDING OUT ABOUT PSYREN DIED OF MYSTERIOUS CAUSES.
HIS APARTMENT WAS RANSACKED AND HIS COMPUTER STOLEN. BUT BEFORE HE DIED...
...HE WROTE IN HIS BLOG THAT HE WAS BEING WATCHED.

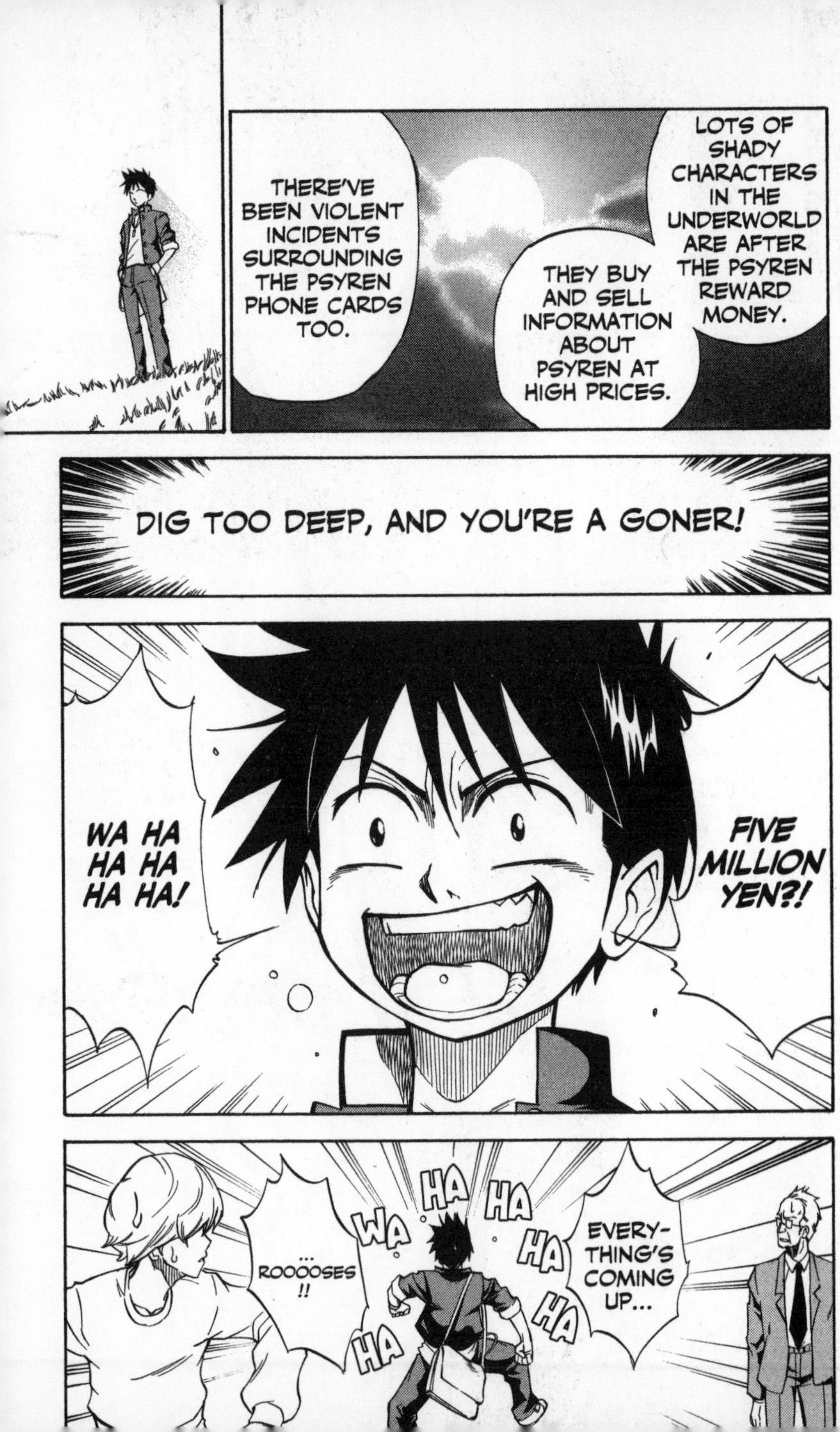
LOTS OF SHADY CHARACTERS IN THE UNDERWORLD ARE AFTER THE PSYREN REWARD MONEY.
THEY BUY AND SELL INFORMATION ABOUT PSYREN AT HIGH PRICES.
THERE'VE BEEN VIOLENT INCIDENTS SURROUNDING THE PSYREN PHONE CARDS TOO.
DIG TOO DEEP, AND YOU'RE A GONER!
FIVE MILLION YEN?!
WA HA HA HA HA HA!
EVERY-THING'S COMING UP...
...ROOOOSES!!
WA HA HA HA HA HA

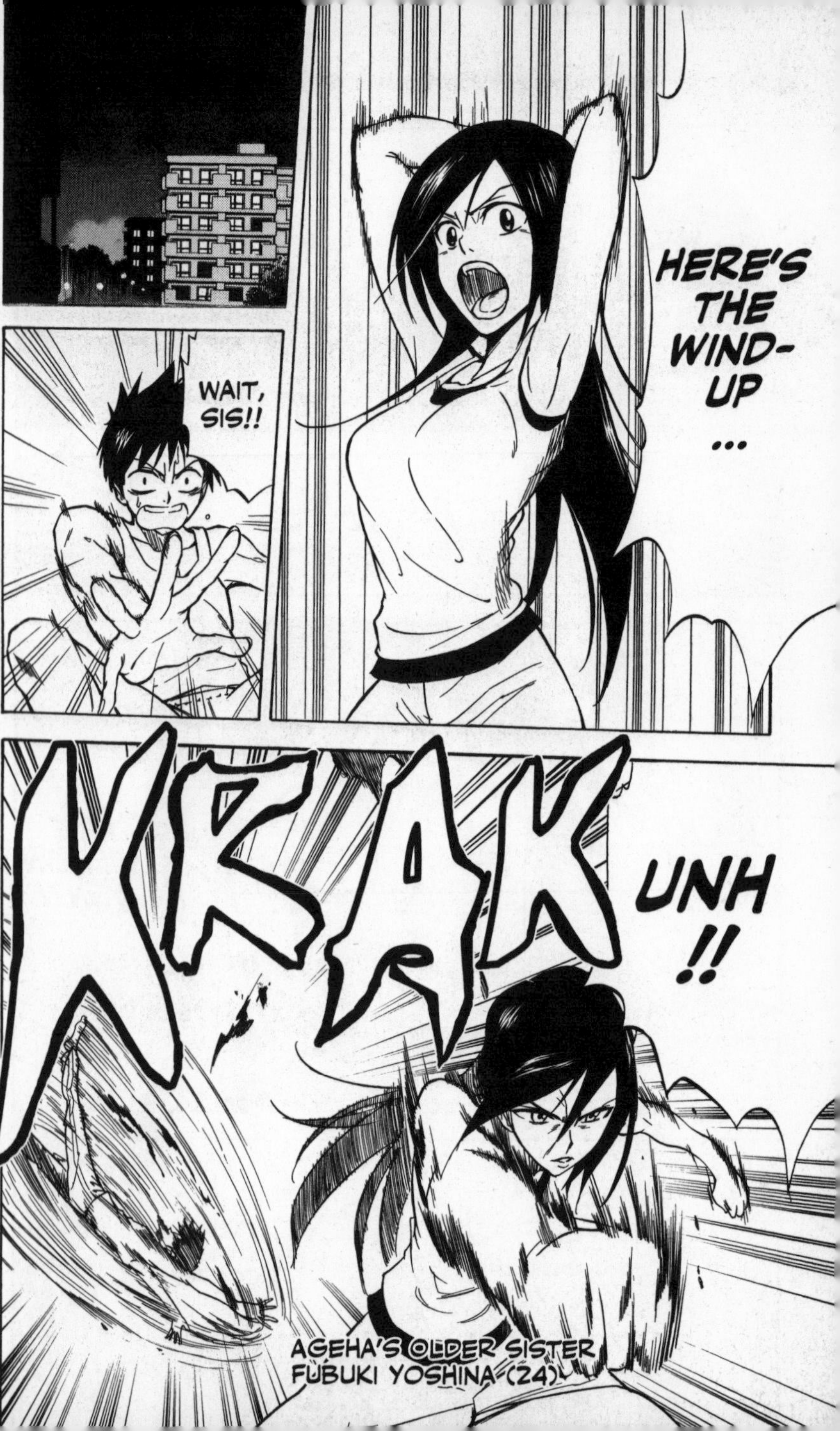
HERE'S THE WIND-UP ...
WAIT, SIS!!
KRAK
UNH !!
AGEHA'S OLDER SISTER
FUBUKI YOSHINA (24)

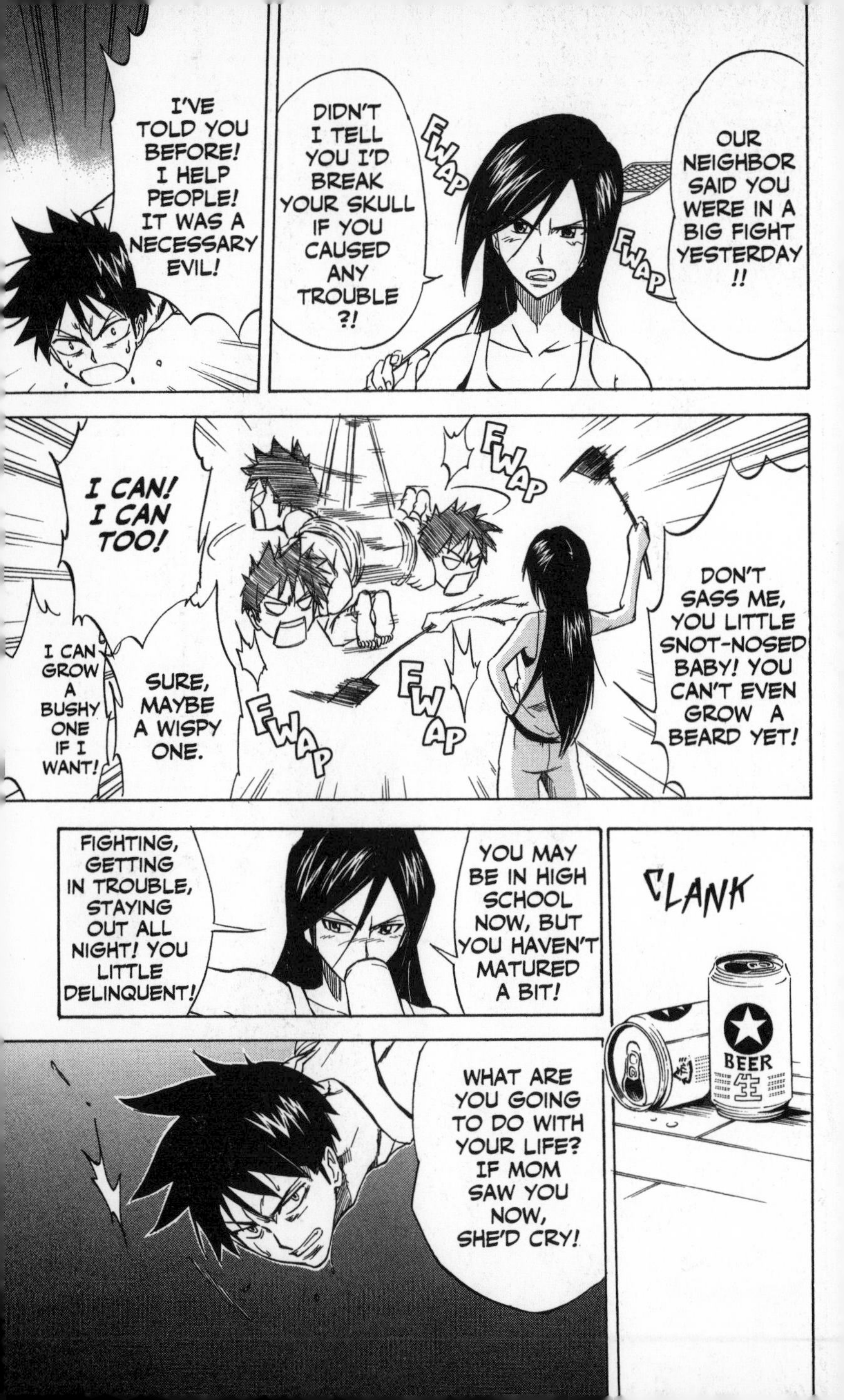
OUR NEIGHBOR SAID YOU WERE IN A BIG FIGHT YESTERDAY!!
FWAP
FWAP
DIDN'T I TELL YOU I'D BREAK YOUR SKULL IF YOU CAUSED ANY TROUBLE?!
I'VE TOLD YOU BEFORE! I HELP PEOPLE! IT WAS A NECESSARY EVIL!
FWAP
DON'T SASS ME, YOU LITTLE SNOT-NOSED BABY! YOU CAN'T EVEN GROW A BEARD YET!
I CAN! I CAN TOO!
FWAP
FWAP
SURE, MAYBE A WISPY ONE.
I CAN GROW A BUSHY ONE IF I WANT!
CLANK
BEER 生
YOU MAY BE IN HIGH SCHOOL NOW, BUT YOU HAVEN'T MATURED A BIT!
FIGHTING, GETTING IN TROUBLE, STAYING OUT ALL NIGHT! YOU LITTLE DELINQUENT!
WHAT ARE YOU GOING TO DO WITH YOUR LIFE? IF MOM SAW YOU NOW, SHE'D CRY!

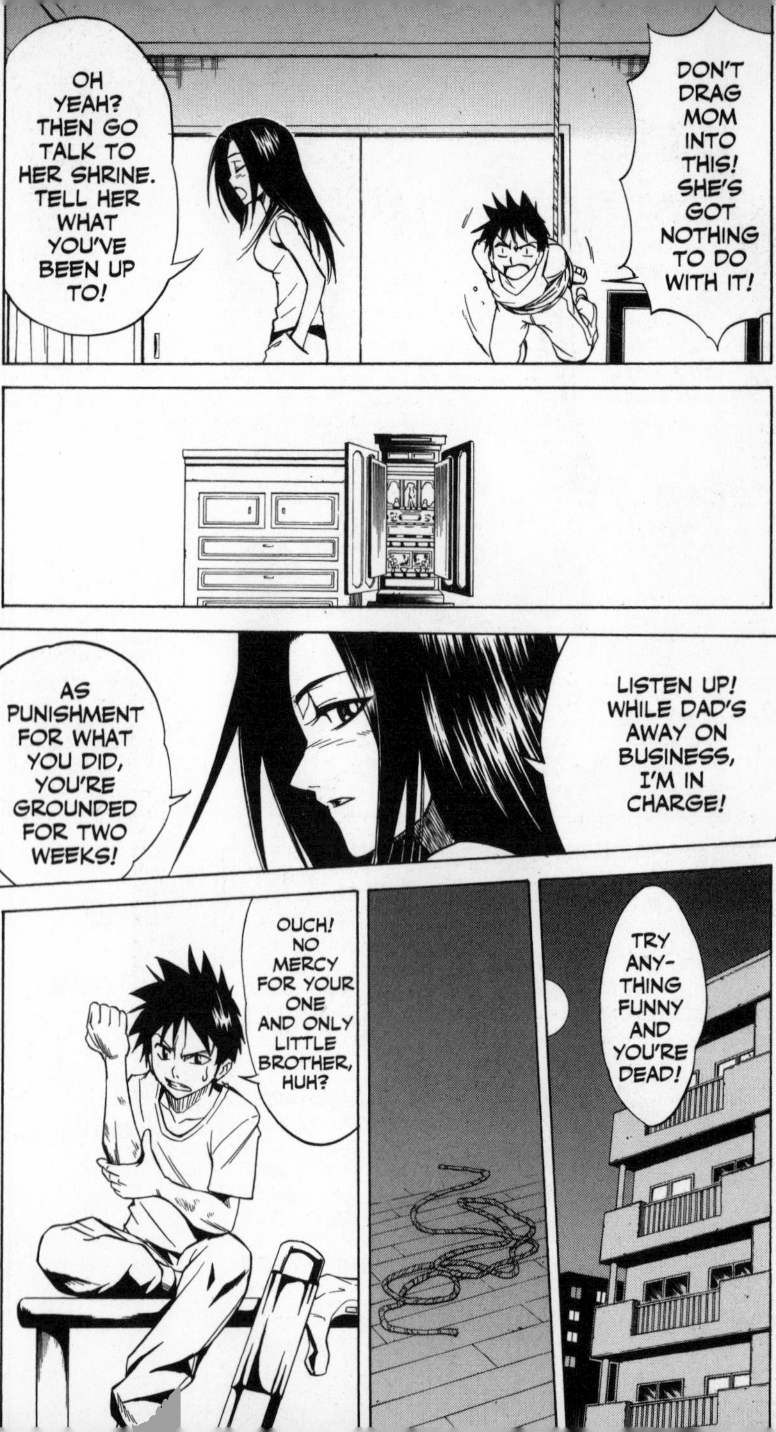
DON'T DRAG MOM INTO THIS! SHE'S GOT NOTHING TO DO WITH IT!
OH YEAH? THEN GO TALK TO HER SHRINE. TELL HER WHAT YOU'VE BEEN UP TO!
LISTEN UP! WHILE DAD'S AWAY ON BUSINESS, I'M IN CHARGE!
AS PUNISHMENT FOR WHAT YOU DID, YOU'RE GROUNDED FOR TWO WEEKS!
TRY ANY-THING FUNNY AND YOU'RE DEAD!
OUCH! NO MERCY FOR YOUR ONE AND ONLY LITTLE BROTHER, HUH?

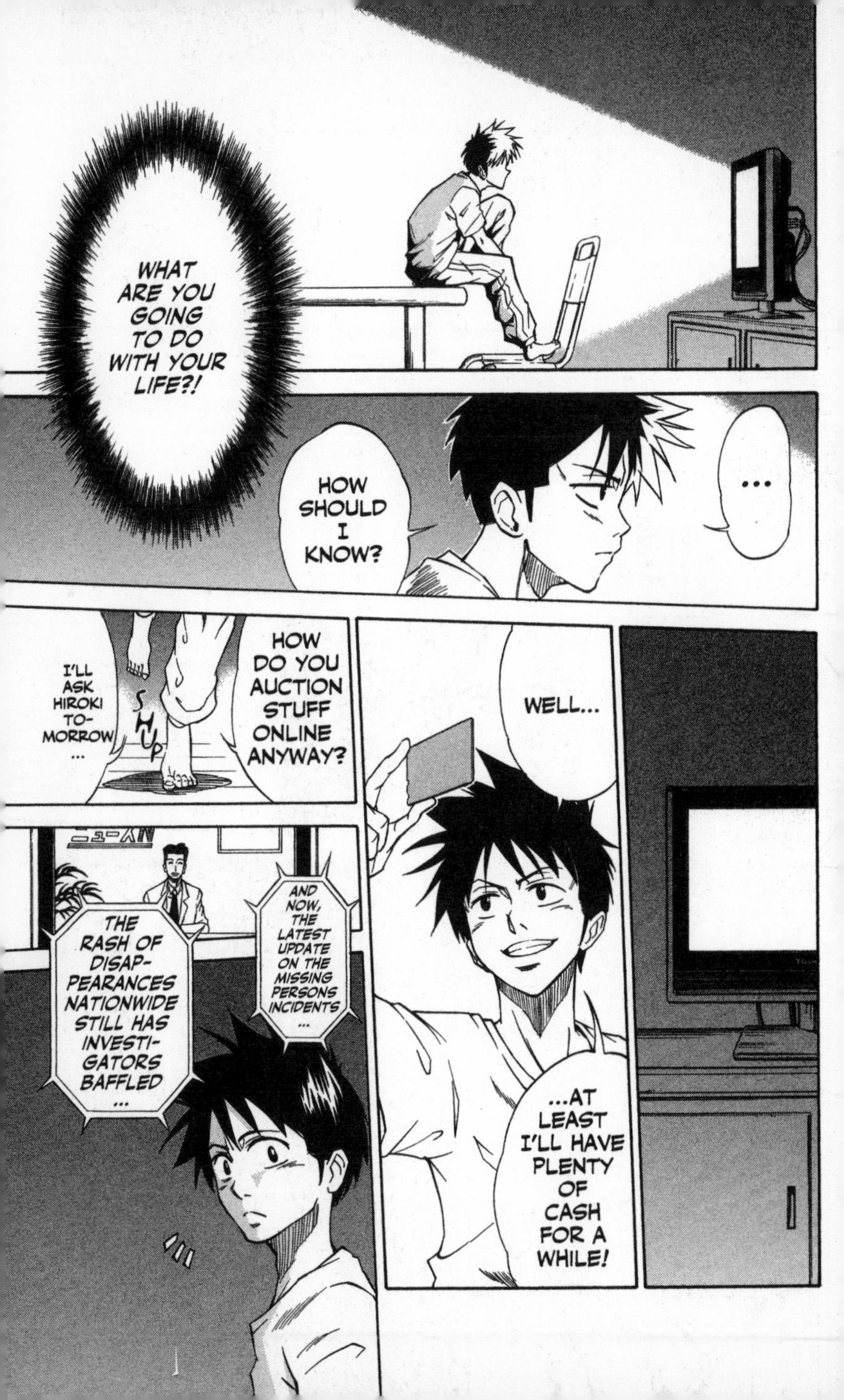
WHAT ARE YOU GOING TO DO WITH YOUR LIFE?!
...
HOW SHOULD I KNOW?
WELL...
...AT LEAST I'LL HAVE PLENTY OF CASH FOR A WHILE!
HOW DO YOU AUCTION STUFF ONLINE ANYWAY?
SHUP
I'LL ASK HIROKI TO-MORROW...
AND NOW, THE LATEST UPDATE ON THE MISSING PERSONS INCIDENTS...
THE RASH OF DISAP-PEARANCES NATIONWIDE STILL HAS INVESTI-GATORS BAFFLED...

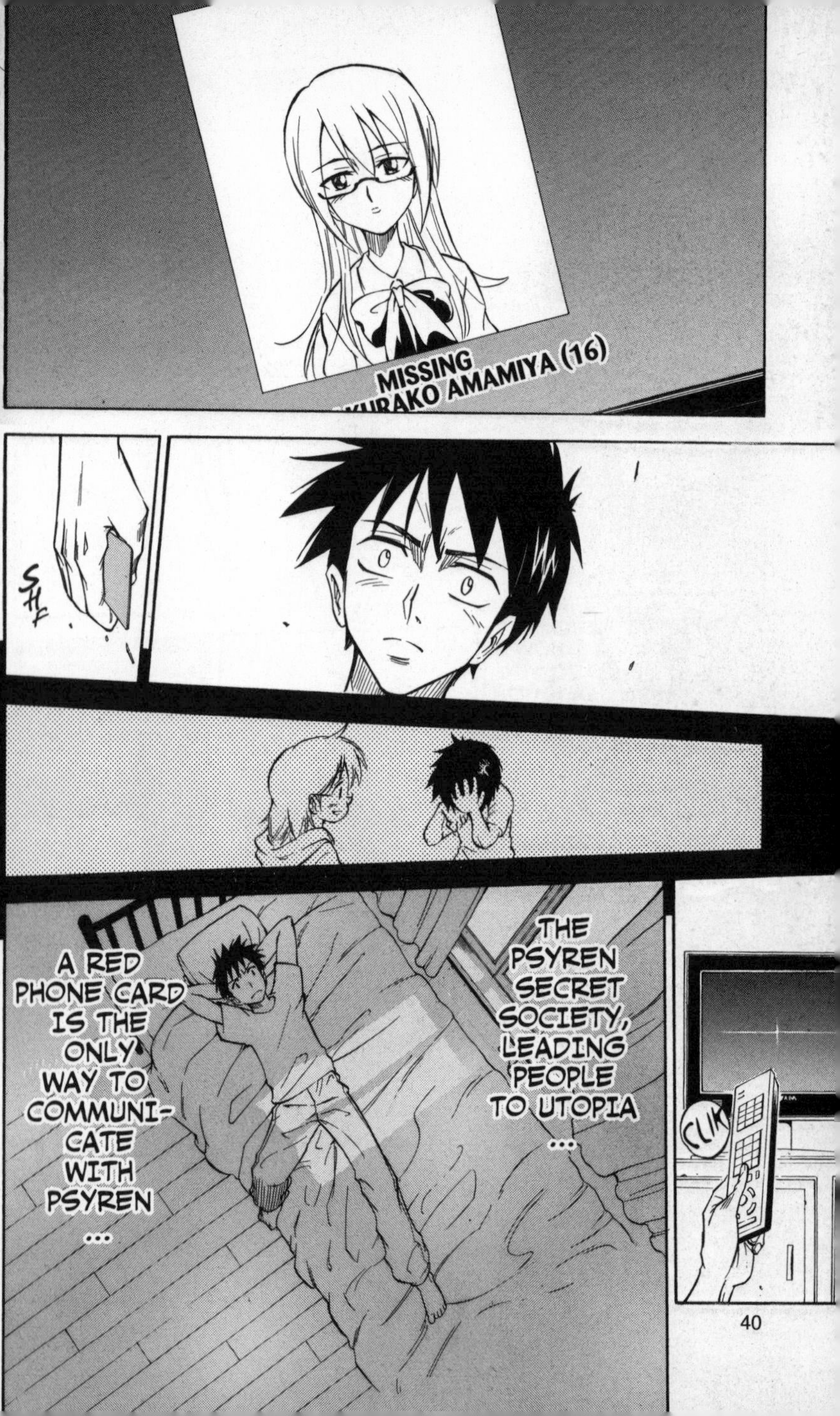
MISSING
KURAKO AMAMIYA (16)
SHF
CLIK
THE PSYREN SECRET SOCIETY, LEADING PEOPLE TO UTOPIA ...
A RED PHONE CARD IS THE ONLY WAY TO COMMUNI-CATE WITH PSYREN ...

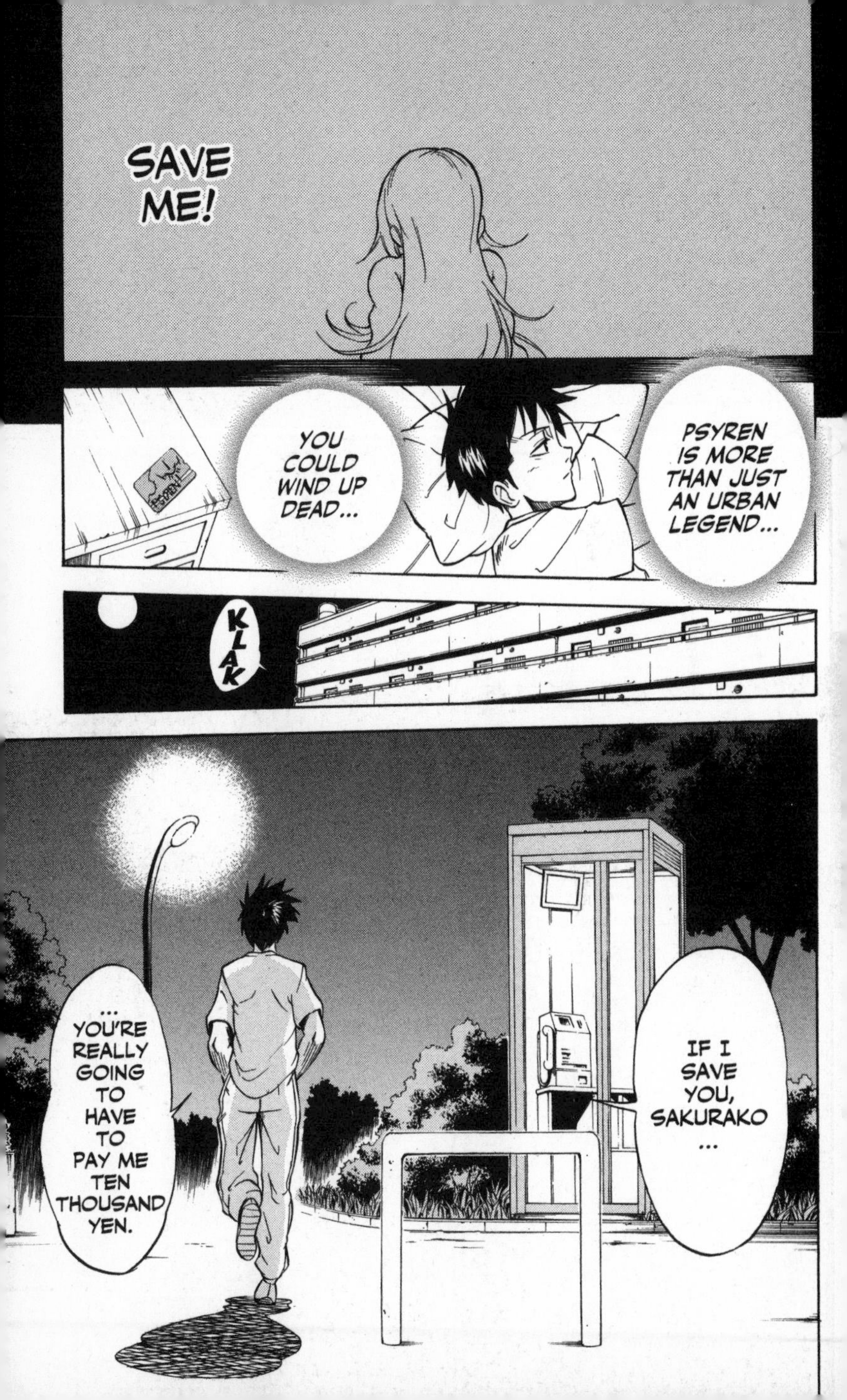
SAVE ME!
PSYREN IS MORE THAN JUST AN URBAN LEGEND...
YOU COULD WIND UP DEAD...
KLAK
IF I SAVE YOU, SAKURAKO...
...YOU'RE REALLY GOING TO HAVE TO PAY ME TEN THOUSAND YEN.

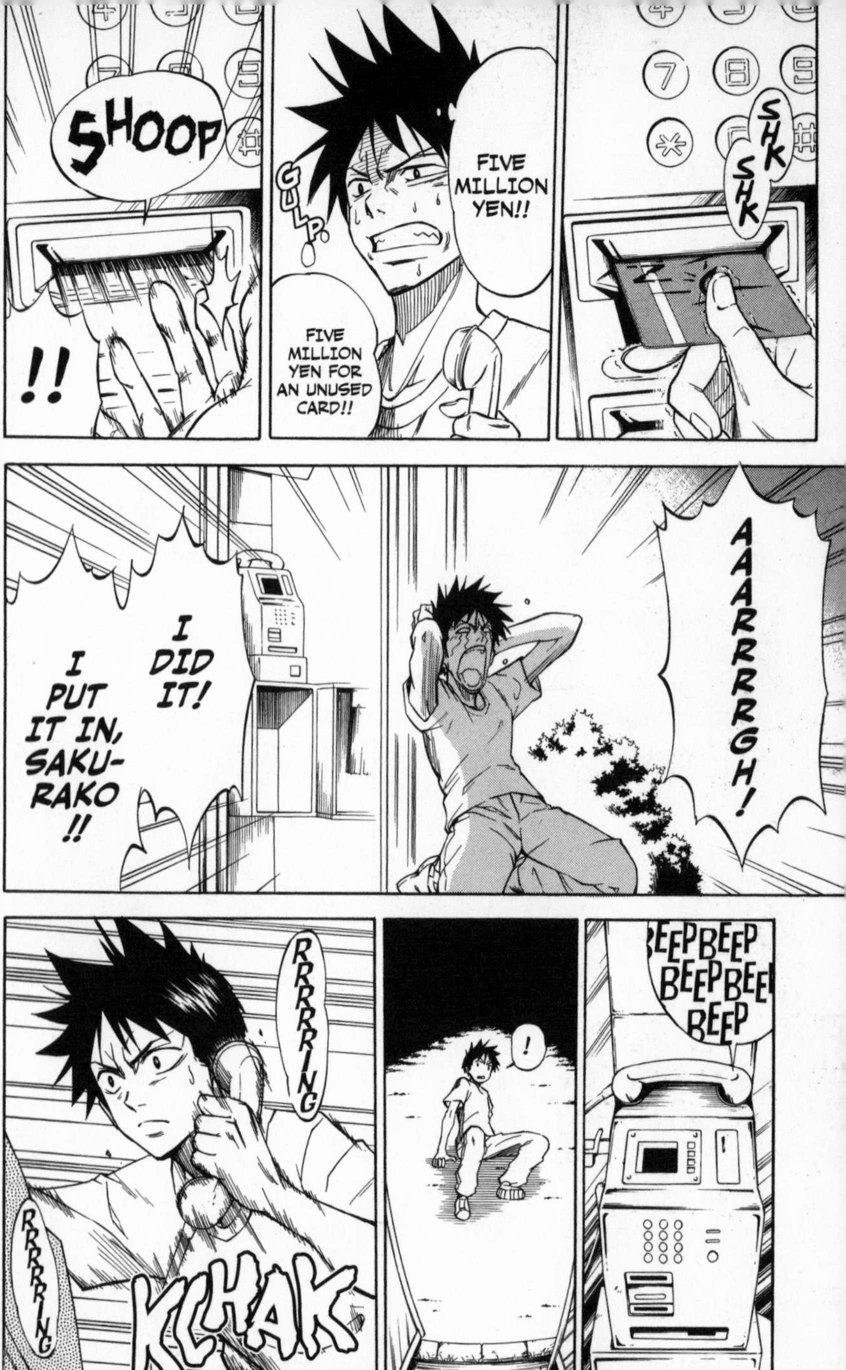
SHK
SHK
FIVE MILLION YEN!!
GULP
FIVE MILLION YEN FOR AN UNUSED CARD!!
SHOOP
!!
AAARRRRRGH!
I DID IT!
I PUT IT IN, SAKURAKO!!
BEEPBEEP BEEPBEEP BEEP
!
RRRRRING
RRRRRING
KCHAK

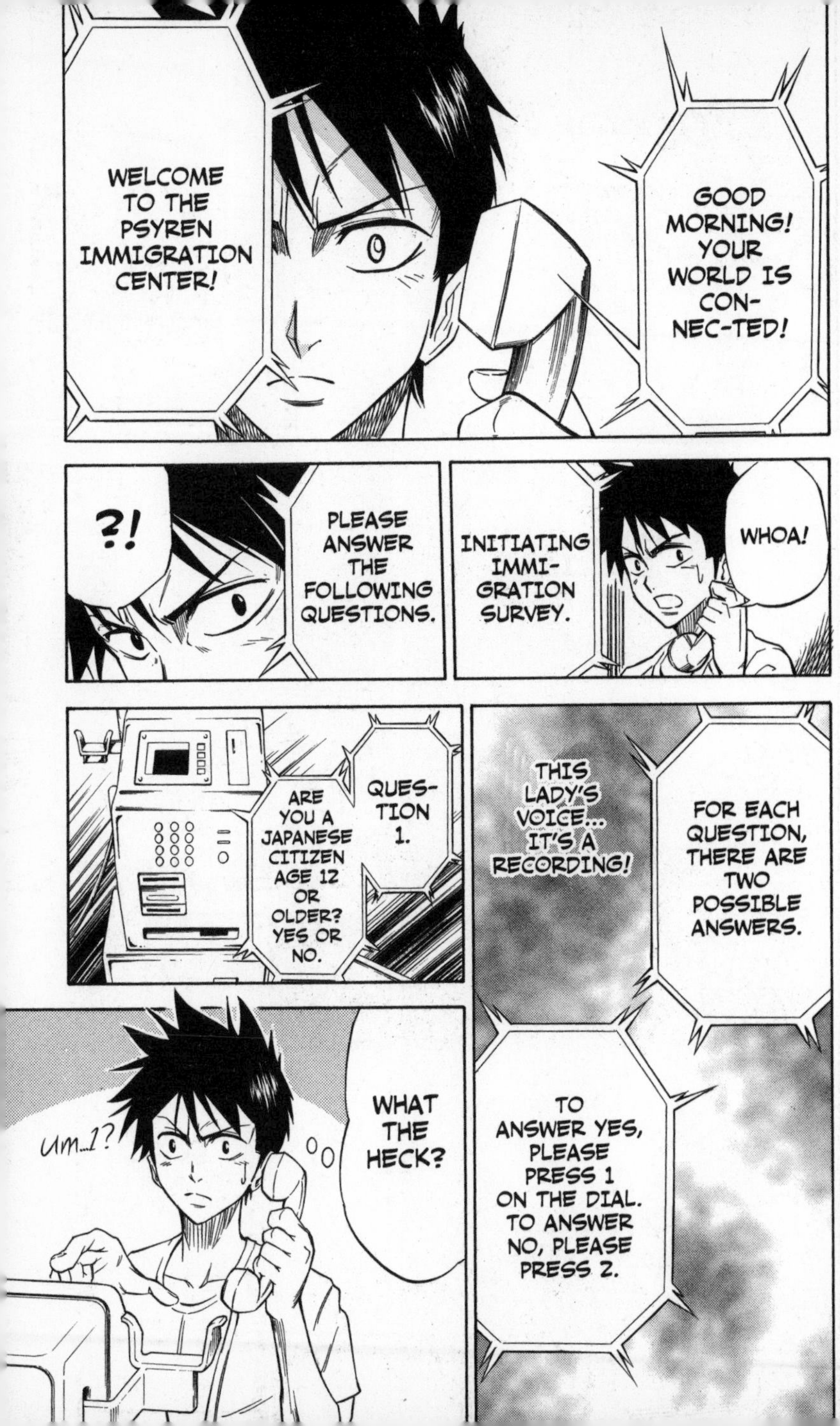
GOOD MORNING! YOUR WORLD IS CON-NEC-TED!
WELCOME TO THE PSYREN IMMIGRATION CENTER!
WHOA!
INITIATING IMMI-GRATION SURVEY.
PLEASE ANSWER THE FOLLOWING QUESTIONS.
?!
FOR EACH QUESTION, THERE ARE TWO POSSIBLE ANSWERS.
THIS LADY'S VOICE... IT'S A RECORDING!
TO ANSWER YES, PLEASE PRESS 1 ON THE DIAL. TO ANSWER NO, PLEASE PRESS 2.
QUES-TION 1.
ARE YOU A JAPANESE CITIZEN AGE 12 OR OLDER? YES OR NO.
WHAT THE HECK?
Um...1?

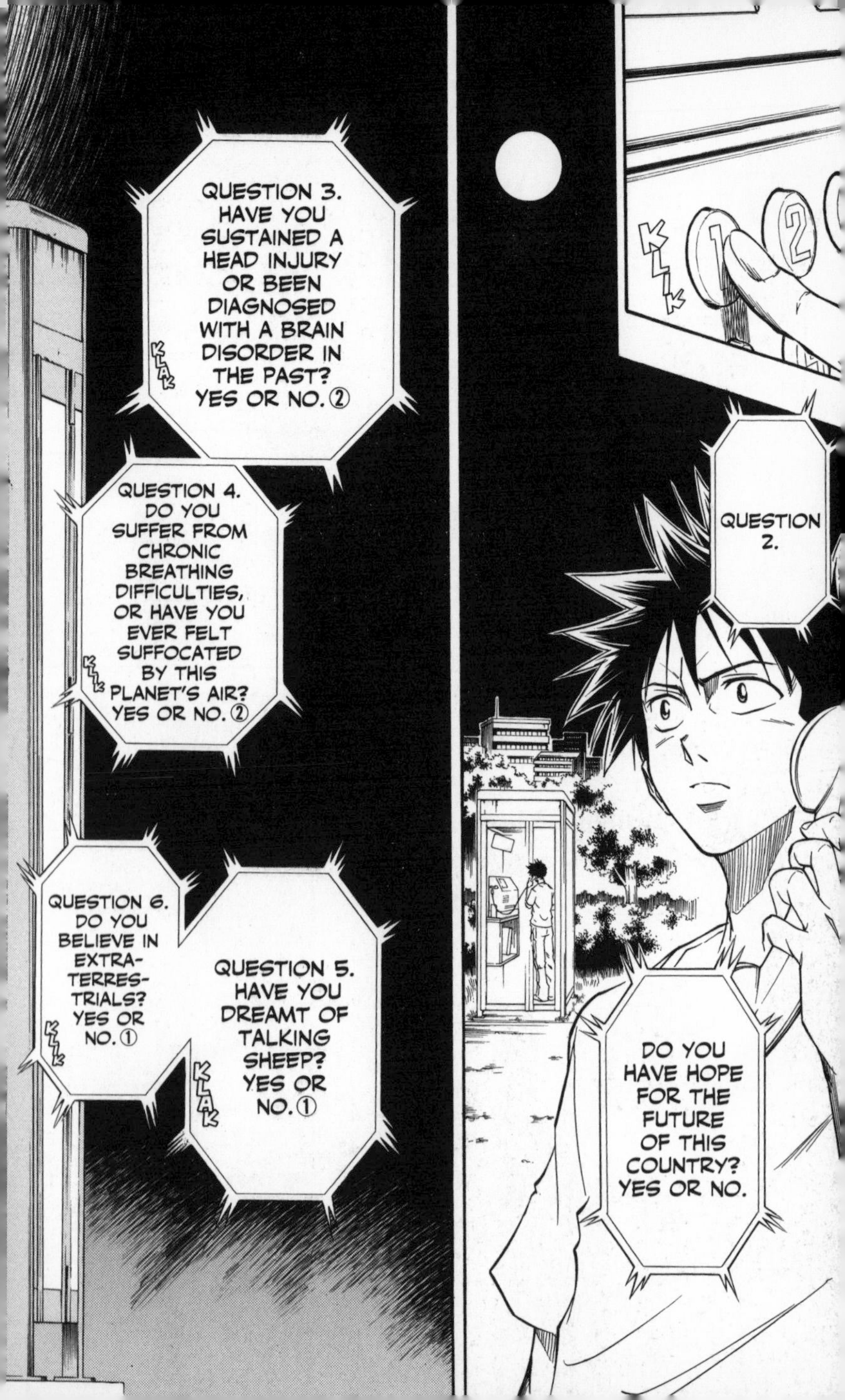
KLIK
QUESTION 2.
DO YOU HAVE HOPE FOR THE FUTURE OF THIS COUNTRY? YES OR NO.
QUESTION 3. HAVE YOU SUSTAINED A HEAD INJURY OR BEEN DIAGNOSED WITH A BRAIN DISORDER IN THE PAST? YES OR NO. ②
KLAK
QUESTION 4. DO YOU SUFFER FROM CHRONIC BREATHING DIFFICULTIES, OR HAVE YOU EVER FELT SUFFOCATED BY THIS PLANET'S AIR? YES OR NO. ②
QUESTION 5. HAVE YOU DREAMT OF TALKING SHEEP? YES OR NO. ①
KLAK
QUESTION 6. DO YOU BELIEVE IN EXTRA-TERRES-TRIALS? YES OR NO. ①

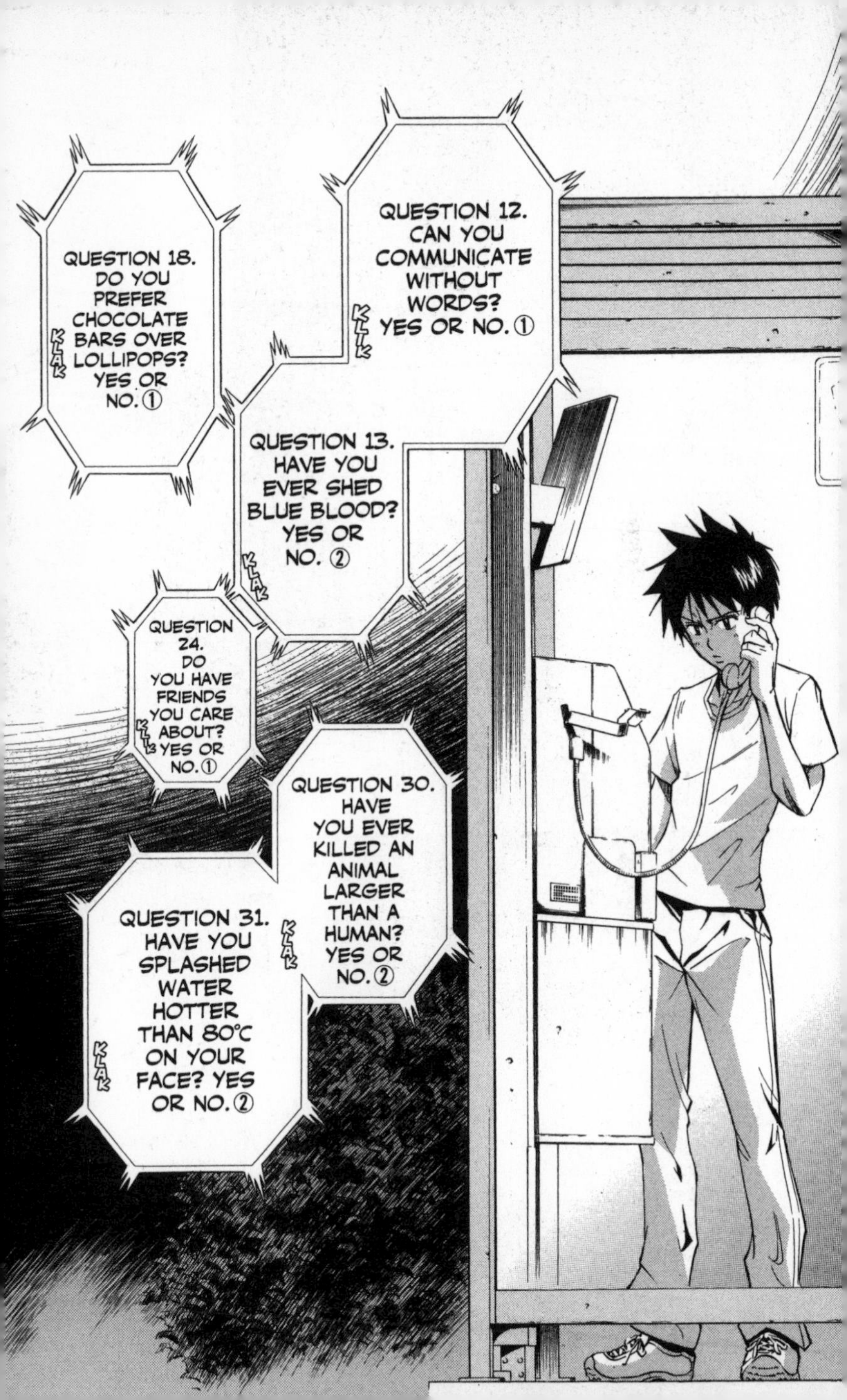
QUESTION 12. CAN YOU COMMUNICATE WITHOUT WORDS? YES OR NO. ①
KLIK
QUESTION 18. DO YOU PREFER CHOCOLATE BARS OVER LOLLIPOPS? YES OR NO. ①
KLAK
QUESTION 13. HAVE YOU EVER SHED BLUE BLOOD? YES OR NO. ②
KLAK
QUESTION 24. DO YOU HAVE FRIENDS YOU CARE ABOUT? YES OR NO. ①
KLIK
QUESTION 30. HAVE YOU EVER KILLED AN ANIMAL LARGER THAN A HUMAN? YES OR NO. ②
KLAK
QUESTION 31. HAVE YOU SPLASHED WATER HOTTER THAN 80°C ON YOUR FACE? YES OR NO. ②
KLAK

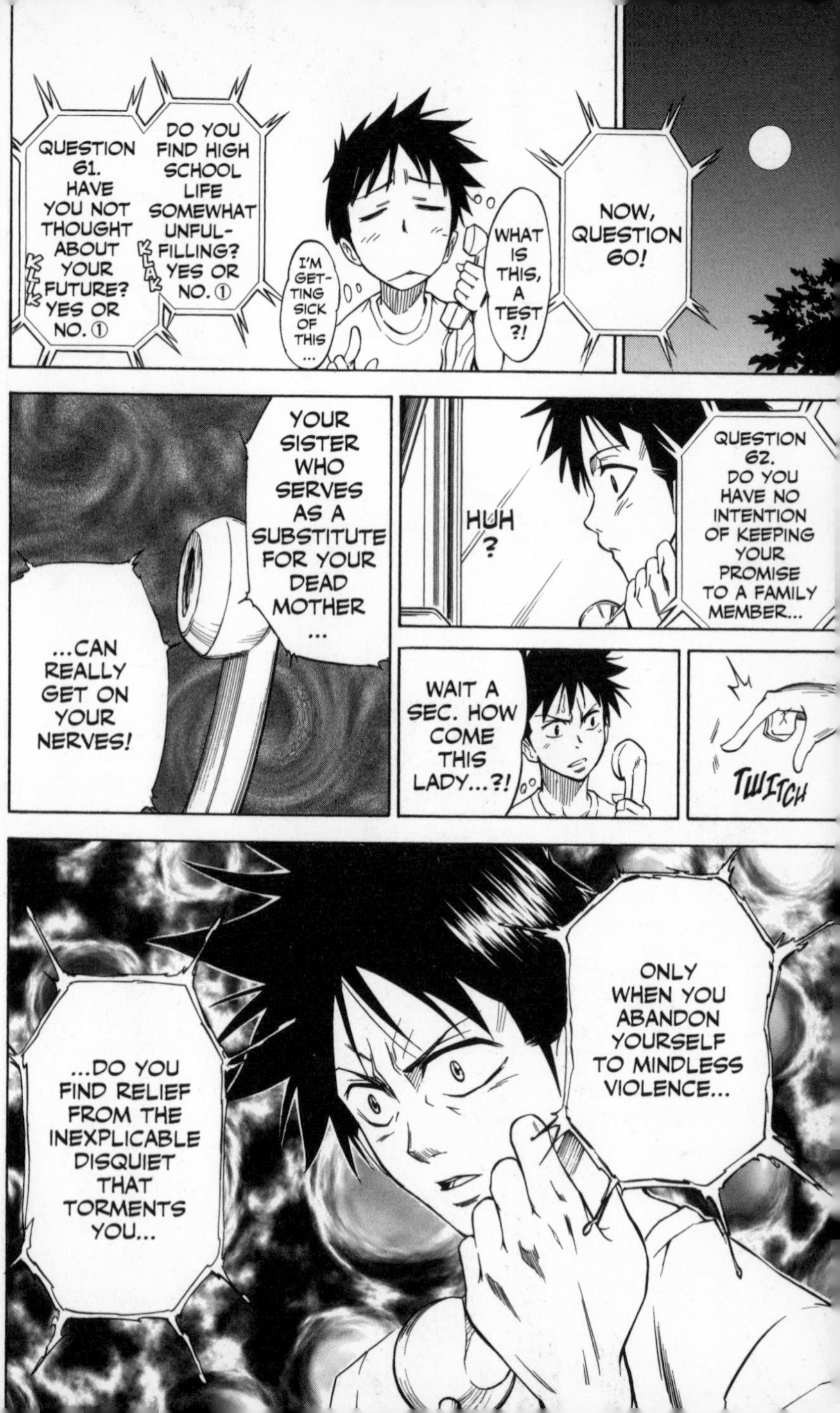
NOW, QUESTION 60!
WHAT IS THIS, A TEST?!
I'M GETTING SICK OF THIS...
DO YOU FIND HIGH SCHOOL LIFE SOMEWHAT UNFULFILLING? YES OR NO. ①
KLAK
QUESTION 61. HAVE YOU NOT THOUGHT ABOUT YOUR FUTURE? YES OR NO. ①
KLIK
QUESTION 62. DO YOU HAVE NO INTENTION OF KEEPING YOUR PROMISE TO A FAMILY MEMBER...
HUH?
TWITCH
WAIT A SEC. HOW COME THIS LADY...?!
YOUR SISTER WHO SERVES AS A SUBSTITUTE FOR YOUR DEAD MOTHER...
...CAN REALLY GET ON YOUR NERVES!
ONLY WHEN YOU ABANDON YOURSELF TO MINDLESS VIOLENCE...
...DO YOU FIND RELIEF FROM THE INEXPLICABLE DISQUIET THAT TORMENTS YOU...

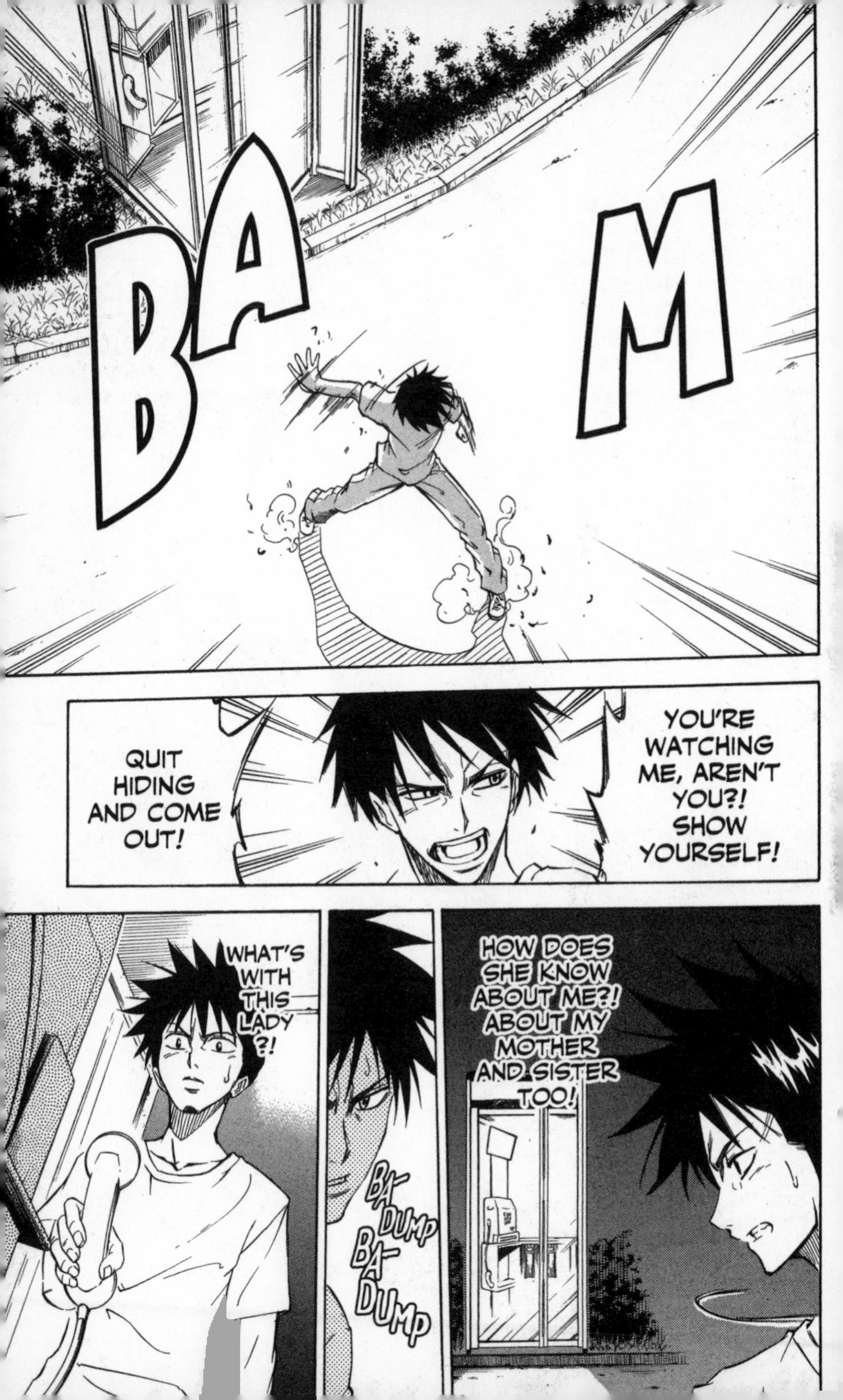
BAM
YOU'RE WATCHING ME, AREN'T YOU?! SHOW YOURSELF!
QUIT HIDING AND COME OUT!
HOW DOES SHE KNOW ABOUT ME?! ABOUT MY MOTHER AND SISTER TOO!
BA-DUMP BA-DUMP
WHAT'S WITH THIS LADY?!

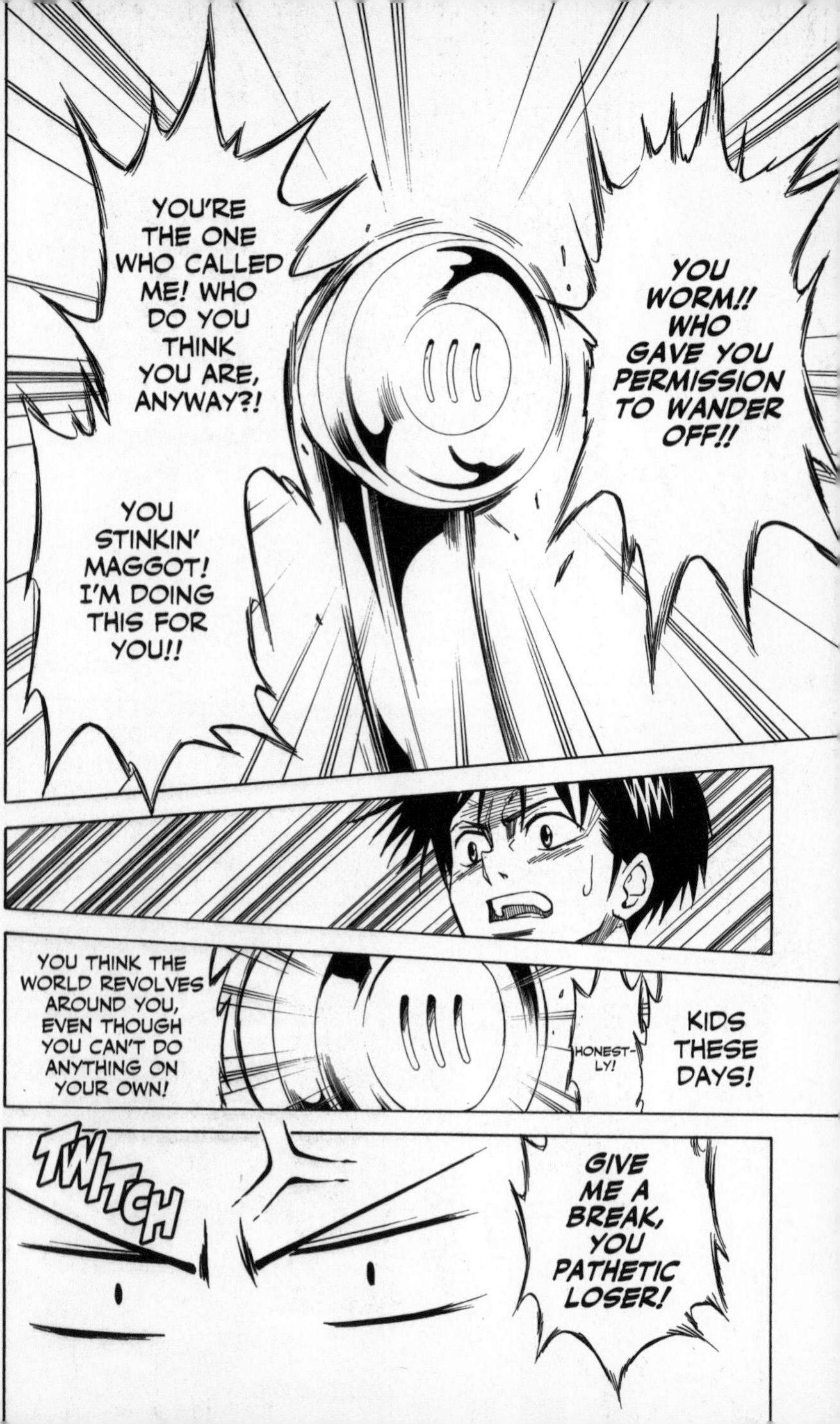
YOU WORM!! WHO GAVE YOU PERMISSION TO WANDER OFF!!
YOU'RE THE ONE WHO CALLED ME! WHO DO YOU THINK YOU ARE, ANYWAY?!
YOU STINKIN' MAGGOT! I'M DOING THIS FOR YOU!!
KIDS THESE DAYS!
HONEST-LY!
YOU THINK THE WORLD REVOLVES AROUND YOU, EVEN THOUGH YOU CAN'T DO ANYTHING ON YOUR OWN!
GIVE ME A BREAK, YOU PATHETIC LOSER!
TWITCH

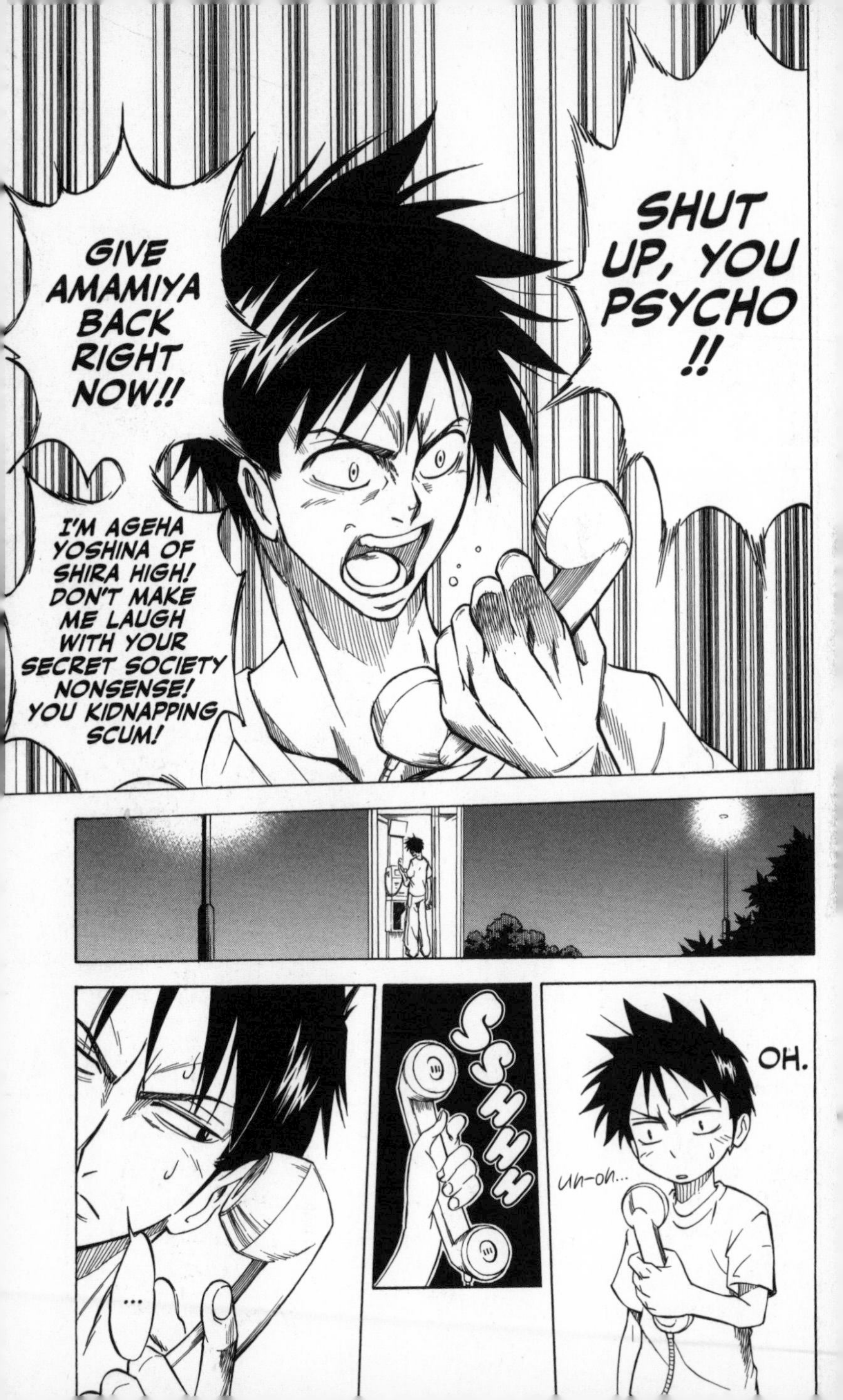
SHUT UP, YOU PSYCHO!!
GIVE AMAMIYA BACK RIGHT NOW!!
I'M AGEHA YOSHINA OF SHIRA HIGH! DON'T MAKE ME LAUGH WITH YOUR SECRET SOCIETY NONSENSE! YOU KIDNAPPING SCUM!
OH.
uh-oh...
SSHHH
...

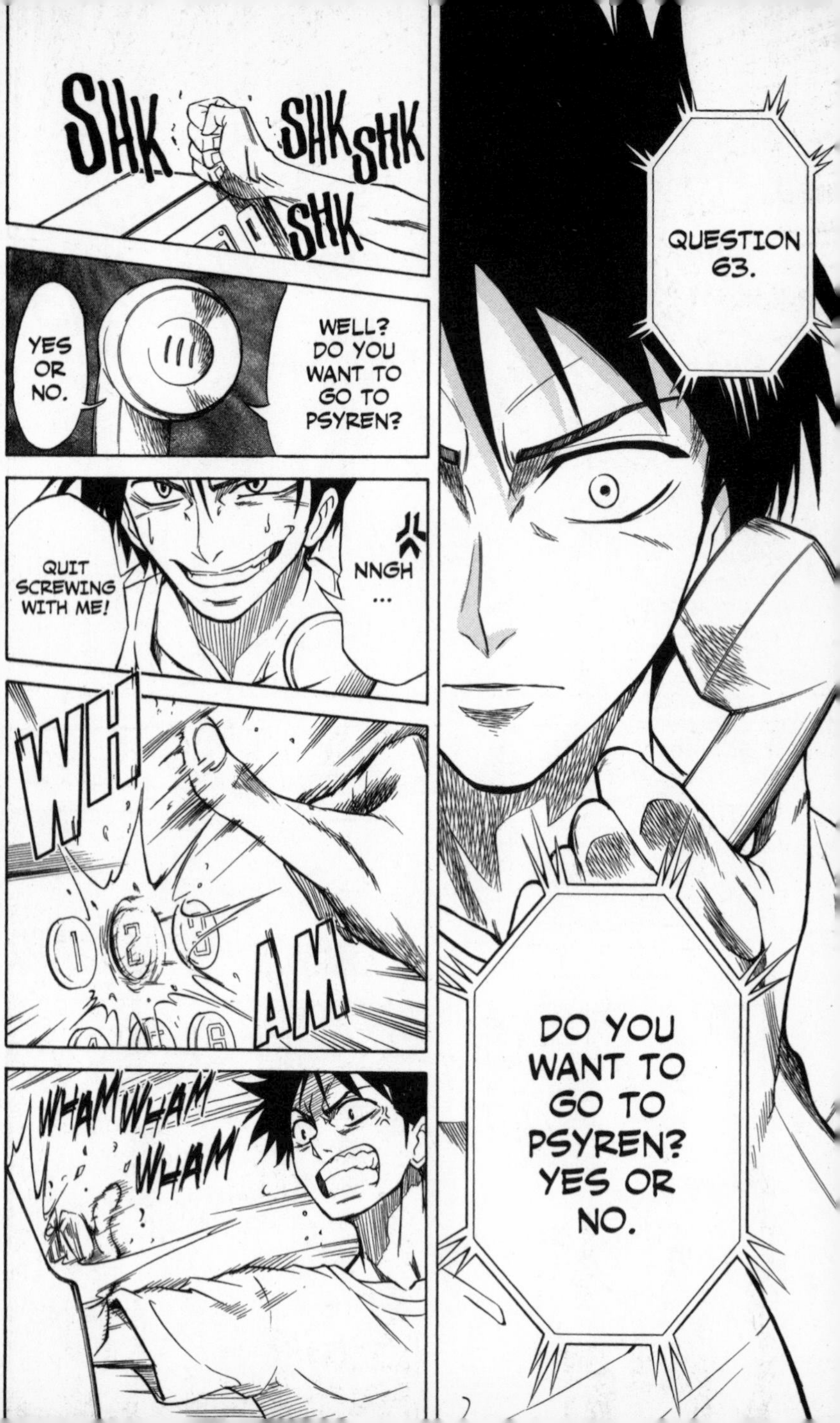
QUESTION 63.
DO YOU WANT TO GO TO PSYREN? YES OR NO.
SHK SHK SHK SHK
WELL? DO YOU WANT TO GO TO PSYREN?
YES OR NO.
NNGH ...
QUIT SCREWING WITH ME!
WH AM
WHAM WHAM WHAM WHAM

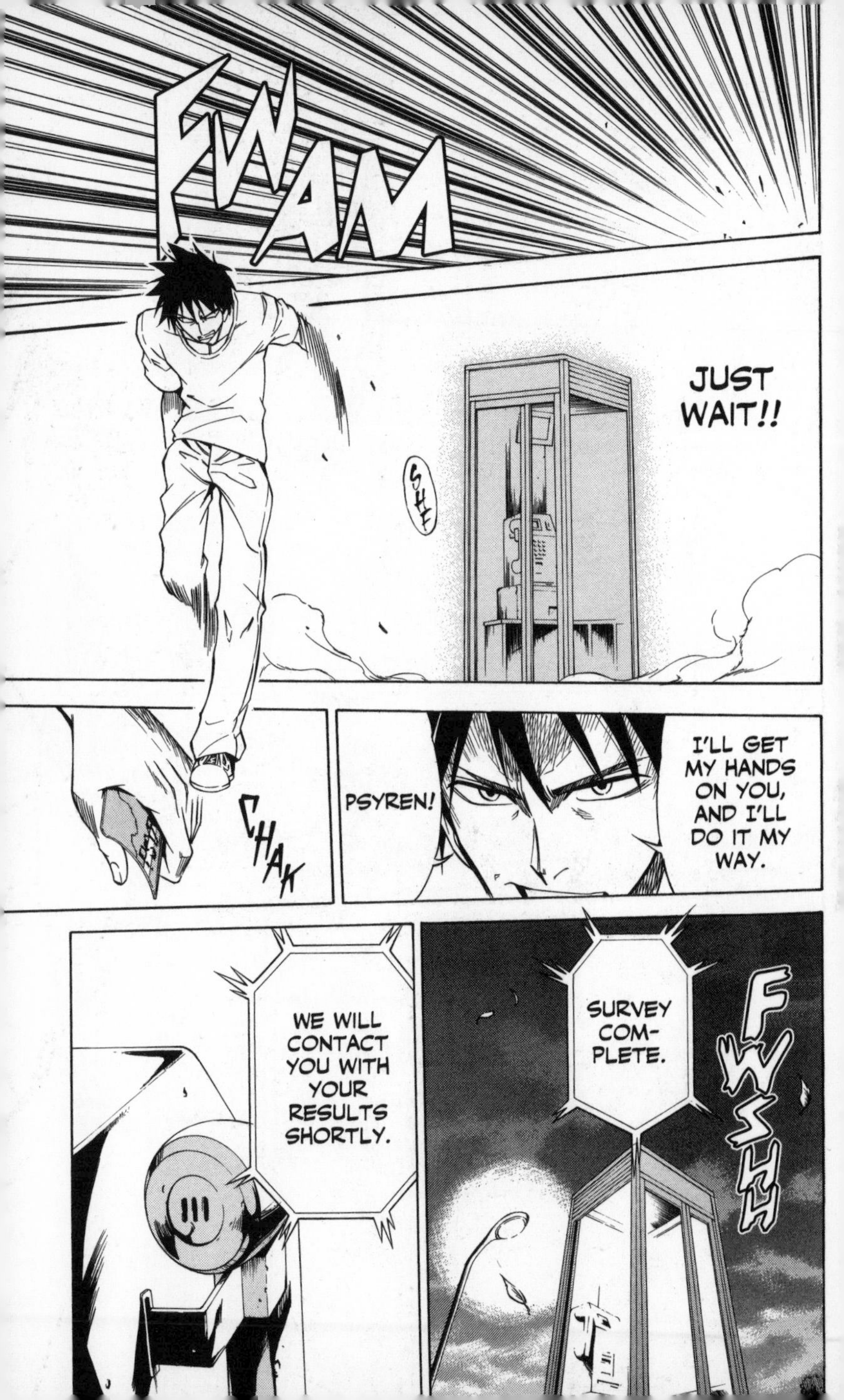
SWAM
JUST WAIT!!
SHF
I'LL GET MY HANDS ON YOU, AND I'LL DO IT MY WAY.
PSYREN!
CHAK
FWSHH
SURVEY COM-PLETE.
WE WILL CONTACT YOU WITH YOUR RESULTS SHORTLY.

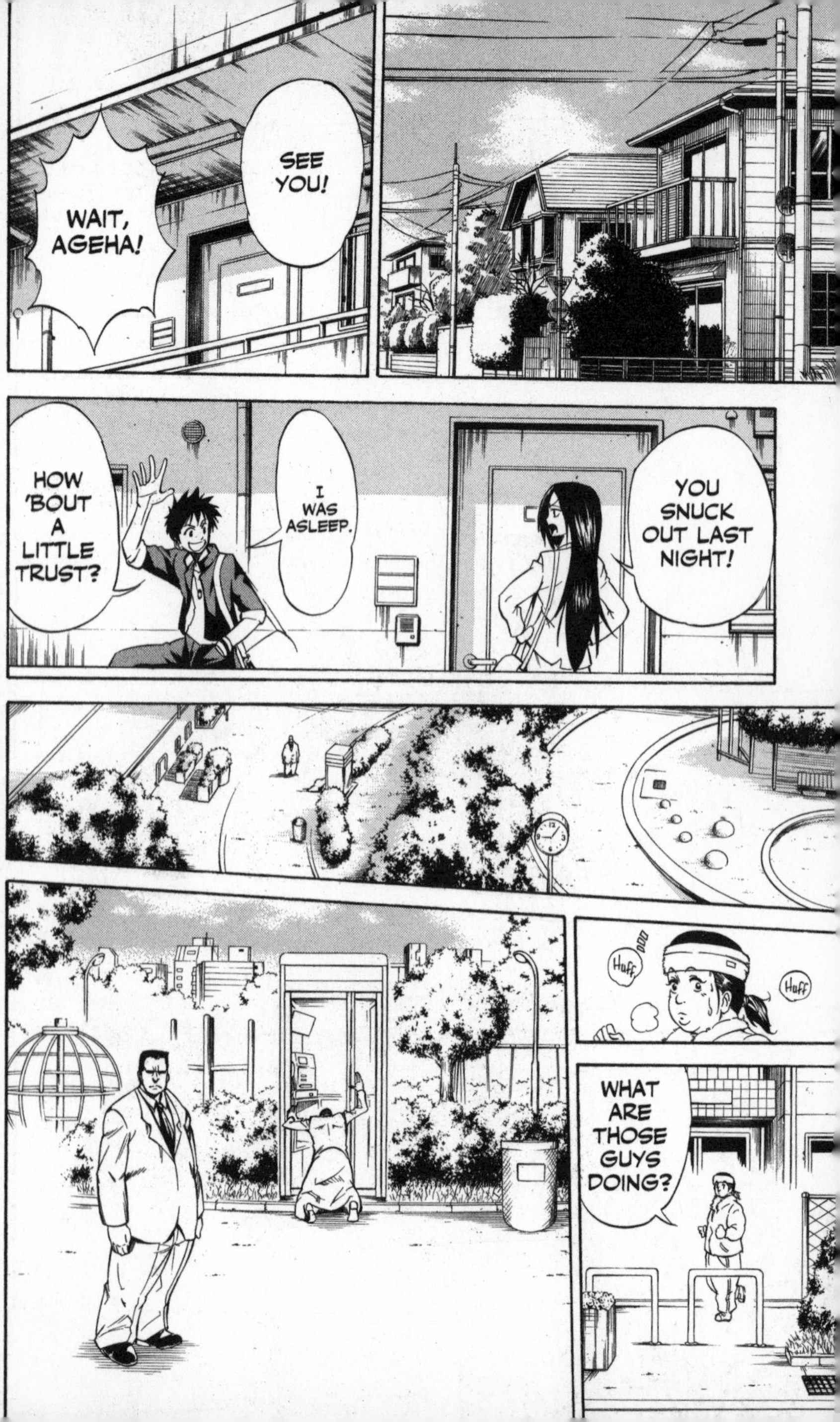
SEE YOU!
WAIT, AGEHA!
YOU SNUCK OUT LAST NIGHT!
I WAS ASLEEP.
HOW 'BOUT A LITTLE TRUST?
Huff
Huff
WHAT ARE THOSE GUYS DOING?

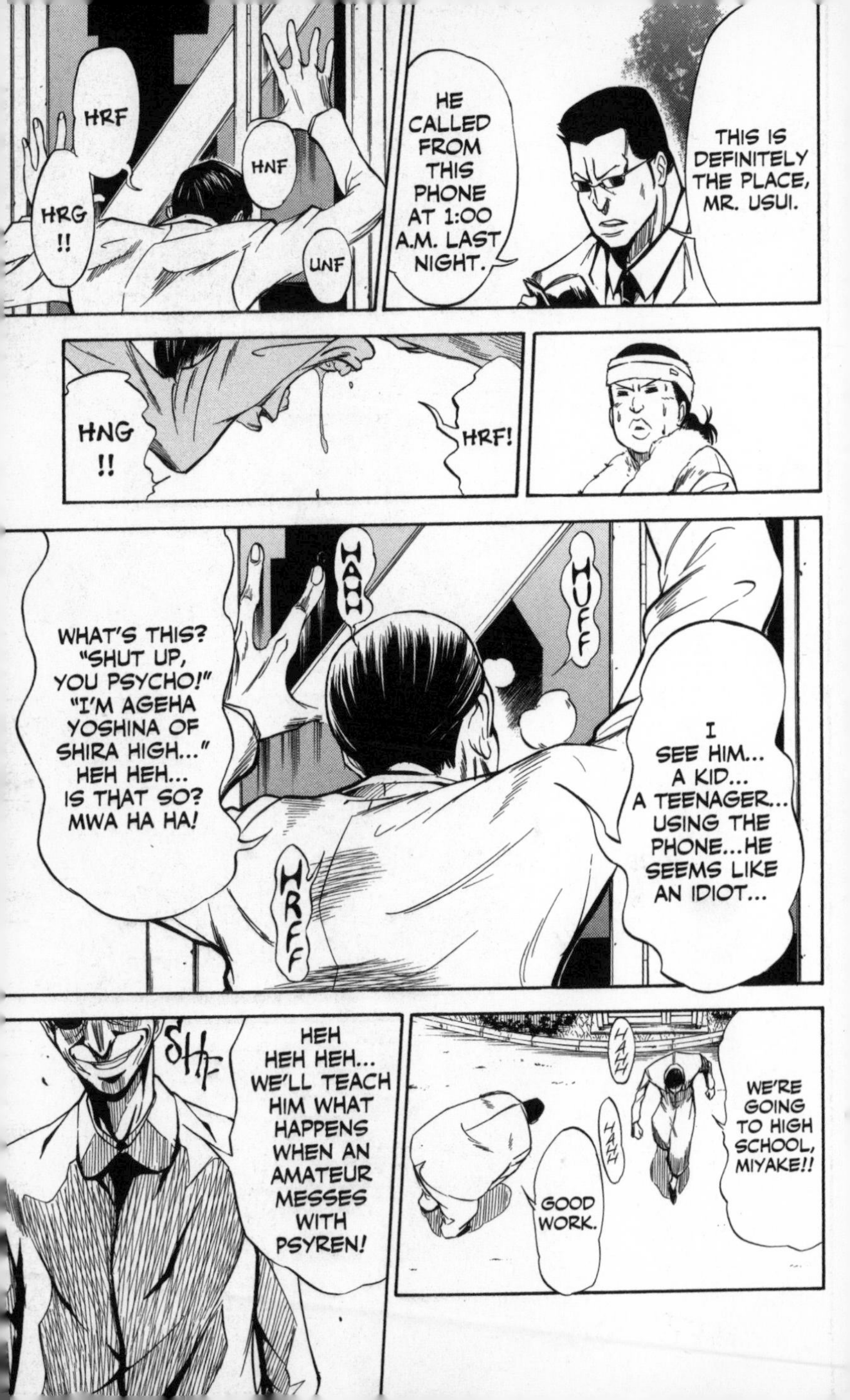
THIS IS DEFINITELY THE PLACE, MR. USUI.
HE CALLED FROM THIS PHONE AT 1:00 A.M. LAST NIGHT.
HNF
UNF
HRF
HRG !!
HRF!
HNG !!
HUFF
HAHH
I SEE HIM... A KID... A TEENAGER... USING THE PHONE...HE SEEMS LIKE AN IDIOT...
WHAT'S THIS? "SHUT UP, YOU PSYCHO!" "I'M AGEHA YOSHINA OF SHIRA HIGH..." HEH HEH... IS THAT SO? MWA HA HA!
HRFF
WE'RE GOING TO HIGH SCHOOL, MIYAKE!!
HAHH
HAHH
GOOD WORK.
HEH HEH HEH... WE'LL TEACH HIM WHAT HAPPENS WHEN AN AMATEUR MESSES WITH PSYREN!
SHF

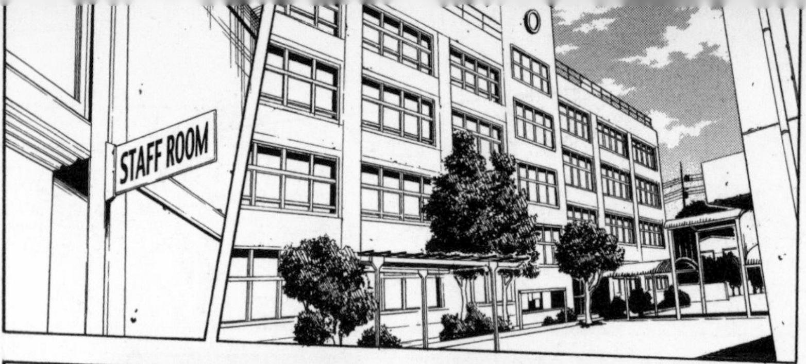
STAFF ROOM

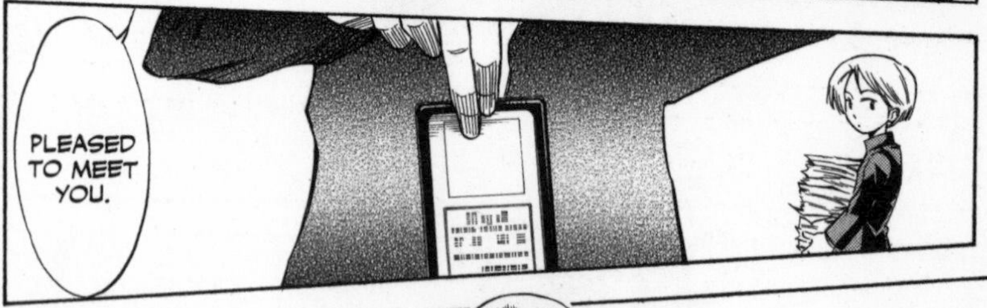
PLEASED TO MEET YOU.

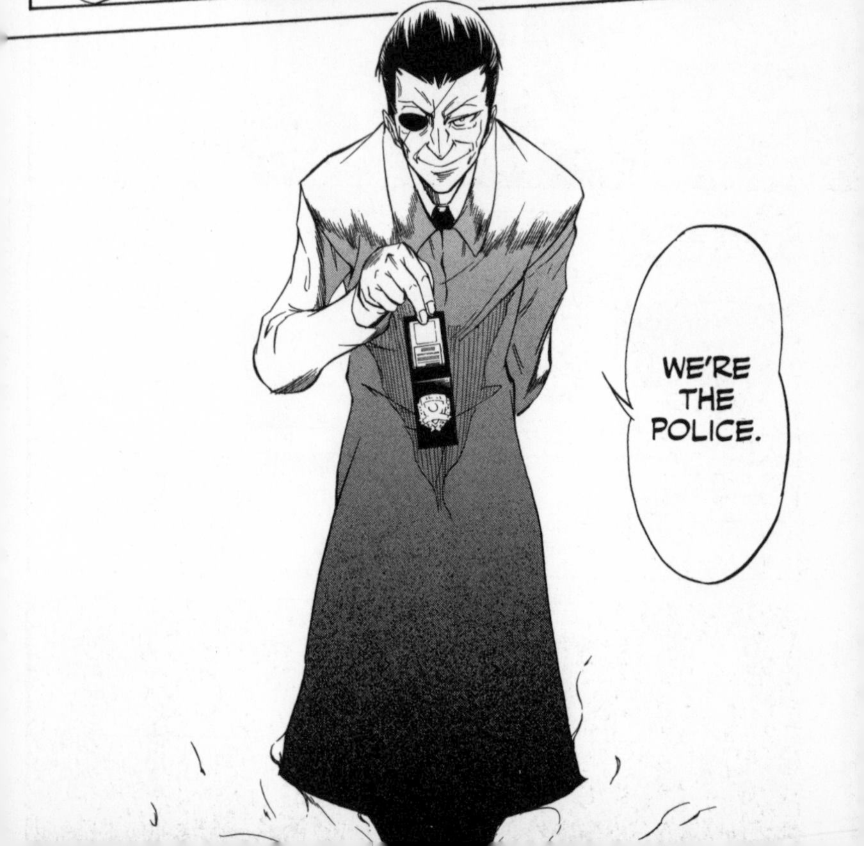
WE'RE THE POLICE.

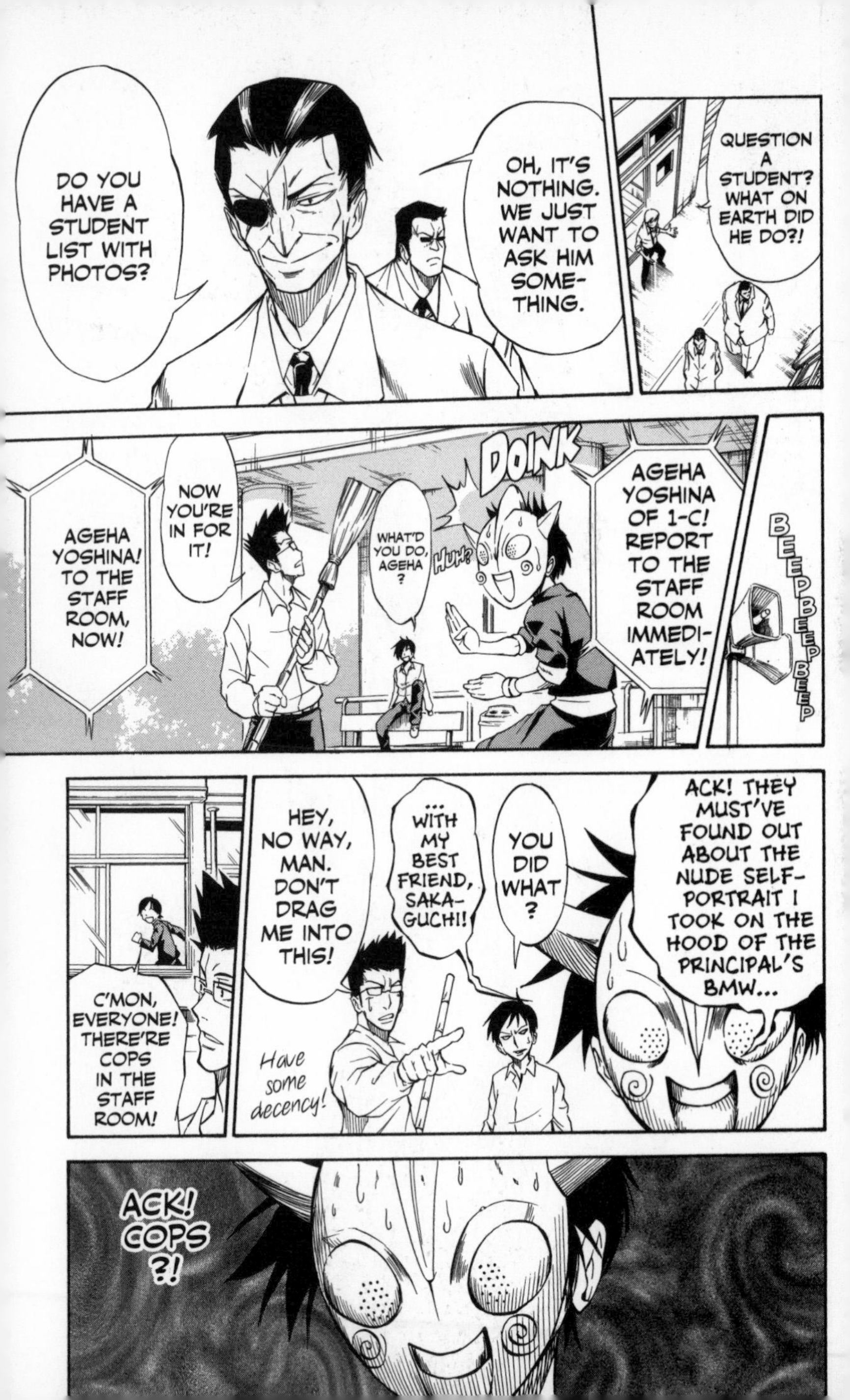
QUESTION A STUDENT? WHAT ON EARTH DID HE DO?!
OH, IT'S NOTHING. WE JUST WANT TO ASK HIM SOME-THING.
DO YOU HAVE A STUDENT LIST WITH PHOTOS?
BEEP BEEP BEEP
AGEHA YOSHINA OF 1-C! REPORT TO THE STAFF ROOM IMMEDI-ATELY!
DOINK
HUH?
WHAT'D YOU DO, AGEHA?
NOW YOU'RE IN FOR IT!
AGEHA YOSHINA! TO THE STAFF ROOM, NOW!
ACK! THEY MUST'VE FOUND OUT ABOUT THE NUDE SELF-PORTRAIT I TOOK ON THE HOOD OF THE PRINCIPAL'S BMW...
YOU DID WHAT?
...WITH MY BEST FRIEND, SAKA-GUCHI!!
HEY, NO WAY, MAN. DON'T DRAG ME INTO THIS!
Have some decency!
C'MON, EVERYONE! THERE'RE COPS IN THE STAFF ROOM!
ACK! COPS ?!

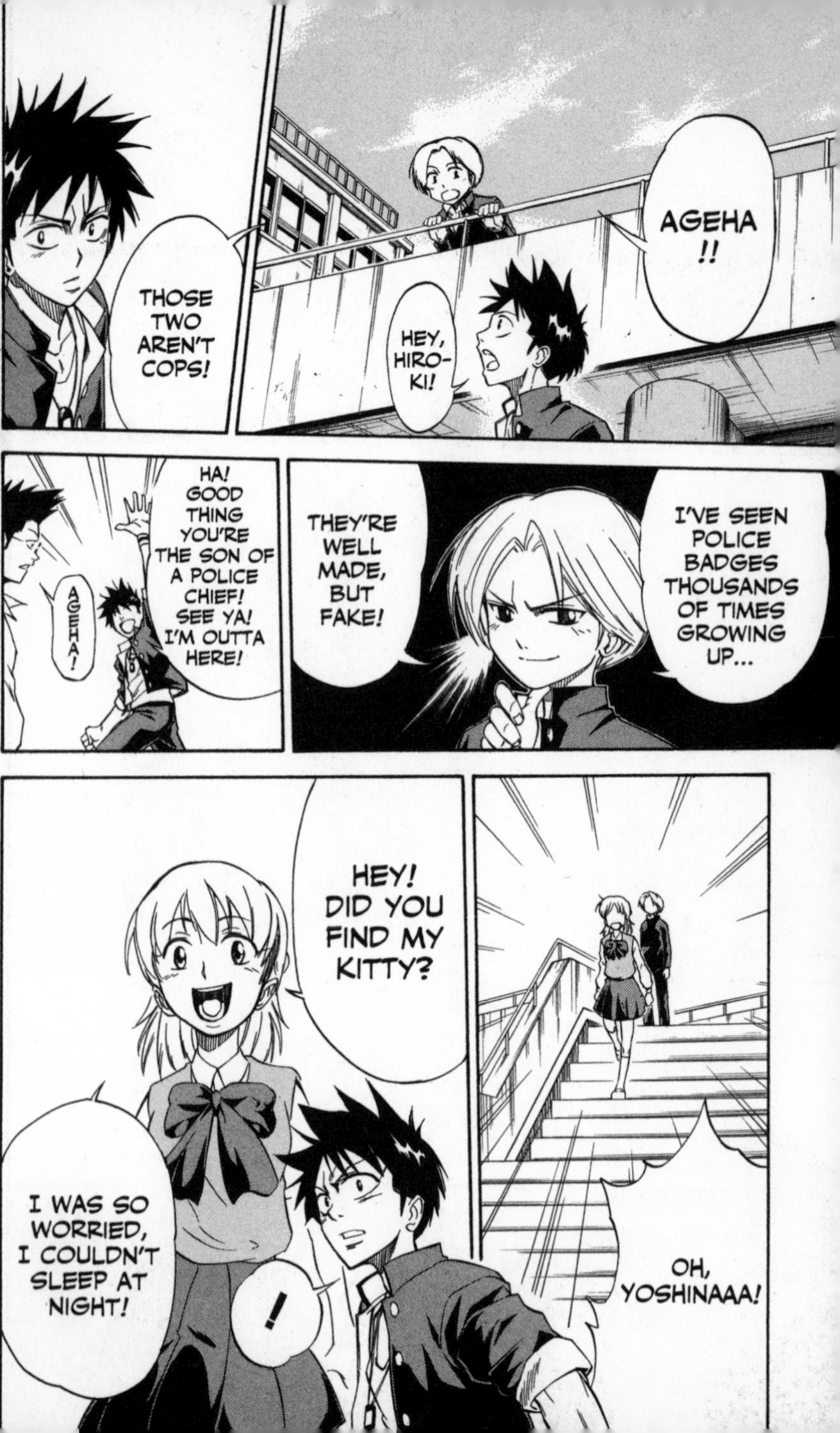
AGEHA!!
HEY, HIRO-KI!
THOSE TWO AREN'T COPS!
I'VE SEEN POLICE BADGES THOUSANDS OF TIMES GROWING UP...
THEY'RE WELL MADE, BUT FAKE!
HA! GOOD THING YOU'RE THE SON OF A POLICE CHIEF! SEE YA! I'M OUTTA HERE!
AGEHA!
OH, YOSHINAAA!
HEY! DID YOU FIND MY KITTY?
I WAS SO WORRIED, I COULDN'T SLEEP AT NIGHT!
!

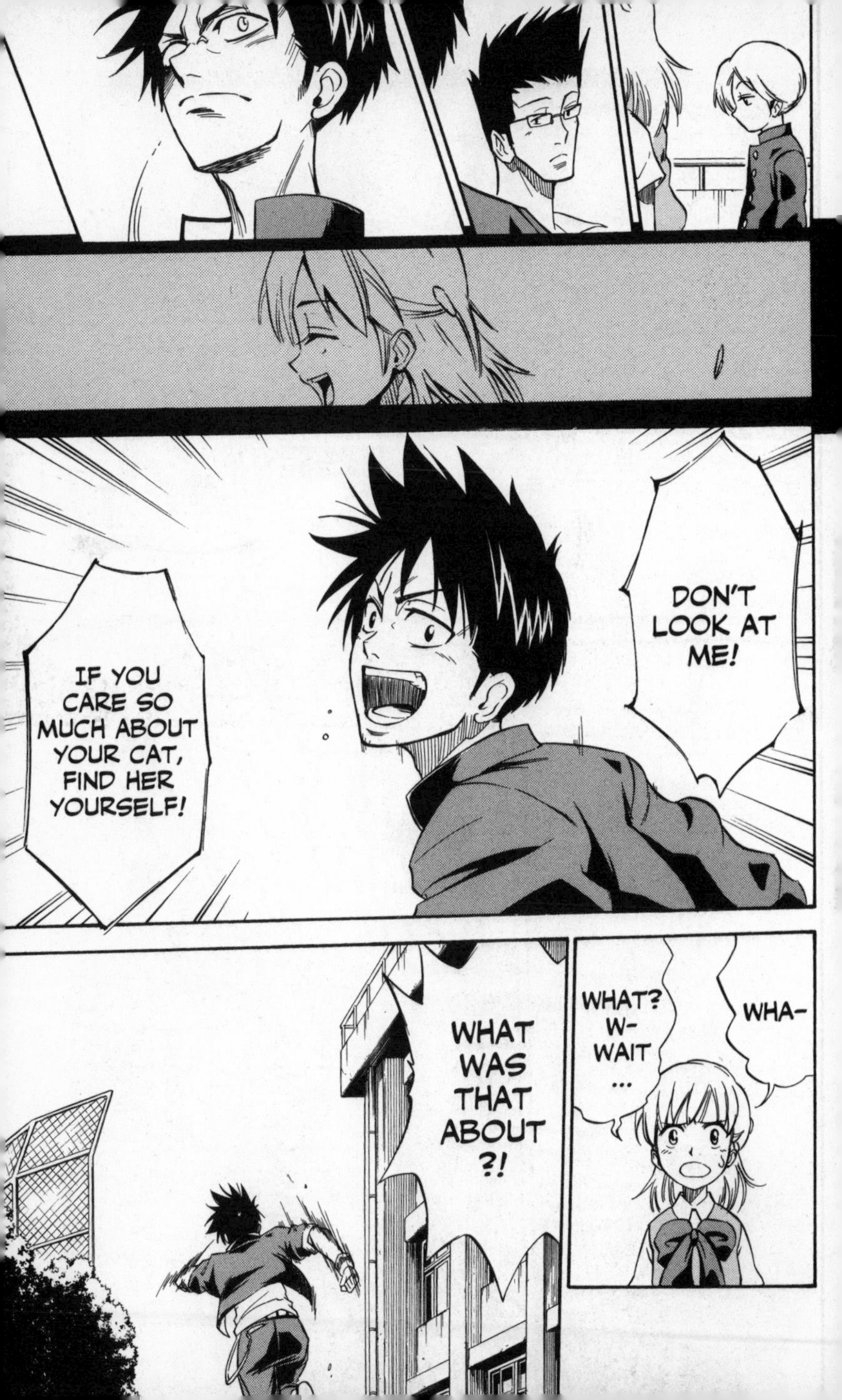
DON'T LOOK AT ME!
IF YOU CARE SO MUCH ABOUT YOUR CAT, FIND HER YOURSELF!
WHA-
WHAT? W-WAIT...
WHAT WAS THAT ABOUT?!

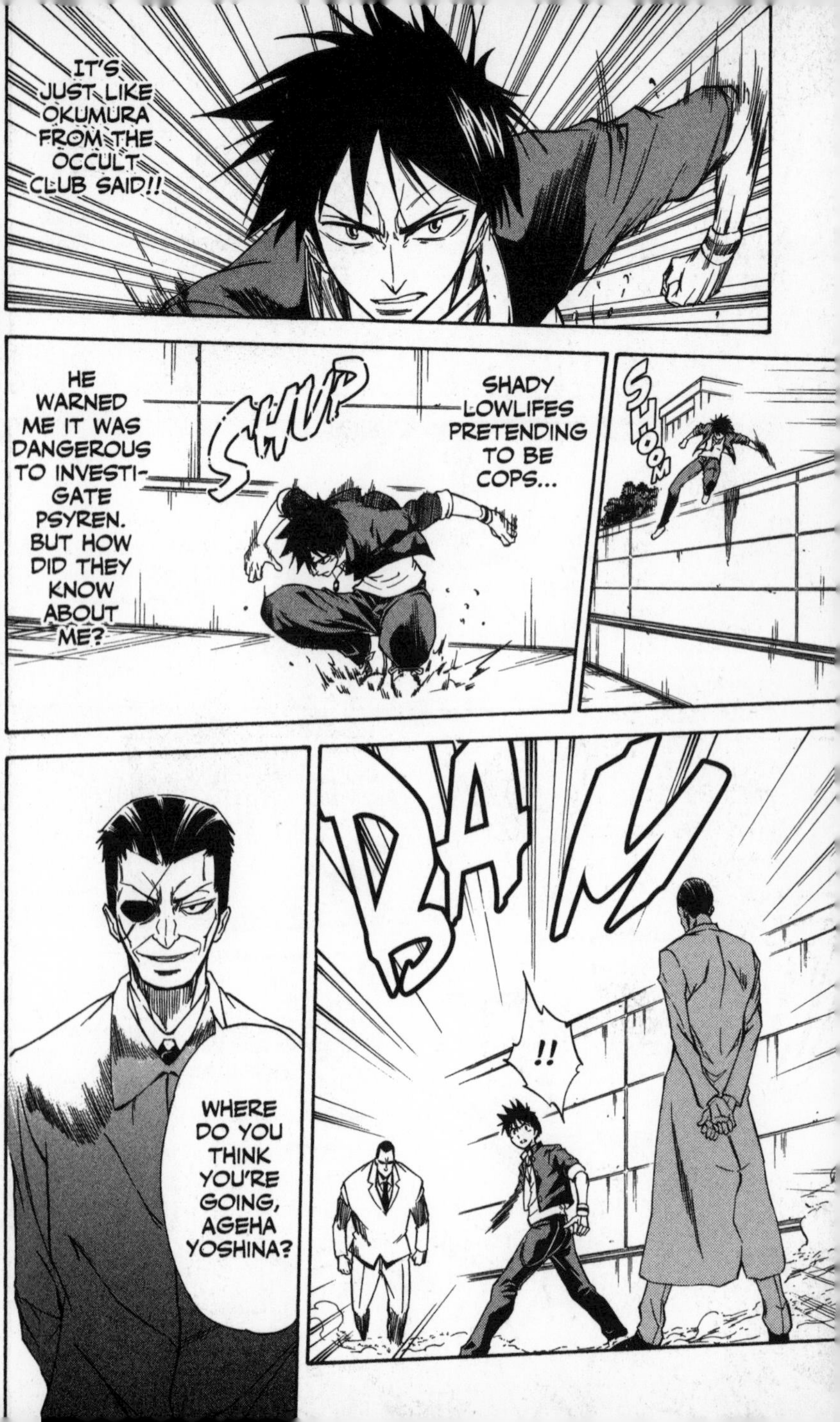
IT'S JUST LIKE OKUMURA FROM THE OCCULT CLUB SAID!!
SHOOM
SHADY LOWLIFES PRETENDING TO BE COPS...
SHUP
HE WARNED ME IT WAS DANGEROUS TO INVESTI-GATE PSYREN. BUT HOW DID THEY KNOW ABOUT ME?
BAM
!!
WHERE DO YOU THINK YOU'RE GOING, AGEHA YOSHINA?

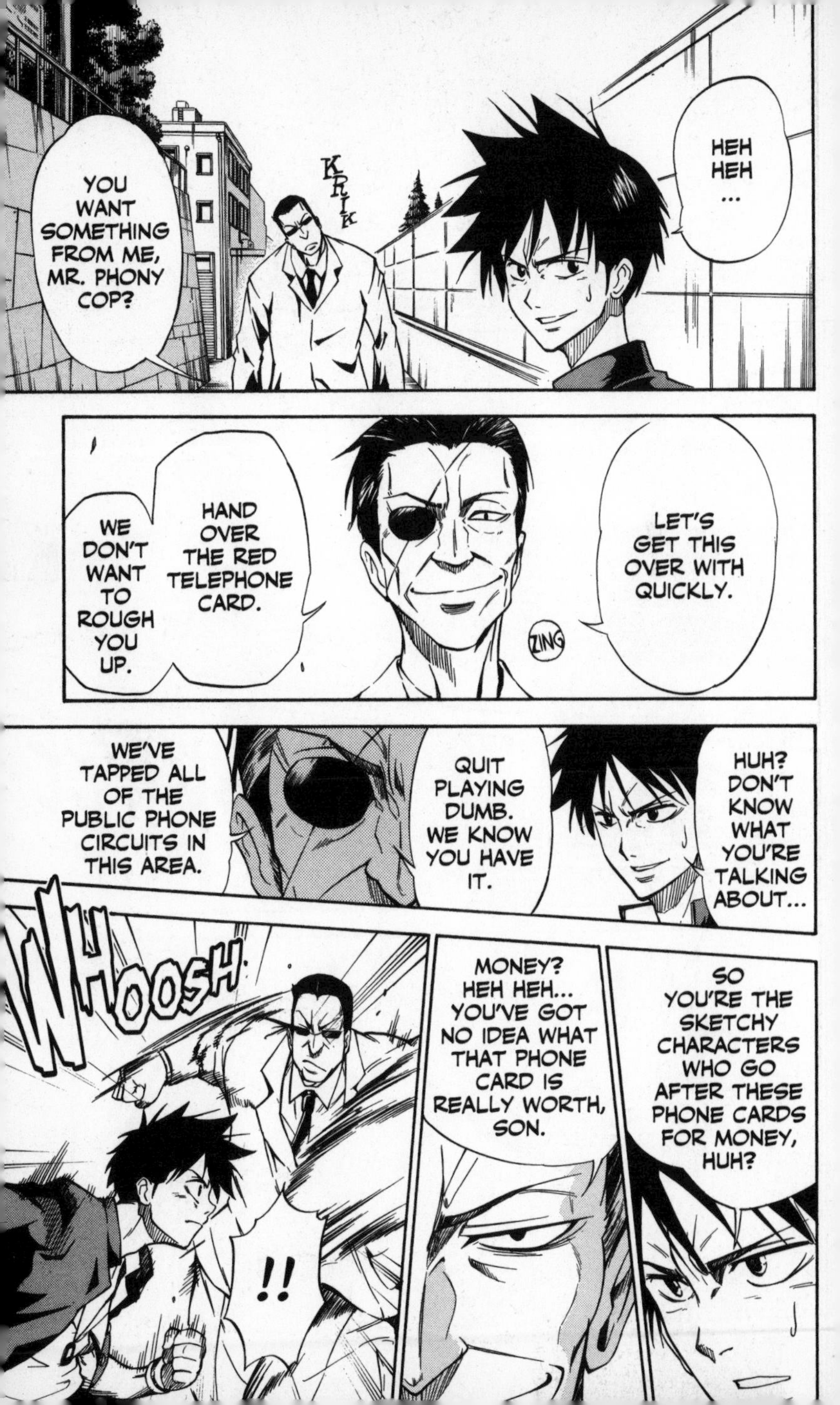
HEH HEH ...
KRIK
YOU WANT SOMETHING FROM ME, MR. PHONY COP?
LET'S GET THIS OVER WITH QUICKLY.
ZING
HAND OVER THE RED TELEPHONE CARD.
WE DON'T WANT TO ROUGH YOU UP.
HUH? DON'T KNOW WHAT YOU'RE TALKING ABOUT...
QUIT PLAYING DUMB. WE KNOW YOU HAVE IT.
WE'VE TAPPED ALL OF THE PUBLIC PHONE CIRCUITS IN THIS AREA.
SO YOU'RE THE SKETCHY CHARACTERS WHO GO AFTER THESE PHONE CARDS FOR MONEY, HUH?
MONEY? HEH HEH... YOU'VE GOT NO IDEA WHAT THAT PHONE CARD IS REALLY WORTH, SON.
WHOOSH
!!

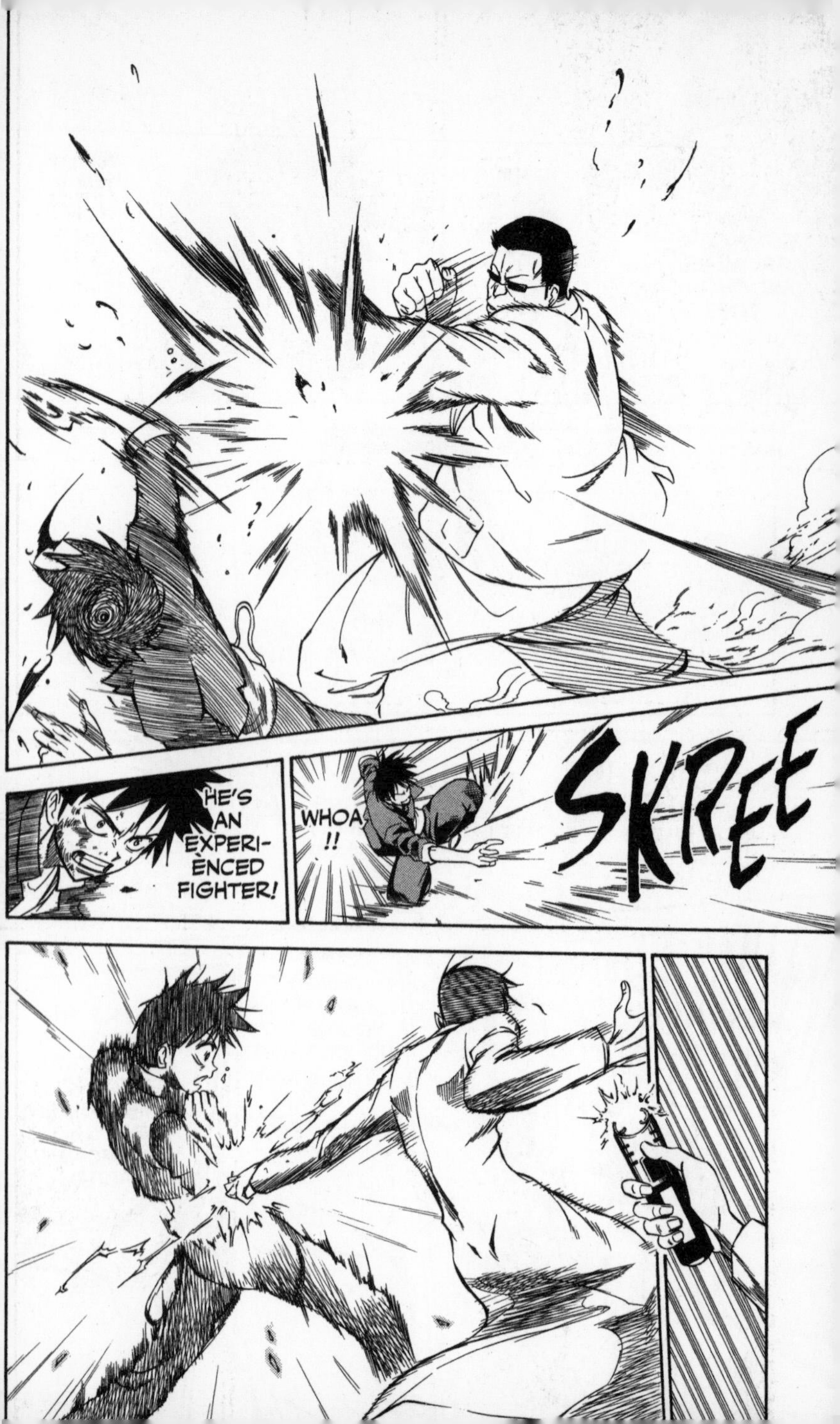
SKREE
WHOA !!
HE'S AN EXPERI-ENCED FIGHTER!

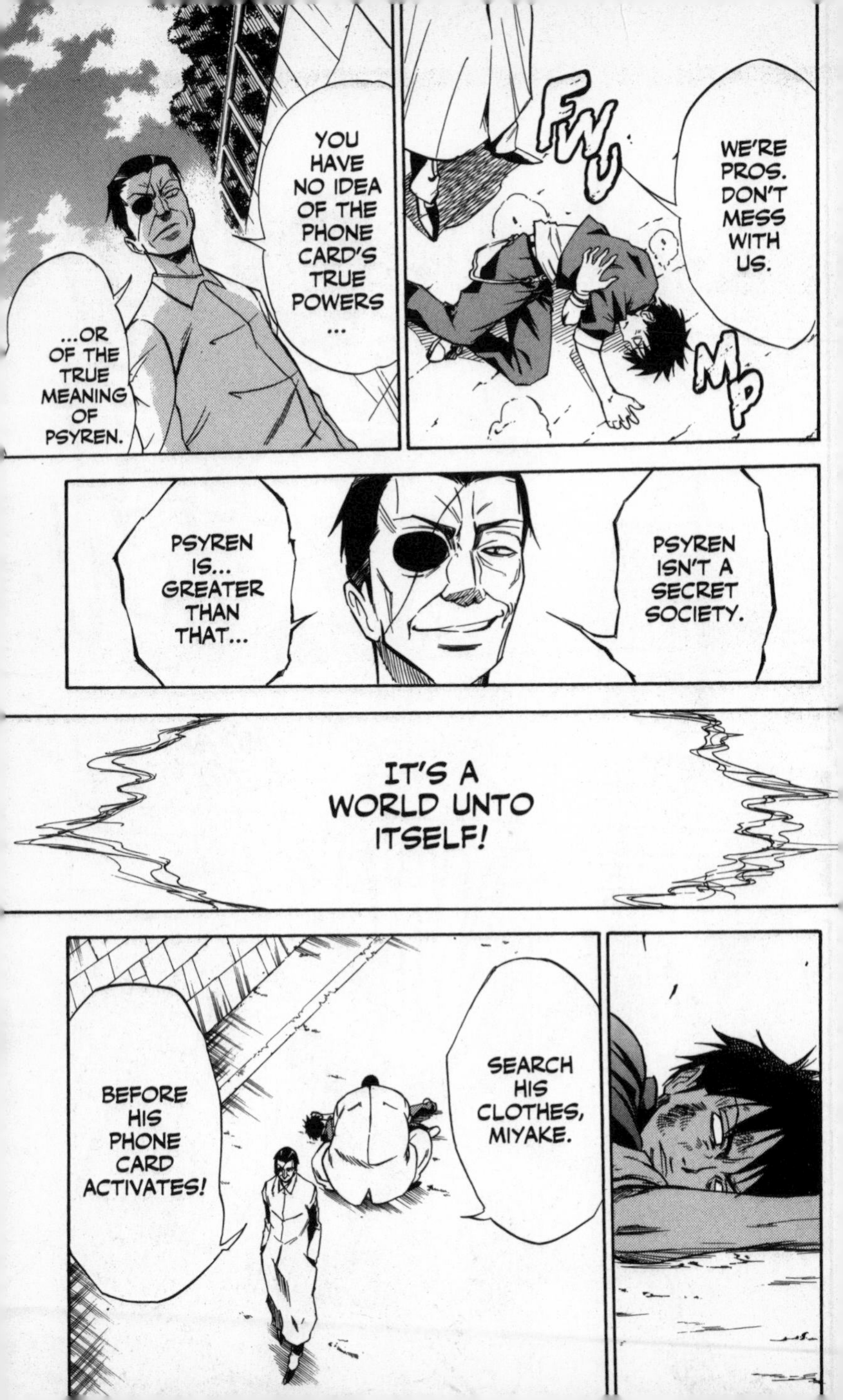
WE'RE PROS. DON'T MESS WITH US.
FWU
MP
YOU HAVE NO IDEA OF THE PHONE CARD'S TRUE POWERS...
...OR OF THE TRUE MEANING OF PSYREN.
PSYREN ISN'T A SECRET SOCIETY.
PSYREN IS... GREATER THAN THAT...
IT'S A WORLD UNTO ITSELF!
SEARCH HIS CLOTHES, MIYAKE.
BEFORE HIS PHONE CARD ACTIVATES!

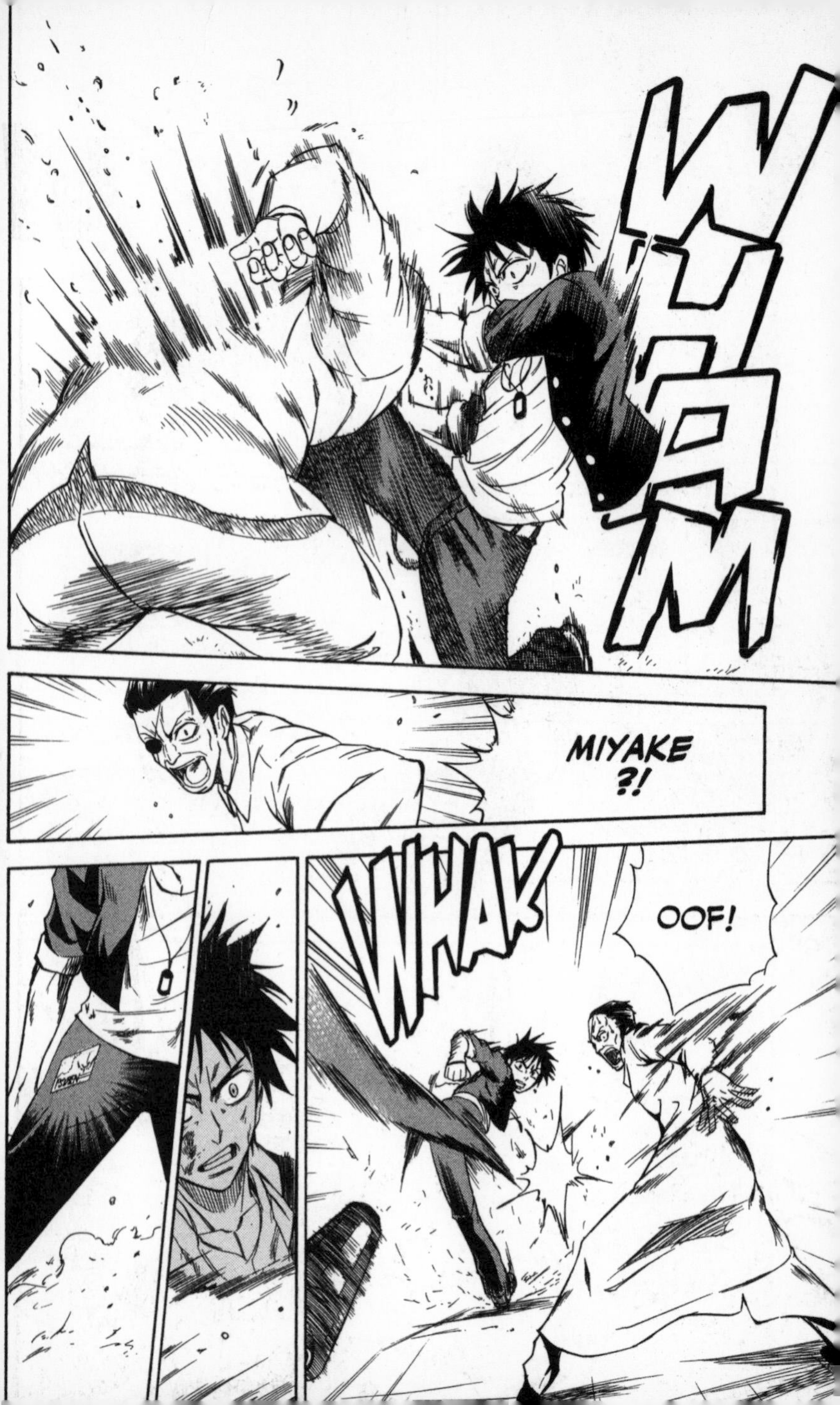
WHAM
MIYAKE ?!
OOF!
WHAK

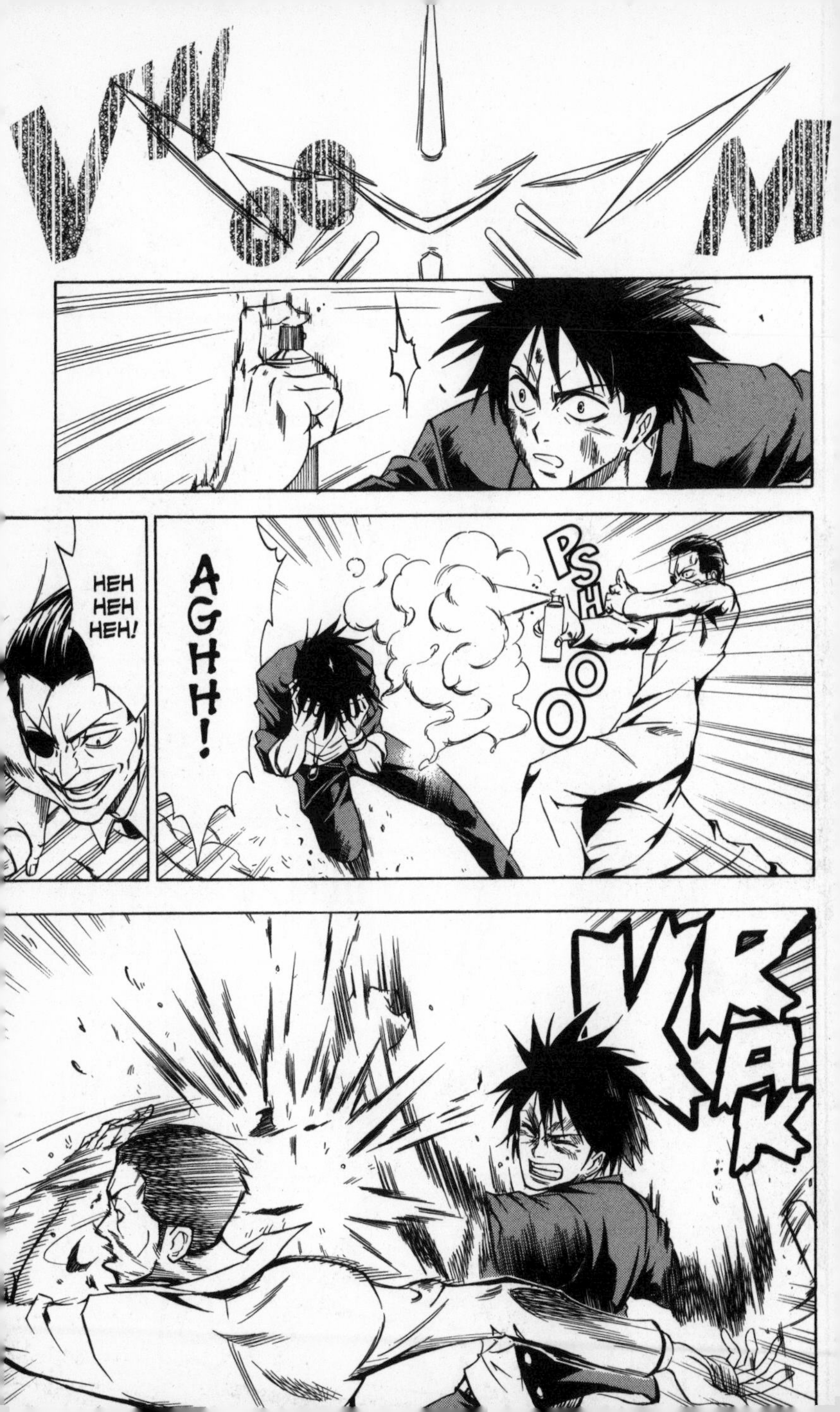
VWOOOM
PSHOOO
AGHH!
HEH HEH HEH!
VRAK

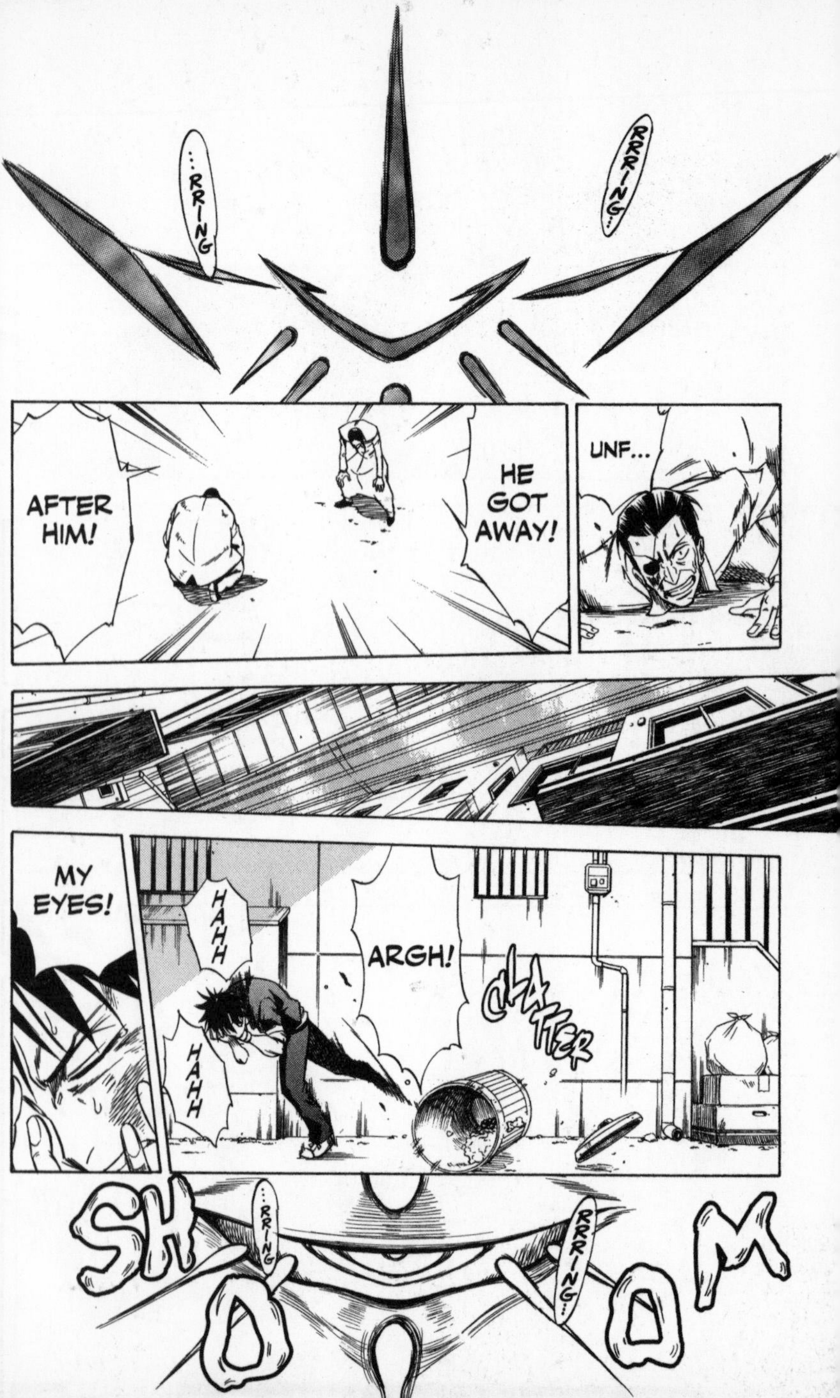
RRRING...
...RRING
UNF...
HE GOT AWAY!
AFTER HIM!
CLATTER
ARGH!
HAHH
HAHH
MY EYES!
RRRING...
...RRING
SHOOOM

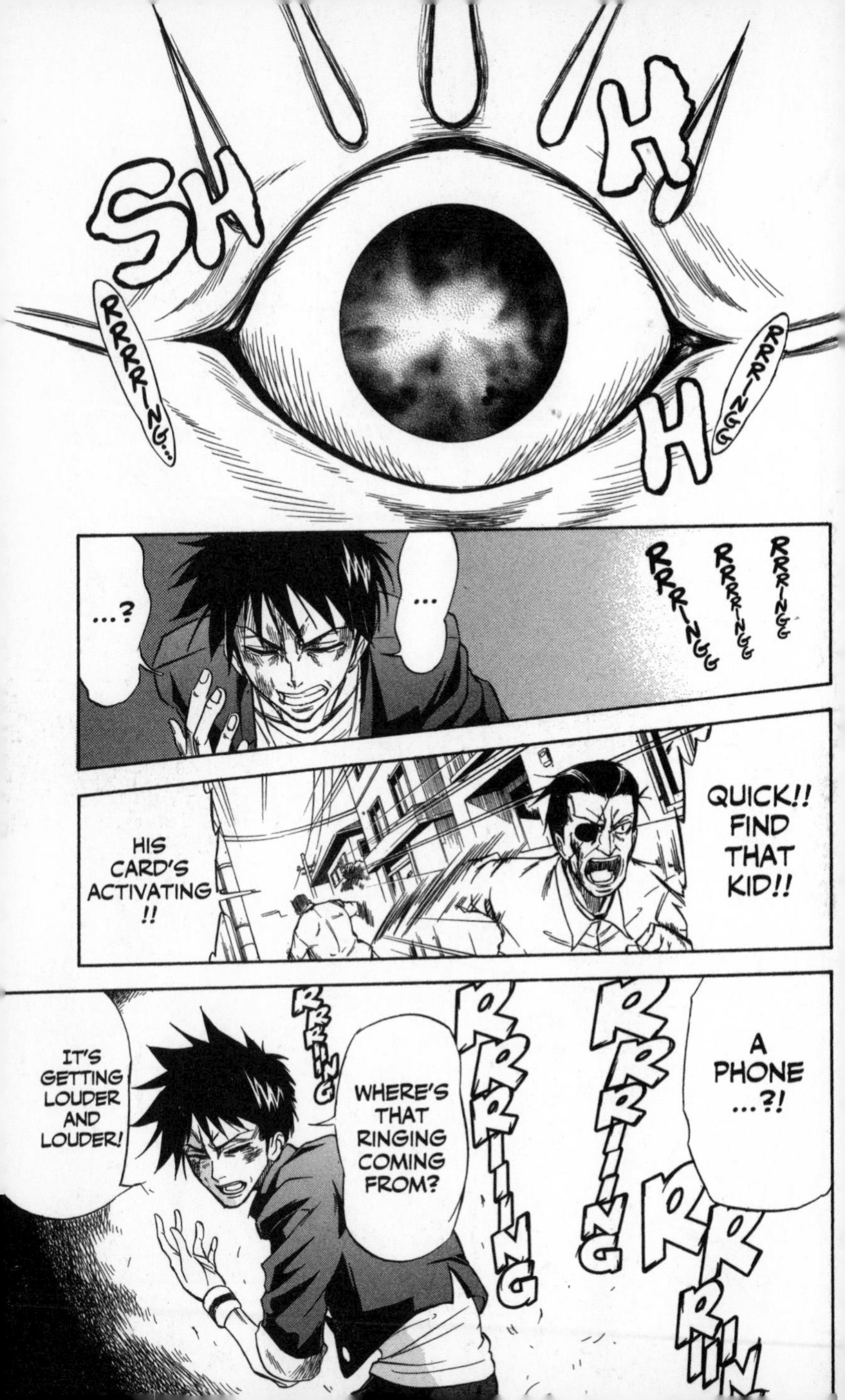
SHUUHH
RRRINGG
RRRRING...
RRRINGG
RRRRINGG
RRRRINGG
...
...?
QUICK!! FIND THAT KID!!
HIS CARD'S ACTIVATING!!
A PHONE ...?!
RRRRING
RRRRING
WHERE'S THAT RINGING COMING FROM?
RRRING
IT'S GETTING LOUDER AND LOUDER!

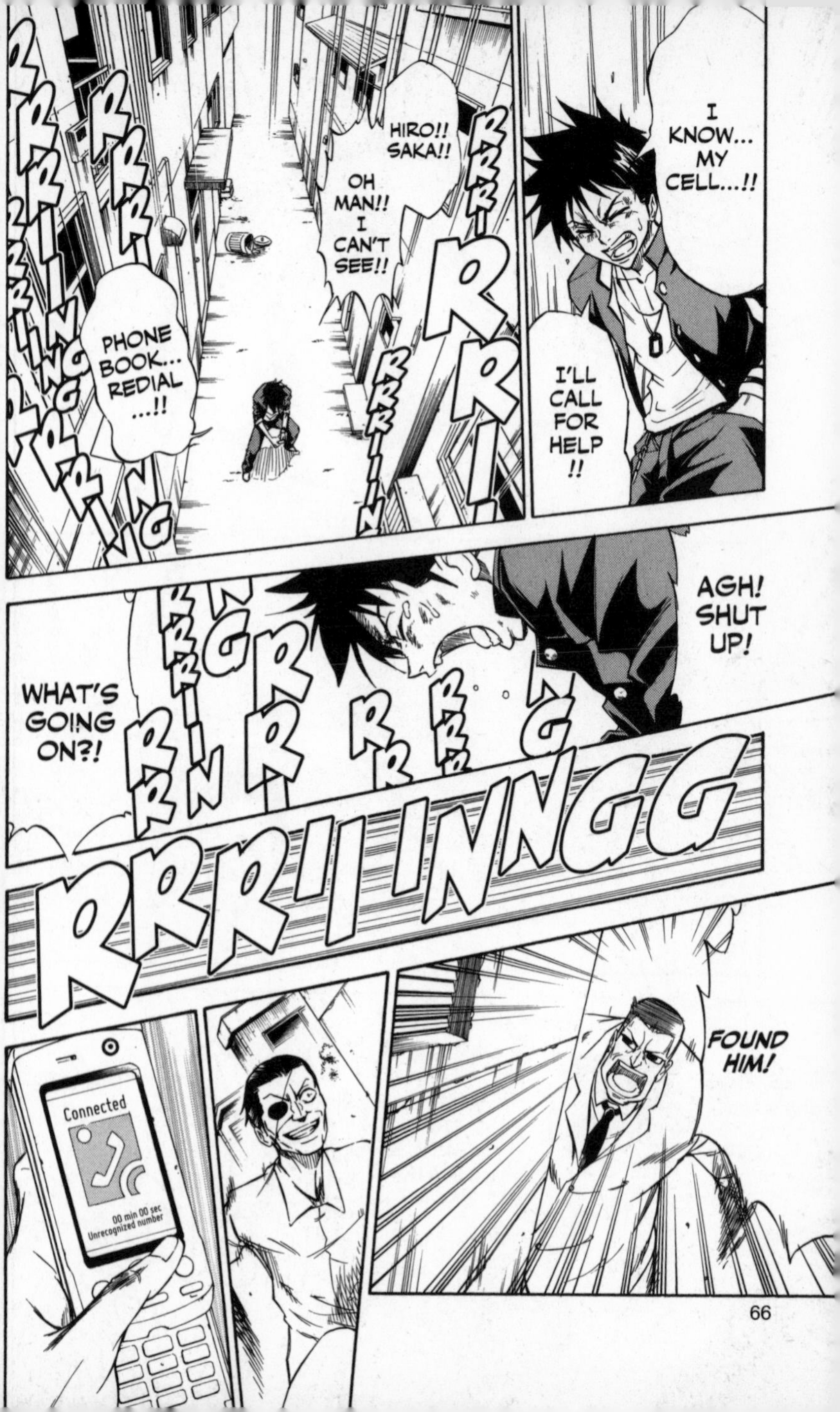
I KNOW... MY CELL...!!
I'LL CALL FOR HELP!!
HIRO!! SAKA!!
OH MAN!! I CAN'T SEE!!
PHONE BOOK... REDIAL ...!!
AGH! SHUT UP!
WHAT'S GOING ON?!
RRRIINNGG
FOUND HIM!
Connected
00 min 00 sec
Unrecognized number

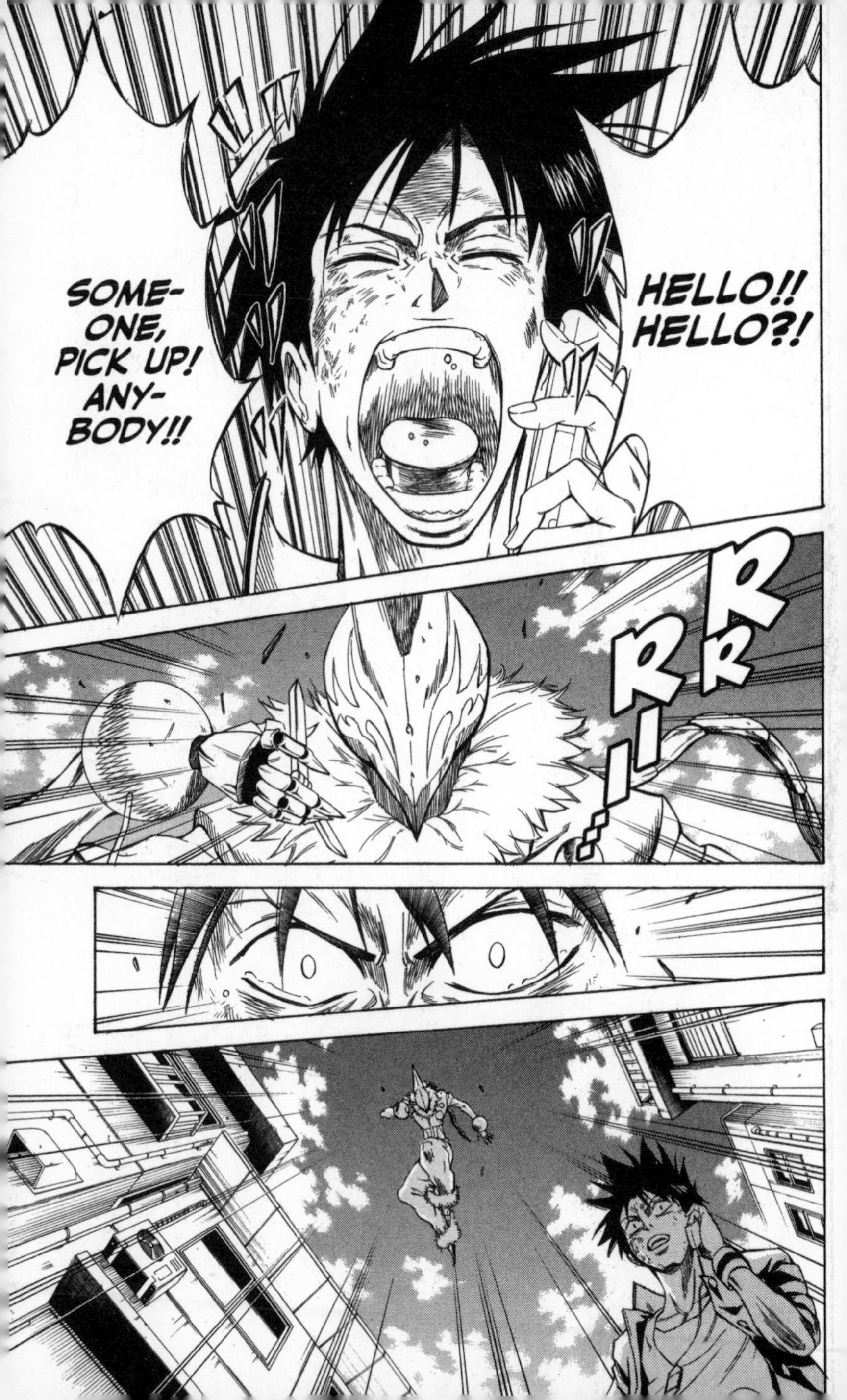
HELLO!! HELLO?!
SOME-ONE, PICK UP! ANY-BODY!!
RRRR!!...

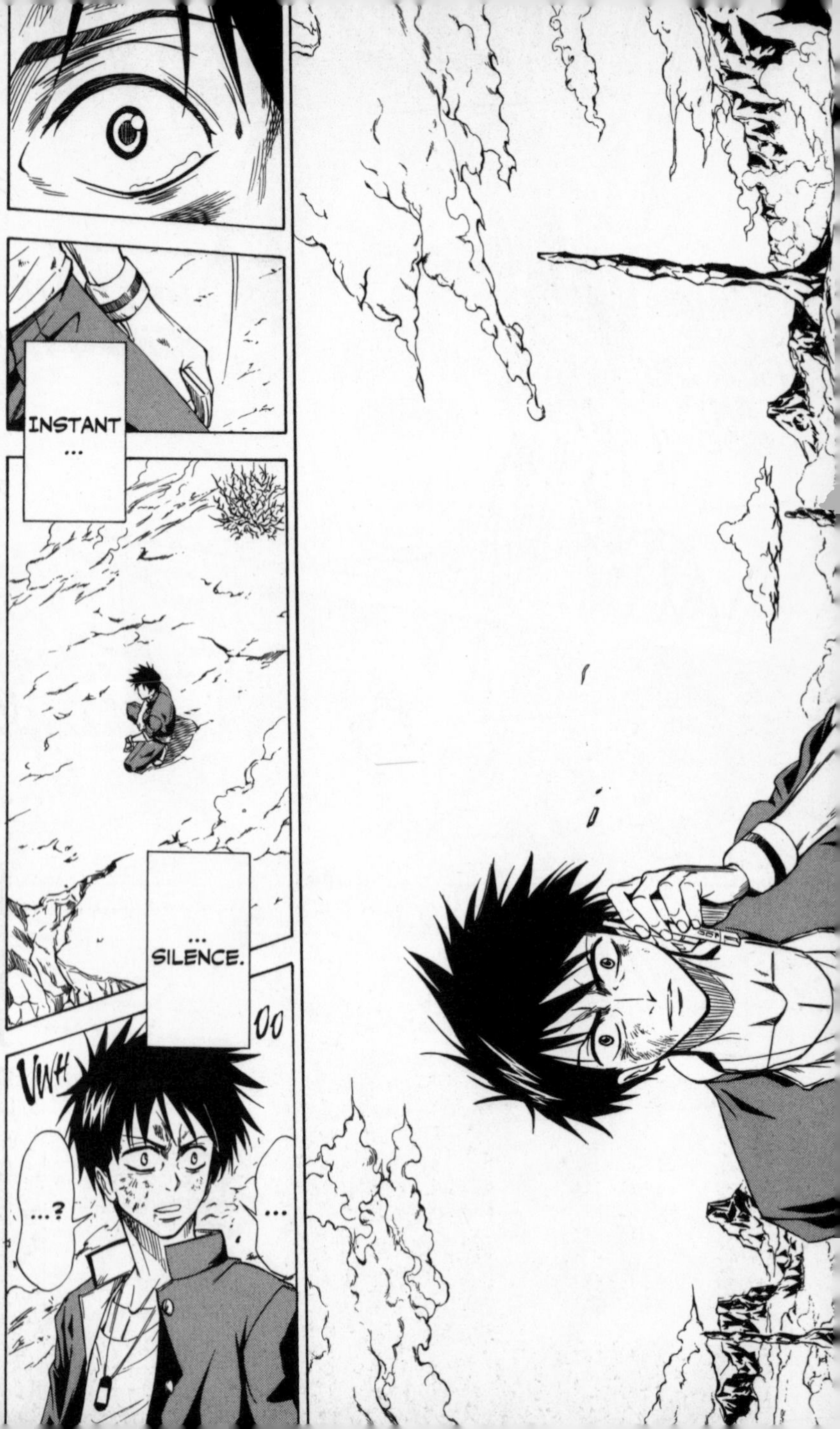
INSTANT ...
... SILENCE.
OO
VWH
...
...?

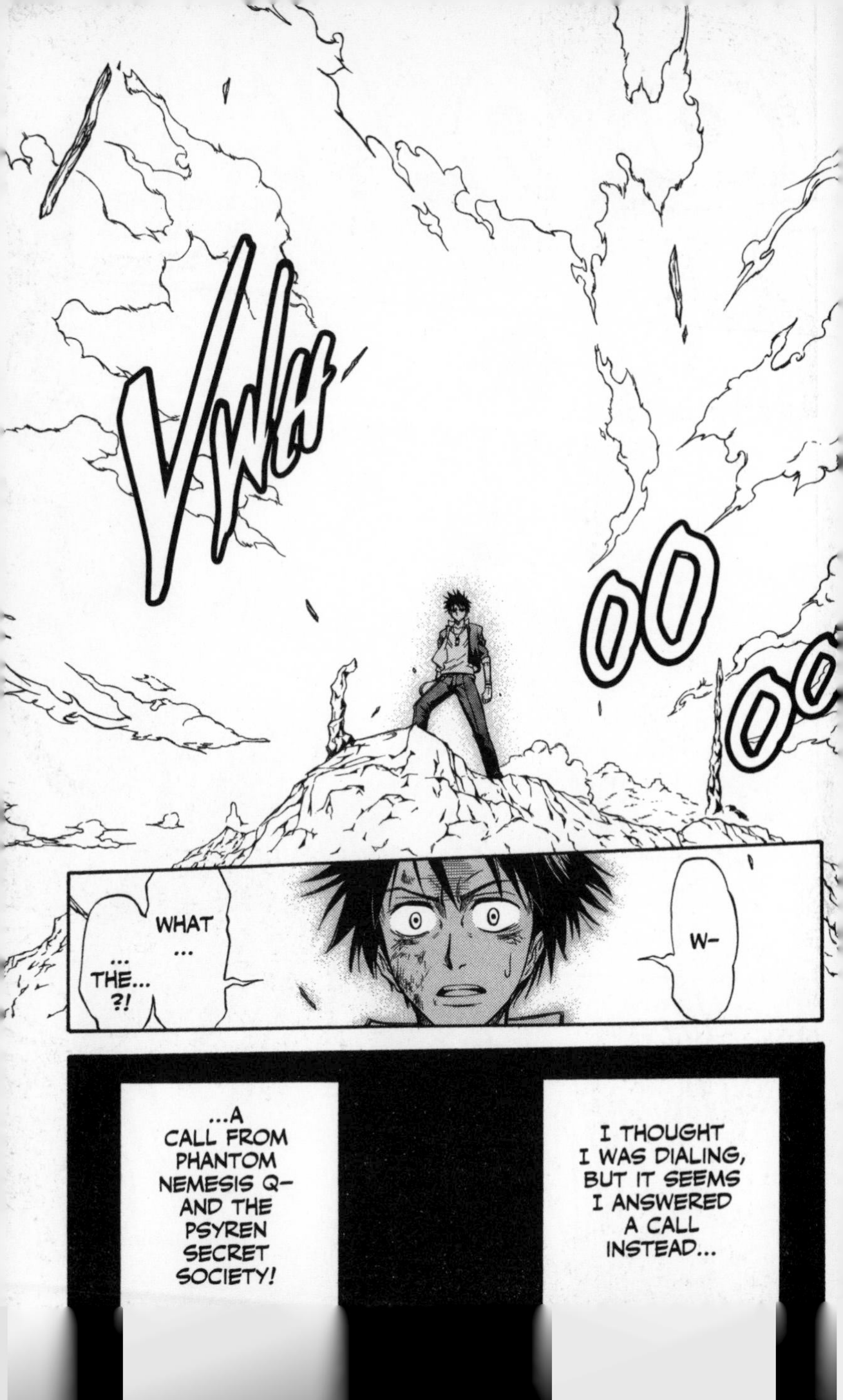
W-
WHAT ... ... THE... ?!
I THOUGHT I WAS DIALING, BUT IT SEEMS I ANSWERED A CALL INSTEAD...
...A CALL FROM PHANTOM NEMESIS Q— AND THE PSYREN SECRET SOCIETY!

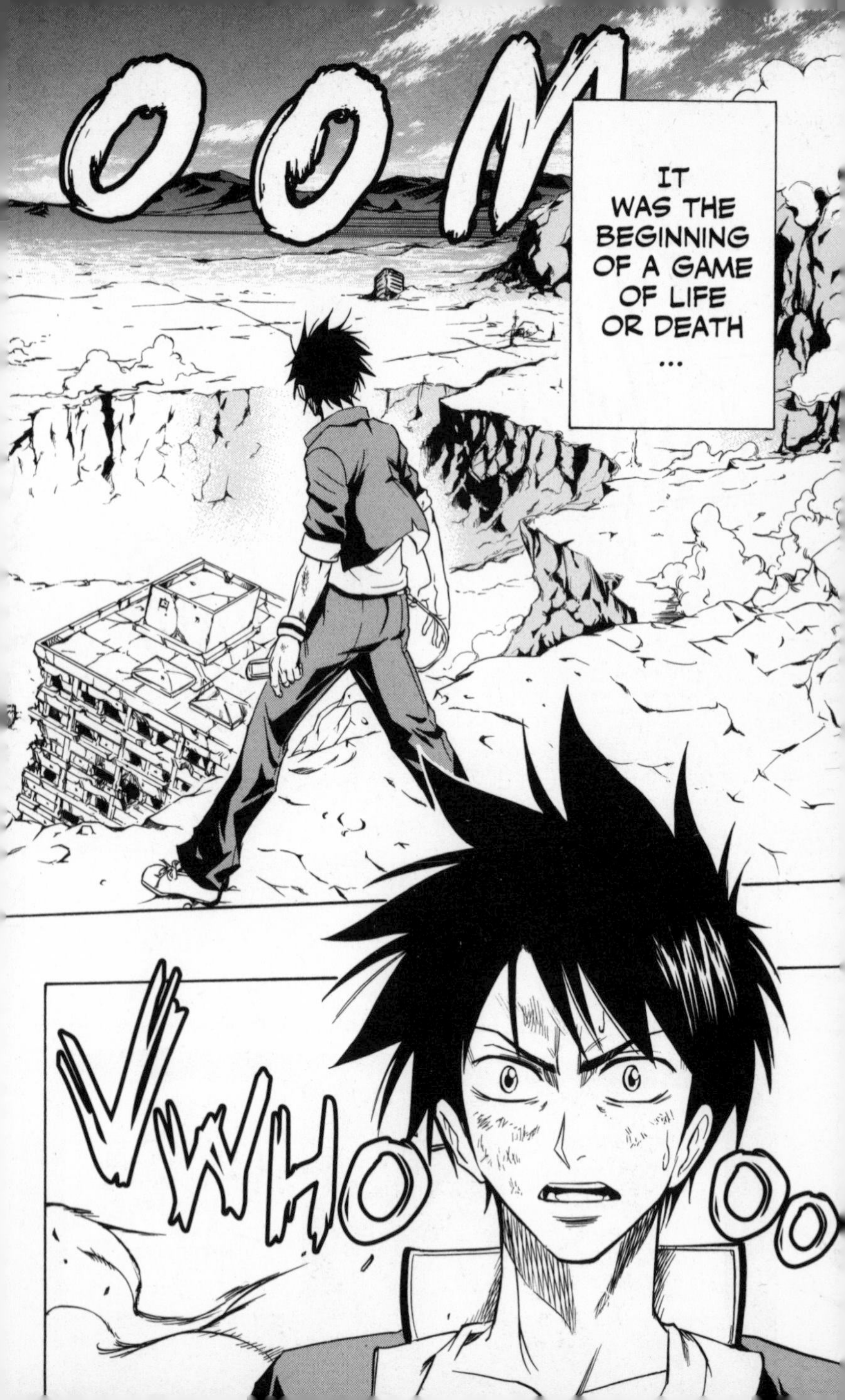
OOOM
IT WAS THE BEGINNING OF A GAME OF LIFE OR DEATH ...
VWHOOOO

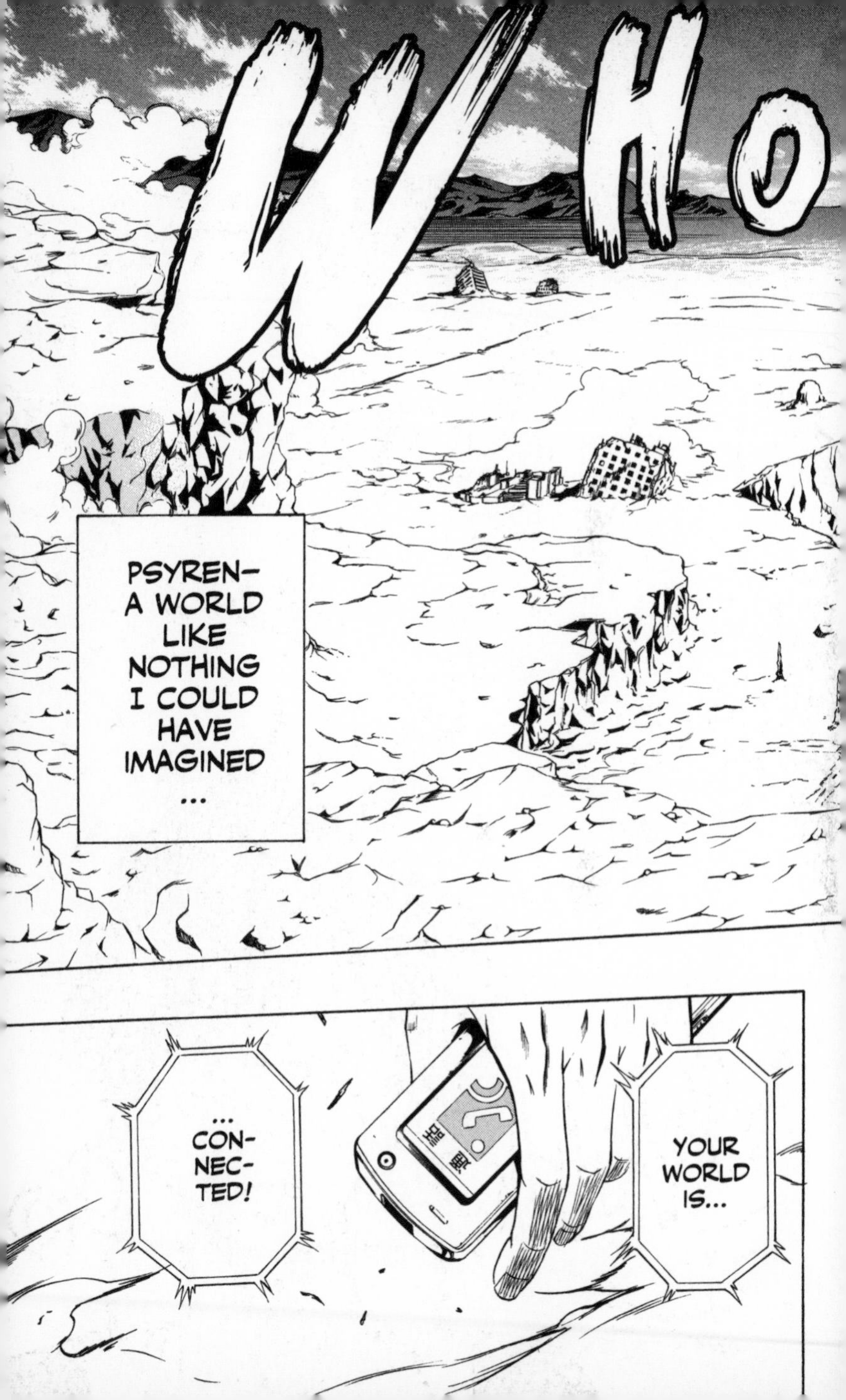
WHO
PSYREN– A WORLD LIKE NOTHING I COULD HAVE IMAGINED ...
YOUR WORLD IS...
... CON- NEC- TED!

< 0 POINTS >

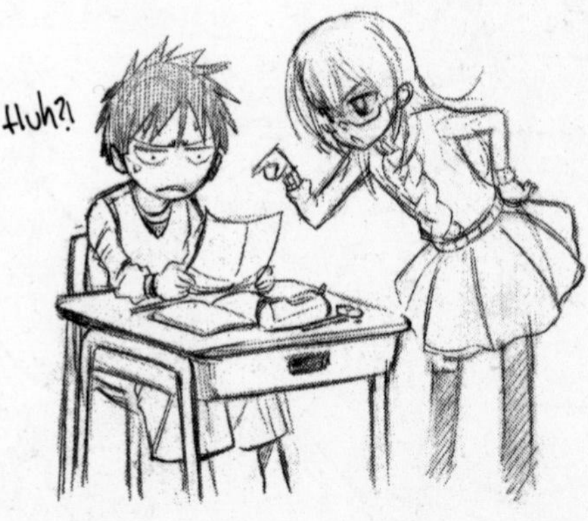
Huh?!

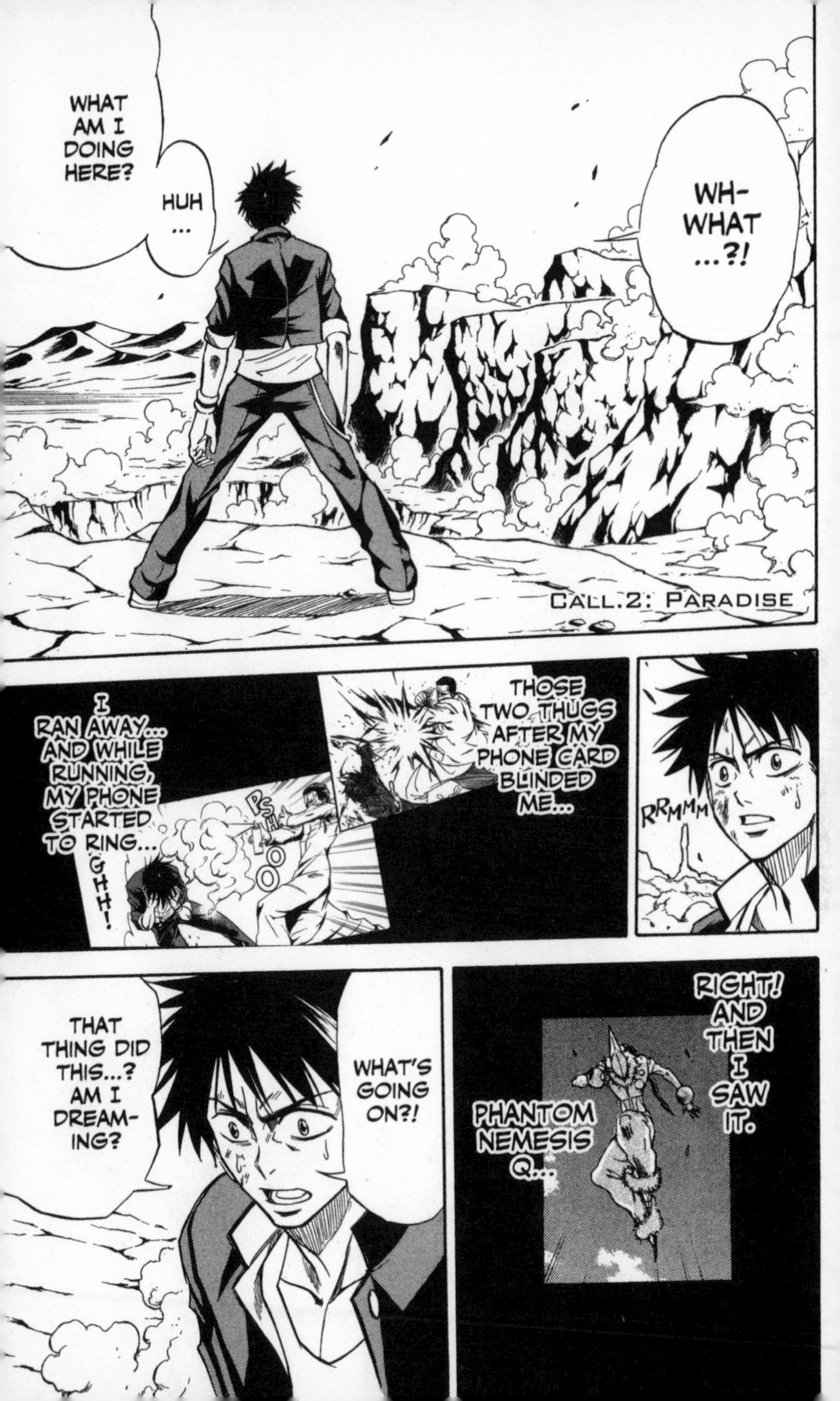
WH- WHAT ...?!
HUH ...
WHAT AM I DOING HERE?
CALL.2: PARADISE
RRMMMM
THOSE TWO THUGS AFTER MY PHONE CARD BLINDED ME...
I RAN AWAY... AND WHILE RUNNING, MY PHONE STARTED TO RING...
PSHOOO
GHH!
RIGHT! AND THEN I SAW IT.
PHANTOM NEMESIS Q...
WHAT'S GOING ON?!
THAT THING DID THIS...? AM I DREAMING?

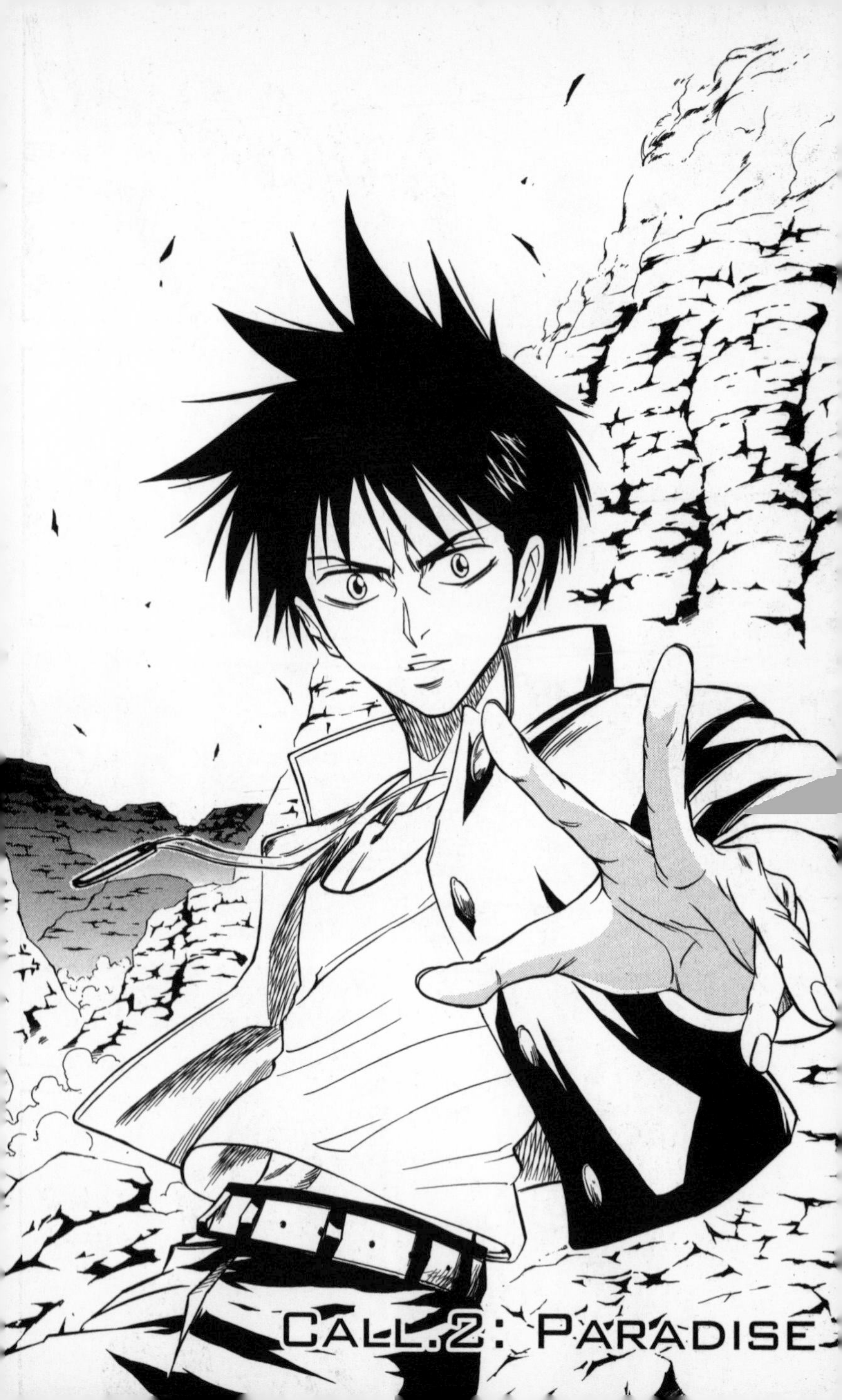
CALL.2: PARADISE

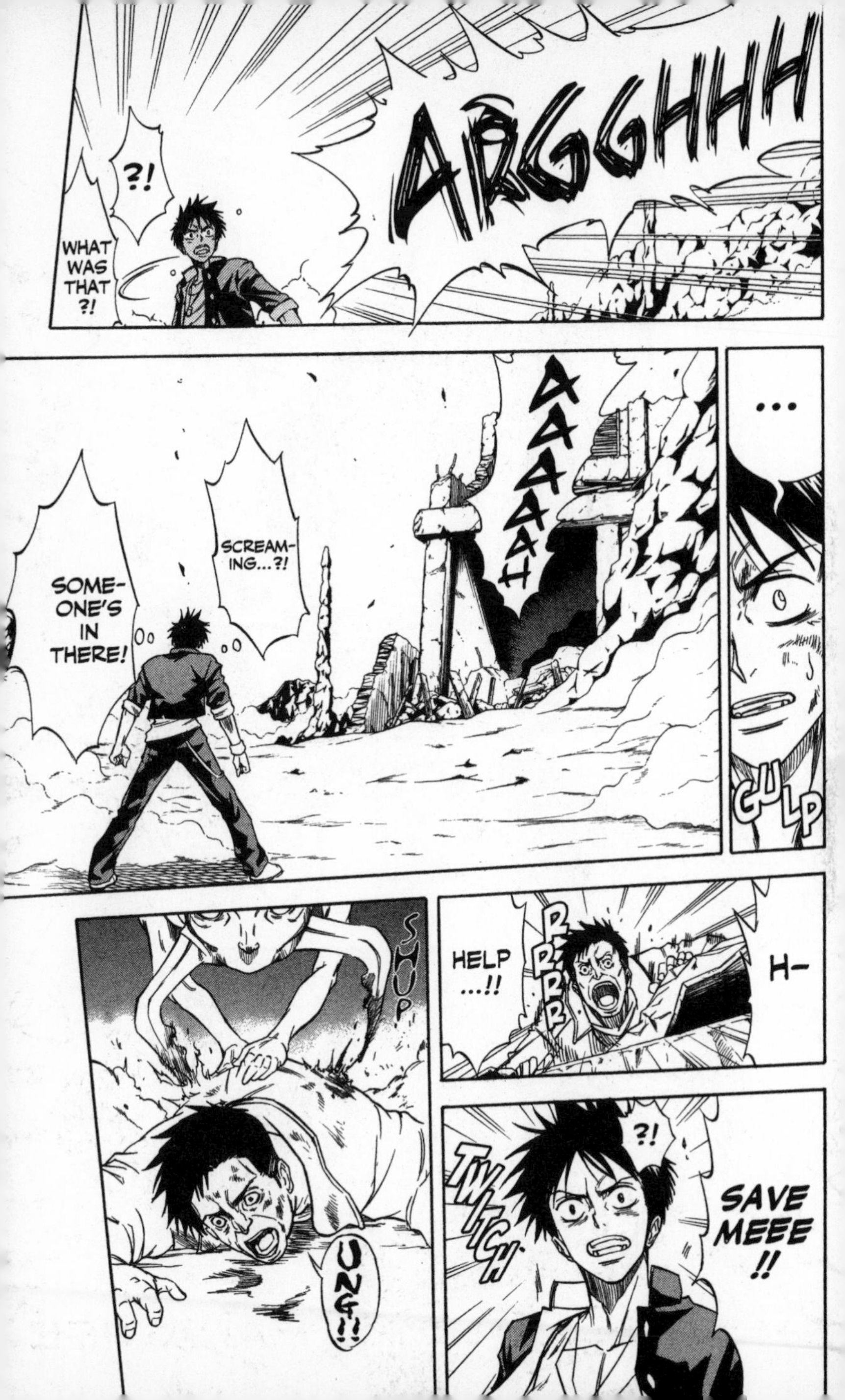
ARGGHHH
?!
WHAT WAS THAT ?!
...
GULP
AAAAAH
SCREAM-ING...?!
SOME-ONE'S IN THERE!
H-
RRRR
HELP ...!!
SAVE MEEE !!
?!
TWITCH
SHUP
UNG!!

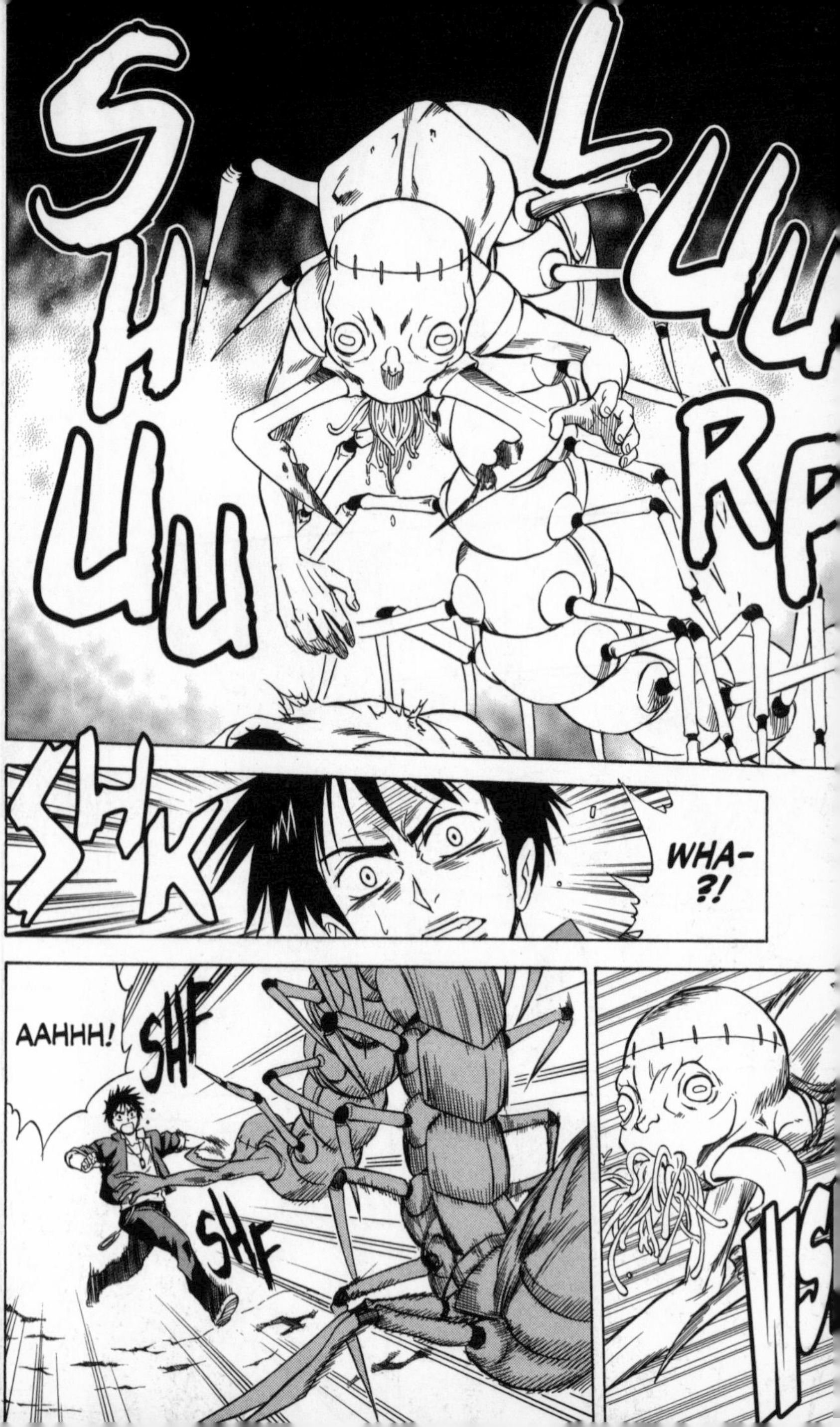
SHUUU
LUURP
SHK
WHA-?!
AAHHH!
SHF
SHF

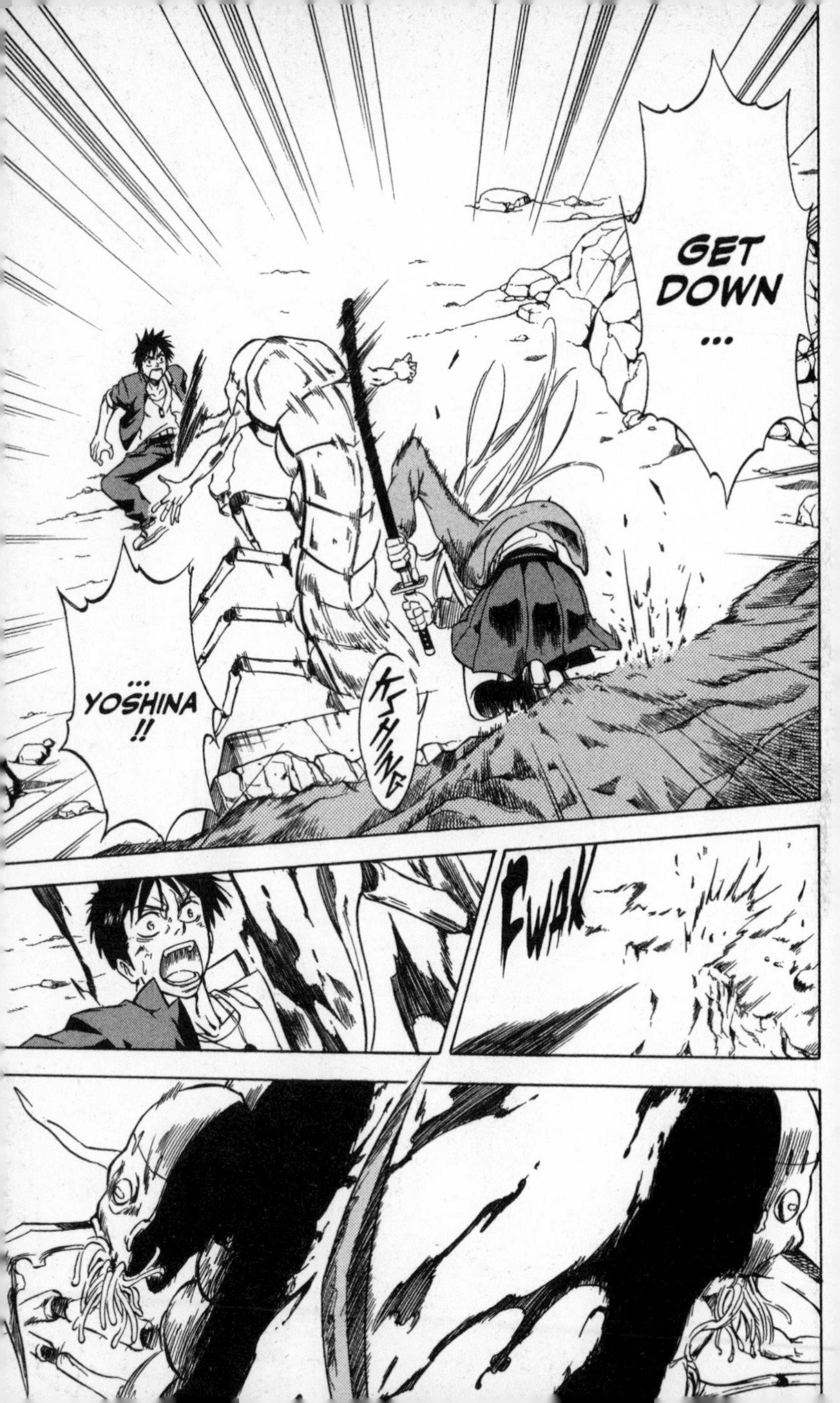
GET DOWN ...
... YOSHINA !!
KSHING
GWAK

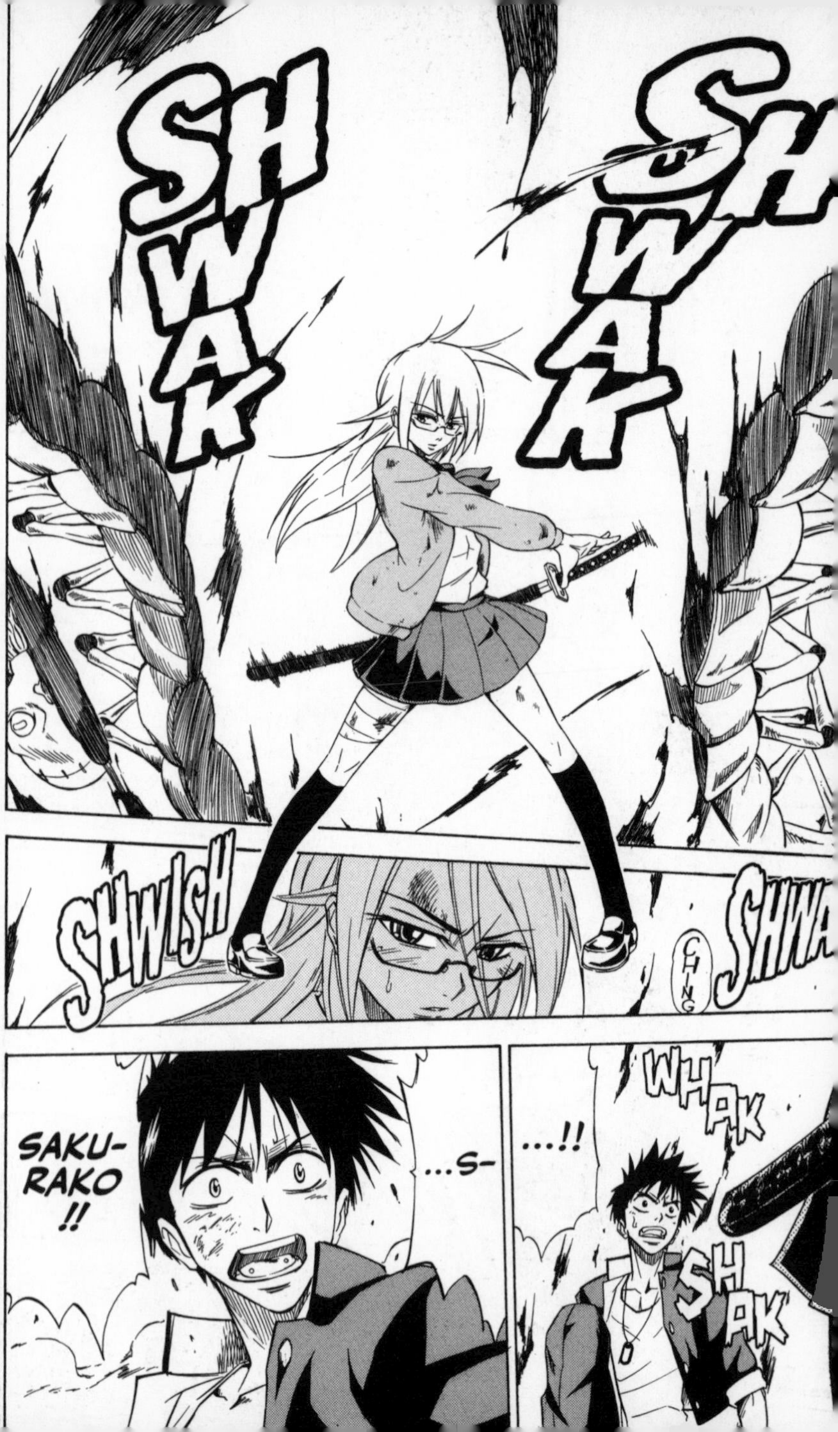
SHWAK
SHWAK
SHWA
CHING
SHWISH
WHAK
...!!
SHAK
...S-
SAKU-RAKO!!

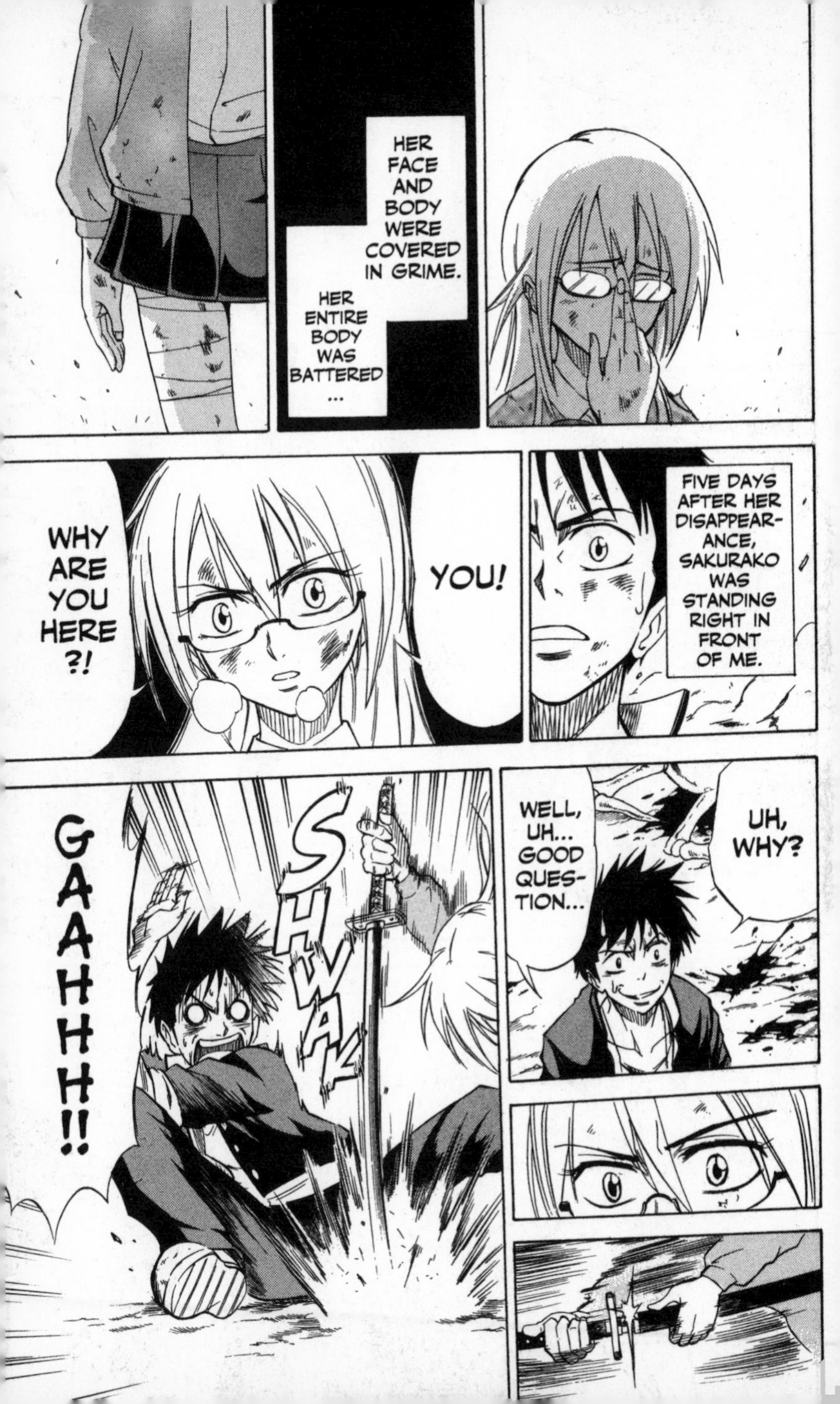
HER FACE AND BODY WERE COVERED IN GRIME.
HER ENTIRE BODY WAS BATTERED...
FIVE DAYS AFTER HER DISAPPEARANCE, SAKURAKO WAS STANDING RIGHT IN FRONT OF ME.
YOU!
WHY ARE YOU HERE?!
UH, WHY?
WELL, UH... GOOD QUESTION...
SHVAK
GAAHHH!!

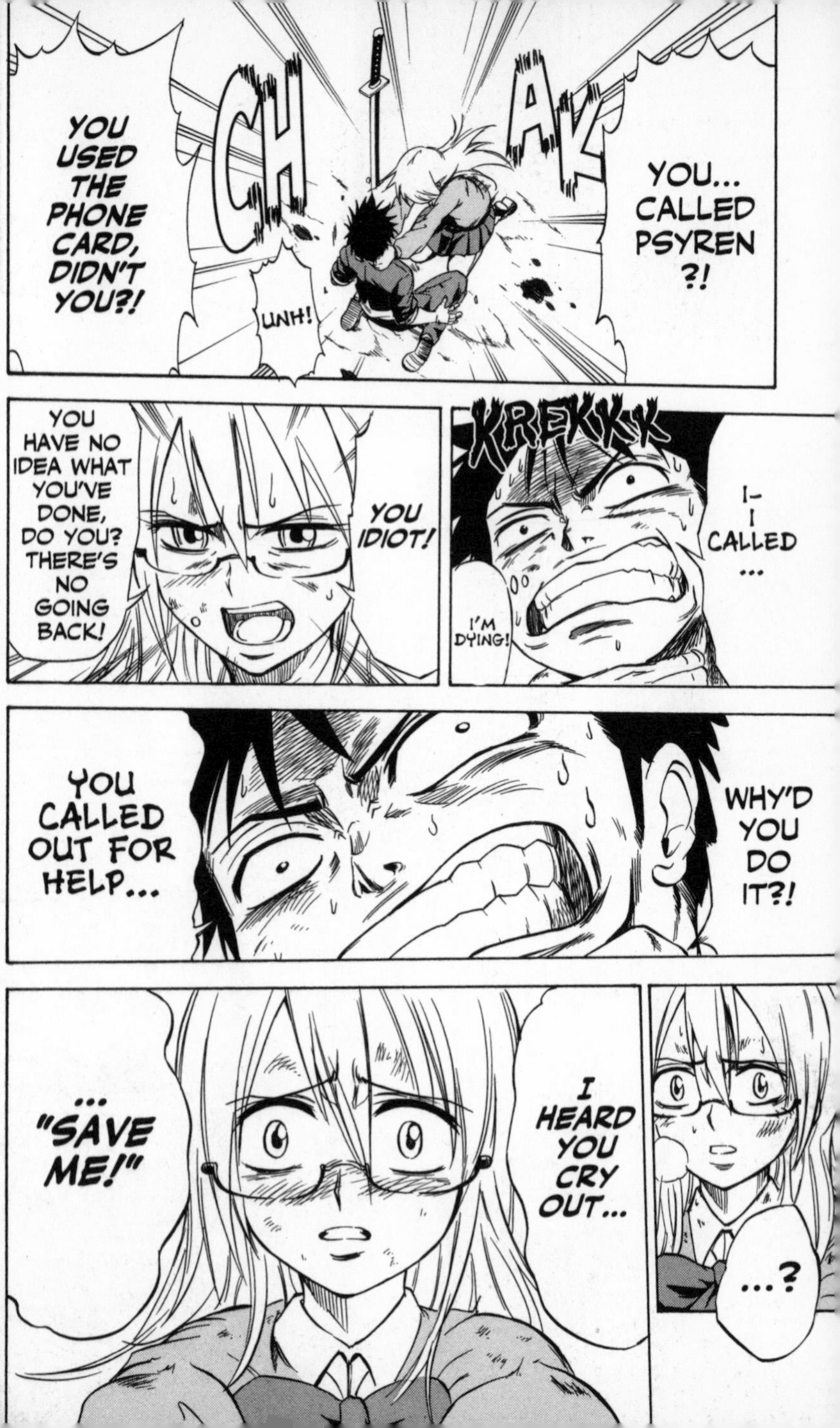
YOU... CALLED PSYREN?!
CHAK
YOU USED THE PHONE CARD, DIDN'T YOU?!
UNH!
KREKKK
I- I CALLED...
I'M DYING!
YOU IDIOT!
YOU HAVE NO IDEA WHAT YOU'VE DONE, DO YOU? THERE'S NO GOING BACK!
WHY'D YOU DO IT?!
YOU CALLED OUT FOR HELP...
...?
I HEARD YOU CRY OUT...
..."SAVE ME!"

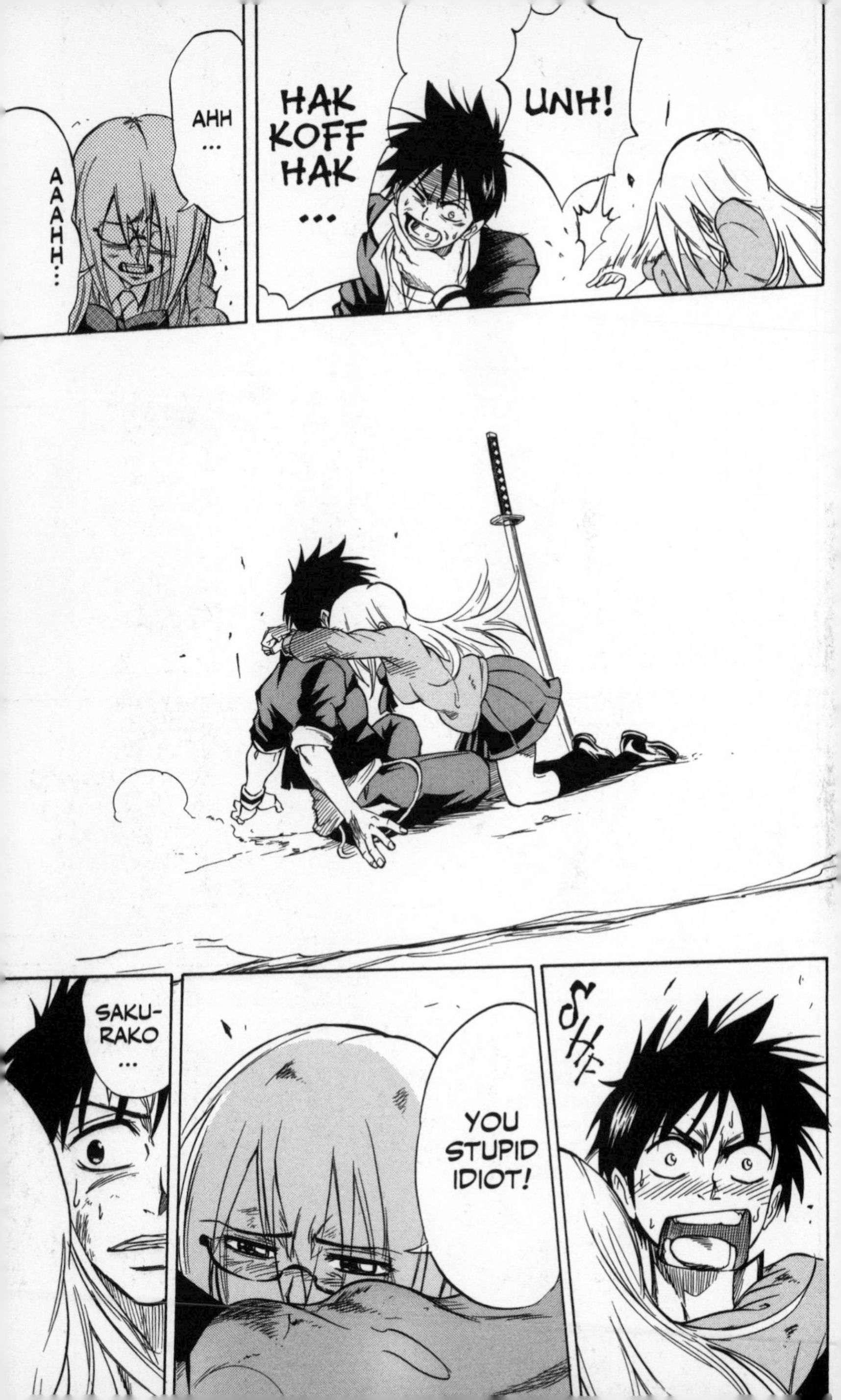
UNH!
HAK KOFF HAK ...
AHH ...
AAAAHH...
SHF
YOU STUPID IDIOT!
SAKU-RAKO ...

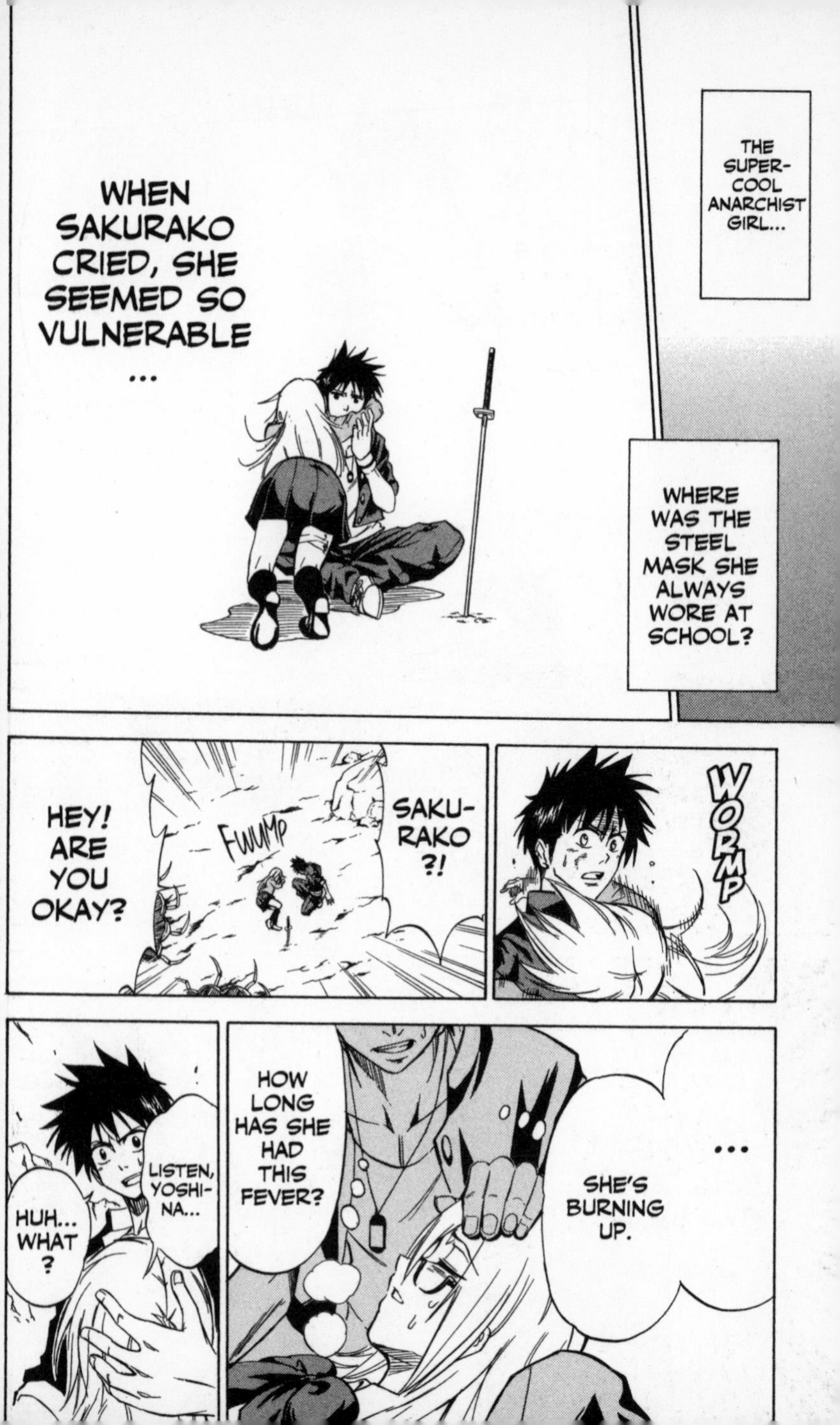
THE SUPER-COOL ANARCHIST GIRL...
WHERE WAS THE STEEL MASK SHE ALWAYS WORE AT SCHOOL?
WHEN SAKURAKO CRIED, SHE SEEMED SO VULNERABLE...
WORMP
SAKU-RAKO?!
FWUMP
HEY! ARE YOU OKAY?
...
SHE'S BURNING UP.
HOW LONG HAS SHE HAD THIS FEVER?
LISTEN, YOSHI-NA...
HUH... WHAT?

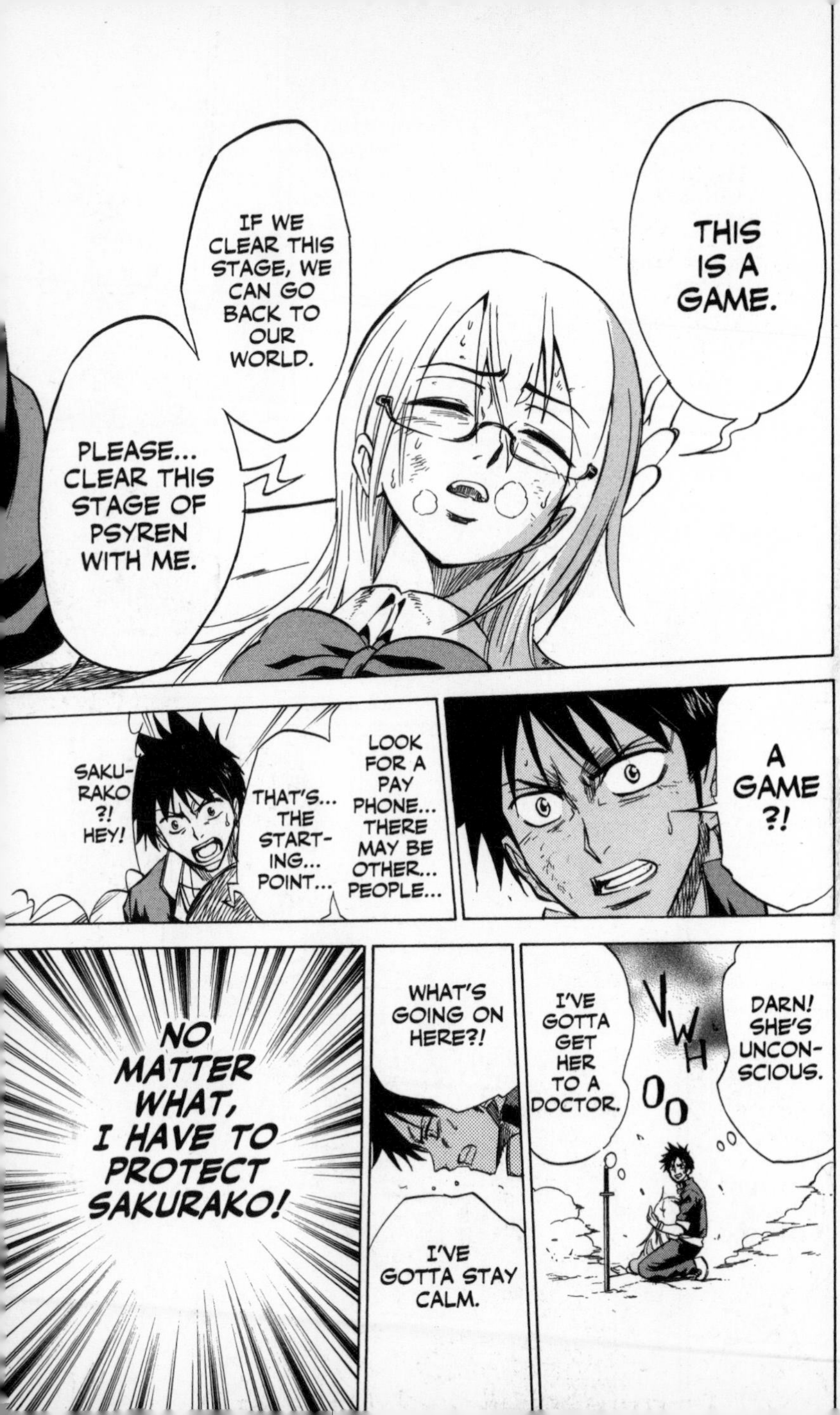
THIS IS A GAME.
IF WE CLEAR THIS STAGE, WE CAN GO BACK TO OUR WORLD.
PLEASE... CLEAR THIS STAGE OF PSYREN WITH ME.
A GAME?!
LOOK FOR A PAY PHONE... THERE MAY BE OTHER... PEOPLE...
THAT'S... THE START-ING... POINT...
SAKU-RAKO?! HEY!
DARN! SHE'S UNCON-SCIOUS.
VWHOO
I'VE GOTTA GET HER TO A DOCTOR.
WHAT'S GOING ON HERE?!
I'VE GOTTA STAY CALM.
NO MATTER WHAT, I HAVE TO PROTECT SAKURAKO!

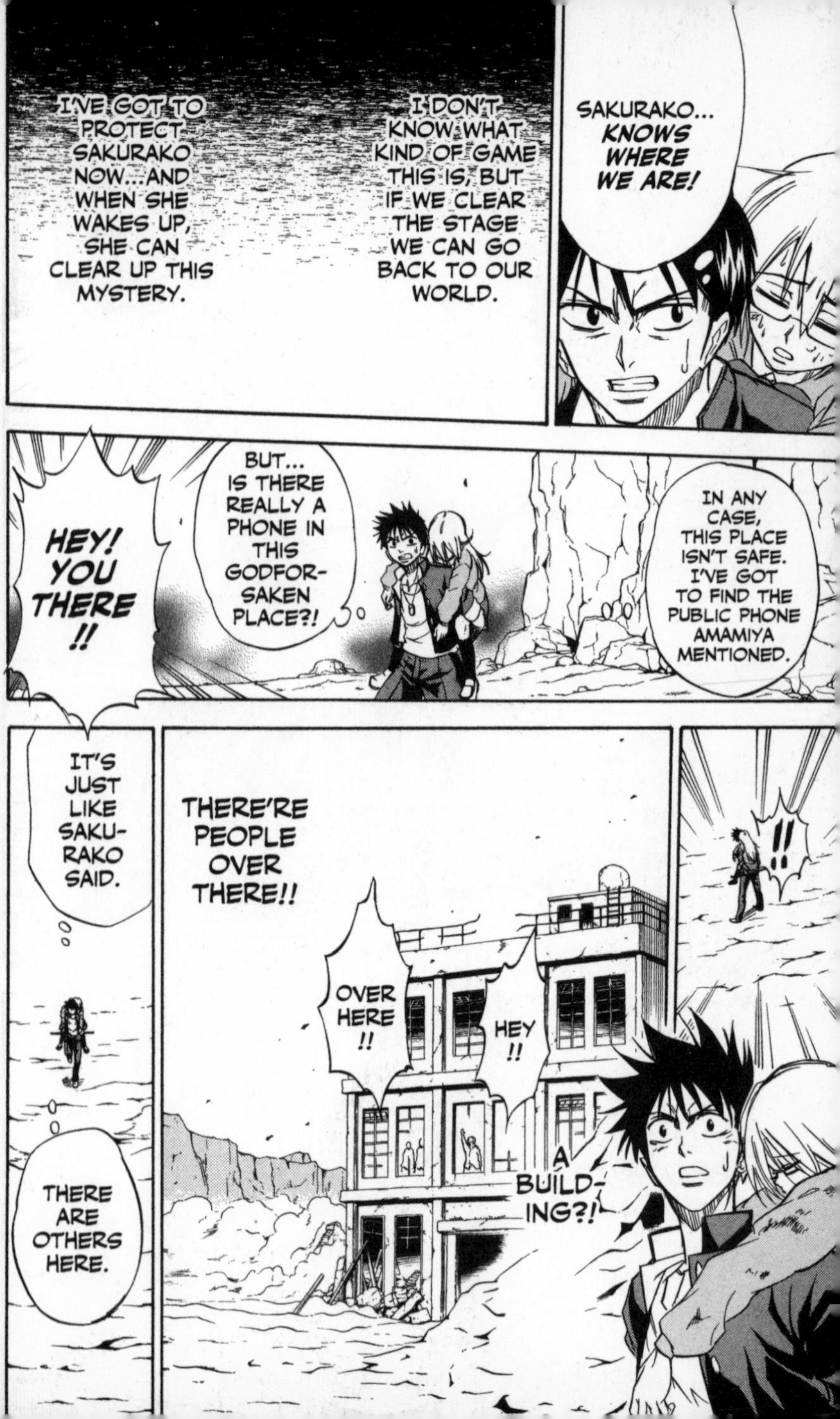
SAKURAKO... KNOWS WHERE WE ARE!
I DON'T KNOW WHAT KIND OF GAME THIS IS, BUT IF WE CLEAR THE STAGE WE CAN GO BACK TO OUR WORLD.
I'VE GOT TO PROTECT SAKURAKO NOW... AND WHEN SHE WAKES UP, SHE CAN CLEAR UP THIS MYSTERY.
IN ANY CASE, THIS PLACE ISN'T SAFE. I'VE GOT TO FIND THE PUBLIC PHONE AMAMIYA MENTIONED.
BUT... IS THERE REALLY A PHONE IN THIS GODFOR-SAKEN PLACE?!
HEY! YOU THERE !!
!!
OVER HERE !!
HEY !!
A BUILD-ING?!
THERE'RE PEOPLE OVER THERE!!
IT'S JUST LIKE SAKU-RAKO SAID.
THERE ARE OTHERS HERE.

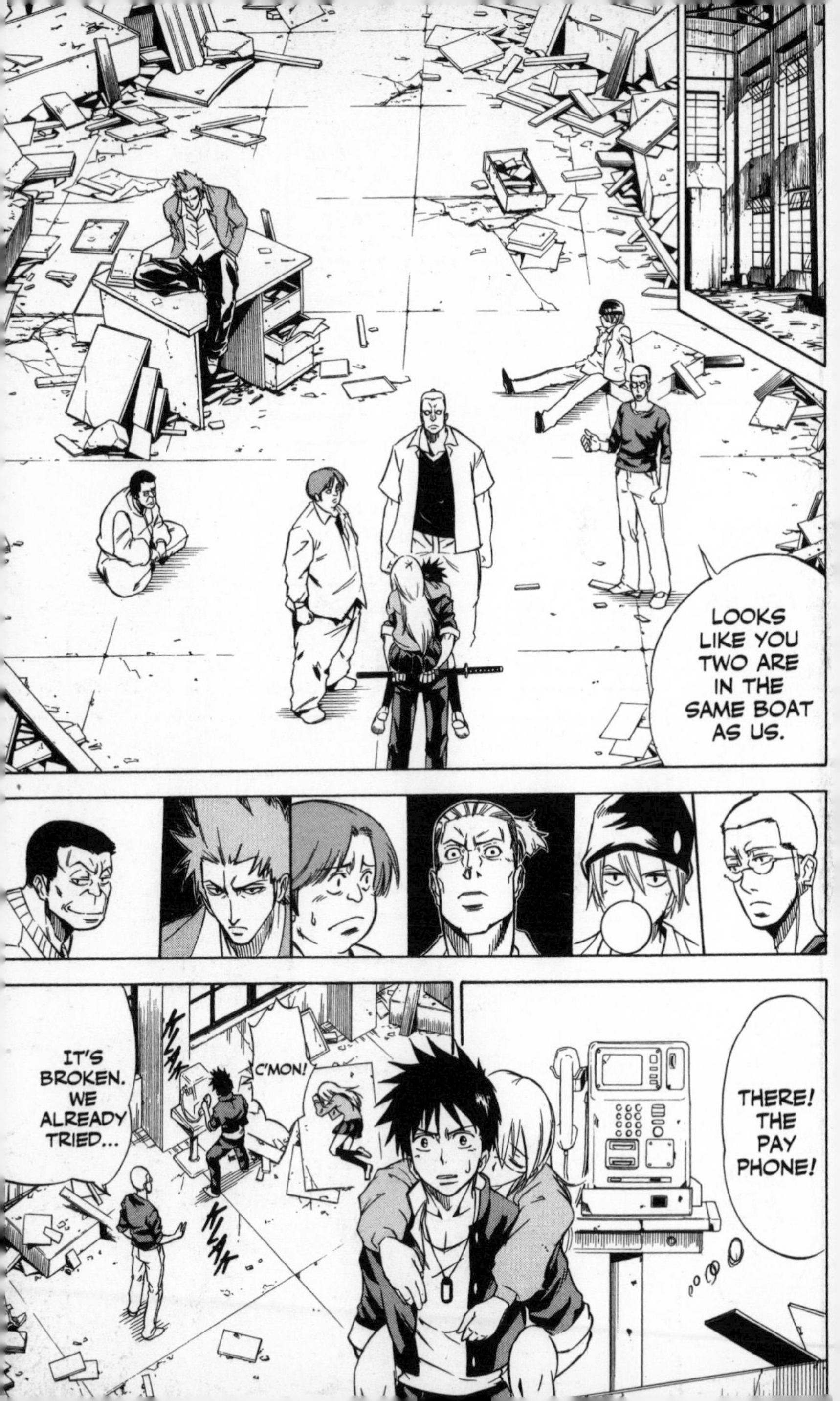
LOOKS LIKE YOU TWO ARE IN THE SAME BOAT AS US.
THERE! THE PAY PHONE!
C'MON!
KLAK
IT'S BROKEN. WE ALREADY TRIED...
KLAK

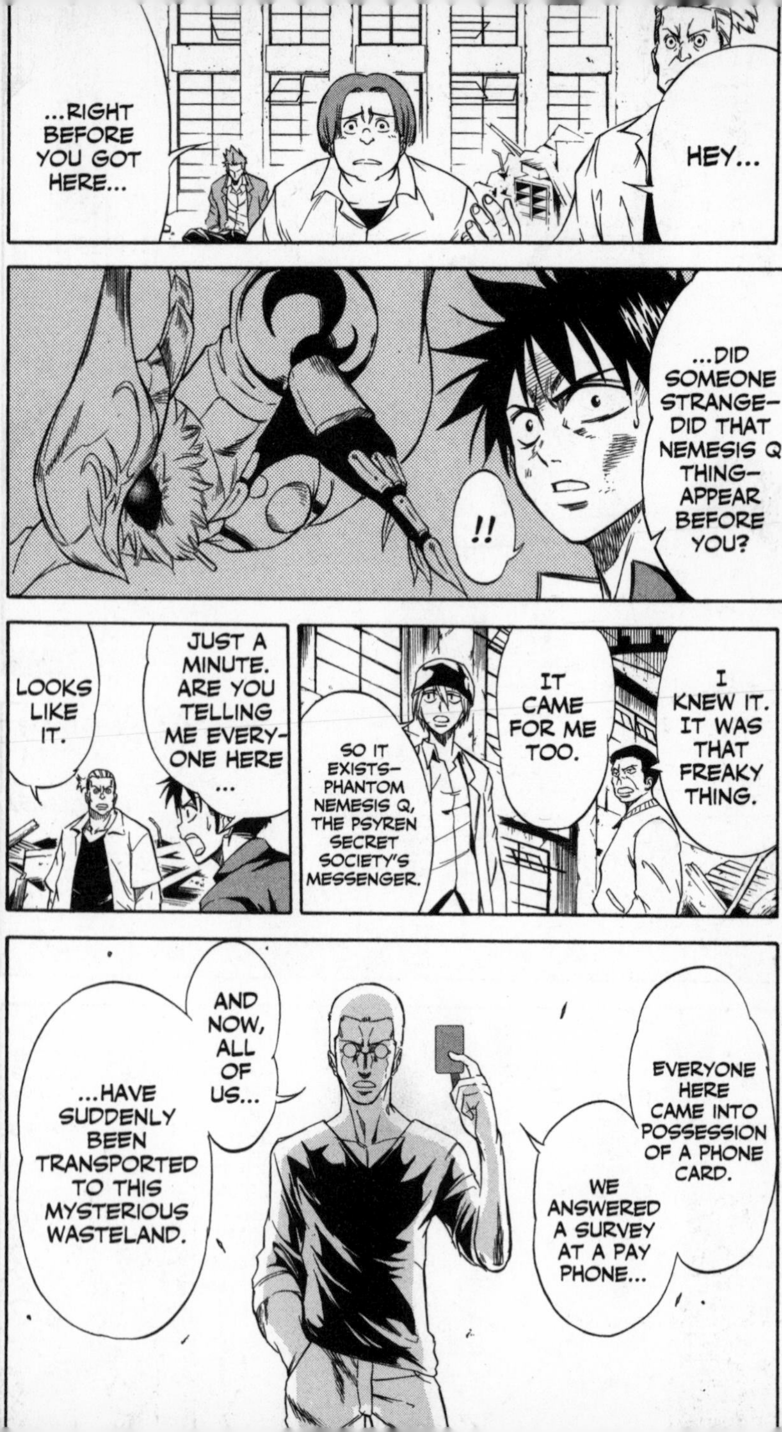
HEY...
...RIGHT BEFORE YOU GOT HERE...
...DID SOMEONE STRANGE—DID THAT NEMESIS Q THING—APPEAR BEFORE YOU?
!!
I KNEW IT. IT WAS THAT FREAKY THING.
IT CAME FOR ME TOO.
SO IT EXISTS—PHANTOM NEMESIS Q, THE PSYREN SECRET SOCIETY'S MESSENGER.
JUST A MINUTE. ARE YOU TELLING ME EVERYONE HERE ...
LOOKS LIKE IT.
EVERYONE HERE CAME INTO POSSESSION OF A PHONE CARD.
WE ANSWERED A SURVEY AT A PAY PHONE...
AND NOW, ALL OF US...
...HAVE SUDDENLY BEEN TRANSPORTED TO THIS MYSTERIOUS WASTELAND.

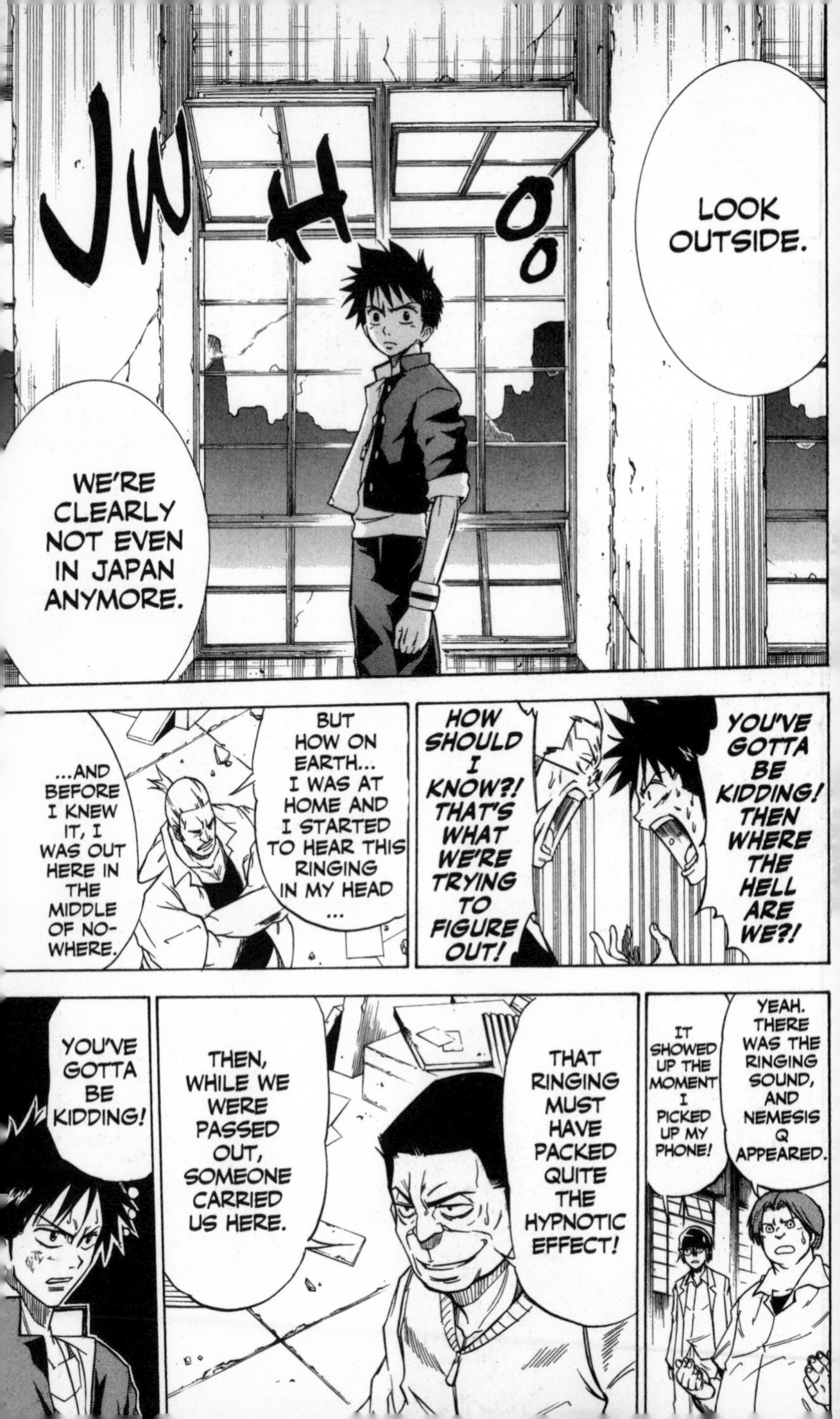
LOOK OUTSIDE.
WE'RE CLEARLY NOT EVEN IN JAPAN ANYMORE.
YOU'VE GOTTA BE KIDDING! THEN WHERE THE HELL ARE WE?!
HOW SHOULD I KNOW?! THAT'S WHAT WE'RE TRYING TO FIGURE OUT!
BUT HOW ON EARTH... I WAS AT HOME AND I STARTED TO HEAR THIS RINGING IN MY HEAD ...
...AND BEFORE I KNEW IT, I WAS OUT HERE IN THE MIDDLE OF NO-WHERE.
YEAH. THERE WAS THE RINGING SOUND, AND NEMESIS Q APPEARED.
IT SHOWED UP THE MOMENT I PICKED UP MY PHONE!
THAT RINGING MUST HAVE PACKED QUITE THE HYPNOTIC EFFECT!
THEN, WHILE WE WERE PASSED OUT, SOMEONE CARRIED US HERE.
YOU'VE GOTTA BE KIDDING!

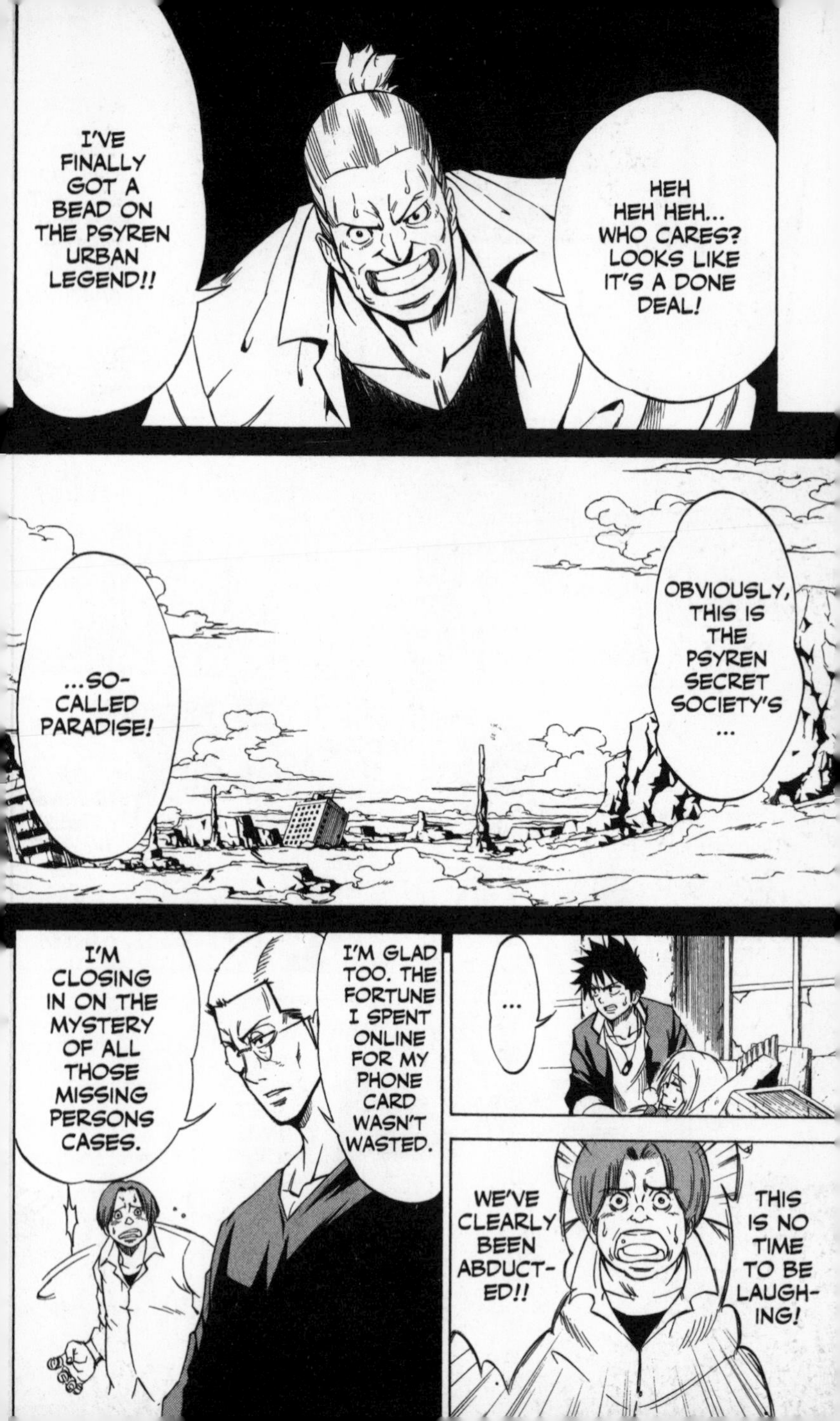
HEH HEH HEH... WHO CARES? LOOKS LIKE IT'S A DONE DEAL!
I'VE FINALLY GOT A BEAD ON THE PSYREN URBAN LEGEND!!
OBVIOUSLY, THIS IS THE PSYREN SECRET SOCIETY'S ...
...SO-CALLED PARADISE!
...
THIS IS NO TIME TO BE LAUGHING!
WE'VE CLEARLY BEEN ABDUCTED!!
I'M GLAD TOO. THE FORTUNE I SPENT ONLINE FOR MY PHONE CARD WASN'T WASTED.
I'M CLOSING IN ON THE MYSTERY OF ALL THOSE MISSING PERSONS CASES.

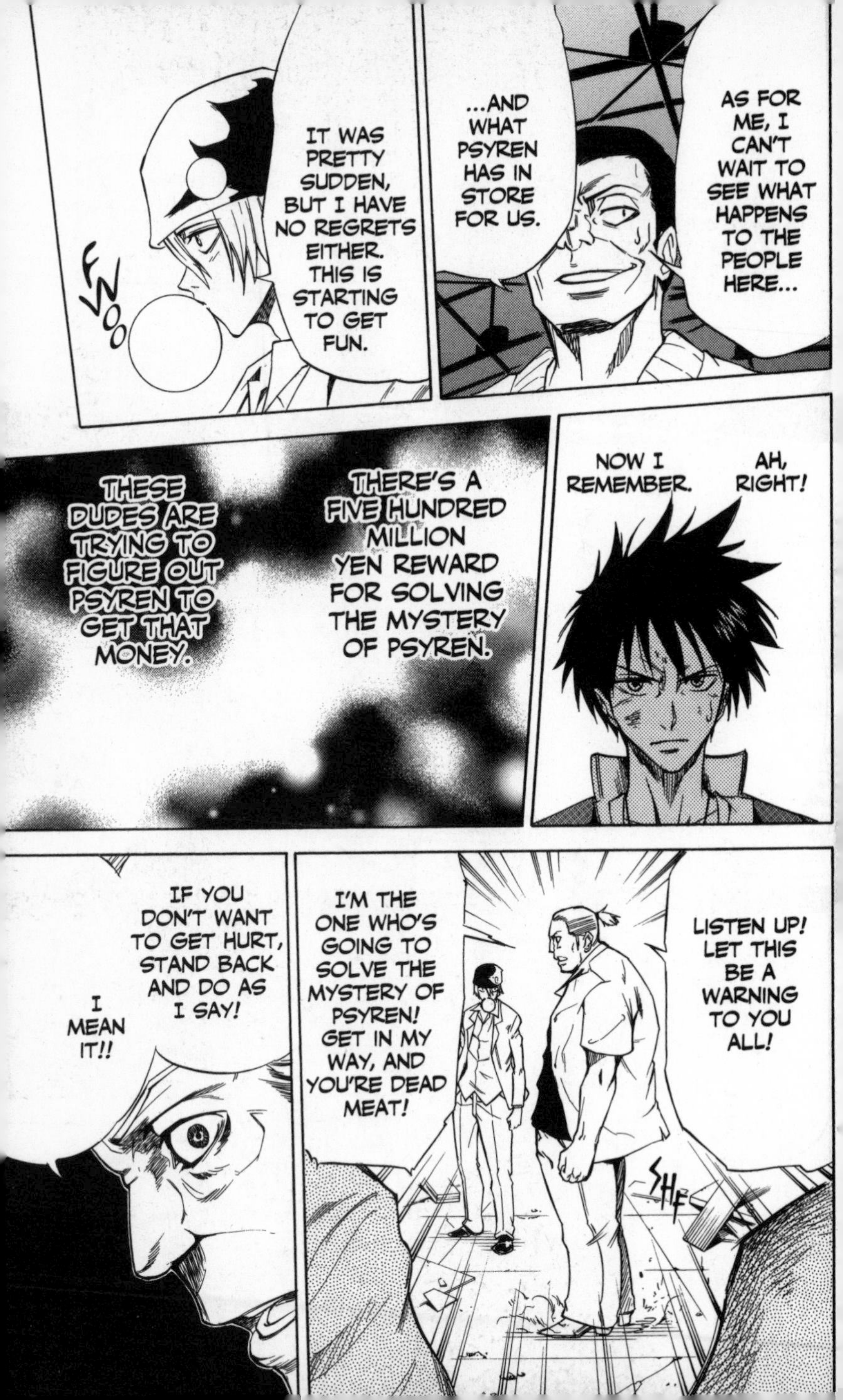
AS FOR ME, I CAN'T WAIT TO SEE WHAT HAPPENS TO THE PEOPLE HERE...
...AND WHAT PSYREN HAS IN STORE FOR US.
IT WAS PRETTY SUDDEN, BUT I HAVE NO REGRETS EITHER. THIS IS STARTING TO GET FUN.
FWOO
AH, RIGHT!
NOW I REMEMBER.
THERE'S A FIVE HUNDRED MILLION YEN REWARD FOR SOLVING THE MYSTERY OF PSYREN.
THESE DUDES ARE TRYING TO FIGURE OUT PSYREN TO GET THAT MONEY.
LISTEN UP! LET THIS BE A WARNING TO YOU ALL!
I'M THE ONE WHO'S GOING TO SOLVE THE MYSTERY OF PSYREN! GET IN MY WAY, AND YOU'RE DEAD MEAT!
SHF
IF YOU DON'T WANT TO GET HURT, STAND BACK AND DO AS I SAY!
I MEAN IT!!

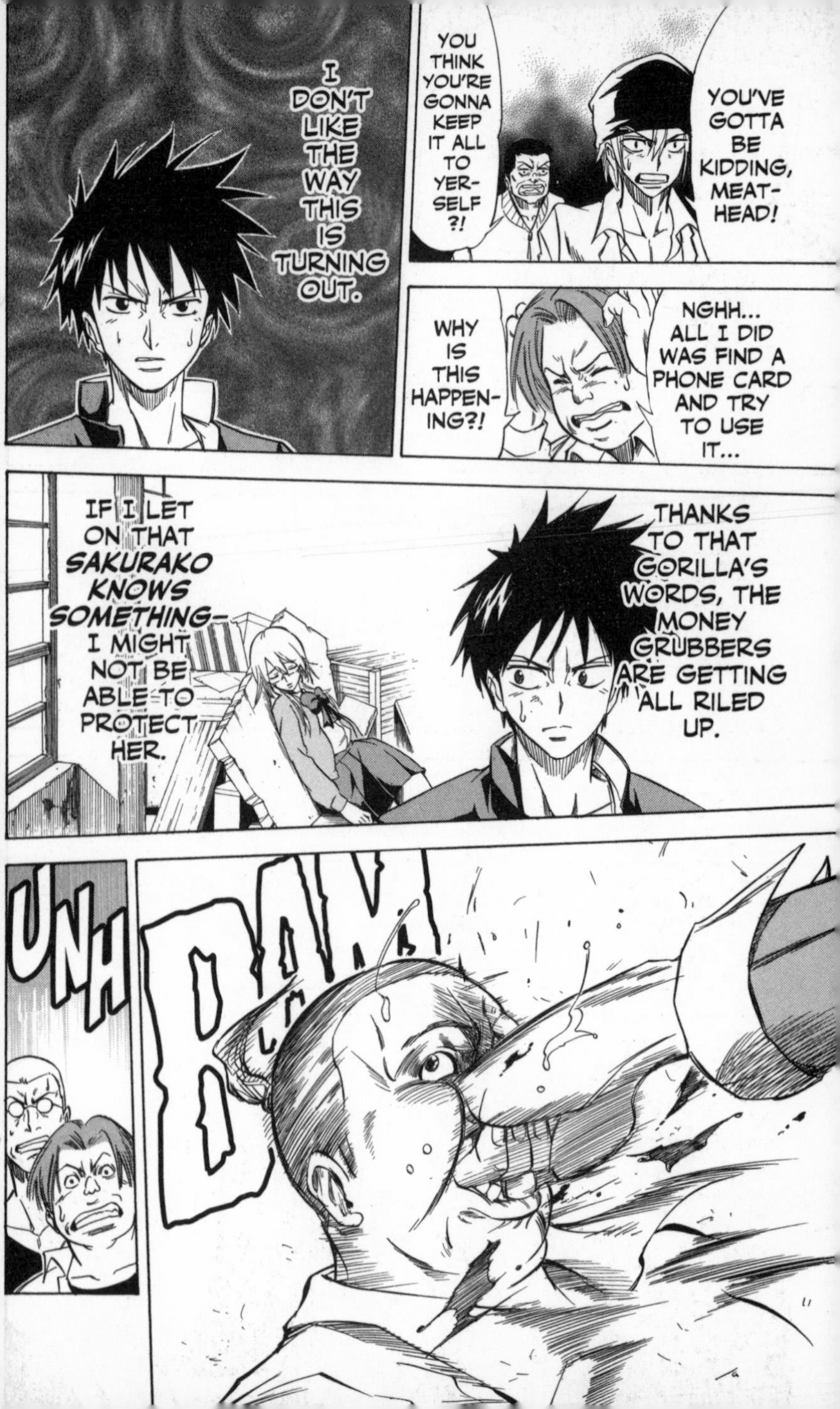
YOU'VE GOTTA BE KIDDING, MEAT-HEAD!
YOU THINK YOU'RE GONNA KEEP IT ALL TO YER-SELF?!
NGHH... ALL I DID WAS FIND A PHONE CARD AND TRY TO USE IT...
WHY IS THIS HAPPEN-ING?!
I DON'T LIKE THE WAY THIS IS TURNING OUT.
THANKS TO THAT GORILLA'S WORDS, THE MONEY GRUBBERS ARE GETTING ALL RILED UP.
IF I LET ON THAT *SAKURAKO KNOWS SOMETHING*– I MIGHT NOT BE ABLE TO PROTECT HER.
BAM
UNH

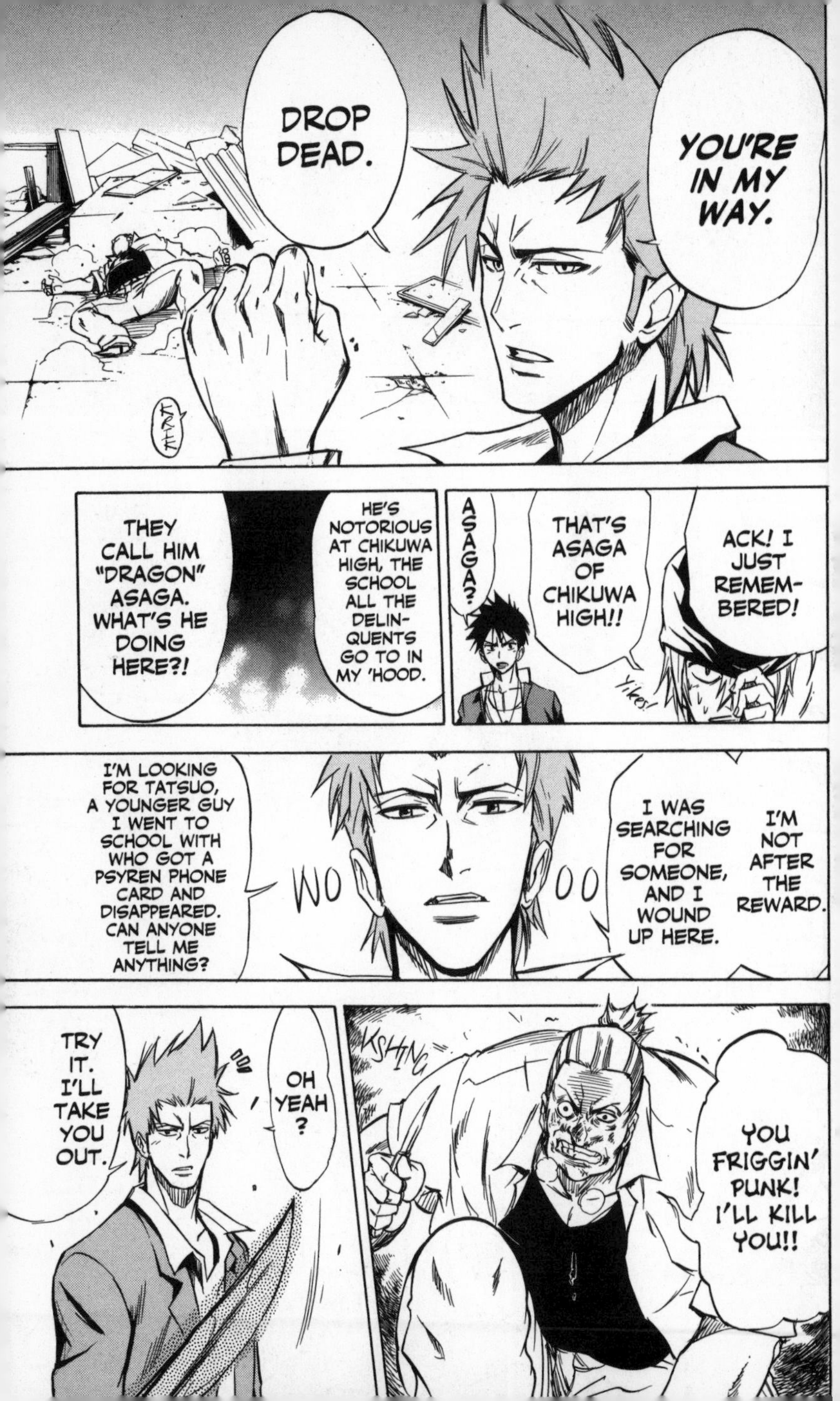
YOU'RE IN MY WAY.
DROP DEAD.
KRIK
ACK! I JUST REMEMBERED!
THAT'S ASAGA OF CHIKUWA HIGH!!
Yikes!
ASAGA?
HE'S NOTORIOUS AT CHIKUWA HIGH, THE SCHOOL ALL THE DELINQUENTS GO TO IN MY 'HOOD.
THEY CALL HIM "DRAGON" ASAGA. WHAT'S HE DOING HERE?!
I'M NOT AFTER THE REWARD.
I WAS SEARCHING FOR SOMEONE, AND I WOUND UP HERE.
I'M LOOKING FOR TATSUO, A YOUNGER GUY I WENT TO SCHOOL WITH WHO GOT A PSYREN PHONE CARD AND DISAPPEARED. CAN ANYONE TELL ME ANYTHING?
KSHING
YOU FRIGGIN' PUNK! I'LL KILL YOU!!
OH YEAH?
TRY IT. I'LL TAKE YOU OUT.

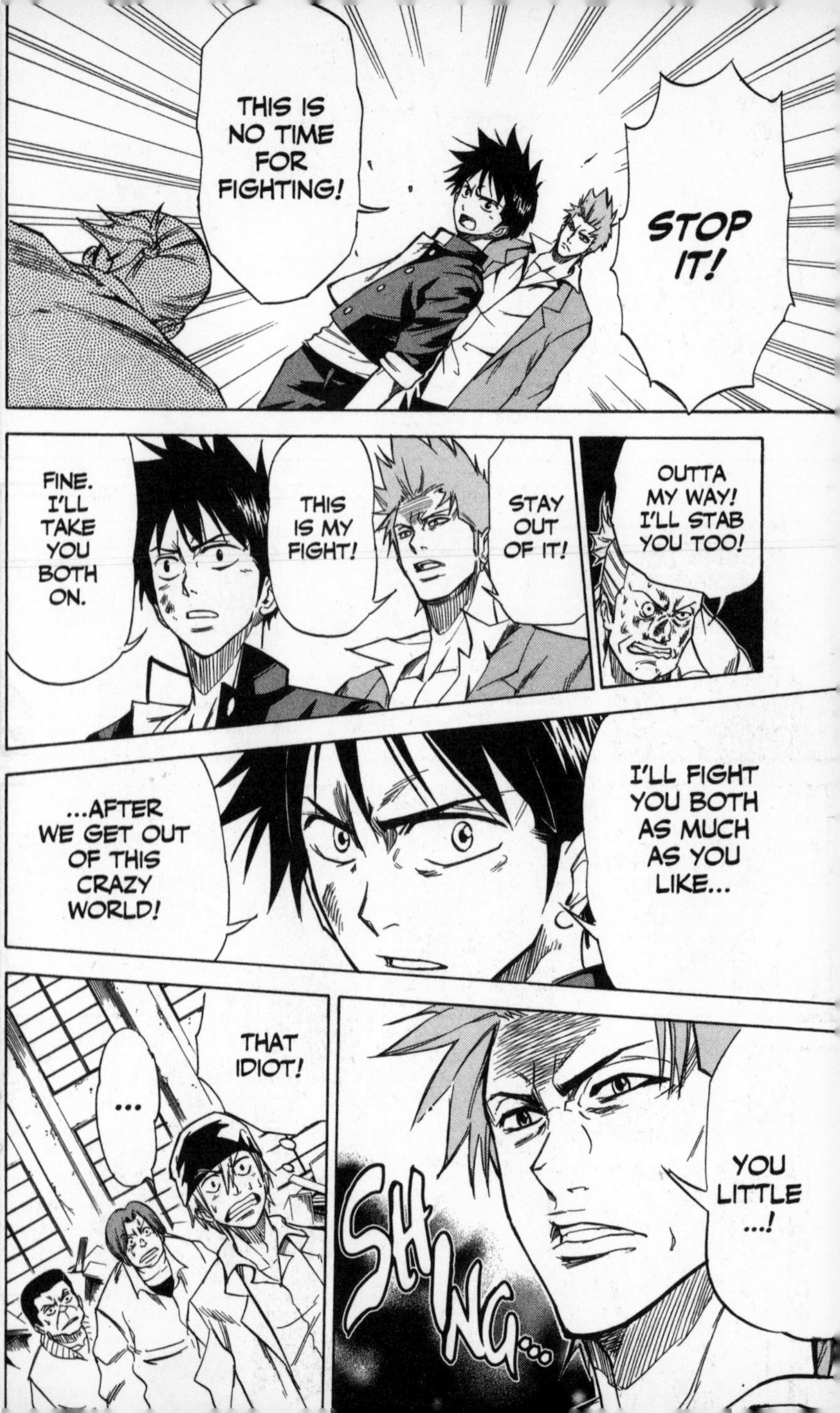
STOP IT!
THIS IS NO TIME FOR FIGHTING!
OUTTA MY WAY! I'LL STAB YOU TOO!
STAY OUT OF IT!
THIS IS MY FIGHT!
FINE. I'LL TAKE YOU BOTH ON.
I'LL FIGHT YOU BOTH AS MUCH AS YOU LIKE...
...AFTER WE GET OUT OF THIS CRAZY WORLD!
YOU LITTLE ...!
SHING...
THAT IDIOT!
...

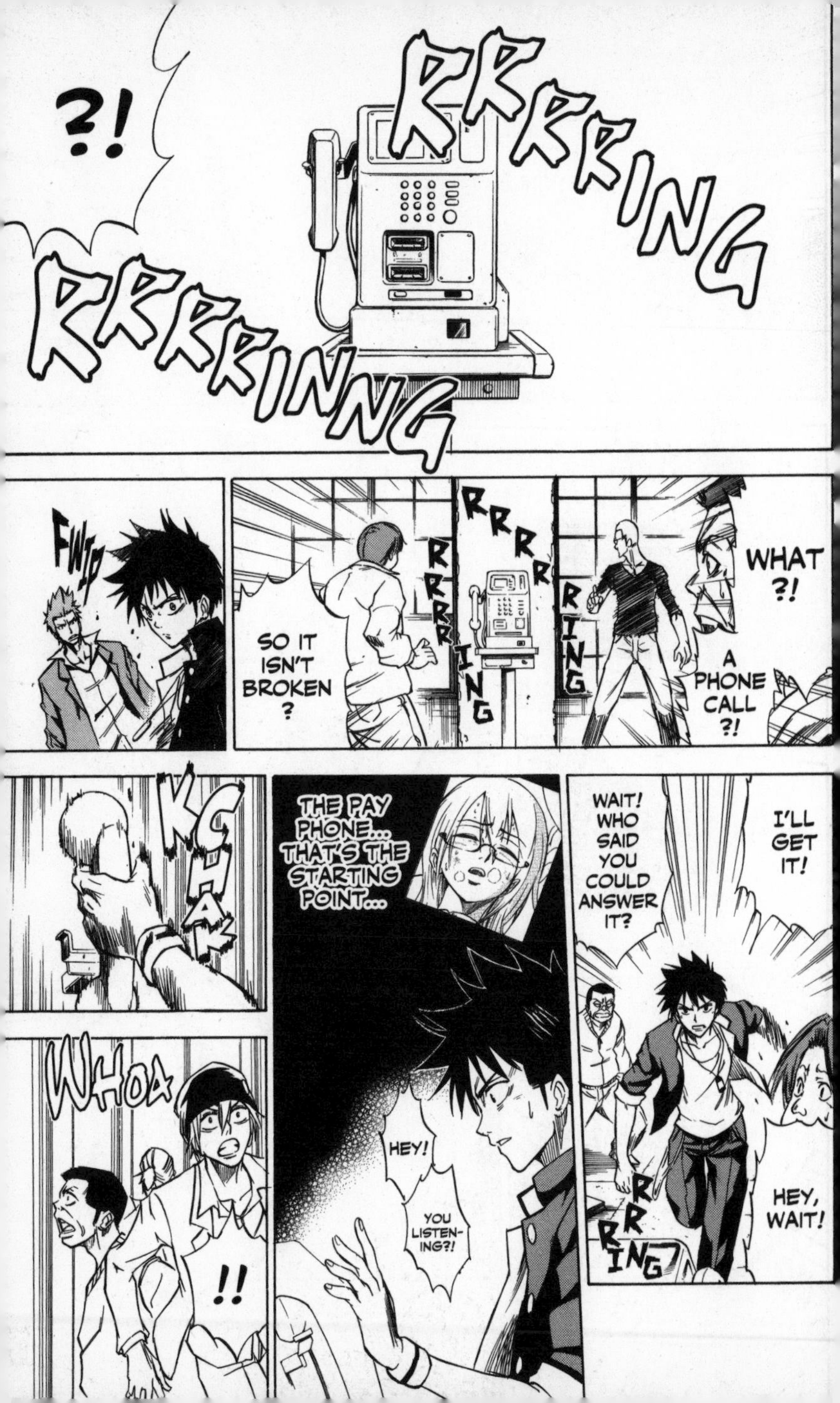

RRRRING
?!
RRRRINNG
WHAT?!
A PHONE CALL?!
RRRRRING
RRRRING
SO IT ISN'T BROKEN?
FWIP
I'LL GET IT!
WAIT! WHO SAID YOU COULD ANSWER IT?
HEY, WAIT!
RRRING
THE PAY PHONE... THAT'S THE STARTING POINT...
HEY!
YOU LISTENING?!
KCHAK
WHOA
!!

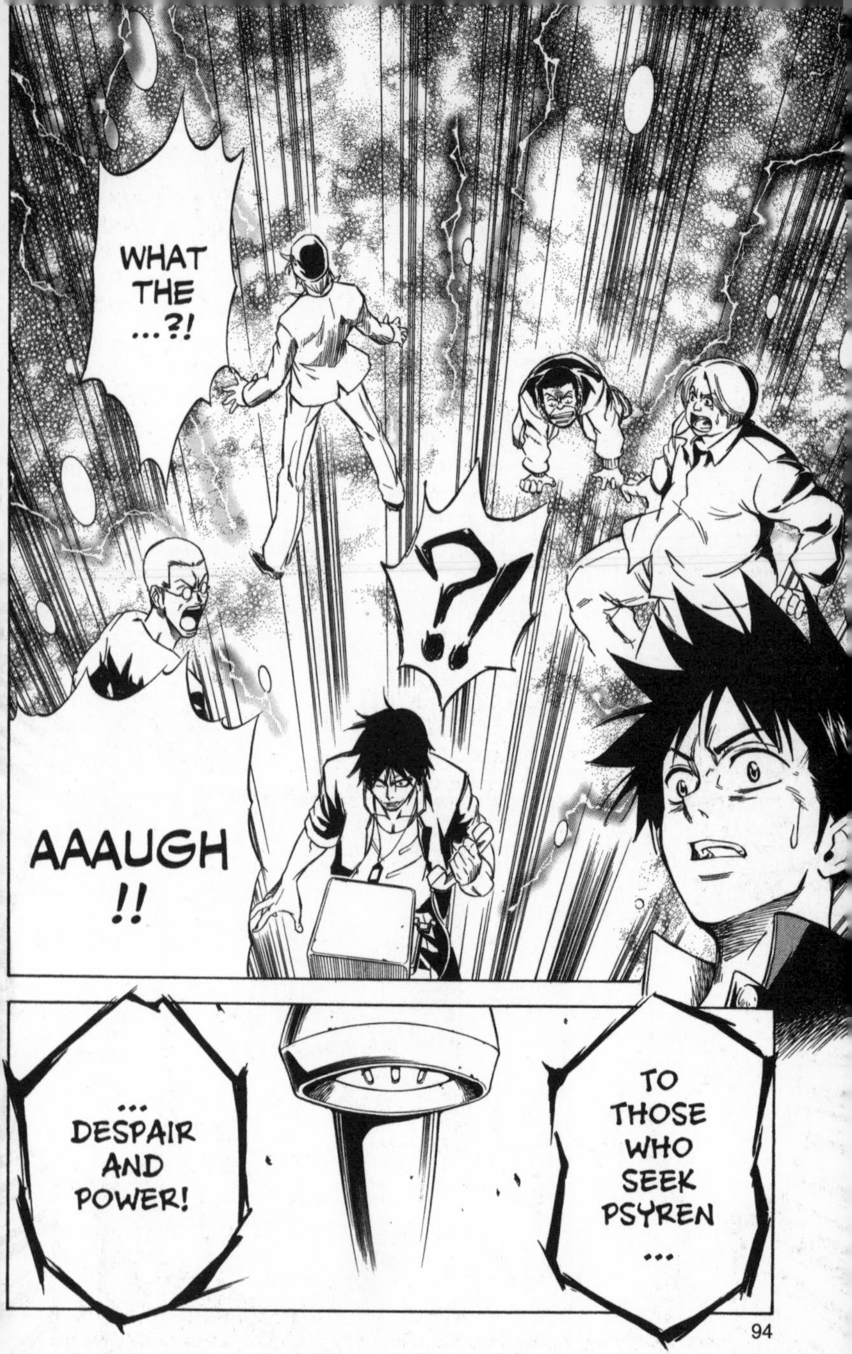
WHAT THE ...?!
?!
AAAUGH !!
TO THOSE WHO SEEK PSYREN ...
... DESPAIR AND POWER!

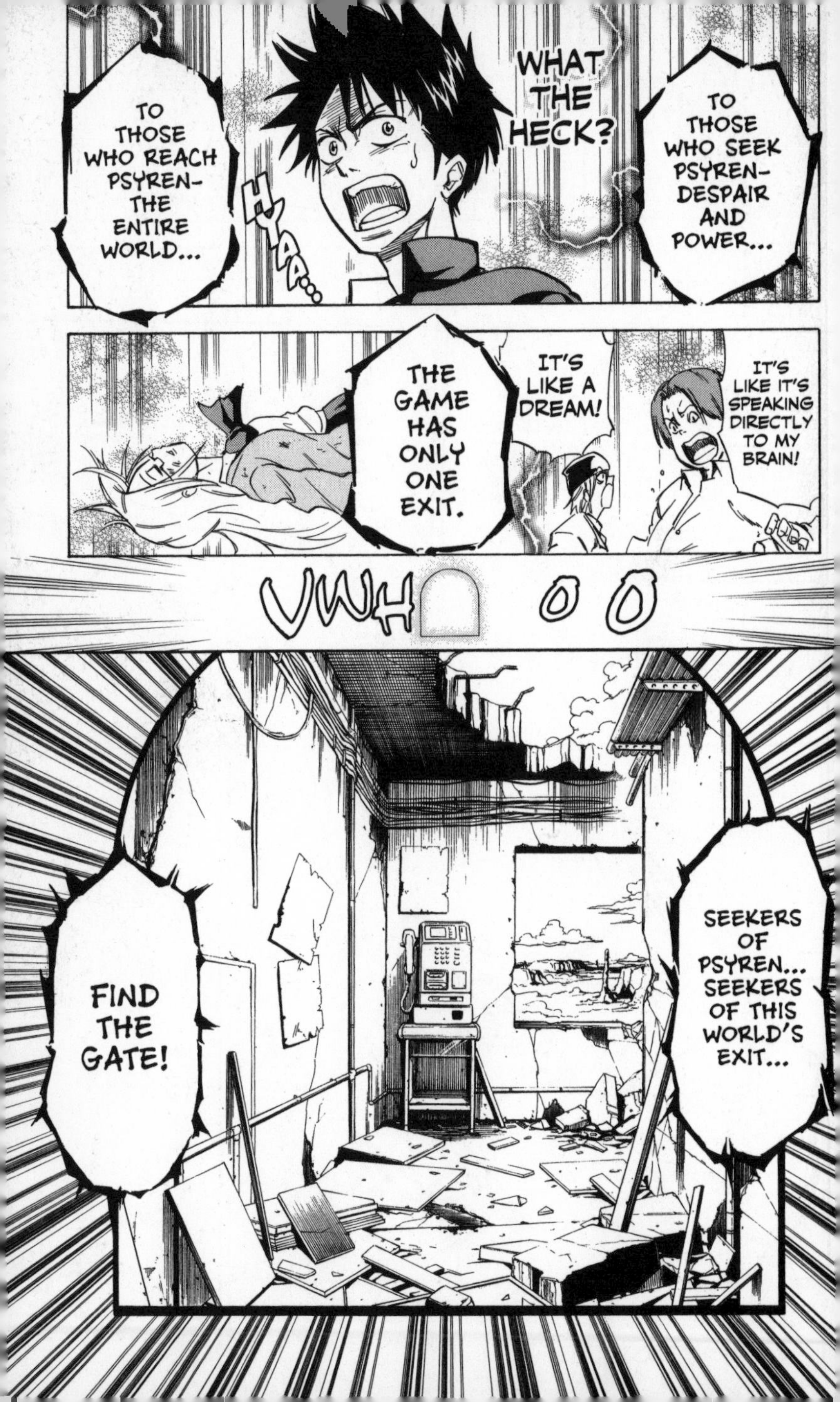
TO THOSE WHO SEEK PSYREN- DESPAIR AND POWER...
WHAT THE HECK?
TO THOSE WHO REACH PSYREN- THE ENTIRE WORLD...
HYAA...
IT'S LIKE IT'S SPEAKING DIRECTLY TO MY BRAIN!
IT'S LIKE A DREAM!
THE GAME HAS ONLY ONE EXIT.
VWH OO
SEEKERS OF PSYREN... SEEKERS OF THIS WORLD'S EXIT...
FIND THE GATE!

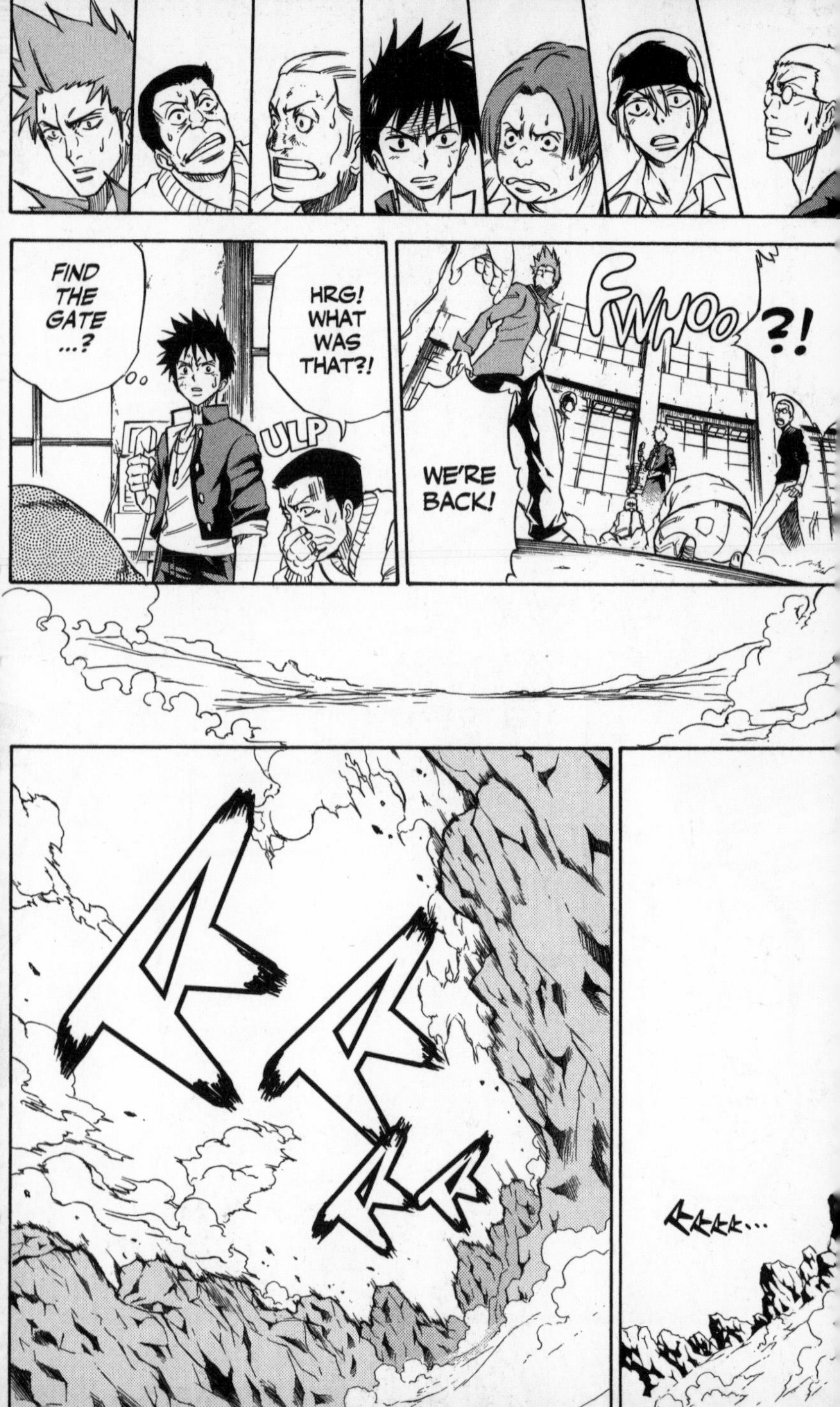
FWHOO
?!
WE'RE BACK!
HRG! WHAT WAS THAT?!
ULP
FIND THE GATE ...?
KRRRR...

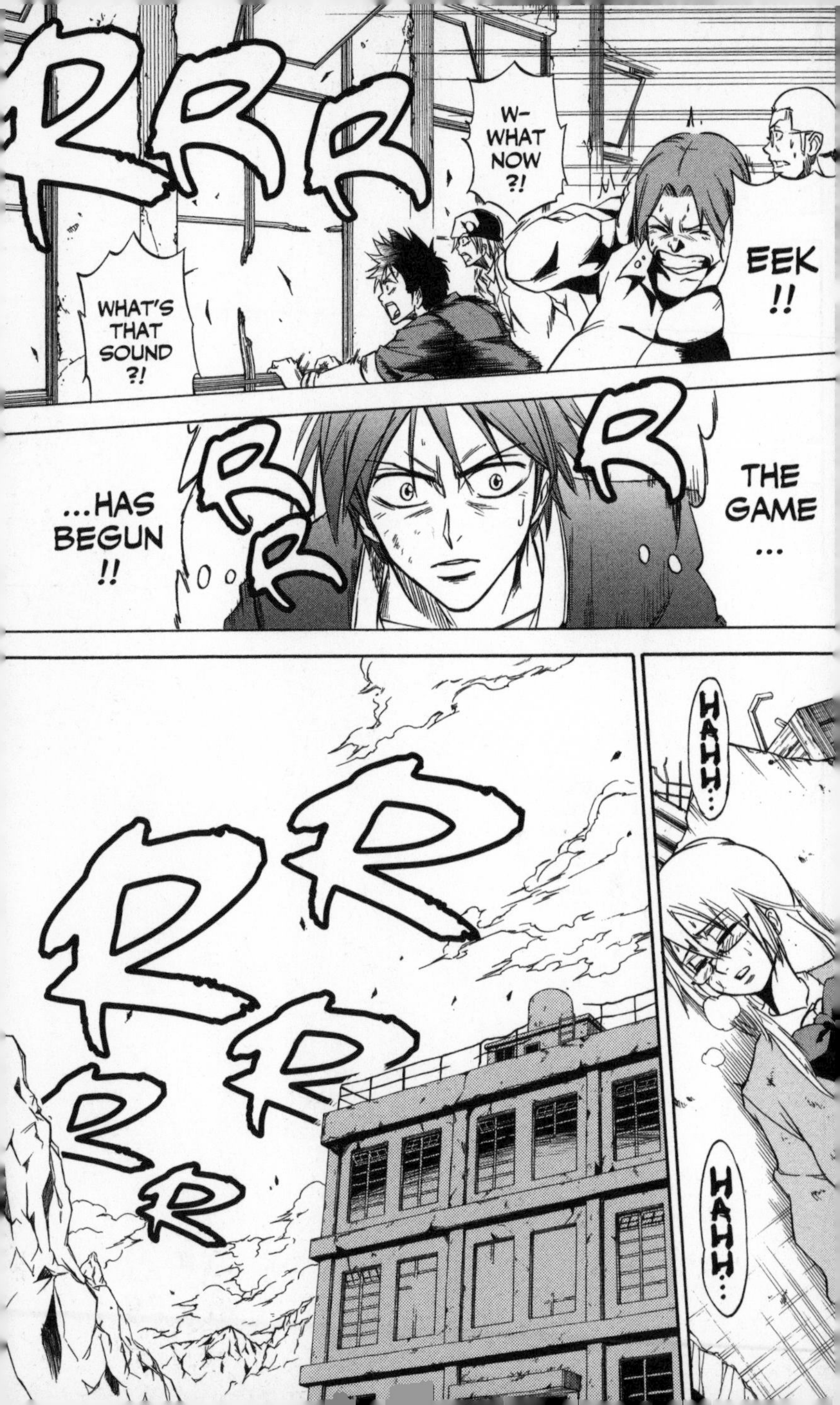

EEK!!
W-WHAT NOW?!
RRR
WHAT'S THAT SOUND?!
RRR
THE GAME...
...HAS BEGUN!!
HAHH...
HAHH...
RRRRR

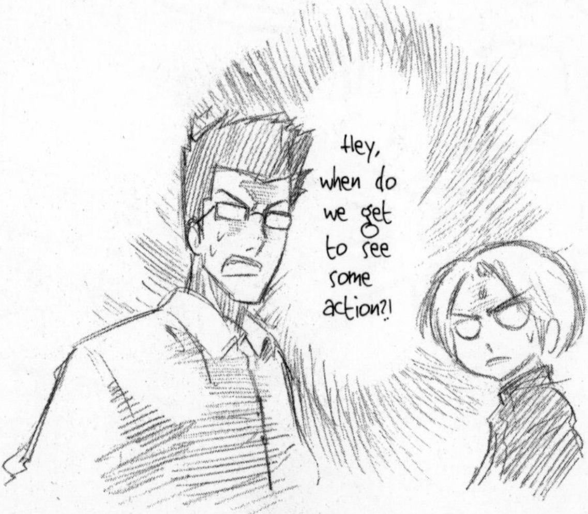
Hey, when do we get to see some action?!

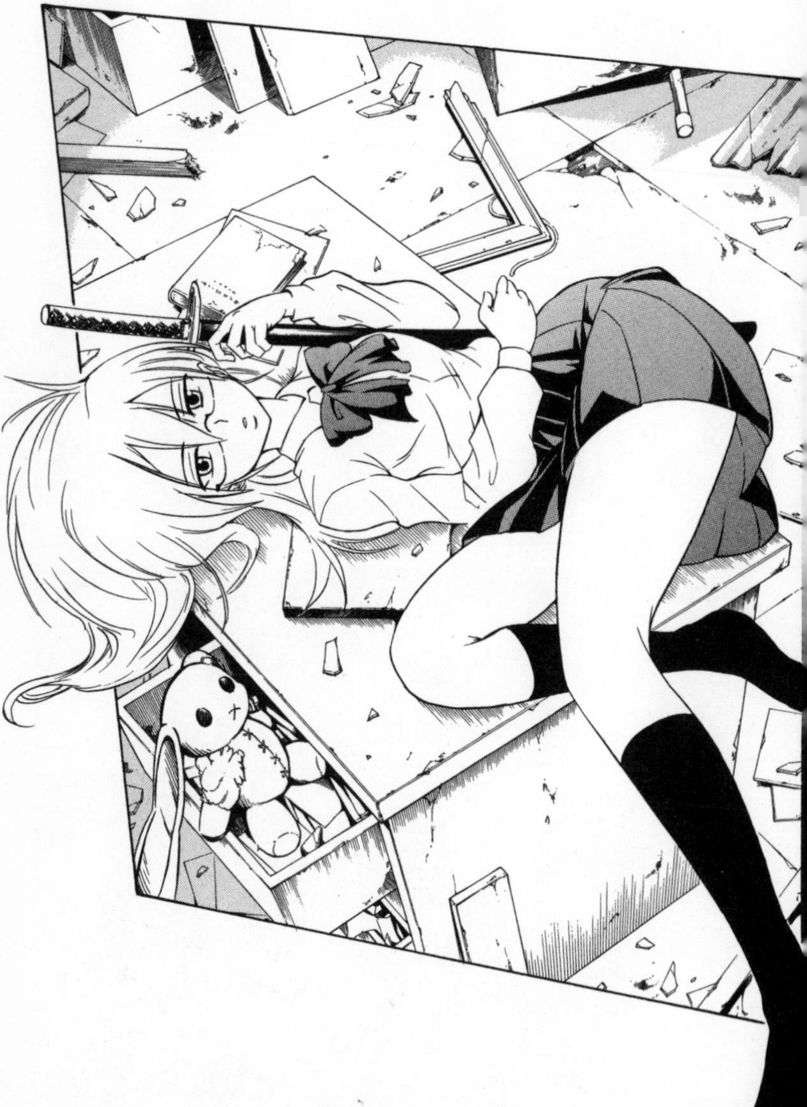

# Call.3: Danger Zone

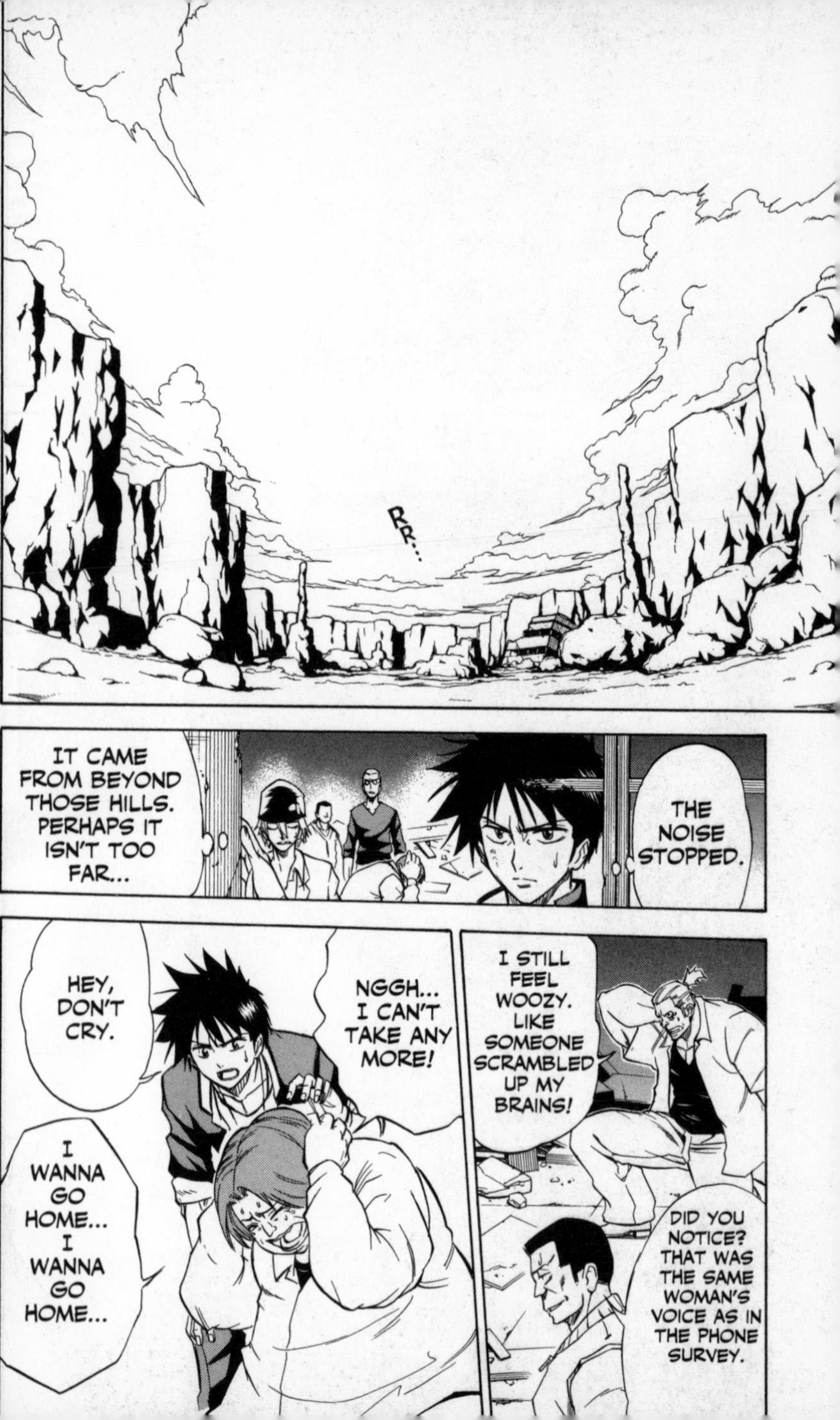
RR...
THE NOISE STOPPED.
IT CAME FROM BEYOND THOSE HILLS. PERHAPS IT ISN'T TOO FAR...
I STILL FEEL WOOZY. LIKE SOMEONE SCRAMBLED UP MY BRAINS!
DID YOU NOTICE? THAT WAS THE SAME WOMAN'S VOICE AS IN THE PHONE SURVEY.
NGGH... I CAN'T TAKE ANY MORE!
HEY, DON'T CRY.
I WANNA GO HOME... I WANNA GO HOME...

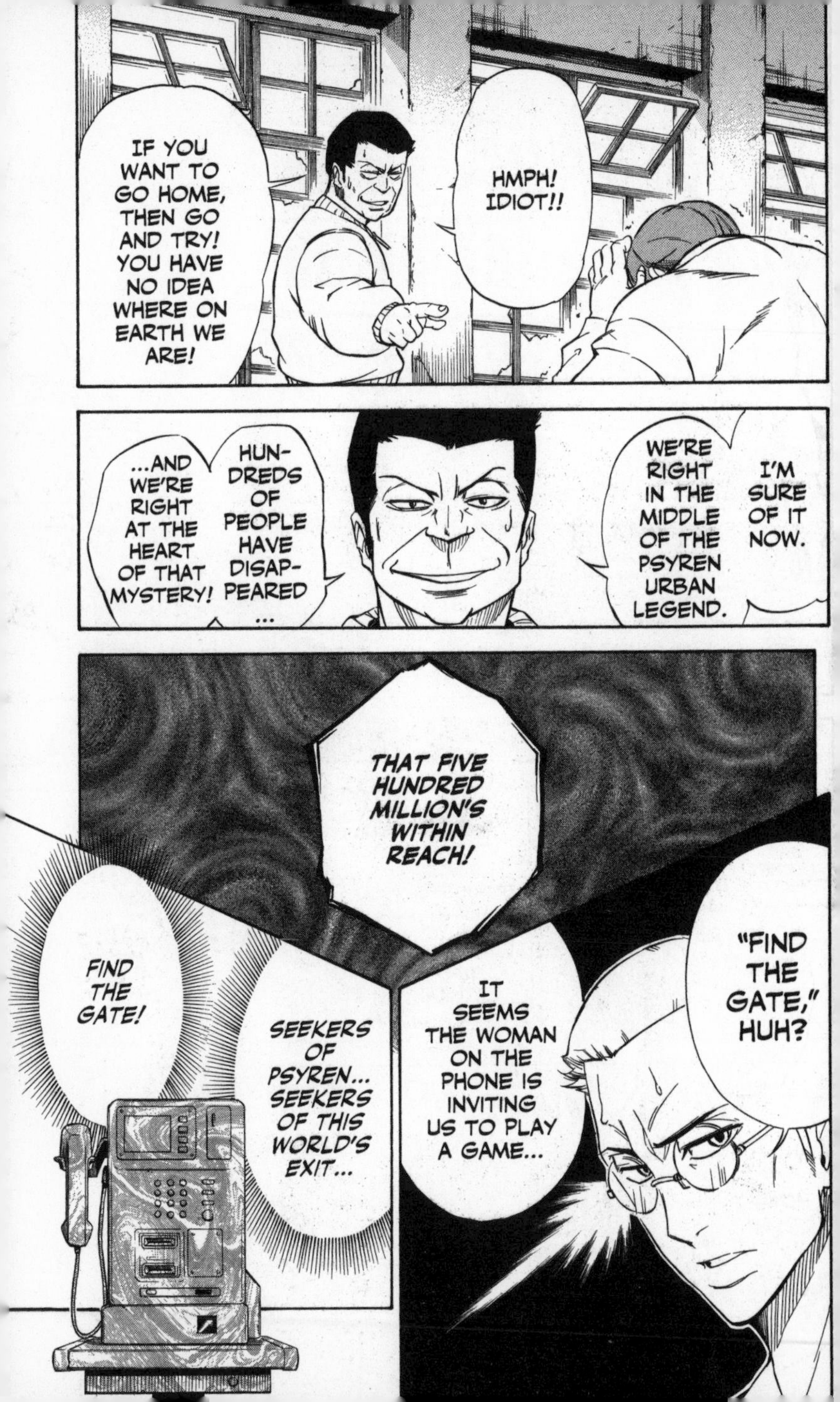
HMPH! IDIOT!!
IF YOU WANT TO GO HOME, THEN GO AND TRY! YOU HAVE NO IDEA WHERE ON EARTH WE ARE!
I'M SURE OF IT NOW.
WE'RE RIGHT IN THE MIDDLE OF THE PSYREN URBAN LEGEND.
HUNDREDS OF PEOPLE HAVE DISAPPEARED...
...AND WE'RE RIGHT AT THE HEART OF THAT MYSTERY!
THAT FIVE HUNDRED MILLION'S WITHIN REACH!
"FIND THE GATE," HUH?
IT SEEMS THE WOMAN ON THE PHONE IS INVITING US TO PLAY A GAME...
SEEKERS OF PSYREN... SEEKERS OF THIS WORLD'S EXIT...
FIND THE GATE!

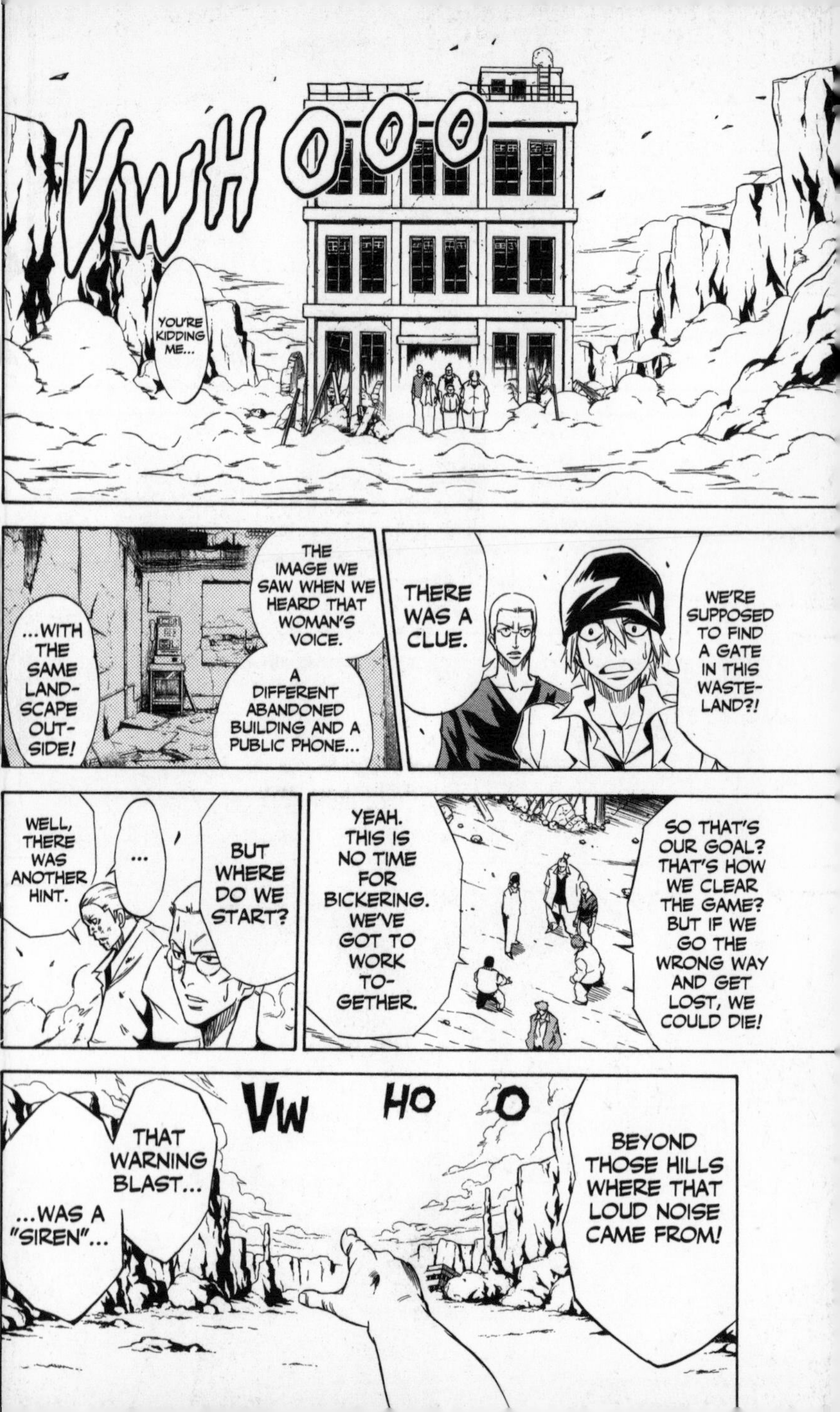
VWHOOO
YOU'RE KIDDING ME...
WE'RE SUPPOSED TO FIND A GATE IN THIS WASTELAND?!
THERE WAS A CLUE.
THE IMAGE WE SAW WHEN WE HEARD THAT WOMAN'S VOICE.
A DIFFERENT ABANDONED BUILDING AND A PUBLIC PHONE...
...WITH THE SAME LANDSCAPE OUTSIDE!
SO THAT'S OUR GOAL? THAT'S HOW WE CLEAR THE GAME? BUT IF WE GO THE WRONG WAY AND GET LOST, WE COULD DIE!
YEAH. THIS IS NO TIME FOR BICKERING. WE'VE GOT TO WORK TOGETHER.
BUT WHERE DO WE START?
...
WELL, THERE WAS ANOTHER HINT.
VW HO O
BEYOND THOSE HILLS WHERE THAT LOUD NOISE CAME FROM!
THAT WARNING BLAST...
...WAS A "SIREN"...

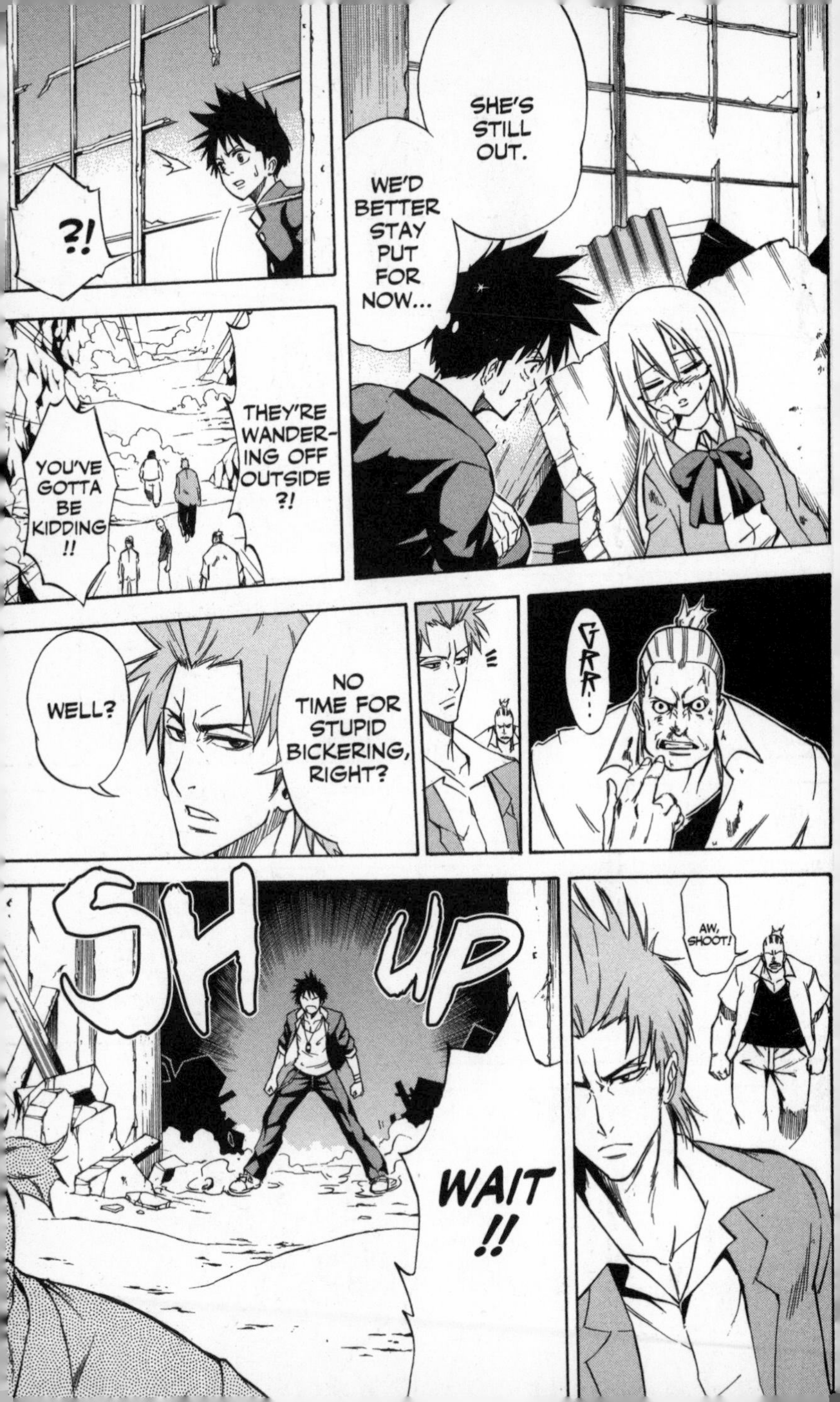
SHE'S STILL OUT.
WE'D BETTER STAY PUT FOR NOW...
?!
THEY'RE WANDERING OFF OUTSIDE ?!
YOU'VE GOTTA BE KIDDING !!
GRR...
NO TIME FOR STUPID BICKERING, RIGHT?
WELL?
AW, SHOOT!
WAIT !!
SHUP

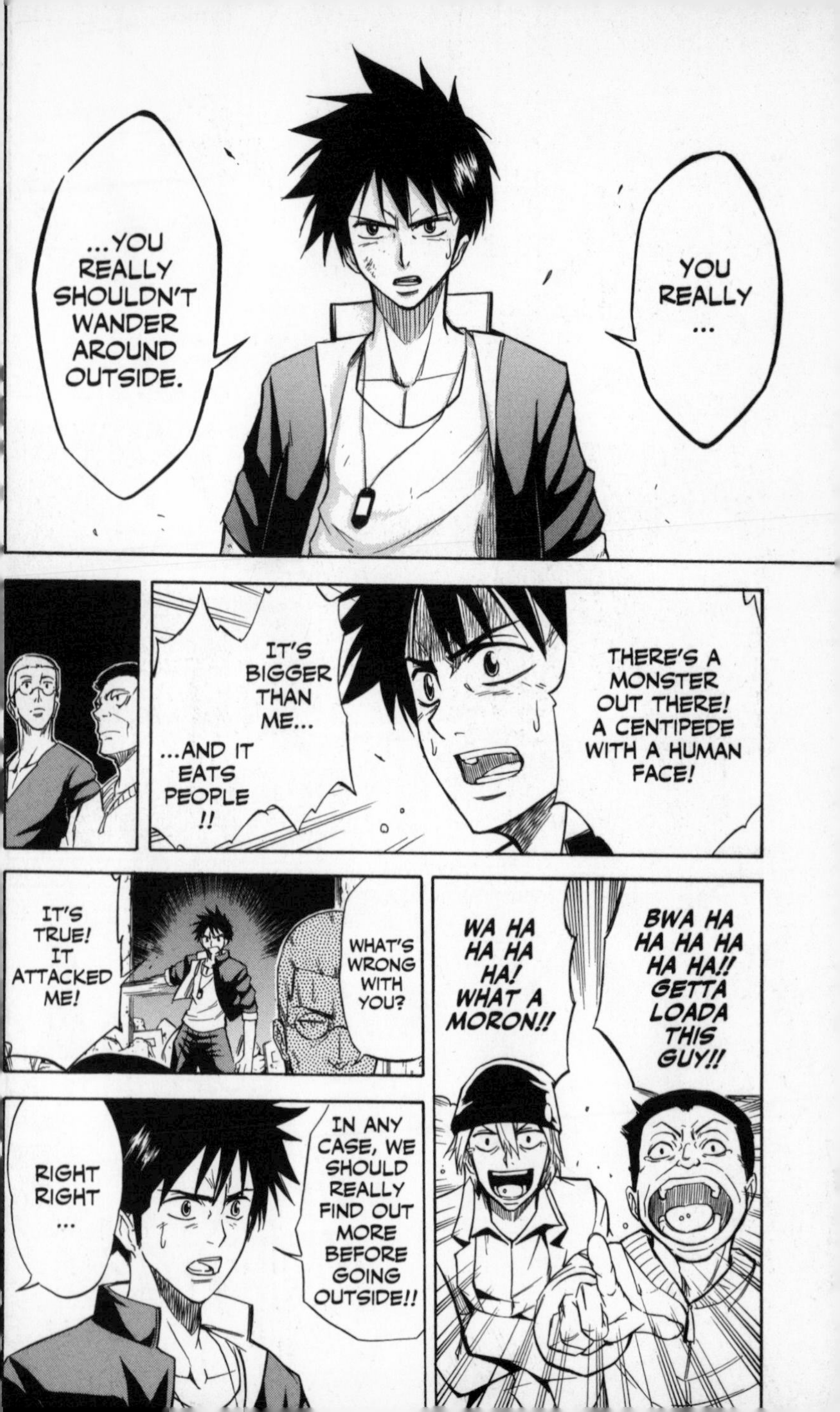
YOU REALLY ...
...YOU REALLY SHOULDN'T WANDER AROUND OUTSIDE.
THERE'S A MONSTER OUT THERE! A CENTIPEDE WITH A HUMAN FACE!
IT'S BIGGER THAN ME...
...AND IT EATS PEOPLE !!
BWA HA HA HA HA HA HA!! GETTA LOADA THIS GUY!!
WA HA HA HA HA! WHAT A MORON!!
WHAT'S WRONG WITH YOU?
IT'S TRUE! IT ATTACKED ME!
IN ANY CASE, WE SHOULD REALLY FIND OUT MORE BEFORE GOING OUTSIDE!!
RIGHT RIGHT ...

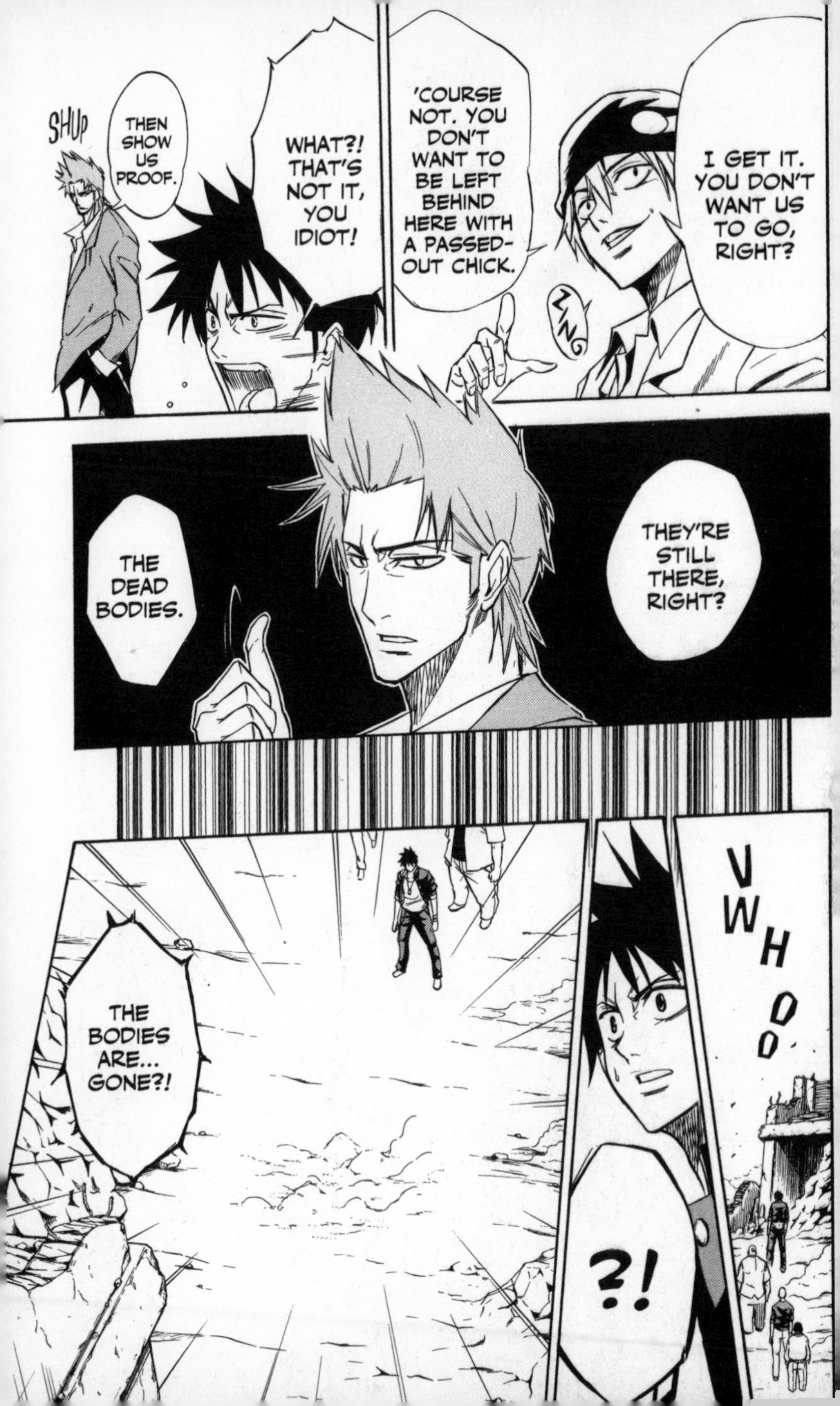
I GET IT. YOU DON'T WANT US TO GO, RIGHT?
ZING
'COURSE NOT. YOU DON'T WANT TO BE LEFT BEHIND HERE WITH A PASSED-OUT CHICK.
WHAT?! THAT'S NOT IT, YOU IDIOT!
SHUP
THEN SHOW US PROOF.
THEY'RE STILL THERE, RIGHT?
THE DEAD BODIES.
VWHOO
?!
THE BODIES ARE... GONE?!

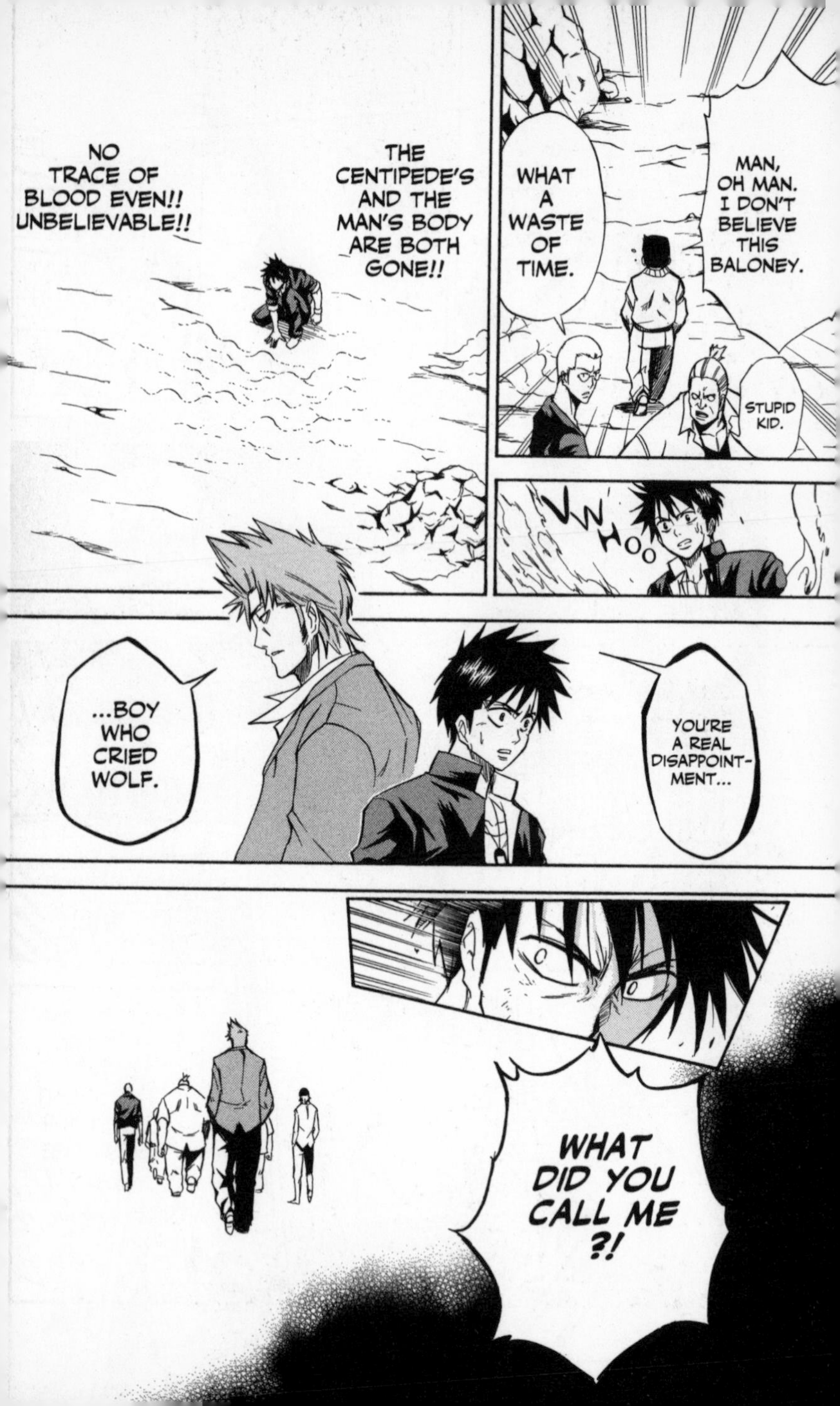
MAN, OH MAN. I DON'T BELIEVE THIS BALONEY.
WHAT A WASTE OF TIME.
STUPID KID.
VWHOO
THE CENTIPEDE'S AND THE MAN'S BODY ARE BOTH GONE!!
NO TRACE OF BLOOD EVEN!! UNBELIEVABLE!!
YOU'RE A REAL DISAPPOINTMENT...
...BOY WHO CRIED WOLF.
WHAT DID YOU CALL ME ?!

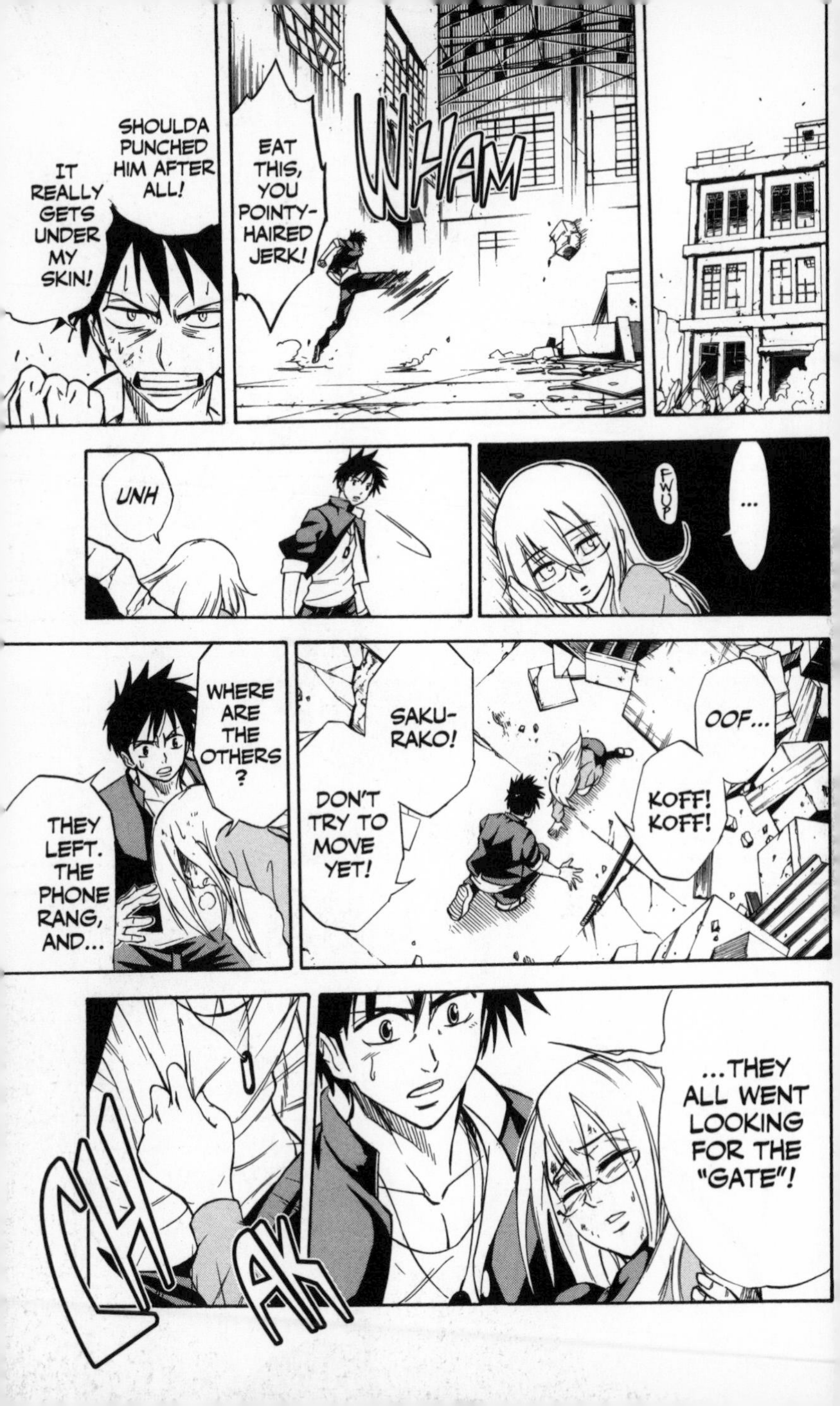
WHAM
EAT THIS, YOU POINTY-HAIRED JERK!
SHOULDA PUNCHED HIM AFTER ALL!
IT REALLY GETS UNDER MY SKIN!
...
FWUP
UNH
OOF...
KOFF! KOFF!
SAKU-RAKO!
DON'T TRY TO MOVE YET!
WHERE ARE THE OTHERS?
THEY LEFT. THE PHONE RANG, AND...
...THEY ALL WENT LOOKING FOR THE "GATE"!
CHAK

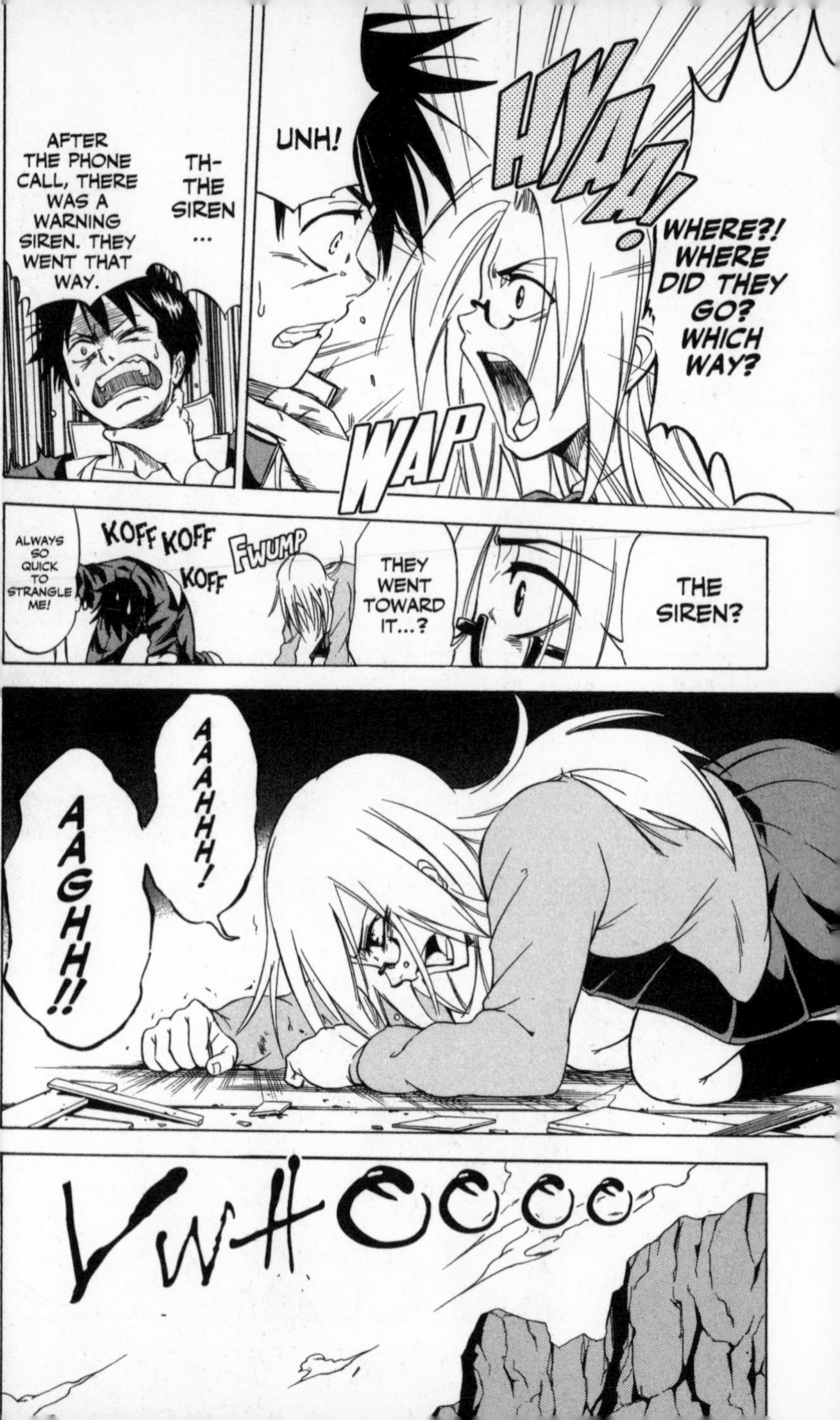
HIYAA!
WHERE?! WHERE DID THEY GO? WHICH WAY?
WAP
UNH!
TH- THE SIREN ...
AFTER THE PHONE CALL, THERE WAS A WARNING SIREN. THEY WENT THAT WAY.
THE SIREN?
THEY WENT TOWARD IT...?
FWUMP
KOFF KOFF KOFF
ALWAYS SO QUICK TO STRANGLE ME!
AAAHHH!
AAGHH!!
VWHEEEEE

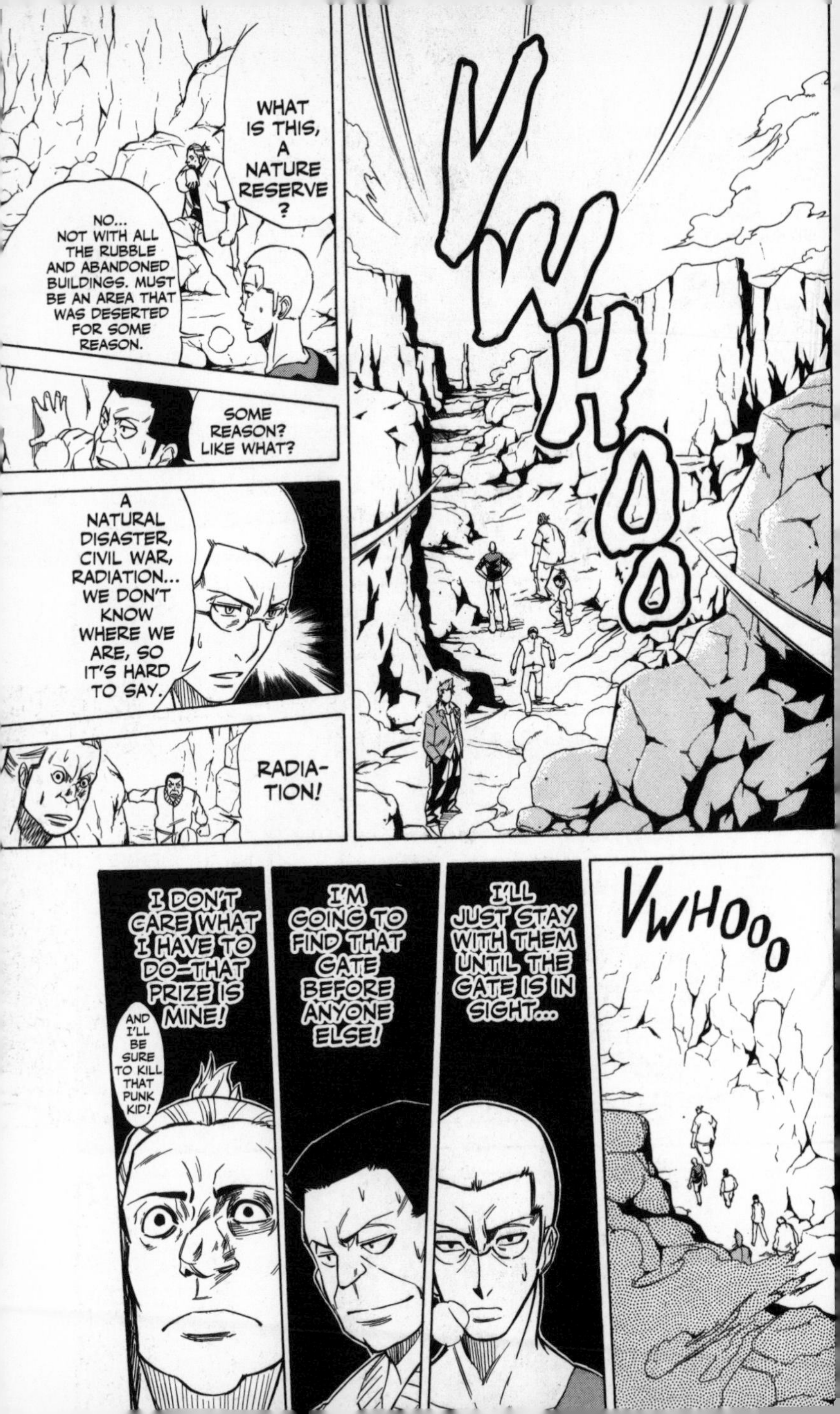
VWHOOO
WHAT IS THIS, A NATURE RESERVE?
NO... NOT WITH ALL THE RUBBLE AND ABANDONED BUILDINGS. MUST BE AN AREA THAT WAS DESERTED FOR SOME REASON.
SOME REASON? LIKE WHAT?
A NATURAL DISASTER, CIVIL WAR, RADIATION... WE DON'T KNOW WHERE WE ARE, SO IT'S HARD TO SAY.
RADIA-TION!
VWHOOO
I'LL JUST STAY WITH THEM UNTIL THE GATE IS IN SIGHT...
I'M GOING TO FIND THAT GATE BEFORE ANYONE ELSE!
I DON'T CARE WHAT I HAVE TO DO—THAT PRIZE IS MINE!
AND I'LL BE SURE TO KILL THAT PUNK KID!

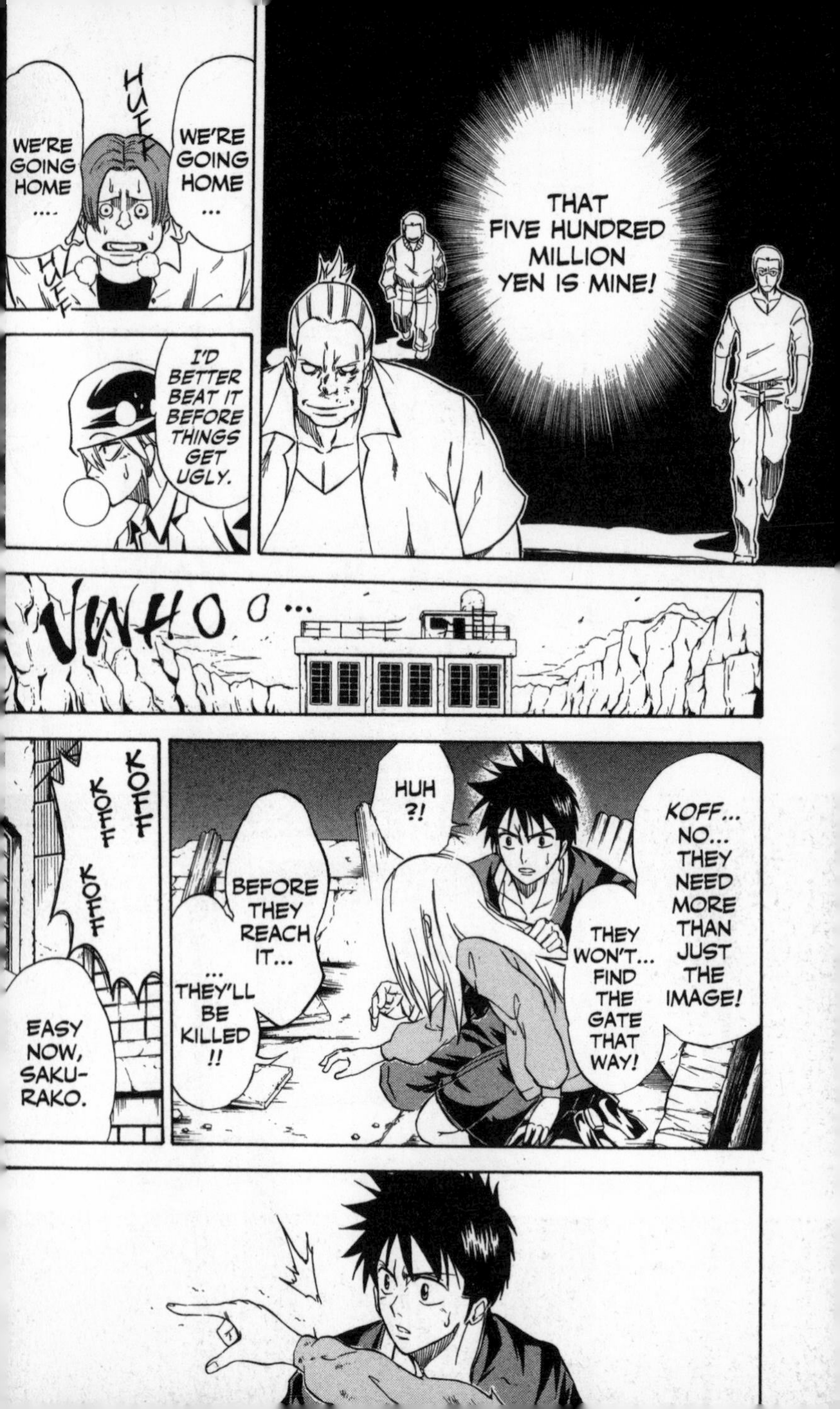

THAT FIVE HUNDRED MILLION YEN IS MINE!
WE'RE GOING HOME ...
HUFF HUFF
WE'RE GOING HOME ....
I'D BETTER BEAT IT BEFORE THINGS GET UGLY.
WHOO...
KOFF... NO... THEY NEED MORE THAN JUST THE IMAGE!
HUH ?!
THEY WON'T... FIND THE GATE THAT WAY!
BEFORE THEY REACH IT...
... THEY'LL BE KILLED !!
KOFF KOFF
KOFF
EASY NOW, SAKU-RAKO.

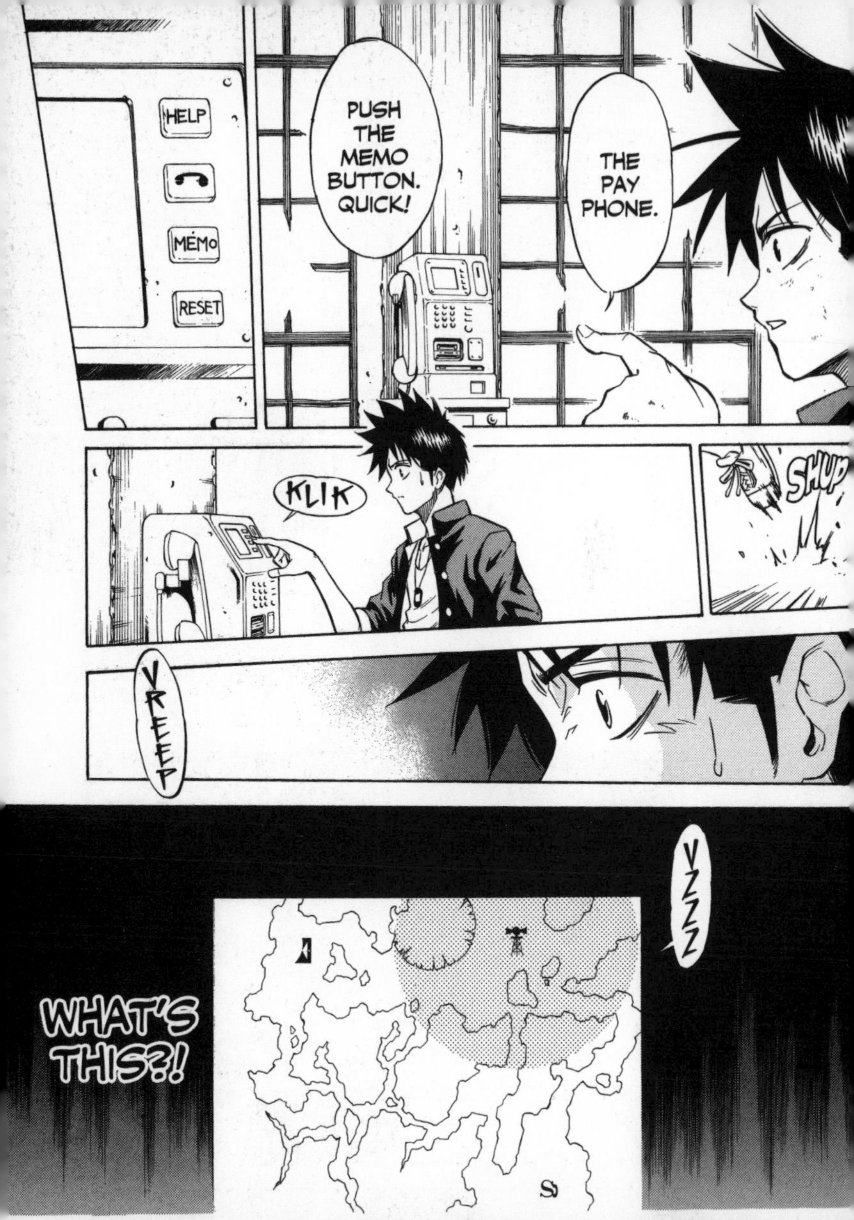

THE PAY PHONE.
PUSH THE MEMO BUTTON. QUICK!
HELP
MEMO
RESET
SHUP
KLIK
VREEEP
VZZZ
WHAT'S THIS?!

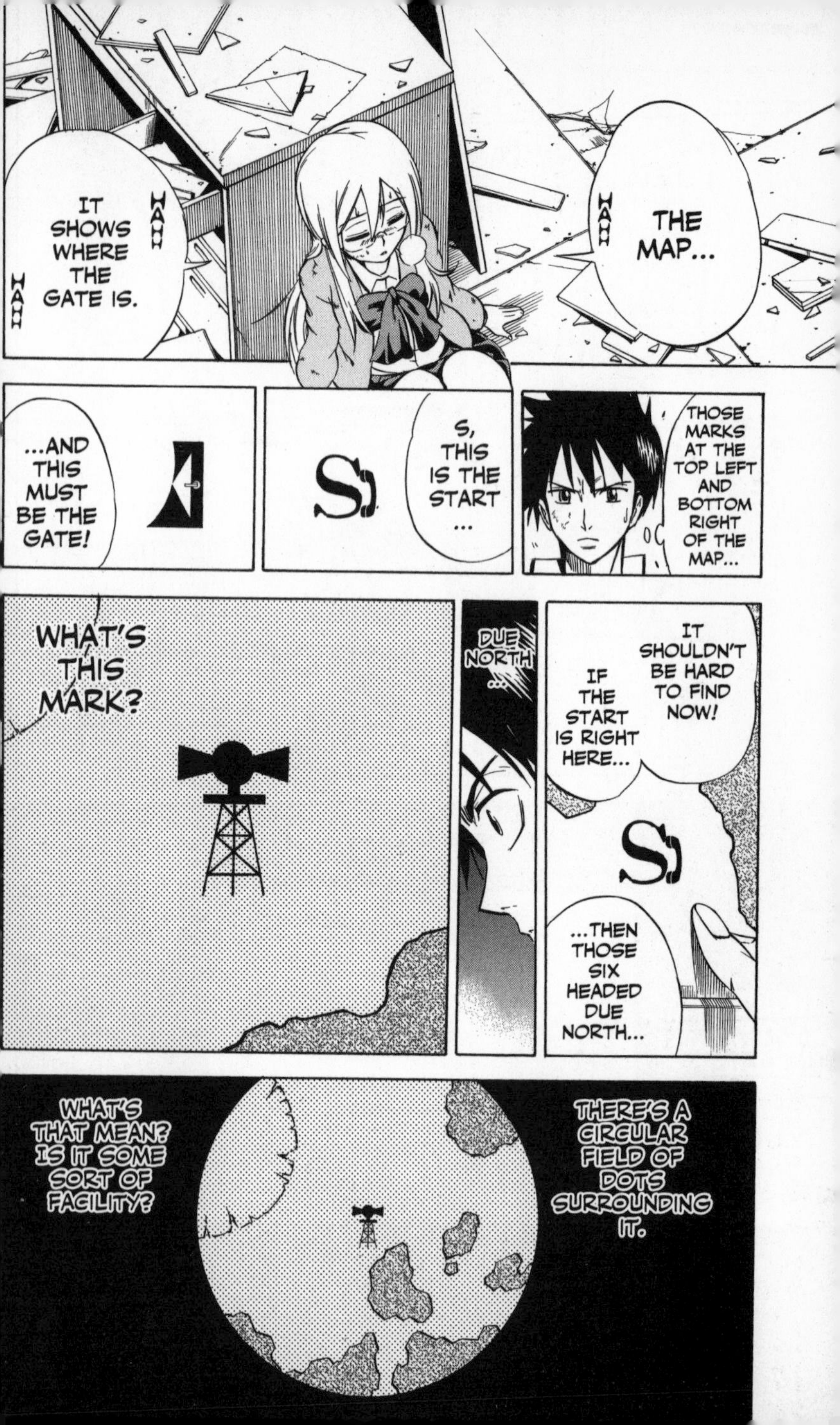
HAHH
THE MAP...
HAHH
IT SHOWS WHERE THE GATE IS.
HAHH
THOSE MARKS AT THE TOP LEFT AND BOTTOM RIGHT OF THE MAP...
S, THIS IS THE START ...
...AND THIS MUST BE THE GATE!
IT SHOULDN'T BE HARD TO FIND NOW!
IF THE START IS RIGHT HERE...
...THEN THOSE SIX HEADED DUE NORTH...
DUE NORTH ...
WHAT'S THIS MARK?
THERE'S A CIRCULAR FIELD OF DOTS SURROUNDING IT.
WHAT'S THAT MEAN? IS IT SOME SORT OF FACILITY?

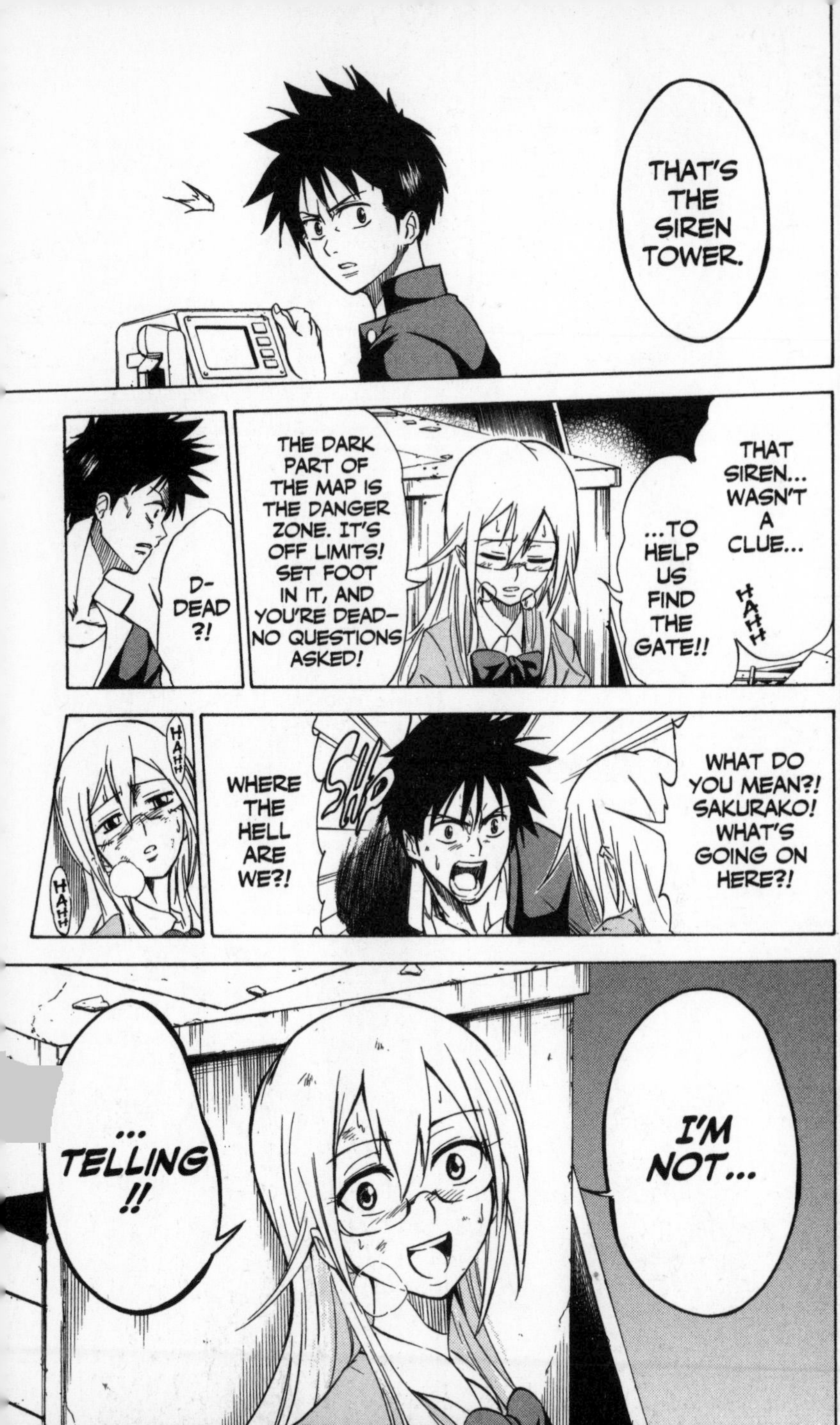
THAT'S THE SIREN TOWER.
THAT SIREN... WASN'T A CLUE...
HAHH
...TO HELP US FIND THE GATE!!
THE DARK PART OF THE MAP IS THE DANGER ZONE. IT'S OFF LIMITS! SET FOOT IN IT, AND YOU'RE DEAD-NO QUESTIONS ASKED!
D-DEAD ?!
WHAT DO YOU MEAN?! SAKURAKO! WHAT'S GOING ON HERE?!
WHERE THE HELL ARE WE?!
HAHH
HAHH
I'M NOT...
...TELLING !!

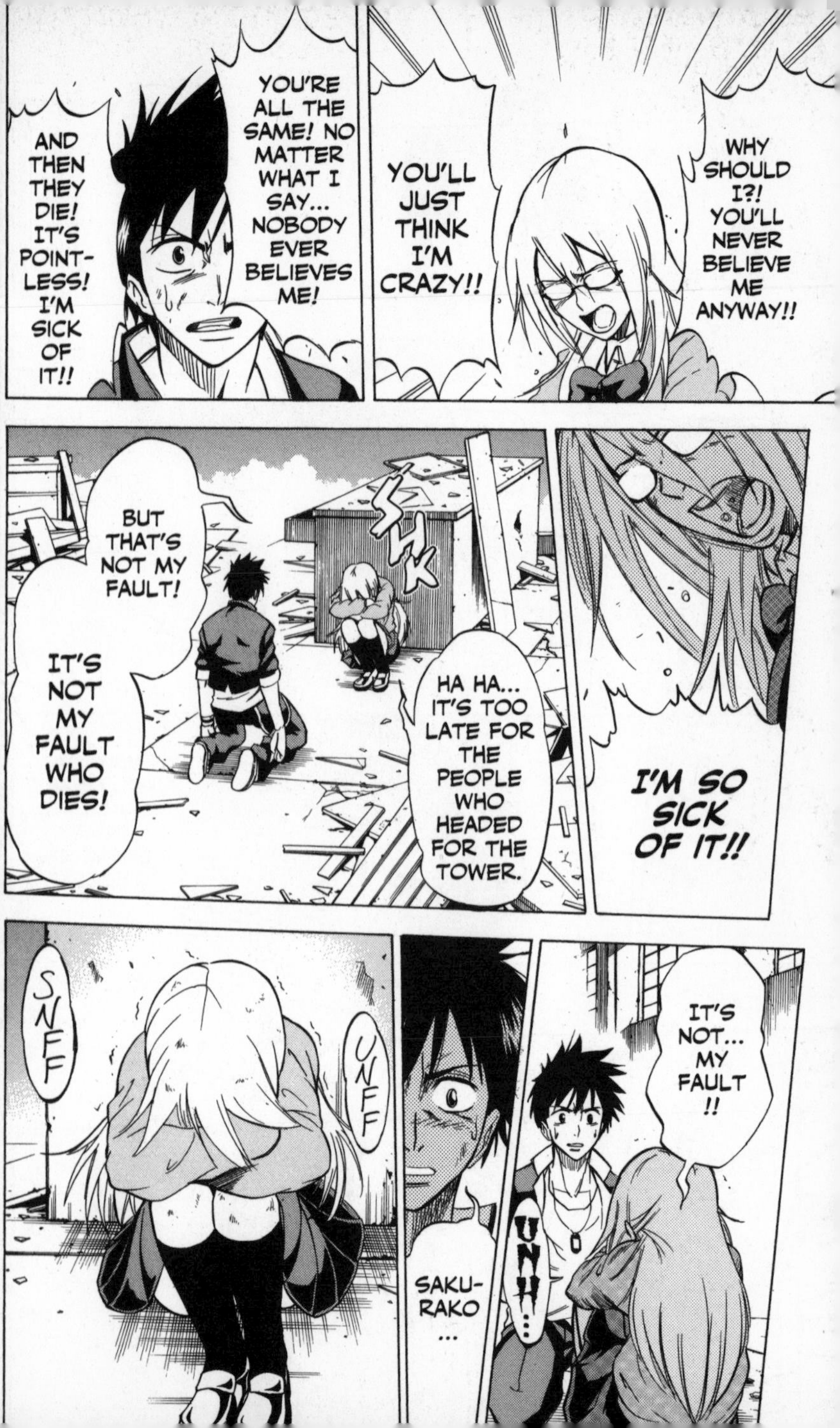
WHY SHOULD I?! YOU'LL NEVER BELIEVE ME ANYWAY!!
YOU'LL JUST THINK I'M CRAZY!!
YOU'RE ALL THE SAME! NO MATTER WHAT I SAY... NOBODY EVER BELIEVES ME!
AND THEN THEY DIE! IT'S POINTLESS! I'M SICK OF IT!!
I'M SO SICK OF IT!!
HA HA... IT'S TOO LATE FOR THE PEOPLE WHO HEADED FOR THE TOWER.
SHK
BUT THAT'S NOT MY FAULT!
IT'S NOT MY FAULT WHO DIES!
IT'S NOT... MY FAULT!!
UNH...
SAKURAKO...
UNFF
SNFF

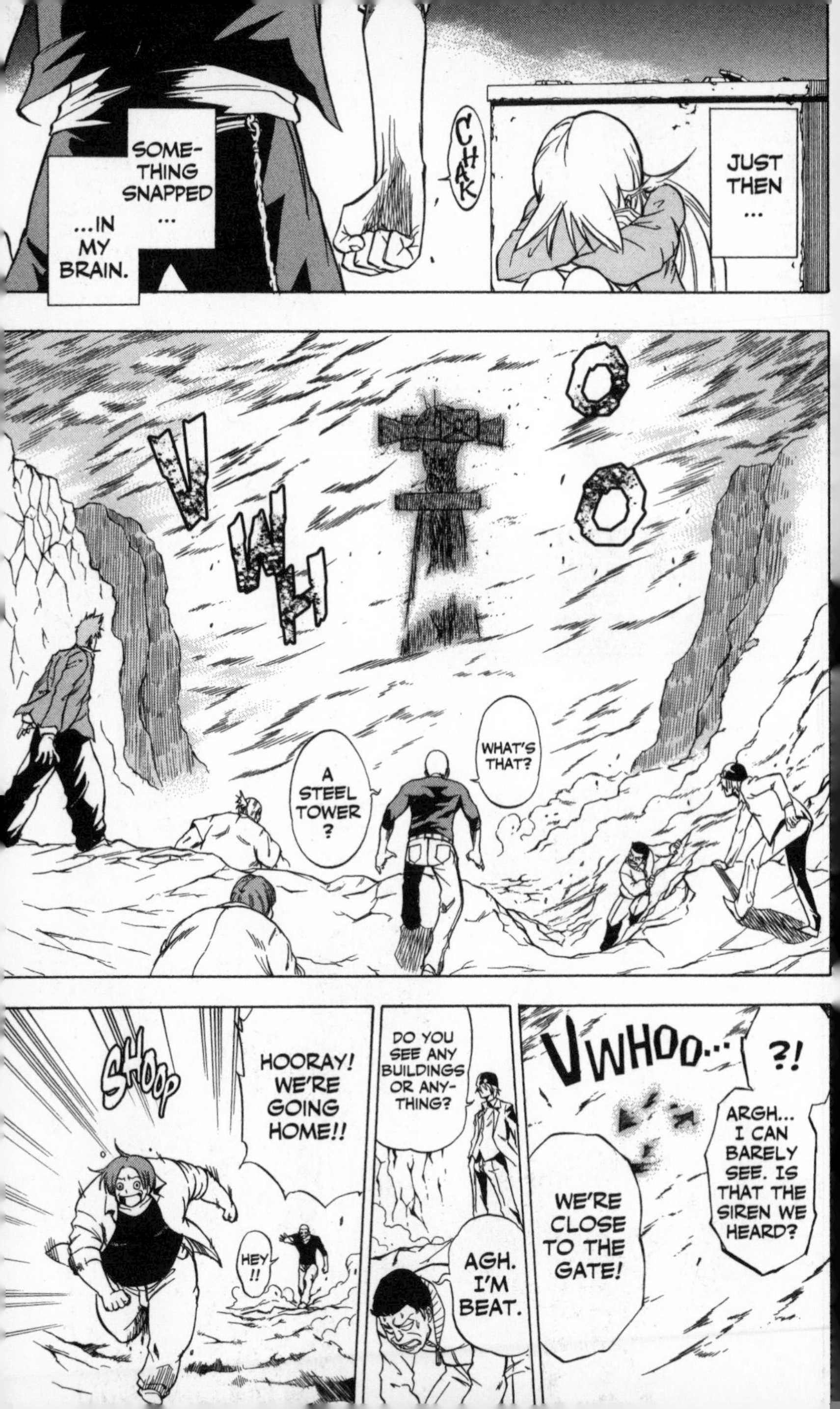
JUST THEN ...
CHAK
SOME-THING SNAPPED ...
...IN MY BRAIN.
VWHOO
WHAT'S THAT?
A STEEL TOWER?
VWHOO...
?!
ARGH... I CAN BARELY SEE. IS THAT THE SIREN WE HEARD?
WE'RE CLOSE TO THE GATE!
AGH. I'M BEAT.
DO YOU SEE ANY BUILDINGS OR ANY-THING?
HOORAY! WE'RE GOING HOME!!
SHOOP
HEY!!

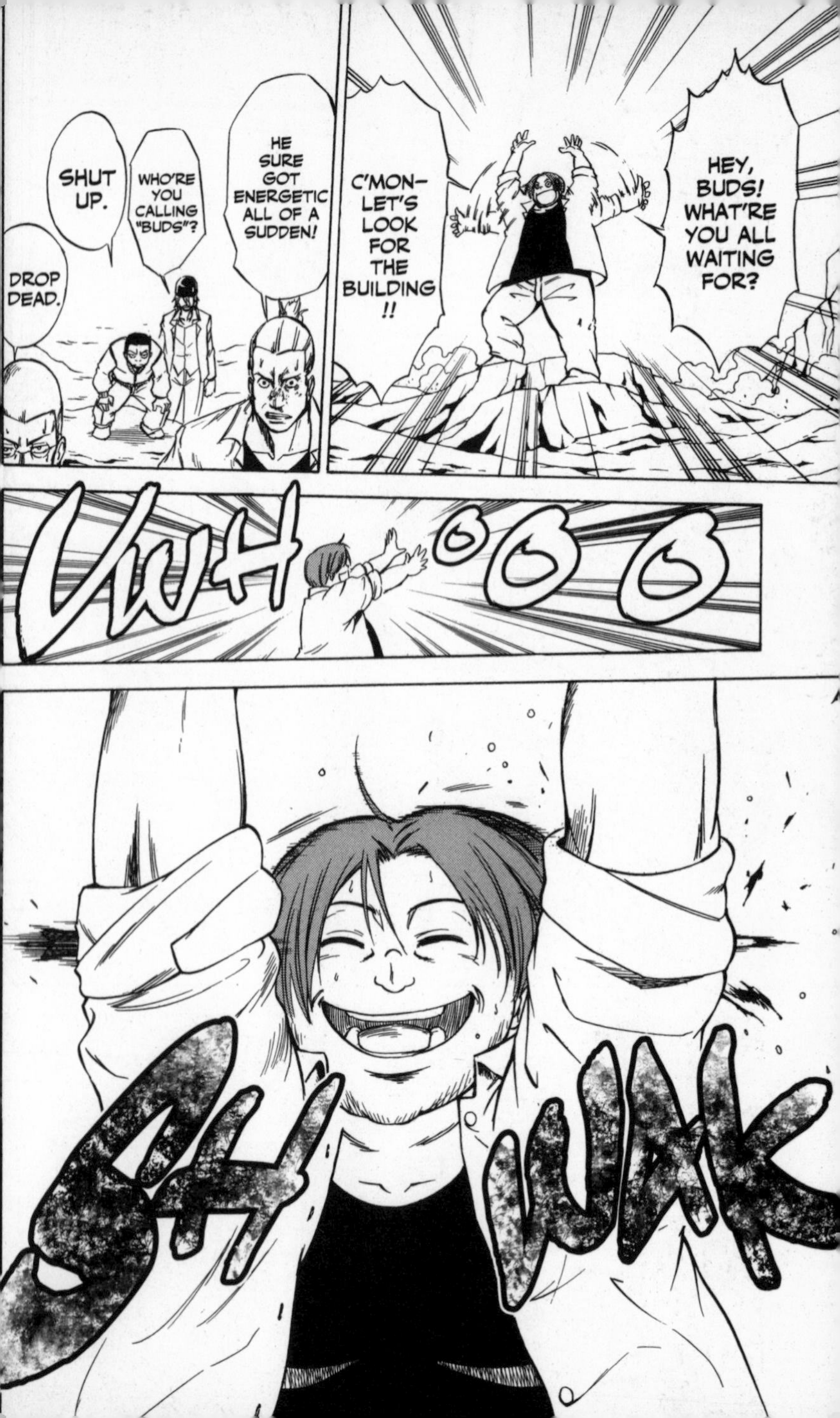
HEY, BUDS! WHAT'RE YOU ALL WAITING FOR?
C'MON— LET'S LOOK FOR THE BUILDING !!
HE SURE GOT ENERGETIC ALL OF A SUDDEN!
WHO'RE YOU CALLING "BUDS"?
SHUT UP.
DROP DEAD.
VWHOOO
SHWAK

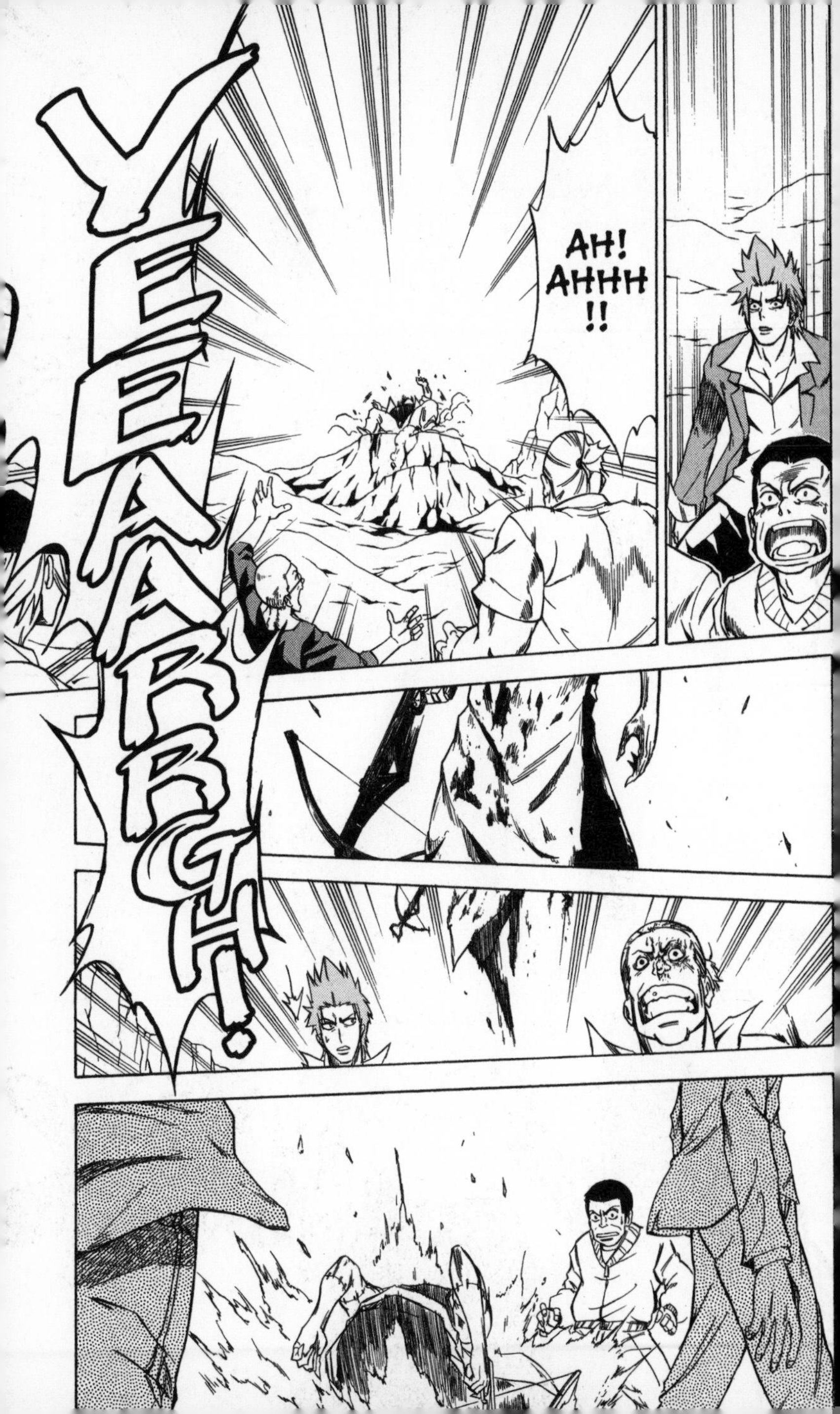
AH! AHHH !!
YEEAAARRGH!

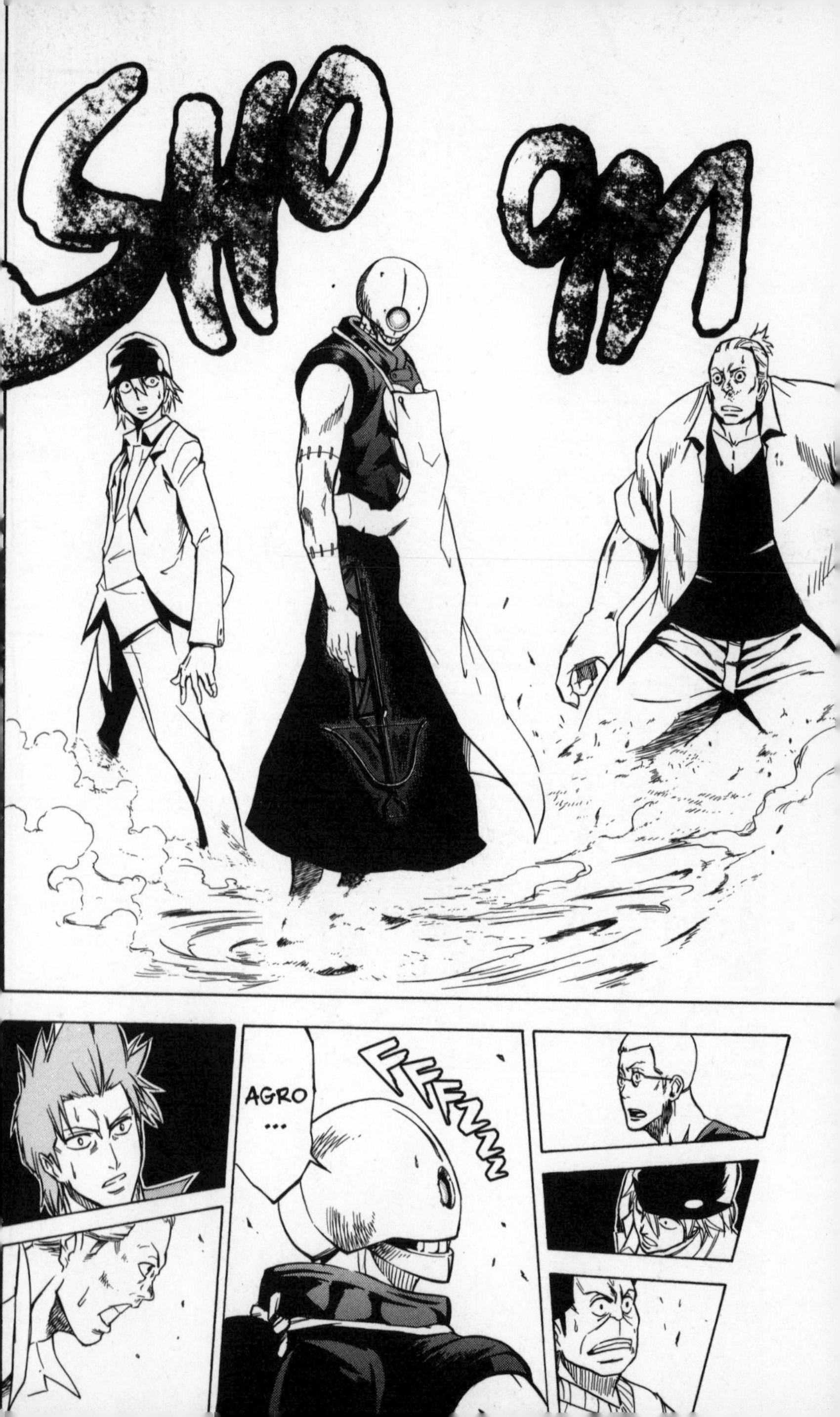
SHOOM
FFFZZZ
AGRO ...

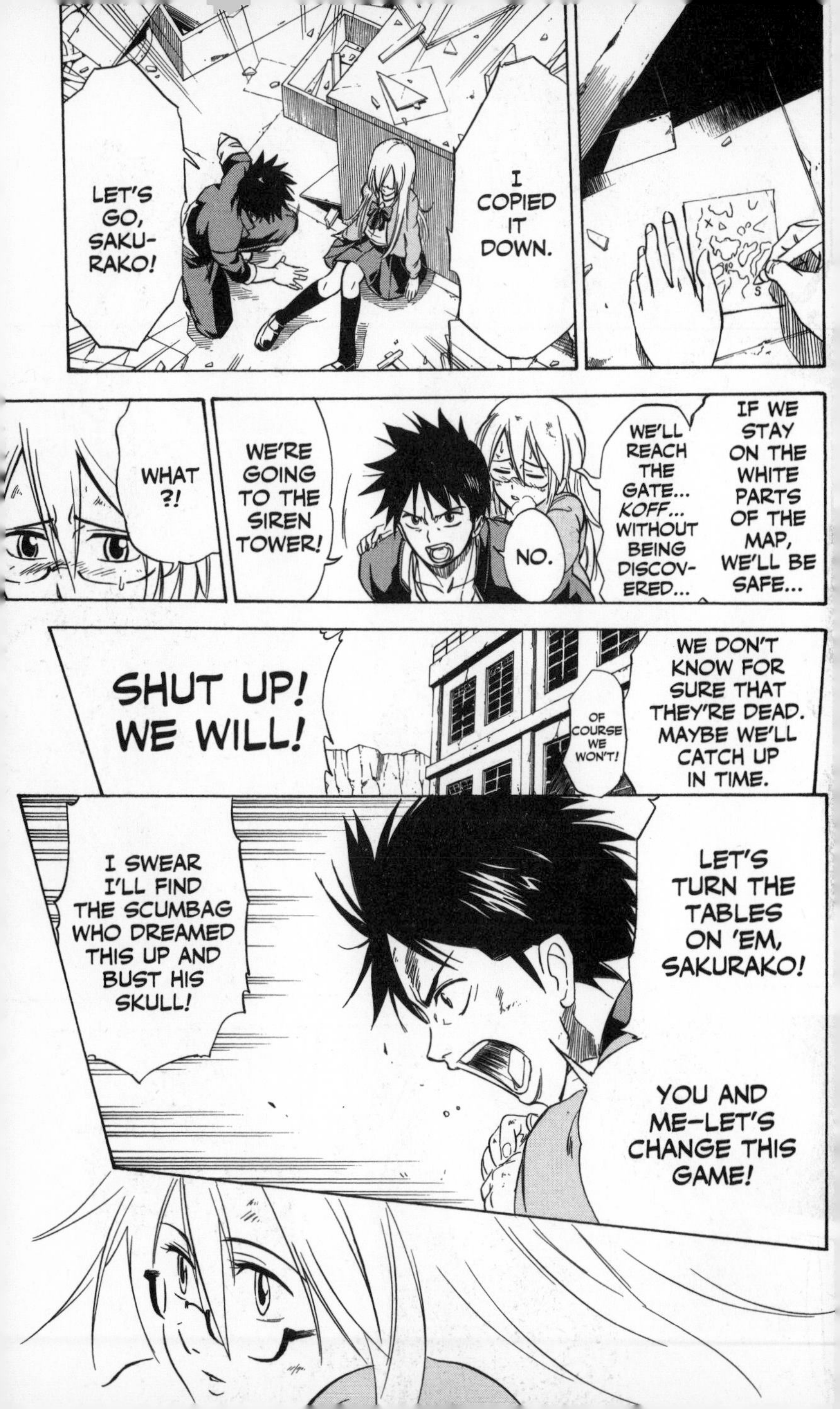
I COPIED IT DOWN.
LET'S GO, SAKURAKO!
IF WE STAY ON THE WHITE PARTS OF THE MAP, WE'LL BE SAFE...
WE'LL REACH THE GATE... *KOFF*... WITHOUT BEING DISCOVERED...
NO.
WE'RE GOING TO THE SIREN TOWER!
WHAT?!
WE DON'T KNOW FOR SURE THAT THEY'RE DEAD. MAYBE WE'LL CATCH UP IN TIME.
OF COURSE WE WON'T!
SHUT UP! WE WILL!
LET'S TURN THE TABLES ON 'EM, SAKURAKO!
I SWEAR I'LL FIND THE SCUMBAG WHO DREAMED THIS UP AND BUST HIS SKULL!
YOU AND ME—LET'S CHANGE THIS GAME!

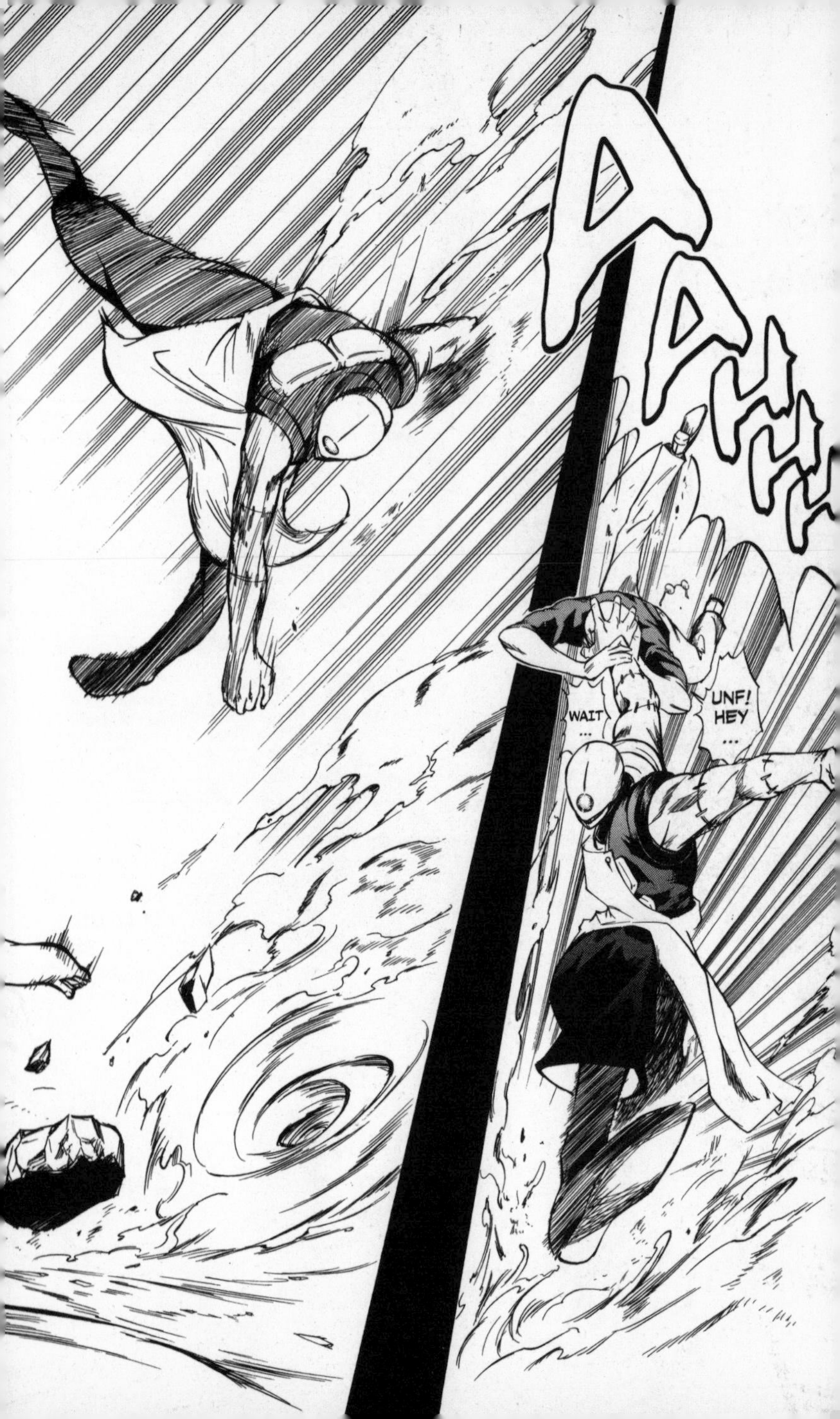
AAAHHH
UNF! HEY ...
WAIT ...

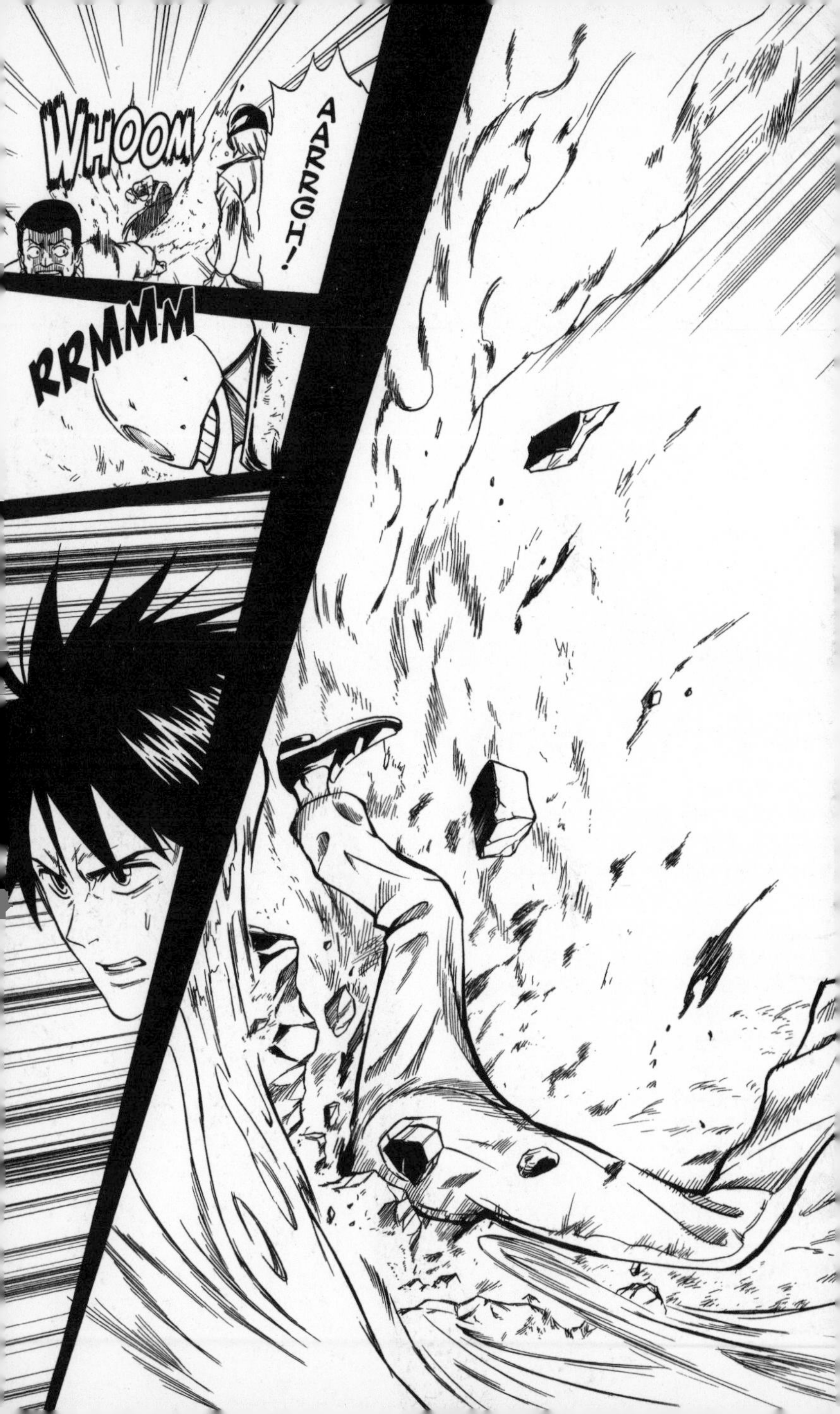
AARRGH!
WHOOM
RRMMM

# AGEHA YOSHINA

BEFORE THE SERIES WAS
SERIALIZED, BACK DURING
THE NAMING STAGE, AGEHA
HAD MEAN-LOOKING EYES.
I QUICKLY DECIDED TO
CHANGE THE SIZE OF HIS
EYES, SO I FOUND DRAWING
HIS EXPRESSIONS AND
REACTIONS DIFFICULT AT FIRST.

NOW, WHEN I DRAW AGEHA
WITH BIGGER EYES, I'M
ALWAYS GLAD I MADE THE
CHANGE. THE EYES OF THE
PROTAGONIST ARE VERY
IMPORTANT! I'M GRATEFUL
TO MY EDITOR FOR THAT
ADVICE.

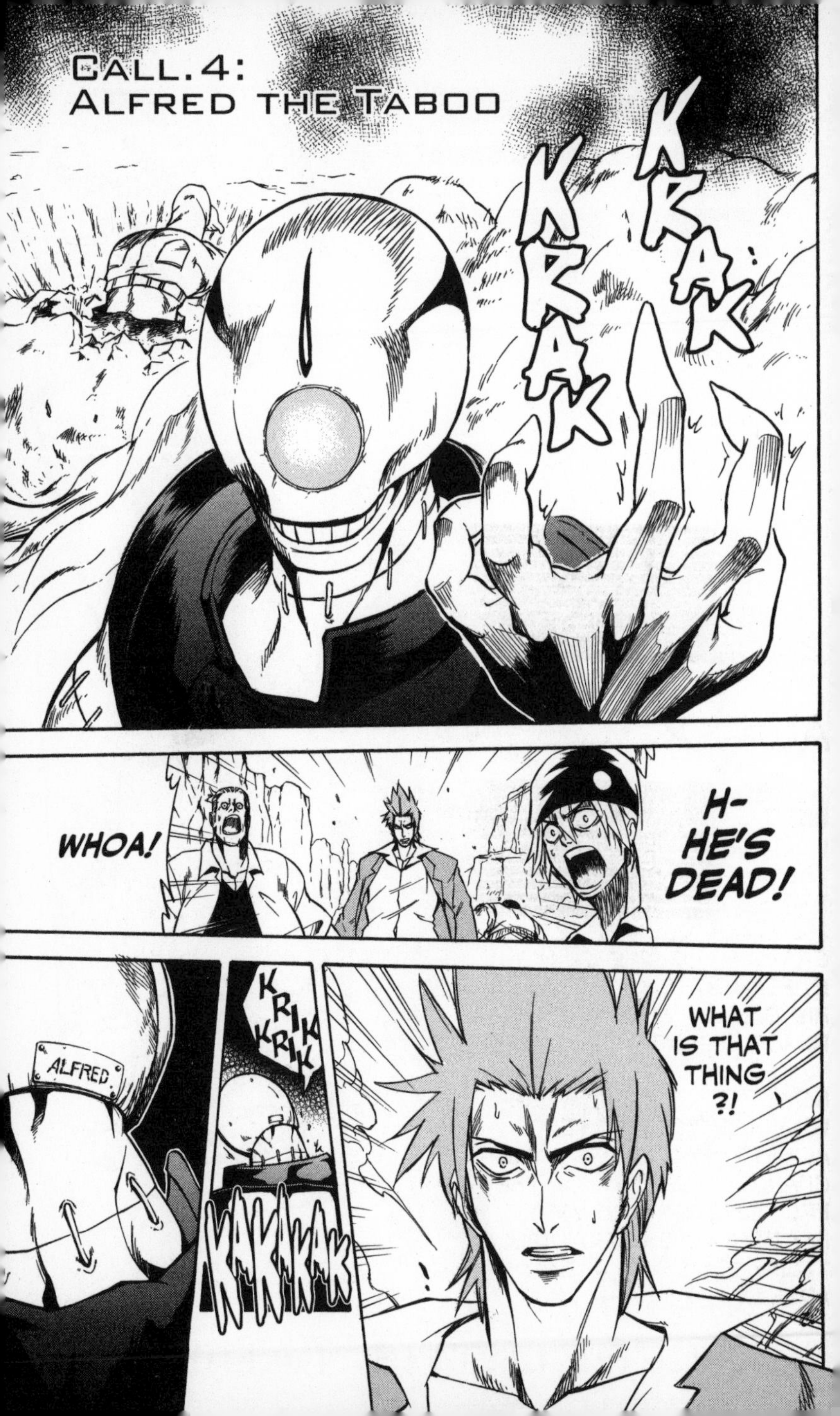
Call.4:
Alfred the Taboo
KRAK
KRAK
H-
HE'S
DEAD!
WHOA!
WHAT
IS THAT
THING
?!
KRIK
KRIK
KAKAKAK
ALFRED

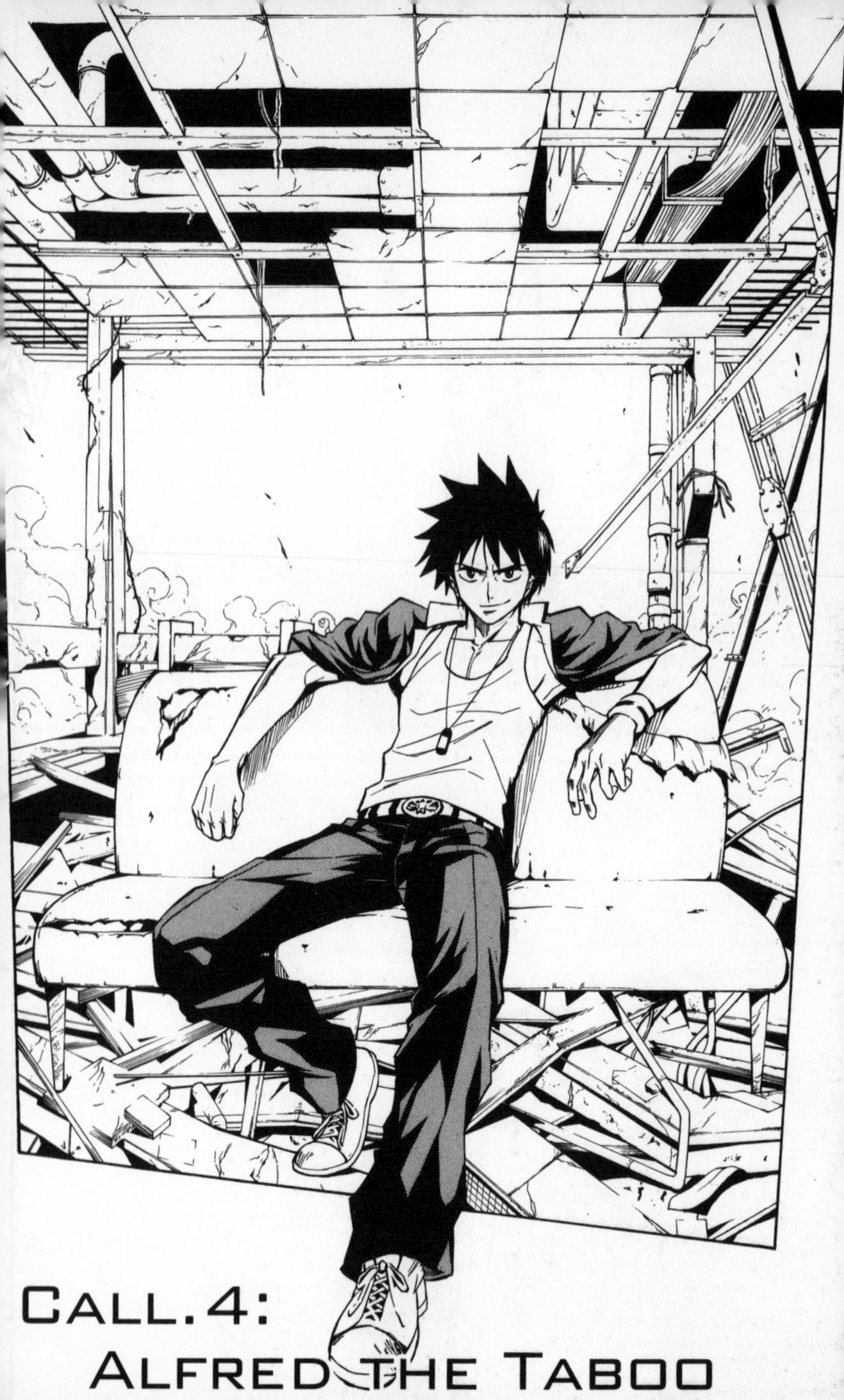

# Call. 4: Alfred the Taboo

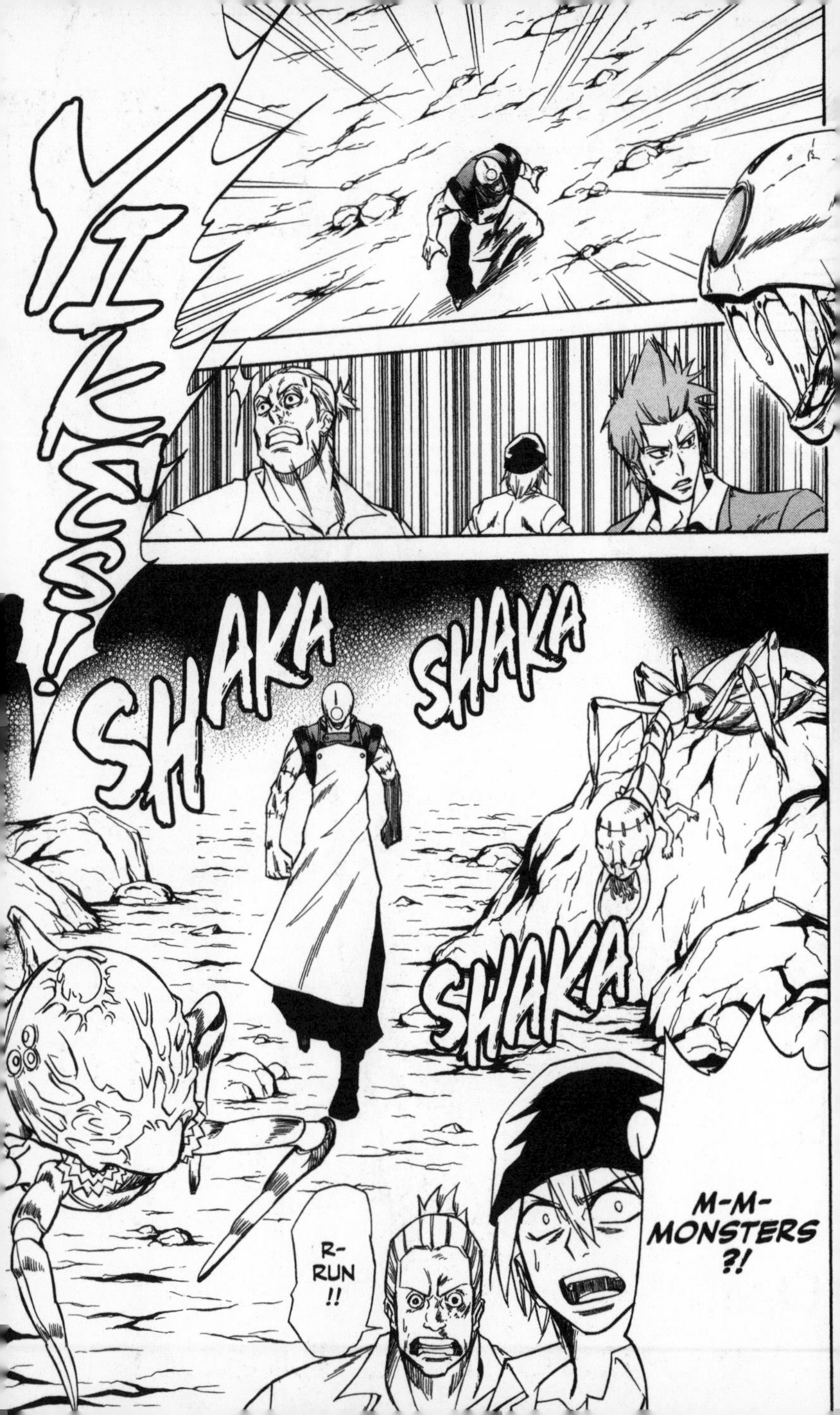
YIIKES!
SHAKA
SHAKA
SHAKA
M-M-MONSTERS?!
R-RUN!!

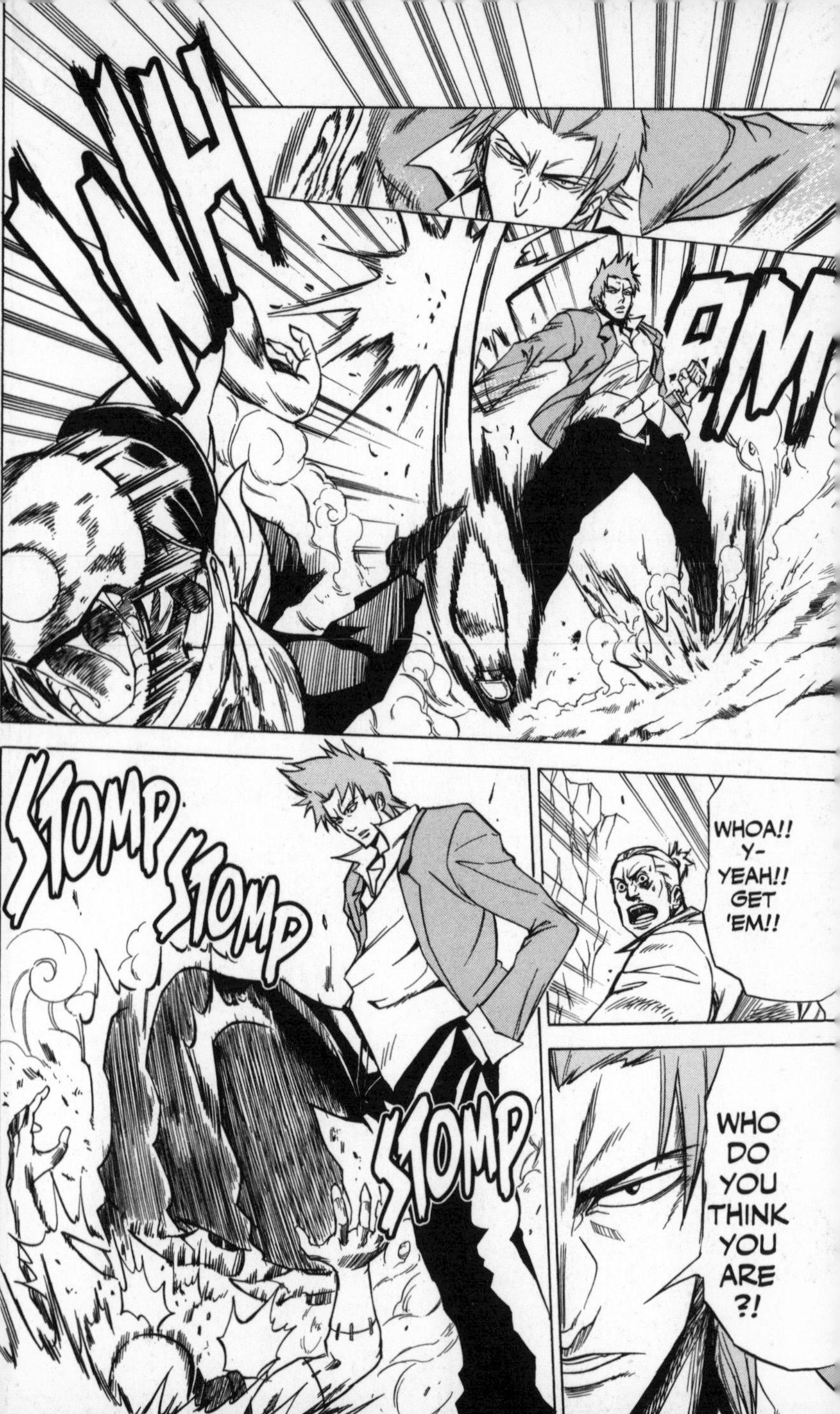
WHOA!! Y-YEAH!! GET 'EM!!
WHO DO YOU THINK YOU ARE?!
STOMP
STOMP
STOMP

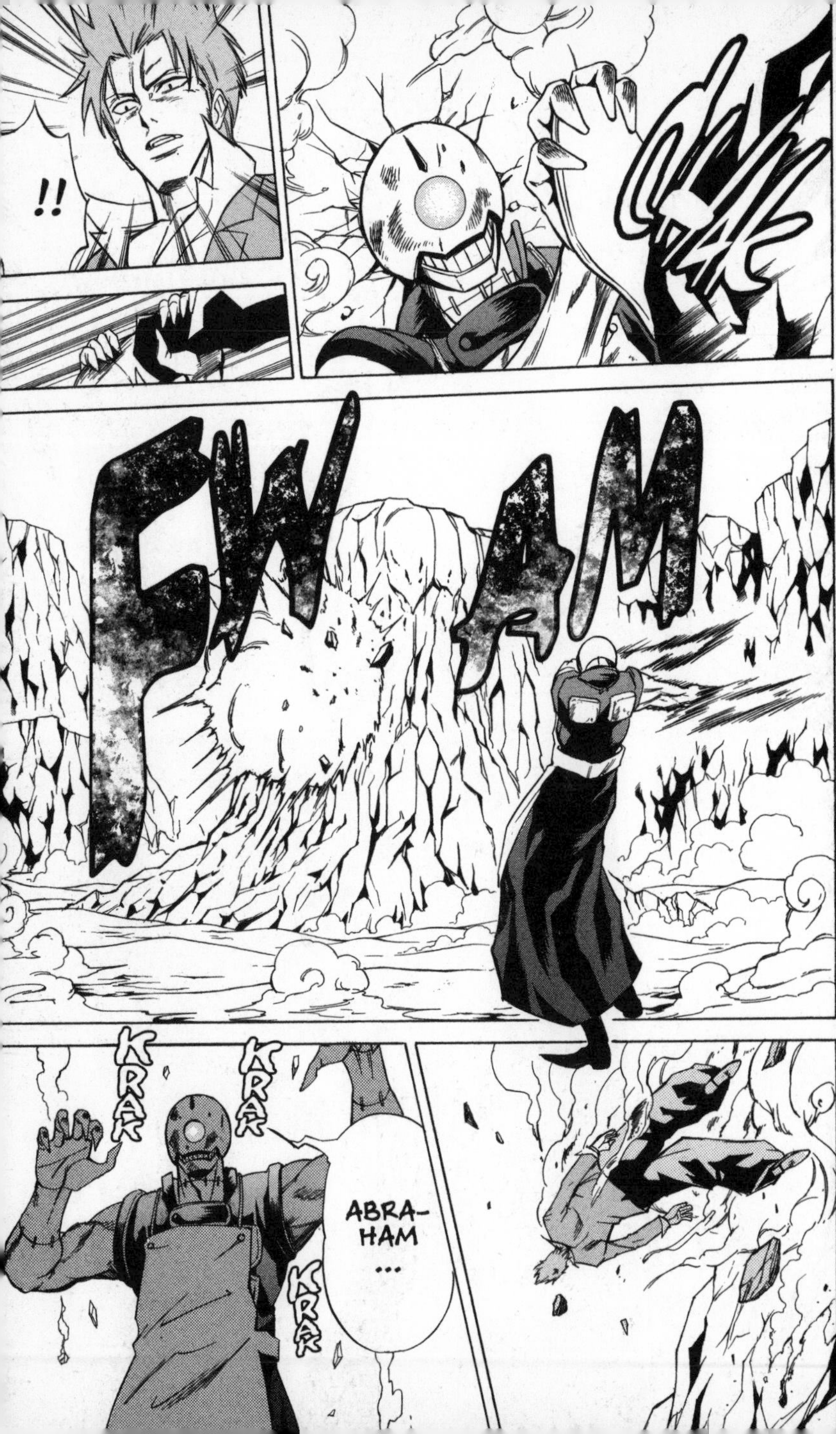
!!
FWAM
KRAK
KRAK
ABRA-HAM ...
KRAK

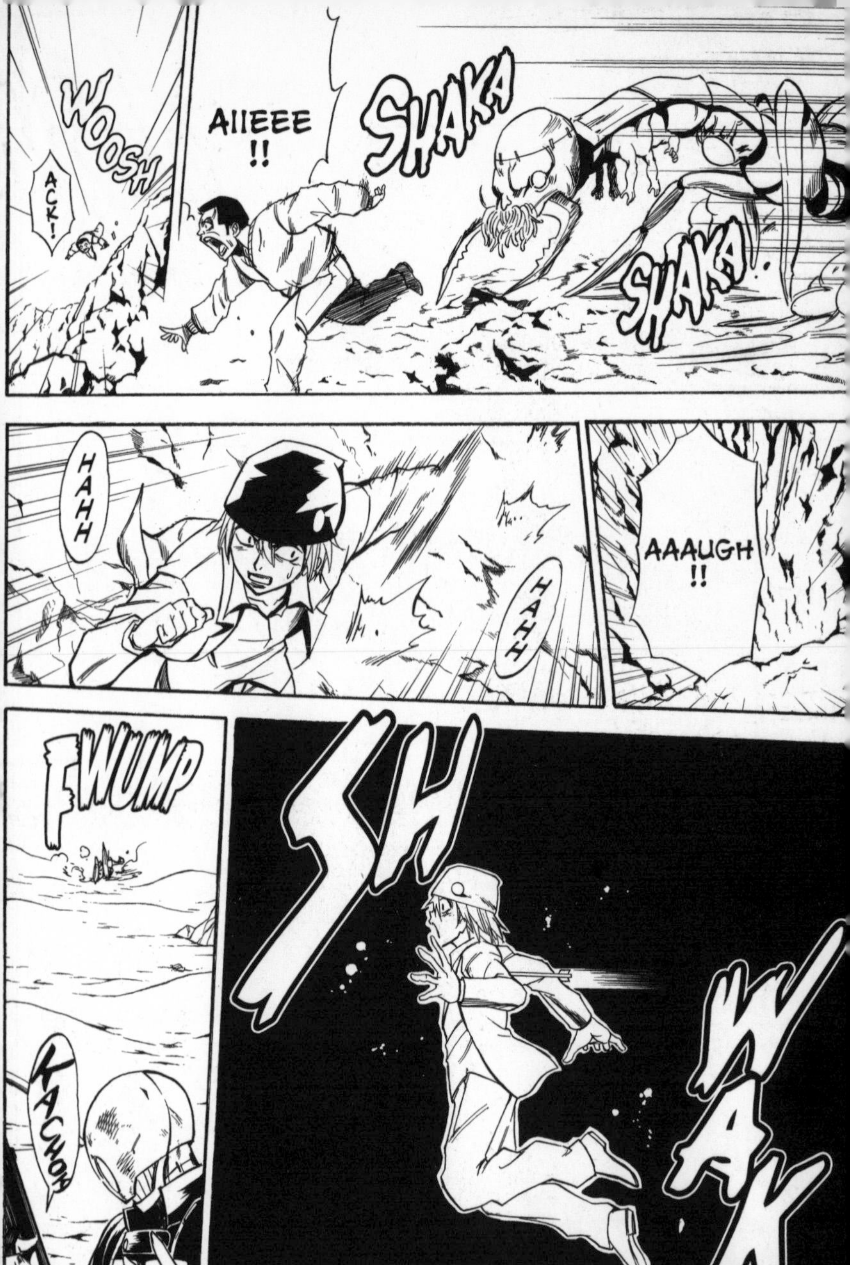
SHAKA
SHAKA
AIIEEE !!
WOOSH
ACK!
AAAUGH !!
HAHH
HAHH
SH
WAK
FWUMP
KACHOK

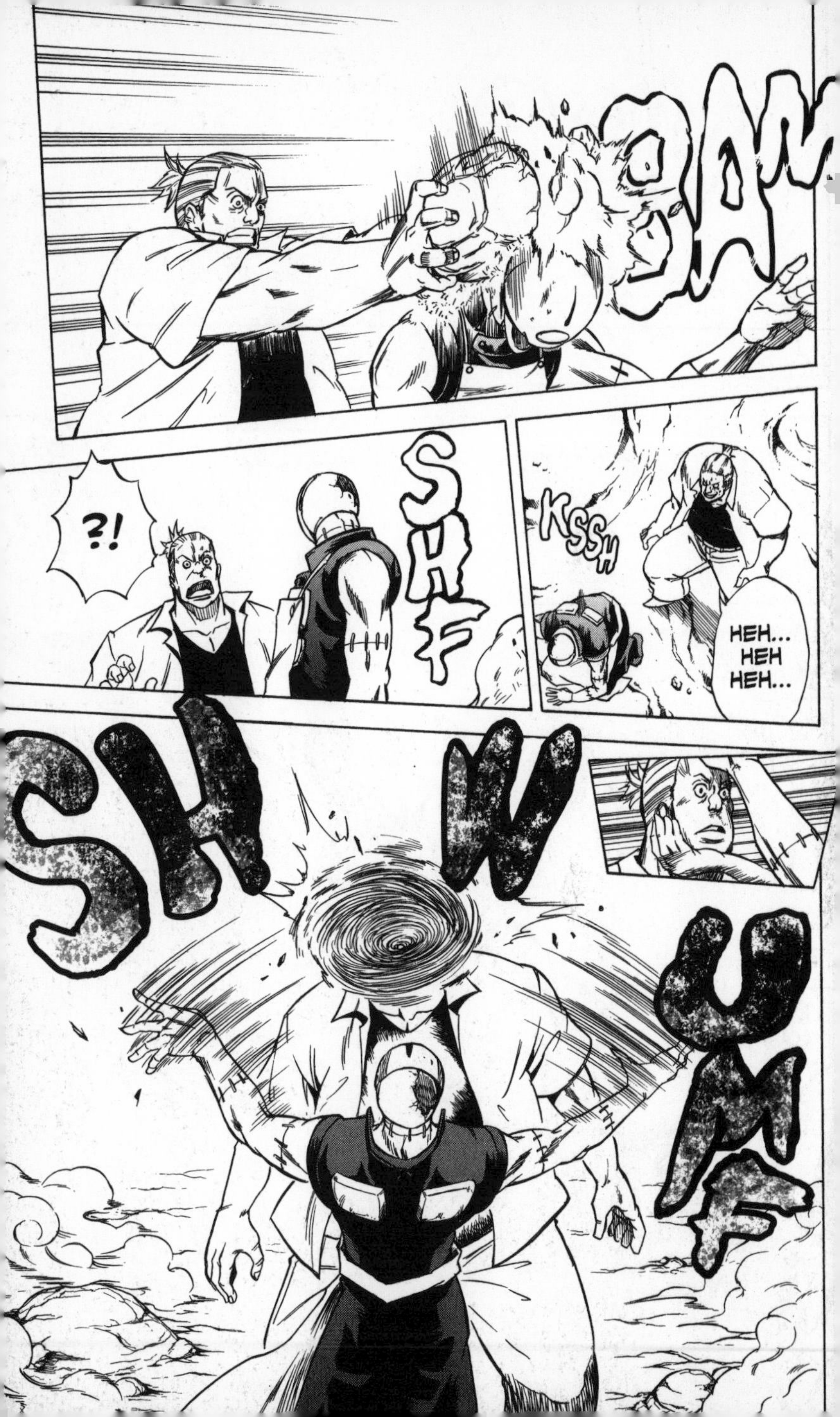
BAM
KSSH
HEH... HEH HEH...
SHFF
?!
SHWUMF

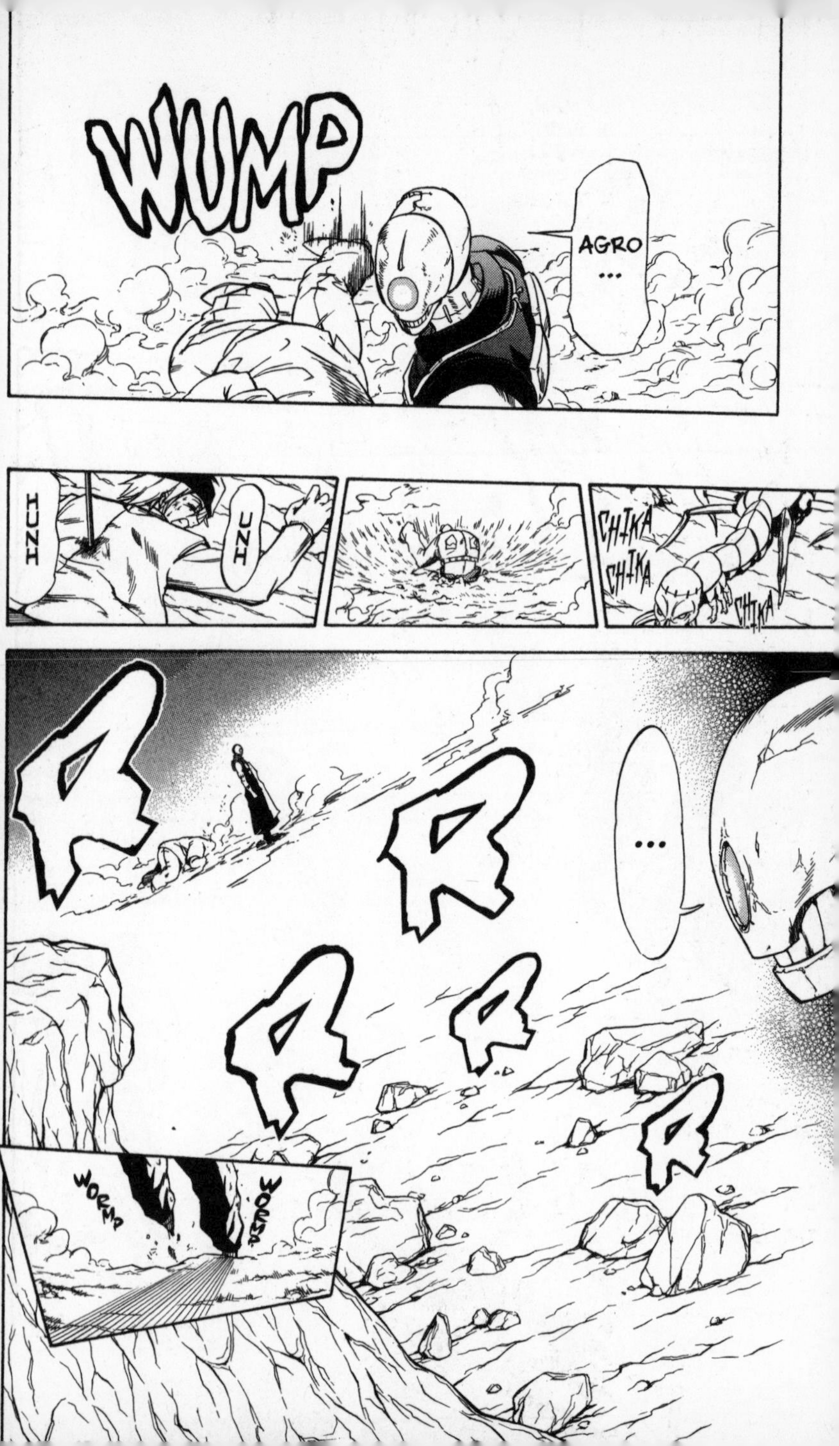
WUMP
AGRO ...
CHIKA CHIKA CHIKA
UNH
HUNH
...
R R R R R
WORM
WORM

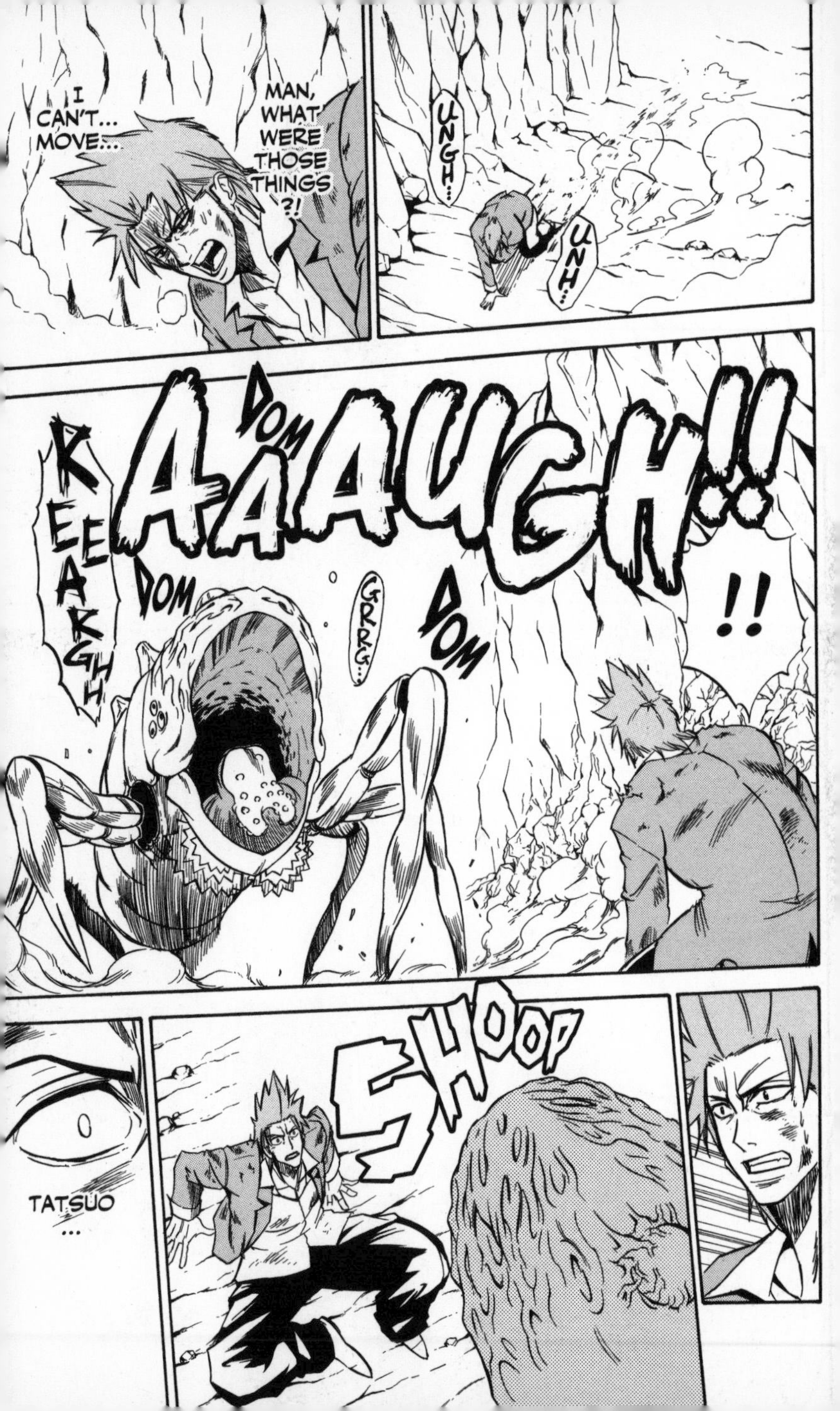
UNGH...
UNH...
MAN, WHAT WERE THOSE THINGS?!
I CAN'T... MOVE...
AAAUGH!!
DOM
DOM
DOM
REEEARGH
GRRRG...
!!
SHOOP
TATSUO...

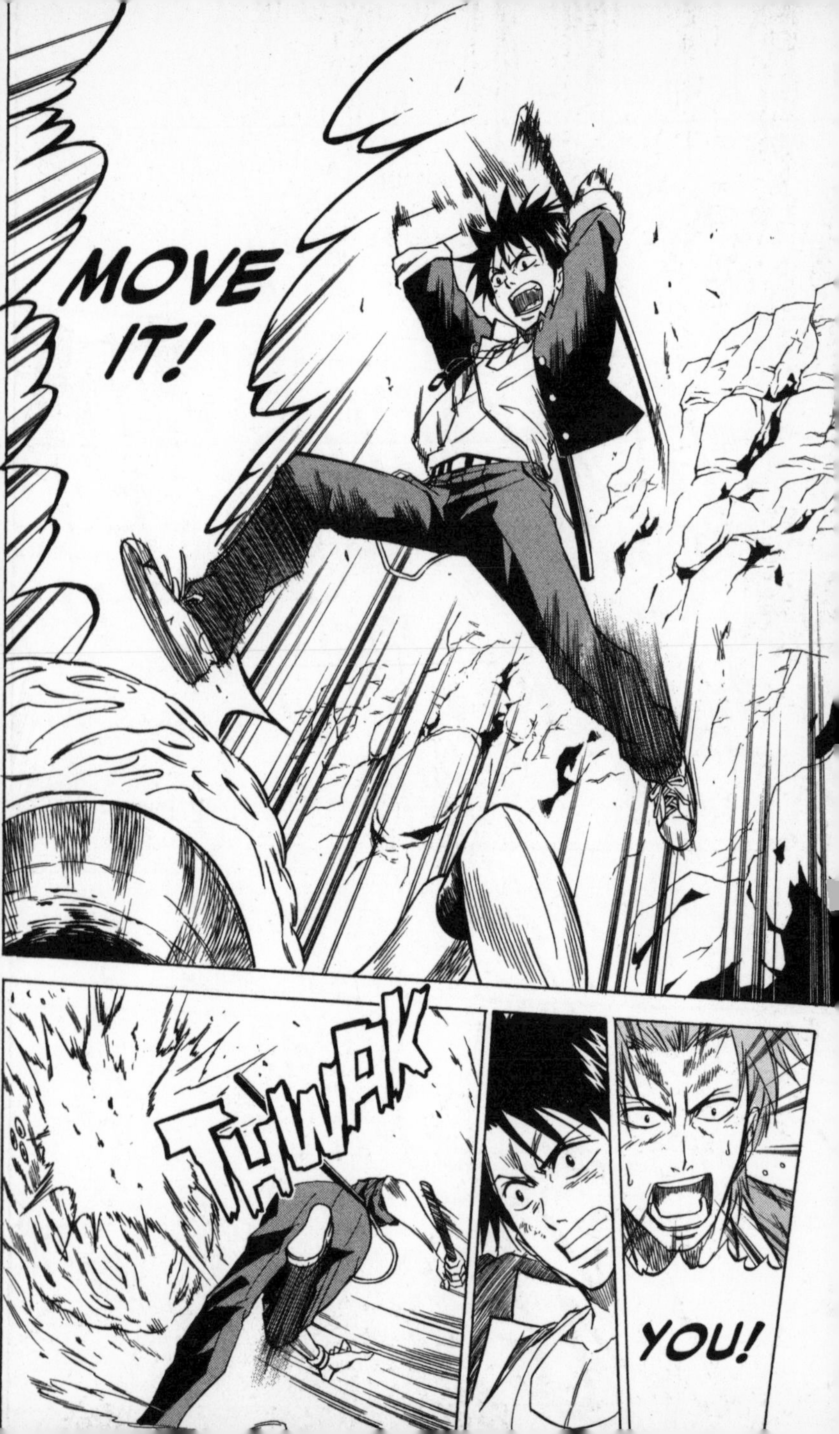
MOVE IT!
YOU!
THWAK

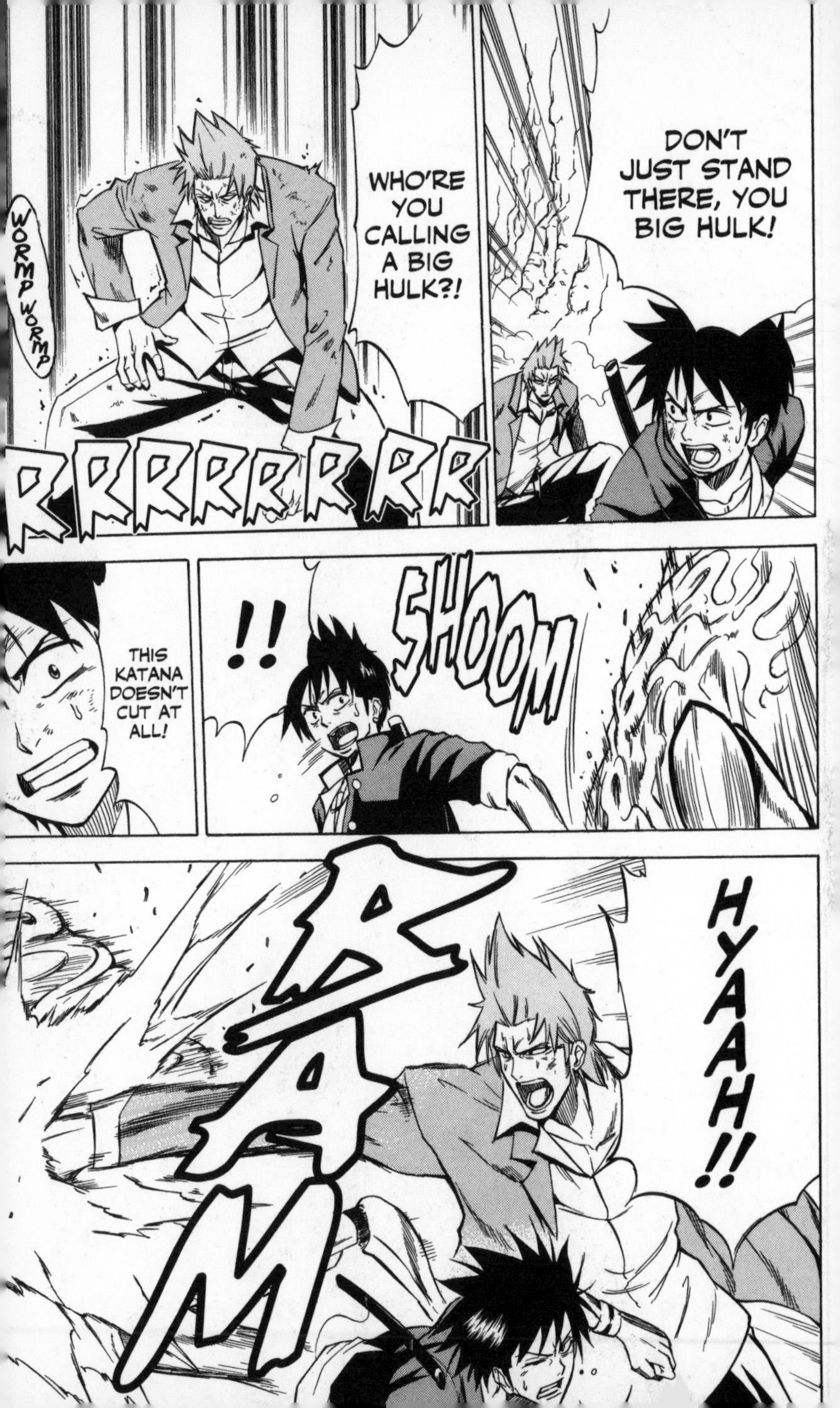
DON'T JUST STAND THERE, YOU BIG HULK!
WHO'RE YOU CALLING A BIG HULK?!
WORMP WORMP
RRRRRRRR
SHOOM
!!
THIS KATANA DOESN'T CUT AT ALL!
HYAAH!!
BAM

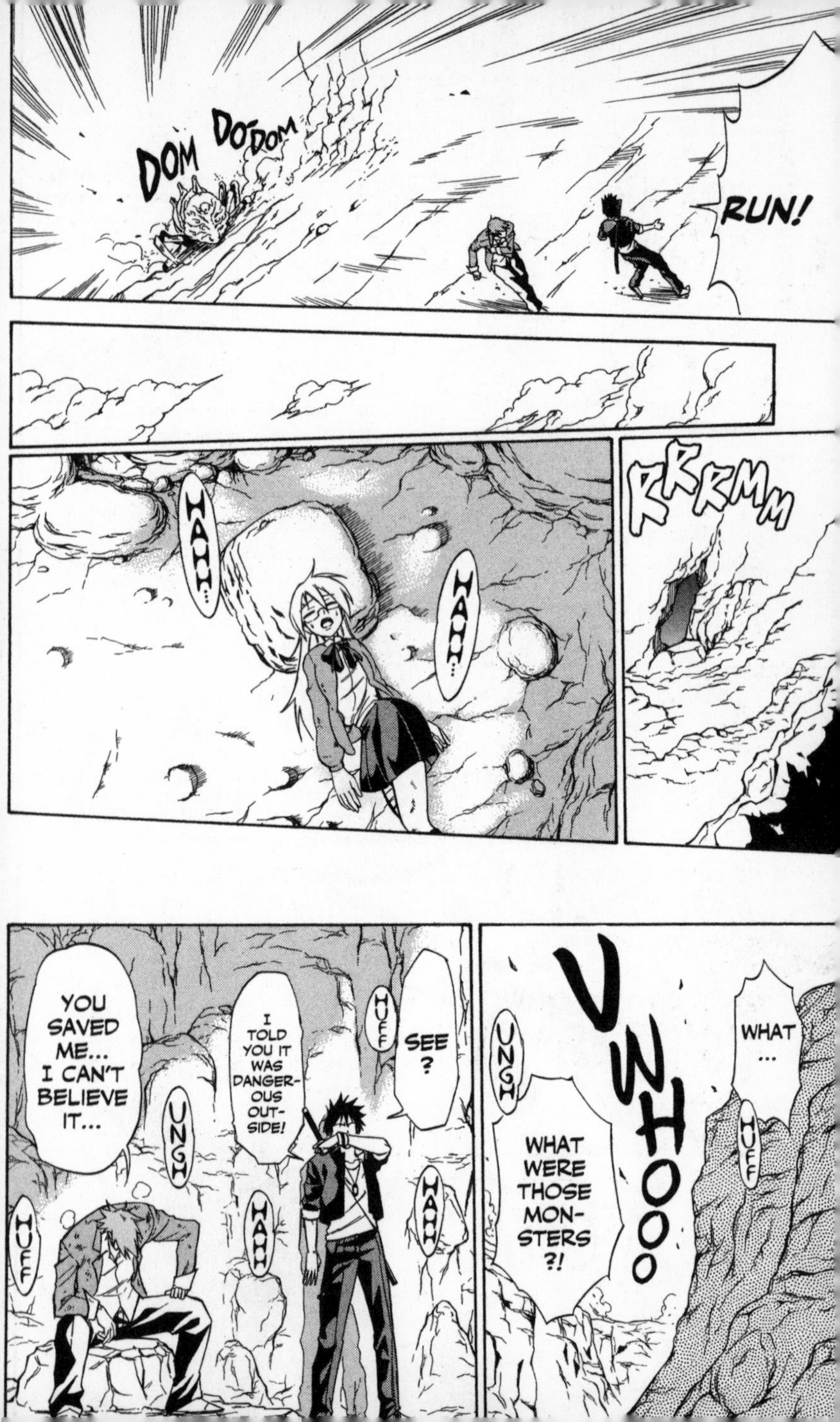
RUN!
DOM DO'DOM
RRRMMM
HAHH...
HAHH...
WHAT...
HUFF
VWHOOOO
UNGH
WHAT WERE THOSE MONSTERS?!
SEE?
HUFF
I TOLD YOU IT WAS DANGER-OUS OUT-SIDE!
HAHH
YOU SAVED ME... I CAN'T BELIEVE IT...
UNGH
HAHH
HUFF

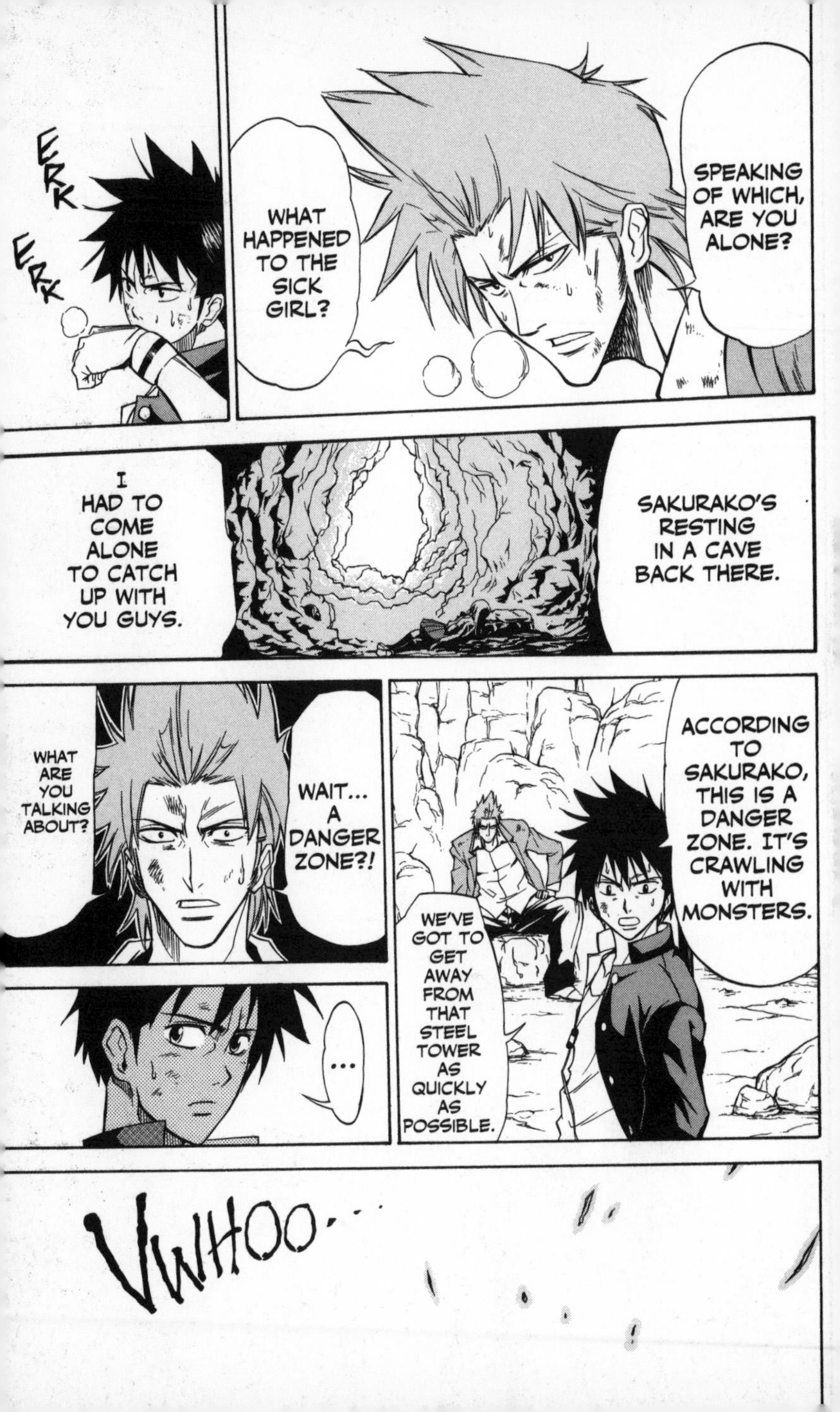
SPEAKING OF WHICH, ARE YOU ALONE?
WHAT HAPPENED TO THE SICK GIRL?
ERK
ERK
SAKURAKO'S RESTING IN A CAVE BACK THERE.
I HAD TO COME ALONE TO CATCH UP WITH YOU GUYS.
ACCORDING TO SAKURAKO, THIS IS A DANGER ZONE. IT'S CRAWLING WITH MONSTERS.
WE'VE GOT TO GET AWAY FROM THAT STEEL TOWER AS QUICKLY AS POSSIBLE.
WAIT... A DANGER ZONE?!
WHAT ARE YOU TALKING ABOUT?
...
VWHOO...

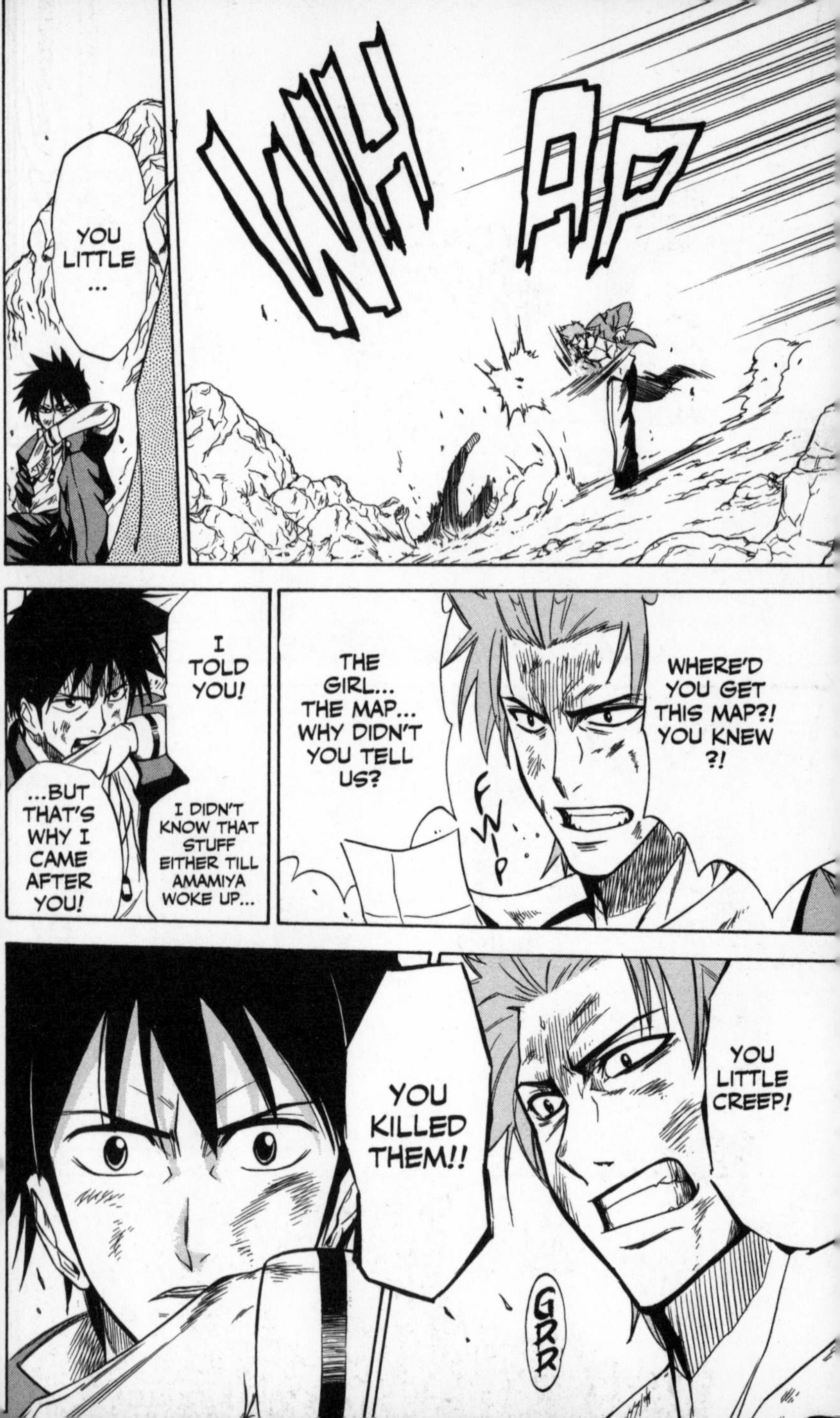
WHAP
YOU LITTLE ...
WHERE'D YOU GET THIS MAP?! YOU KNEW ?!
FWIP
THE GIRL... THE MAP... WHY DIDN'T YOU TELL US?
I TOLD YOU!
I DIDN'T KNOW THAT STUFF EITHER TILL AMAMIYA WOKE UP...
...BUT THAT'S WHY I CAME AFTER YOU!
YOU LITTLE CREEP!
GRR
YOU KILLED THEM!!

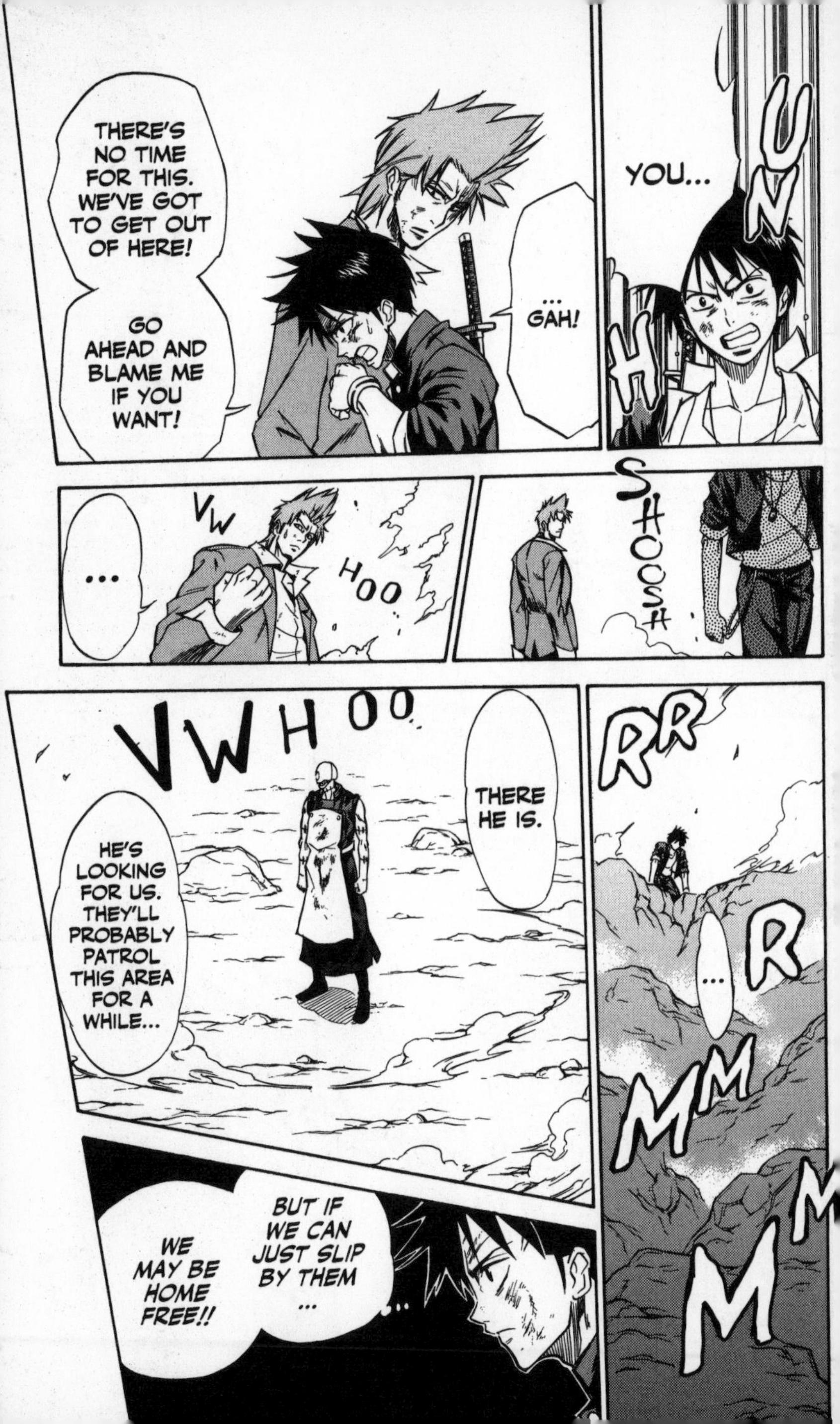
HNNU
YOU...
...GAH!
THERE'S NO TIME FOR THIS. WE'VE GOT TO GET OUT OF HERE!
GO AHEAD AND BLAME ME IF YOU WANT!
SHOOSH
VWHOO
...
RRRMMMMM
...
THERE HE IS.
VWHOO
HE'S LOOKING FOR US. THEY'LL PROBABLY PATROL THIS AREA FOR A WHILE...
BUT IF WE CAN JUST SLIP BY THEM...
WE MAY BE HOME FREE!!

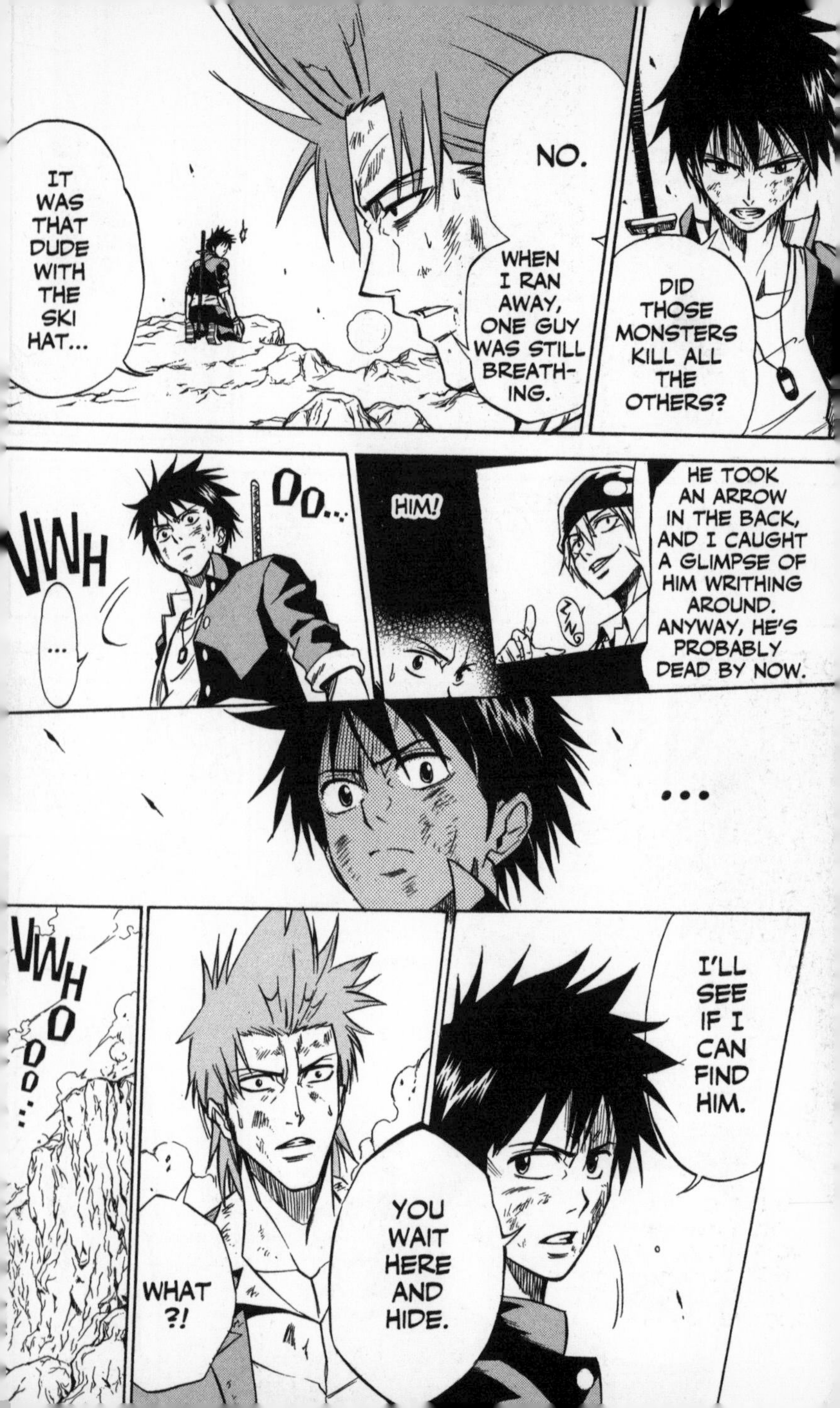
DID THOSE MONSTERS KILL ALL THE OTHERS?
NO.
WHEN I RAN AWAY, ONE GUY WAS STILL BREATHING.
IT WAS THAT DUDE WITH THE SKI HAT...
HE TOOK AN ARROW IN THE BACK, AND I CAUGHT A GLIMPSE OF HIM WRITHING AROUND. ANYWAY, HE'S PROBABLY DEAD BY NOW.
ZING
HIM!
OO...
VWH
...
...
I'LL SEE IF I CAN FIND HIM.
YOU WAIT HERE AND HIDE.
WHAT?!
VWHOOOO...

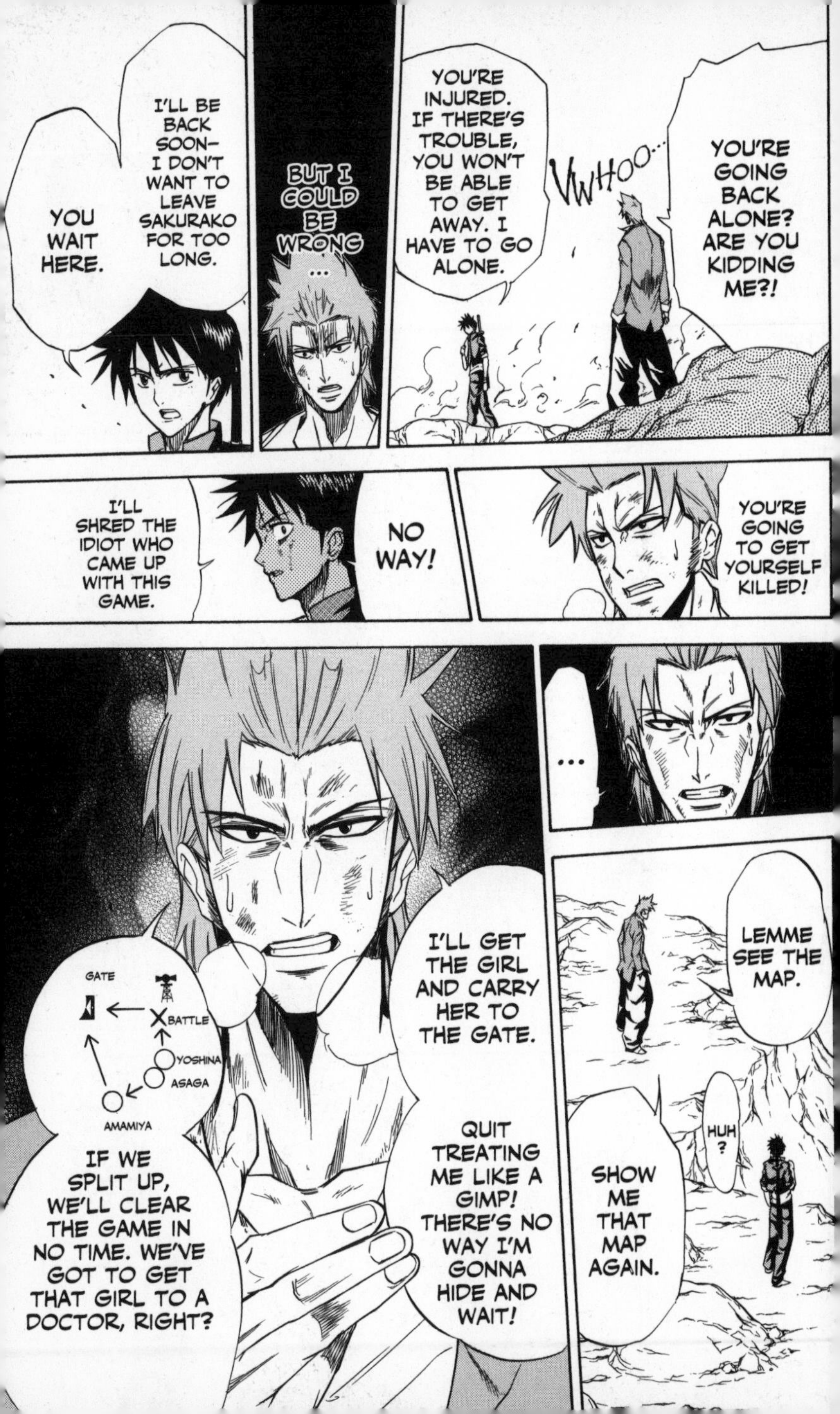
YOU'RE GOING BACK ALONE? ARE YOU KIDDING ME?!
VWHOO...
YOU'RE INJURED. IF THERE'S TROUBLE, YOU WON'T BE ABLE TO GET AWAY. I HAVE TO GO ALONE.
BUT I COULD BE WRONG ...
I'LL BE BACK SOON— I DON'T WANT TO LEAVE SAKURAKO FOR TOO LONG.
YOU WAIT HERE.
YOU'RE GOING TO GET YOURSELF KILLED!
NO WAY!
I'LL SHRED THE IDIOT WHO CAME UP WITH THIS GAME.
...
LEMME SEE THE MAP.
HUH?
SHOW ME THAT MAP AGAIN.
I'LL GET THE GIRL AND CARRY HER TO THE GATE.
QUIT TREATING ME LIKE A GIMP! THERE'S NO WAY I'M GONNA HIDE AND WAIT!
GATE
BATTLE
YOSHINA
ASAGA
AMAMIYA
IF WE SPLIT UP, WE'LL CLEAR THE GAME IN NO TIME. WE'VE GOT TO GET THAT GIRL TO A DOCTOR, RIGHT?

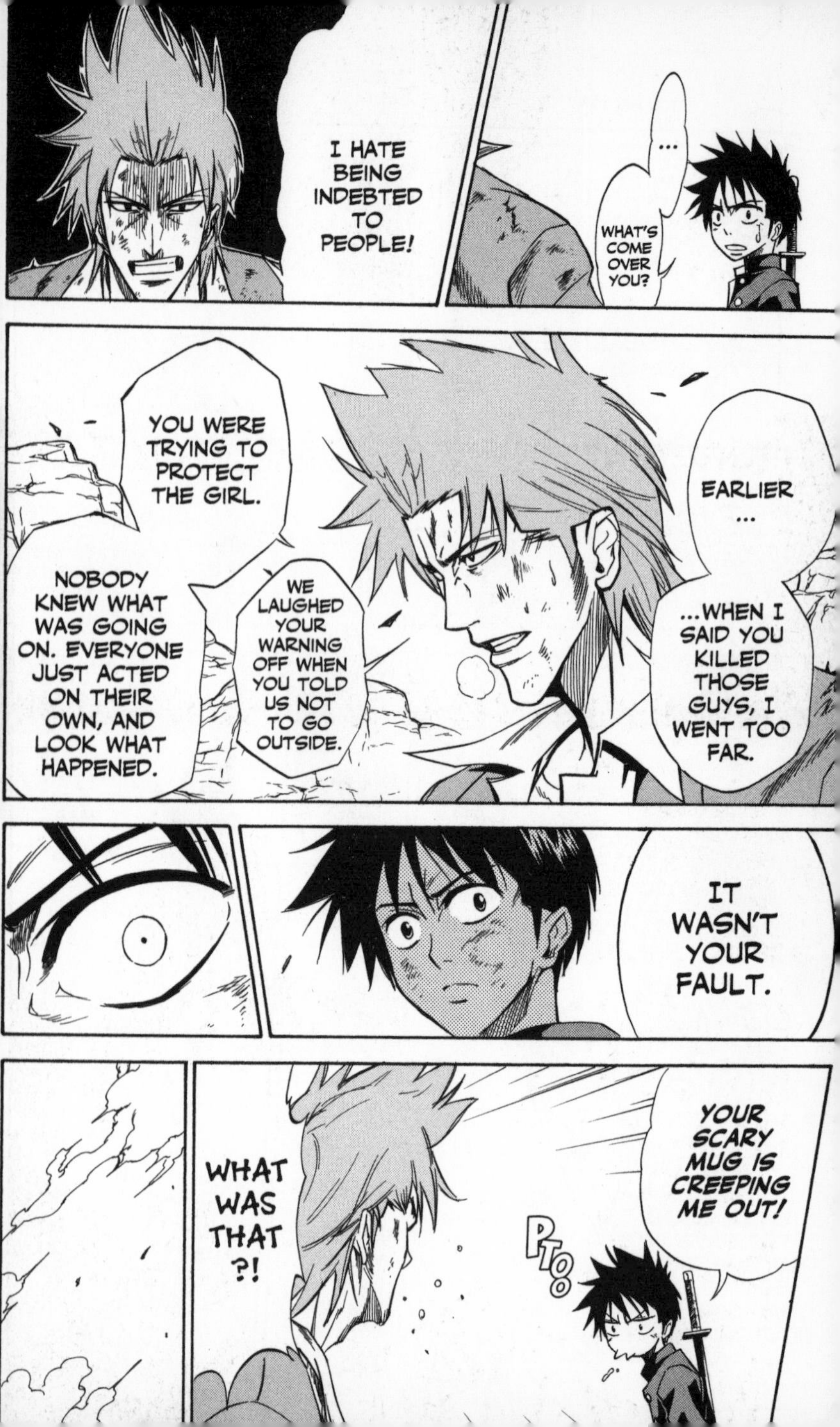
...
WHAT'S COME OVER YOU?
I HATE BEING INDEBTED TO PEOPLE!
EARLIER...
...WHEN I SAID YOU KILLED THOSE GUYS, I WENT TOO FAR.
YOU WERE TRYING TO PROTECT THE GIRL.
WE LAUGHED YOUR WARNING OFF WHEN YOU TOLD US NOT TO GO OUTSIDE.
NOBODY KNEW WHAT WAS GOING ON. EVERYONE JUST ACTED ON THEIR OWN, AND LOOK WHAT HAPPENED.
IT WASN'T YOUR FAULT.
YOUR SCARY MUG IS CREEPING ME OUT!
PTOO
WHAT WAS THAT?!

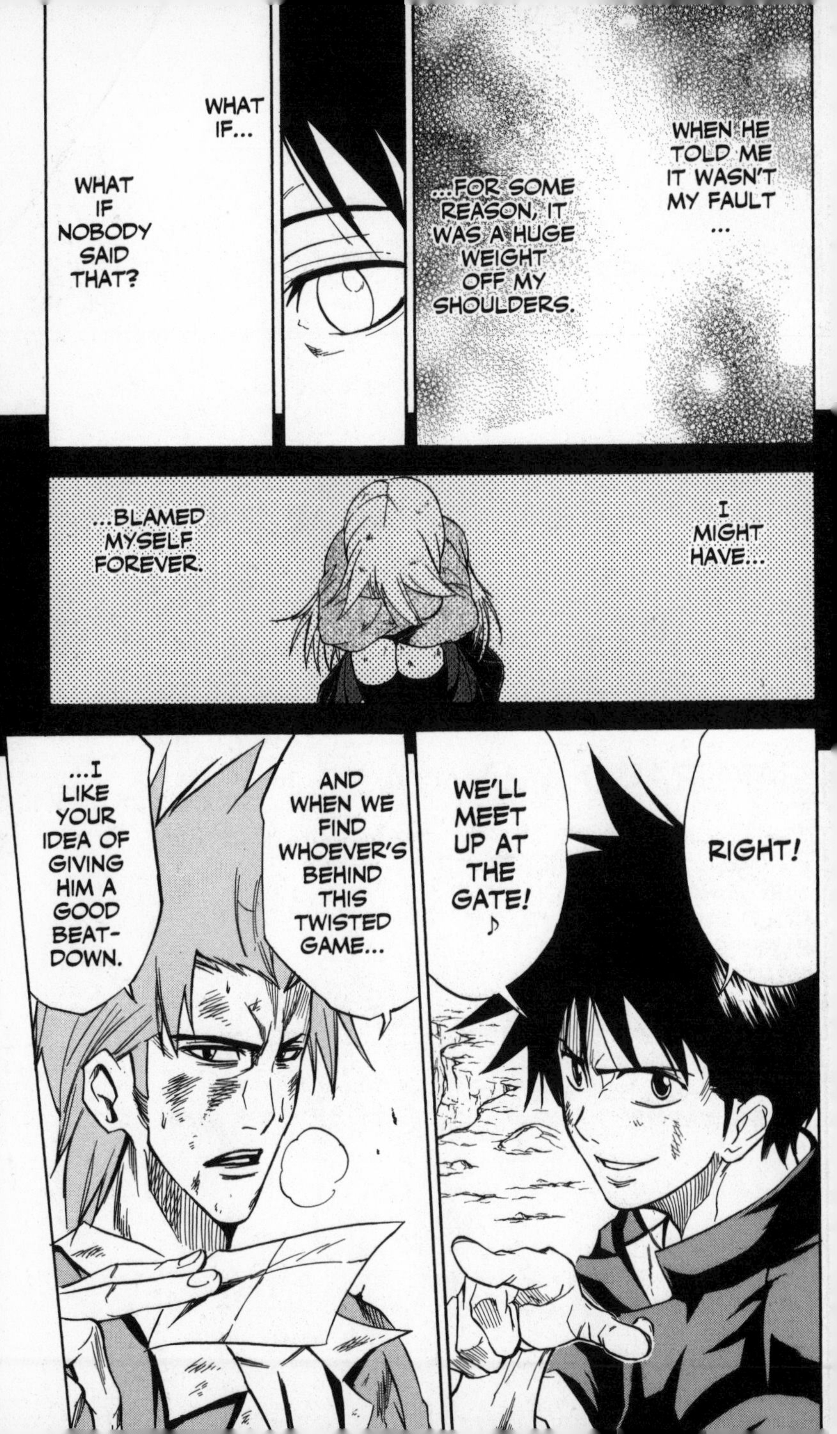
WHEN HE TOLD ME IT WASN'T MY FAULT ...
...FOR SOME REASON, IT WAS A HUGE WEIGHT OFF MY SHOULDERS.
WHAT IF...
WHAT IF NOBODY SAID THAT?
I MIGHT HAVE...
...BLAMED MYSELF FOREVER.
RIGHT!
WE'LL MEET UP AT THE GATE! ♪
AND WHEN WE FIND WHOEVER'S BEHIND THIS TWISTED GAME...
...I LIKE YOUR IDEA OF GIVING HIM A GOOD BEAT-DOWN.

# SAKURAKO AMAMIYA

FORMERLY MISS POPULAR,
SHE IS NOW ANTISOCIAL AND
COLD DUE TO PAST TRAGIC
EVENTS. SHE ENJOYS
READING ANYTHING AND
EVERYTHING. SHE LOVES
STRAWBERRIES, STRAWBERRY-
FLAVORED RICE CAKE AND
SHORT CAKE, BUT SHE
HATES WASABI.

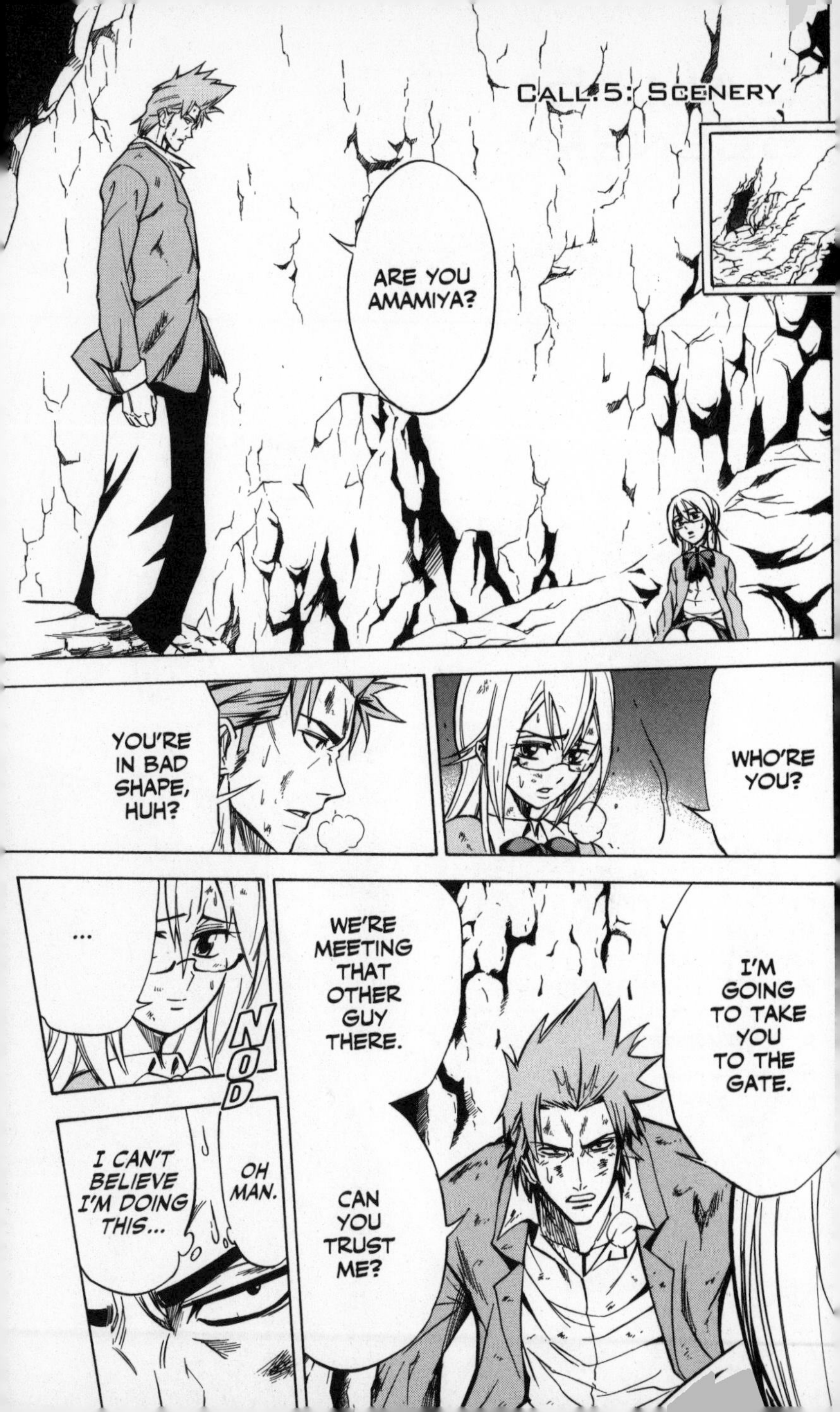
CALL 5: SCENERY
ARE YOU AMAMIYA?
WHO'RE YOU?
YOU'RE IN BAD SHAPE, HUH?
I'M GOING TO TAKE YOU TO THE GATE.
WE'RE MEETING THAT OTHER GUY THERE.
CAN YOU TRUST ME?
...
NOD
OH MAN.
I CAN'T BELIEVE I'M DOING THIS...

# Call. 5: Scenery

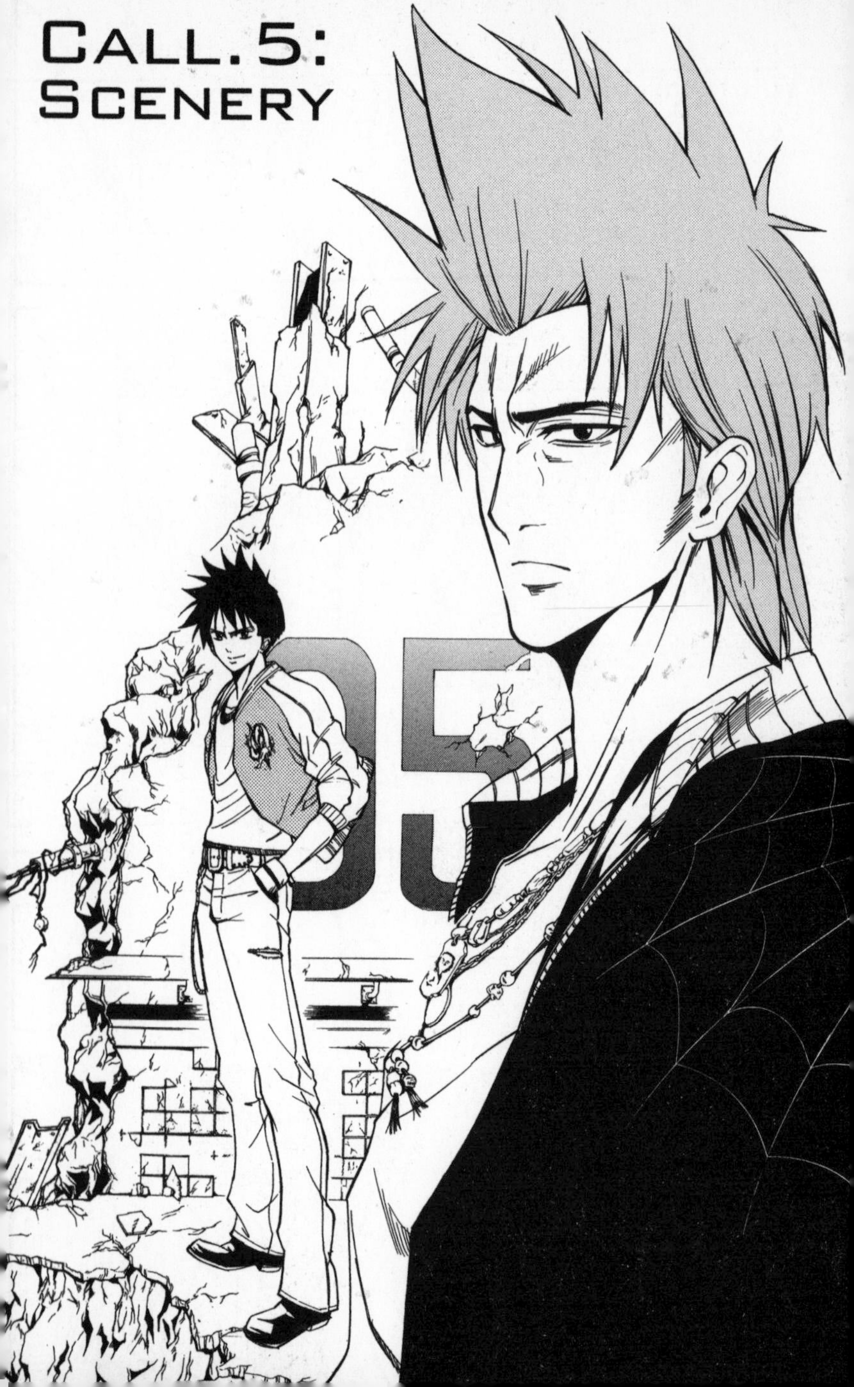

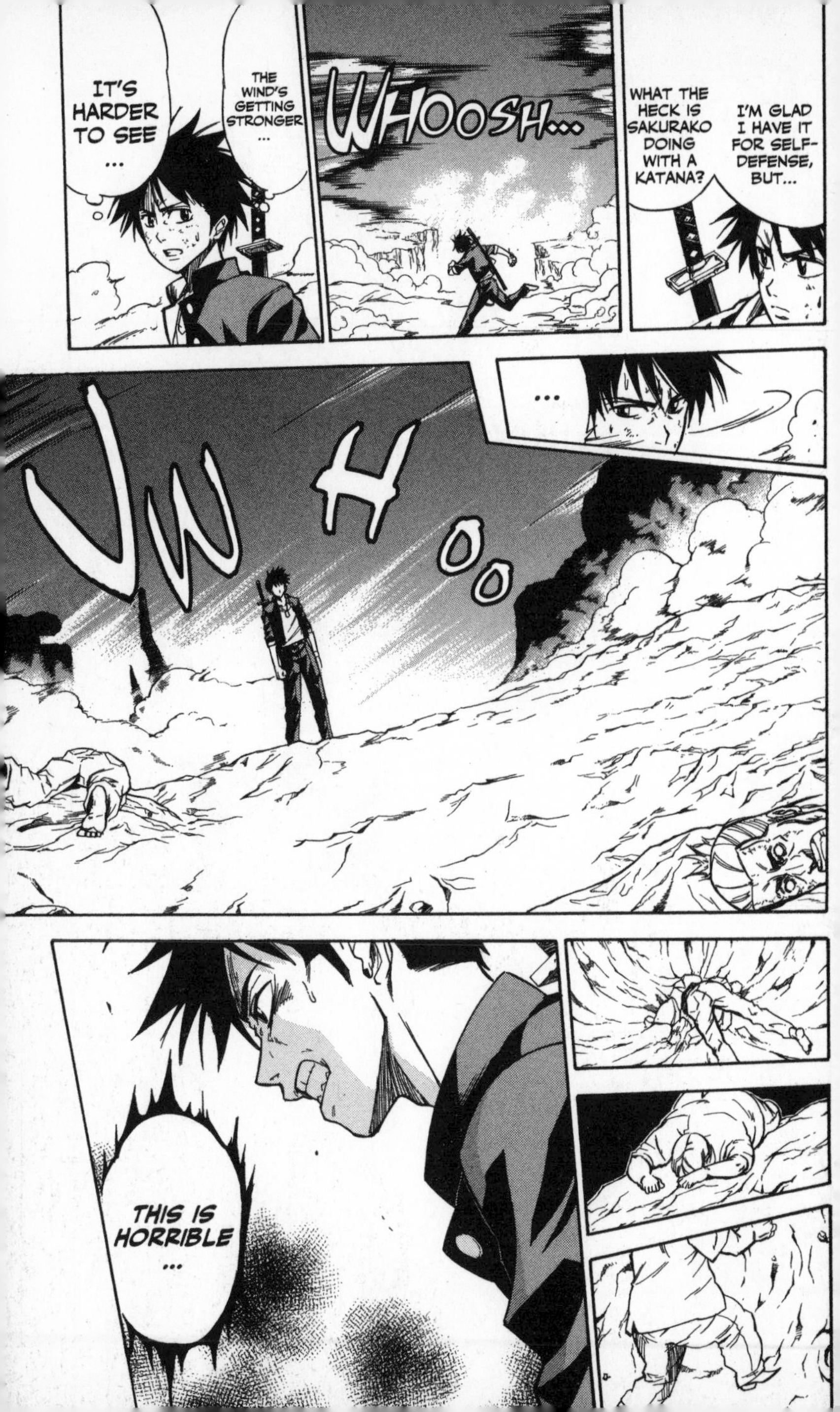
I'M GLAD I HAVE IT FOR SELF-DEFENSE, BUT...
WHAT THE HECK IS SAKURAKO DOING WITH A KATANA?
WHOOSH...
THE WIND'S GETTING STRONGER...
IT'S HARDER TO SEE...
...
THIS IS HORRIBLE...

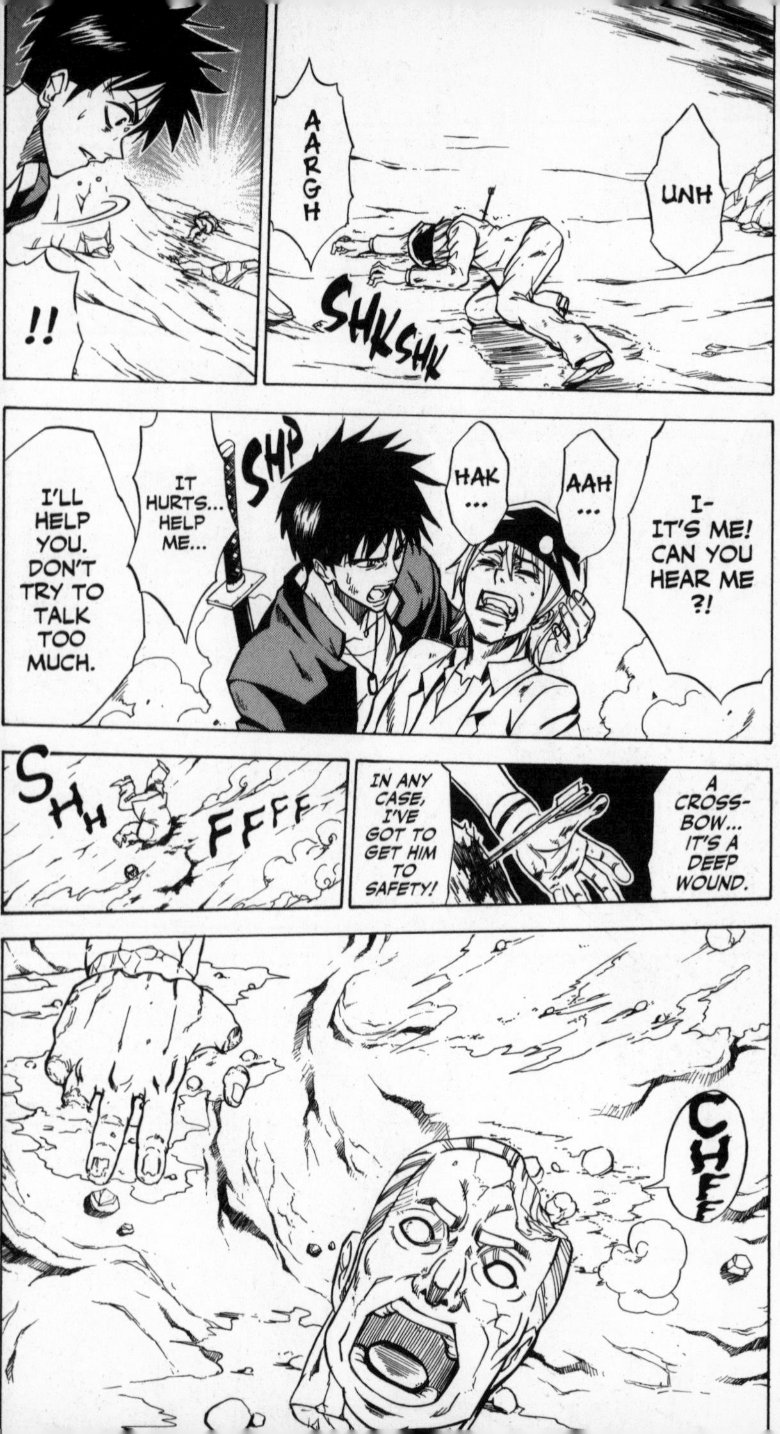
UNH
AARGH
SHKSHK
!!
I- IT'S ME! CAN YOU HEAR ME?!
AAH...
HAK...
SHP
IT HURTS... HELP ME...
I'LL HELP YOU. DON'T TRY TO TALK TOO MUCH.
A CROSSBOW... IT'S A DEEP WOUND.
IN ANY CASE, I'VE GOT TO GET HIM TO SAFETY!
SHH
FFFF
CHFF

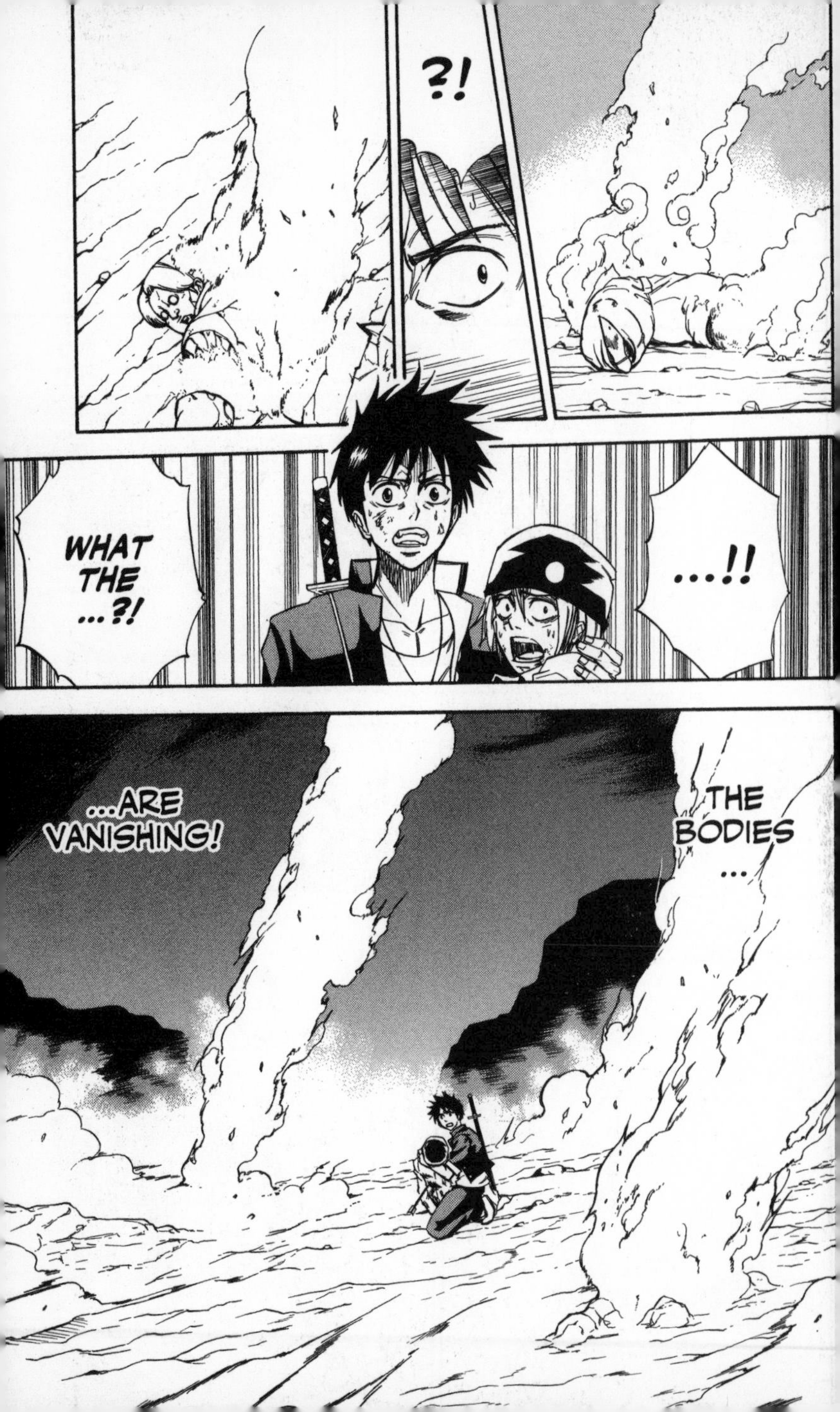
?!
...!!
WHAT THE ...?!
THE BODIES ...
...ARE VANISHING!

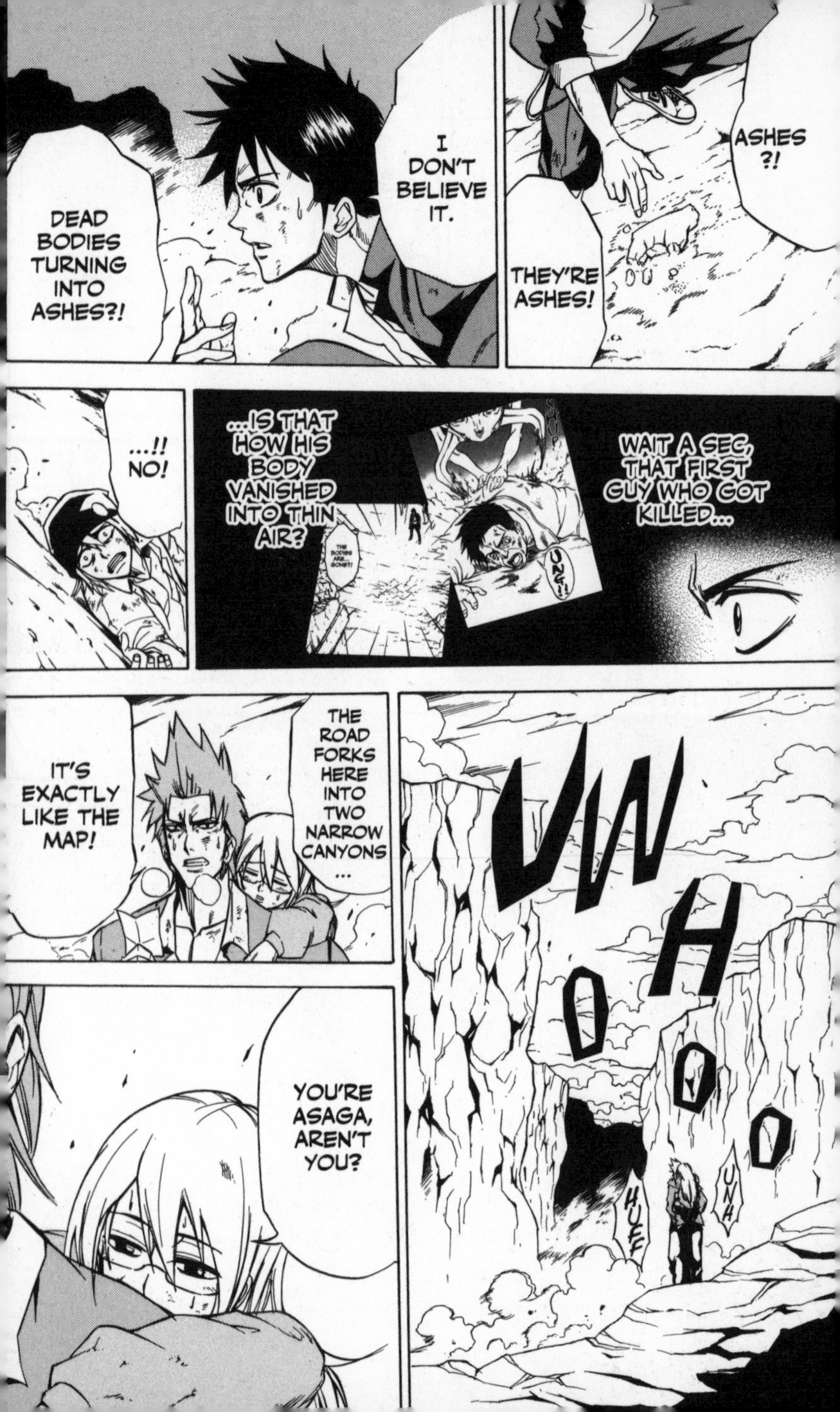
ASHES ?!
THEY'RE ASHES!
I DON'T BELIEVE IT.
DEAD BODIES TURNING INTO ASHES?!
WAIT A SEC, THAT FIRST GUY WHO GOT KILLED...
UNG!!
...IS THAT HOW HIS BODY VANISHED INTO THIN AIR?
...!! NO!
VWHOOOO
UNH
HUFF
THE ROAD FORKS HERE INTO TWO NARROW CANYONS ...
IT'S EXACTLY LIKE THE MAP!
YOU'RE ASAGA, AREN'T YOU?

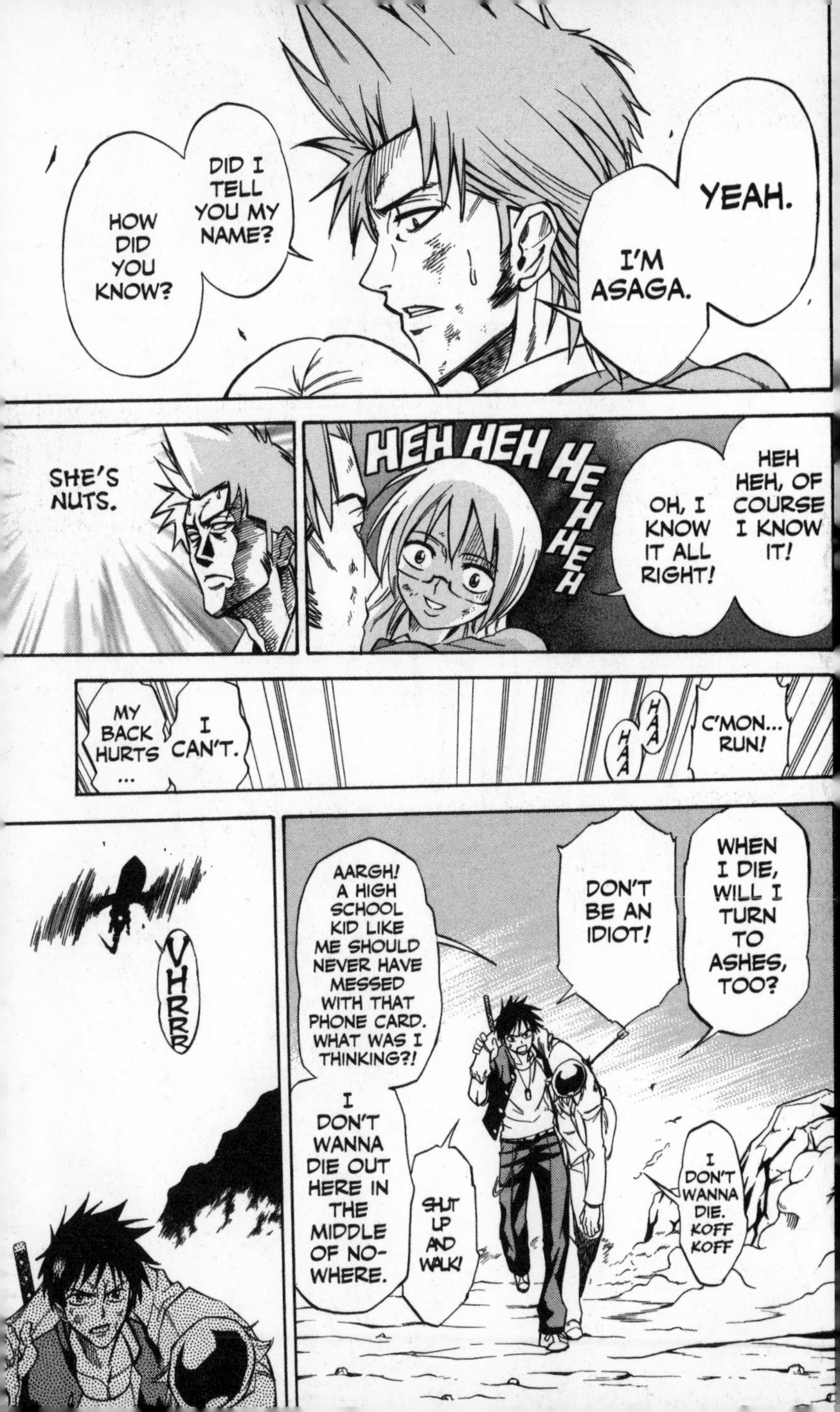
YEAH.
I'M ASAGA.
DID I TELL YOU MY NAME?
HOW DID YOU KNOW?
HEH HEH, OF COURSE I KNOW IT!
OH, I KNOW IT ALL RIGHT!
HEH HEH HEHHHEH
SHE'S NUTS.
C'MON... RUN!
HAA HAA
I CAN'T.
MY BACK HURTS...
WHEN I DIE, WILL I TURN TO ASHES, TOO?
DON'T BE AN IDIOT!
AARGH! A HIGH SCHOOL KID LIKE ME SHOULD NEVER HAVE MESSED WITH THAT PHONE CARD. WHAT WAS I THINKING?!
I DON'T WANNA DIE. KOFF KOFF
SHUT UP AND WALK!
I DON'T WANNA DIE OUT HERE IN THE MIDDLE OF NO-WHERE.
VHRRR

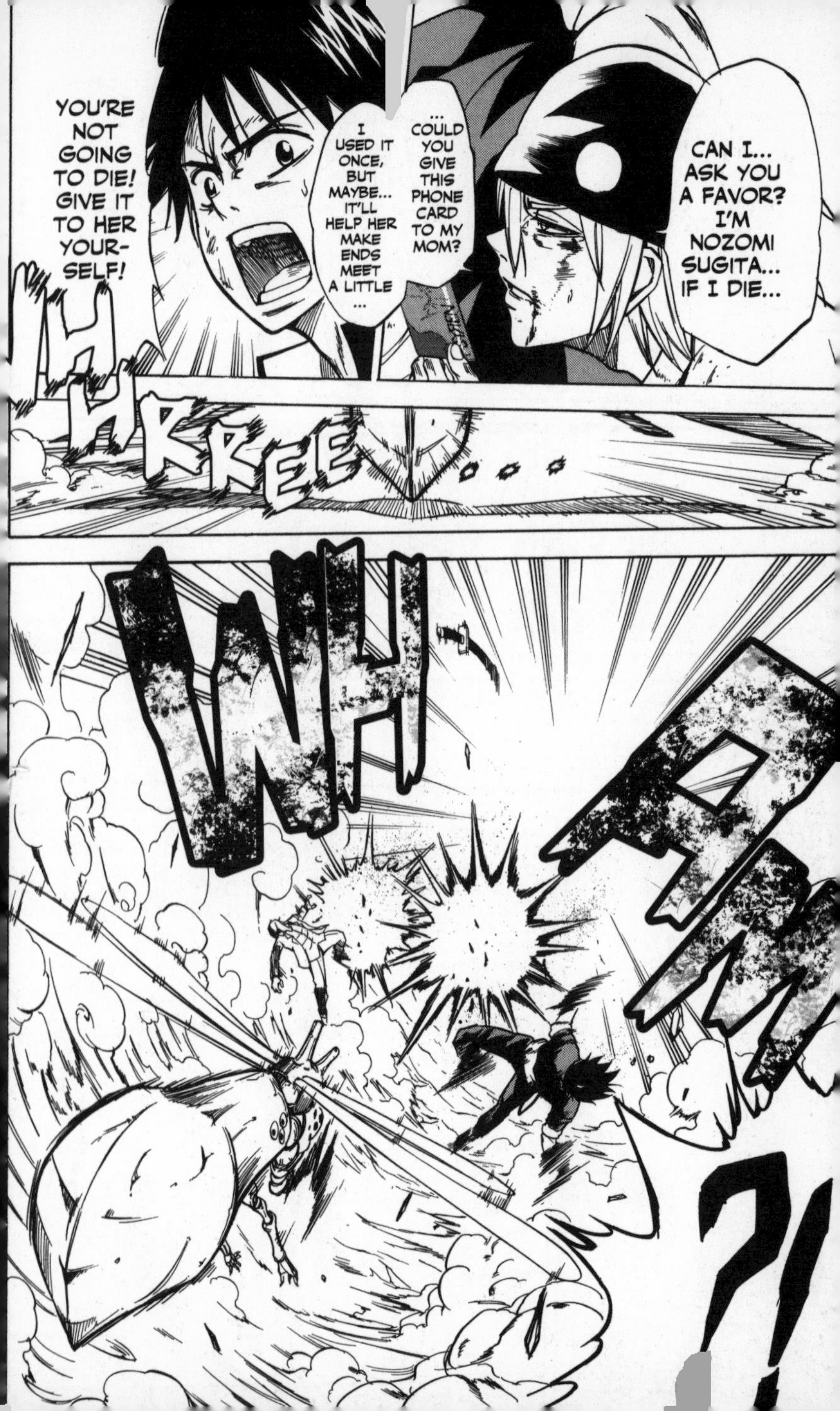
CAN I... ASK YOU A FAVOR? I'M NOZOMI SUGITA... IF I DIE...
... COULD YOU GIVE THIS PHONE CARD TO MY MOM?
I USED IT ONCE, BUT MAYBE... IT'LL HELP HER MAKE ENDS MEET A LITTLE ...
YOU'RE NOT GOING TO DIE! GIVE IT TO HER YOURSELF!
HHREEE...
WHAM
?!

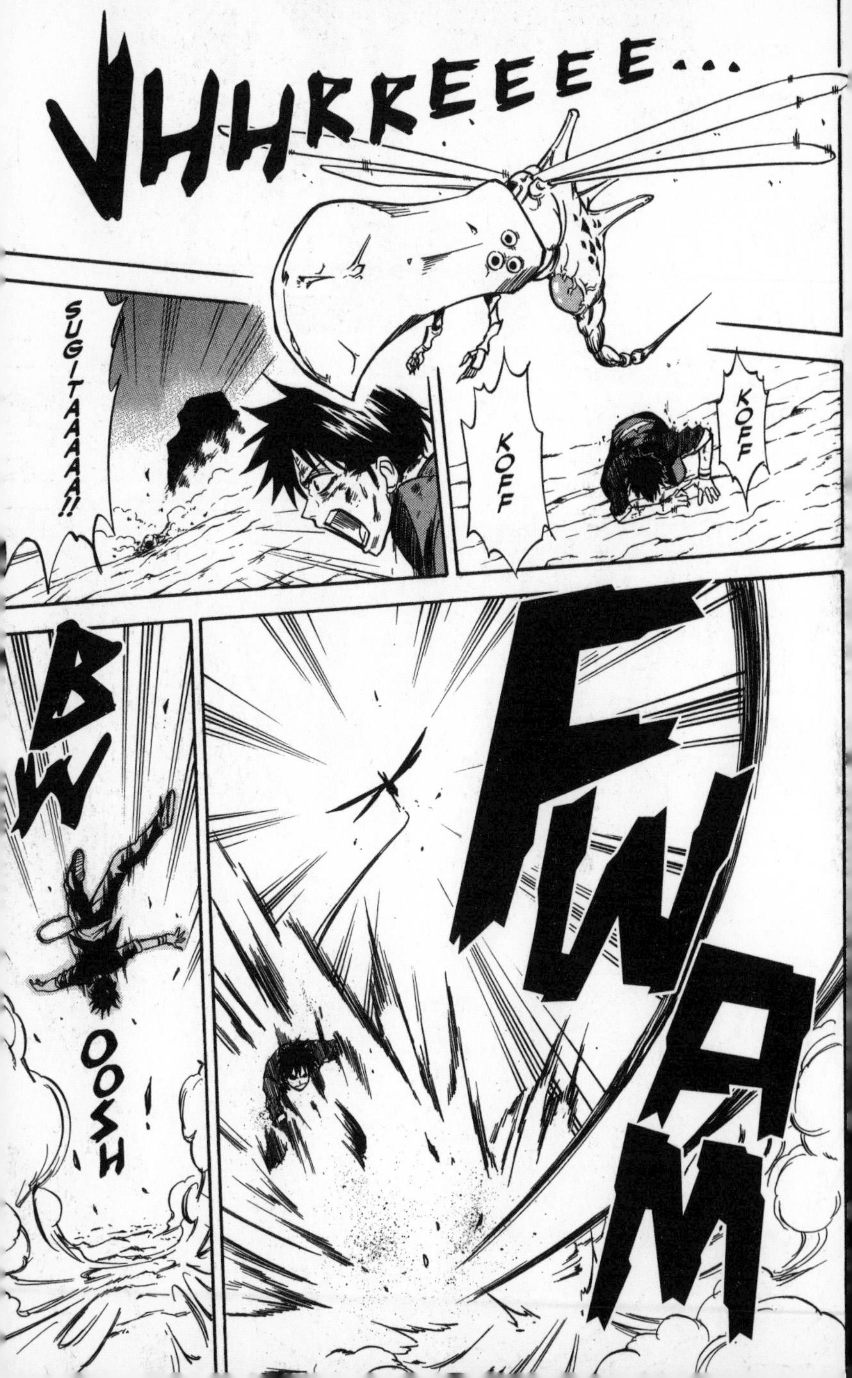
VHHRREEEEE...
KOFF
KOFF
SUGITAAAAAA!!
FWAM
BWOOSH!

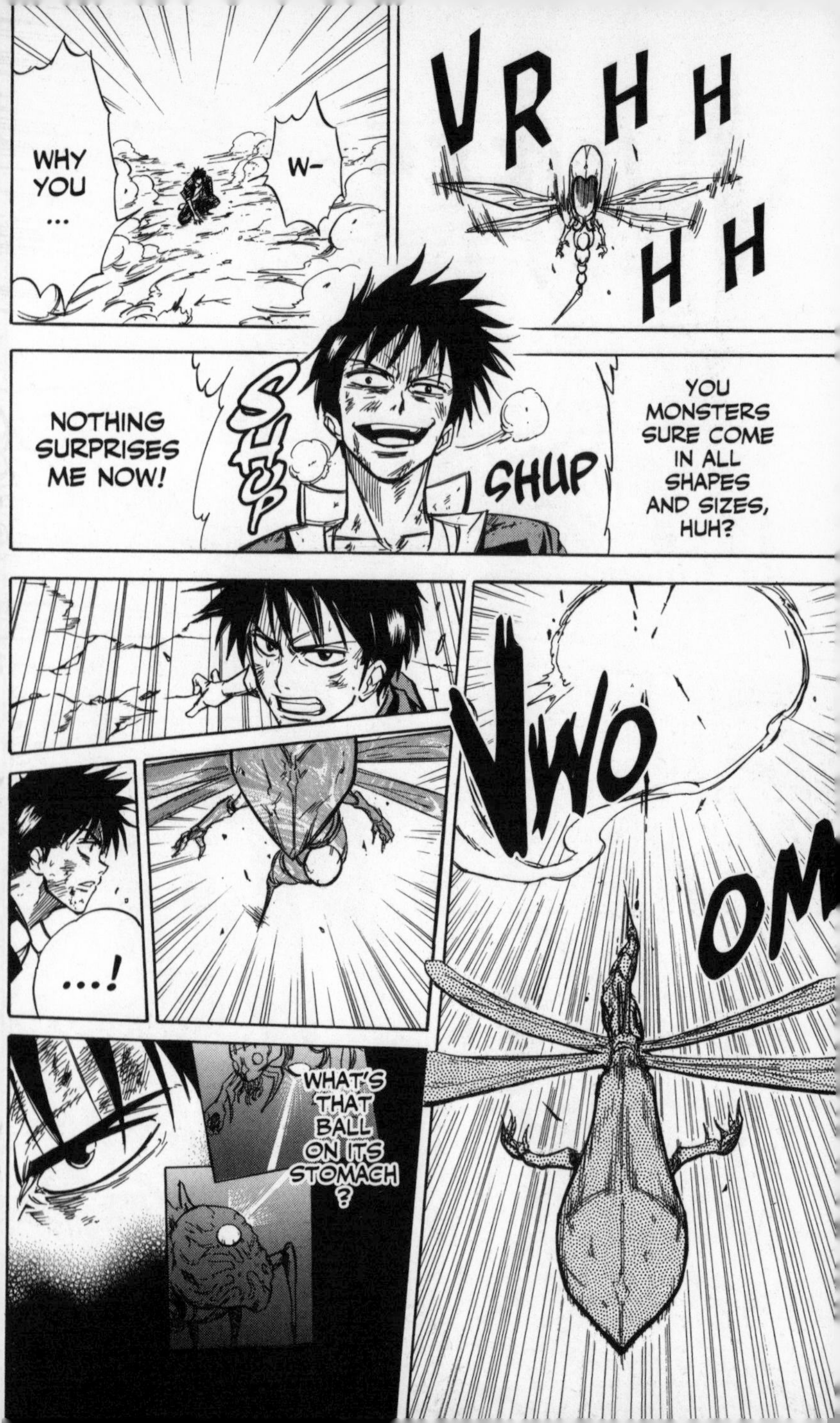
VRHHHH
W-
WHY YOU ...
YOU MONSTERS SURE COME IN ALL SHAPES AND SIZES, HUH?
SHUP
SHUP
NOTHING SURPRISES ME NOW!
VWOOM
...!
WHAT'S THAT BALL ON ITS STOMACH?

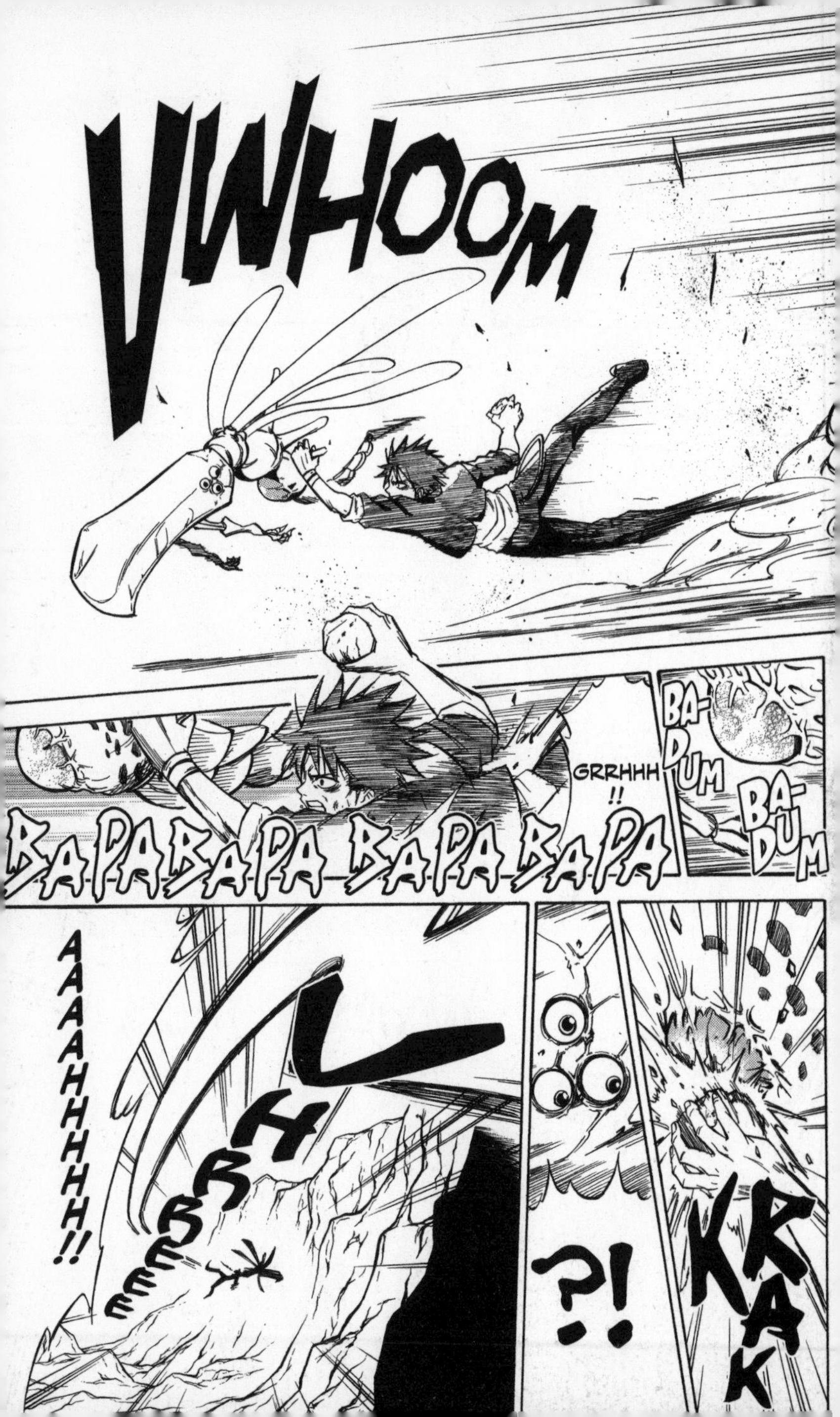
VWHOOM
BA-DUM
BA-DUM
GRRHHH!!
BAPABAPA BAPABAPA
KRAK
?!
AAAAHHHHHH!!
VHRREEE

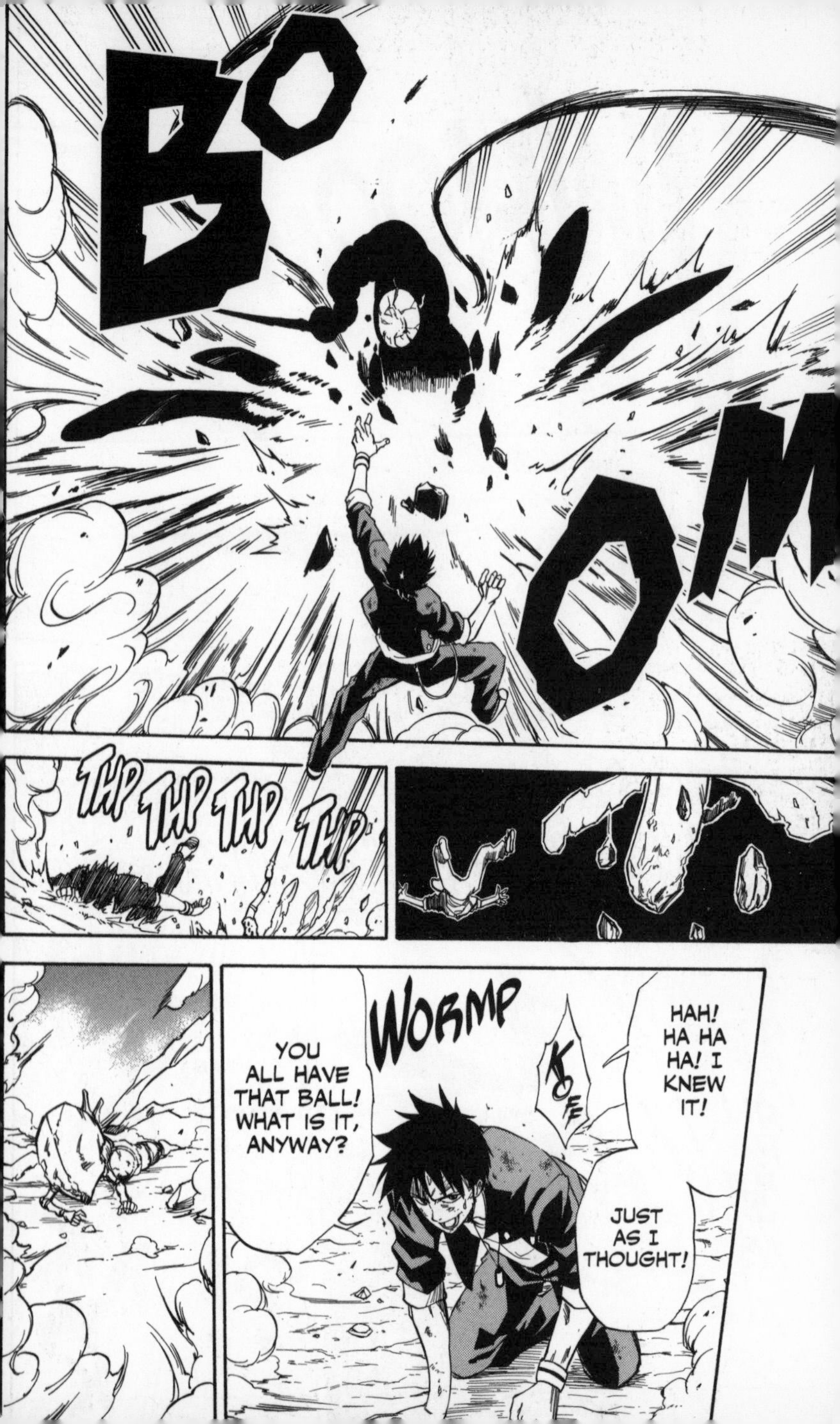
BOOOM
THP THP THP THP
HAH! HA HA HA! I KNEW IT!
KOFF
WORMP
JUST AS I THOUGHT!
YOU ALL HAVE THAT BALL! WHAT IS IT, ANYWAY?

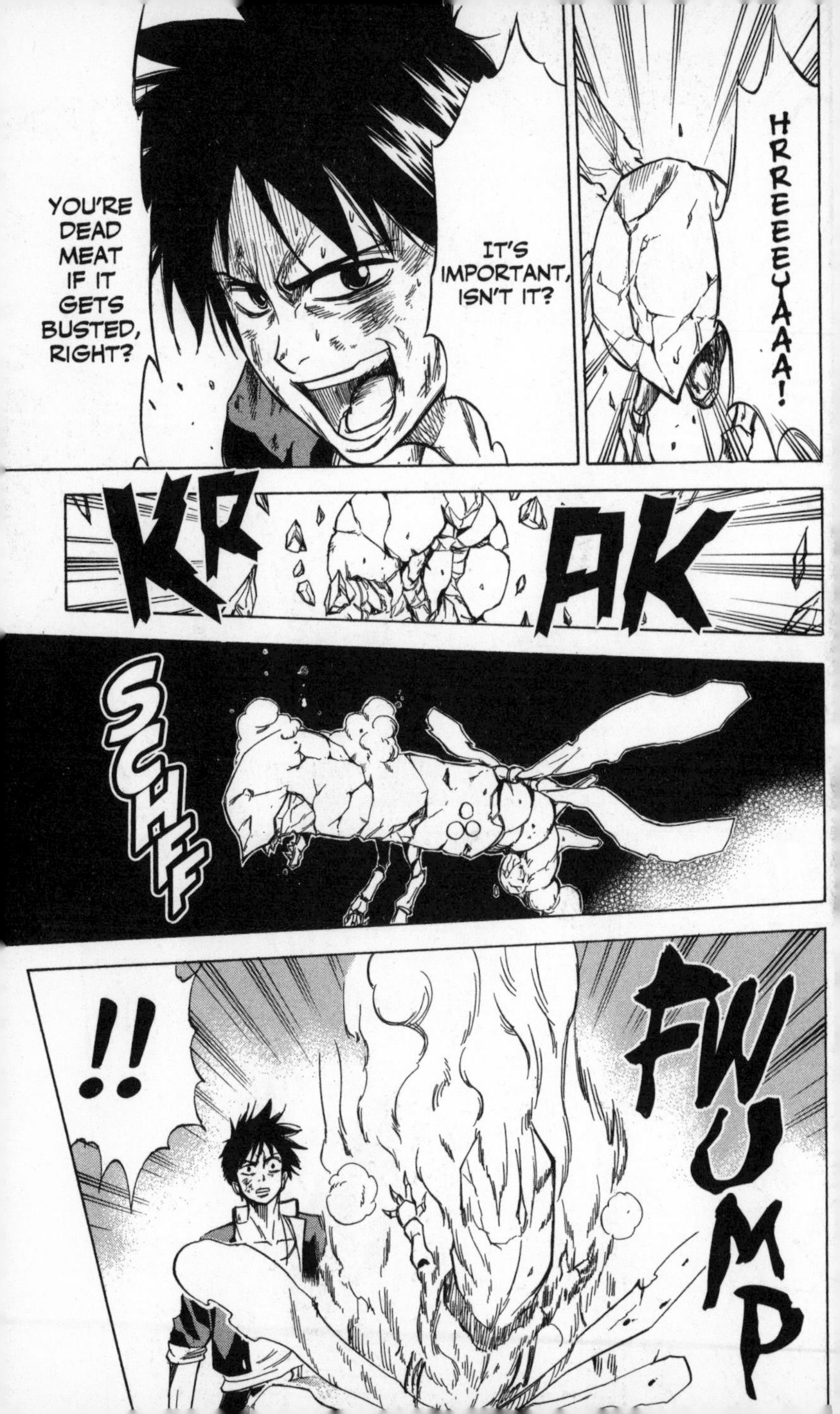
HRREEEYAAAA!
IT'S IMPORTANT, ISN'T IT?
YOU'RE DEAD MEAT IF IT GETS BUSTED, RIGHT?
KRAK
SCHFF
FWUMP
!!

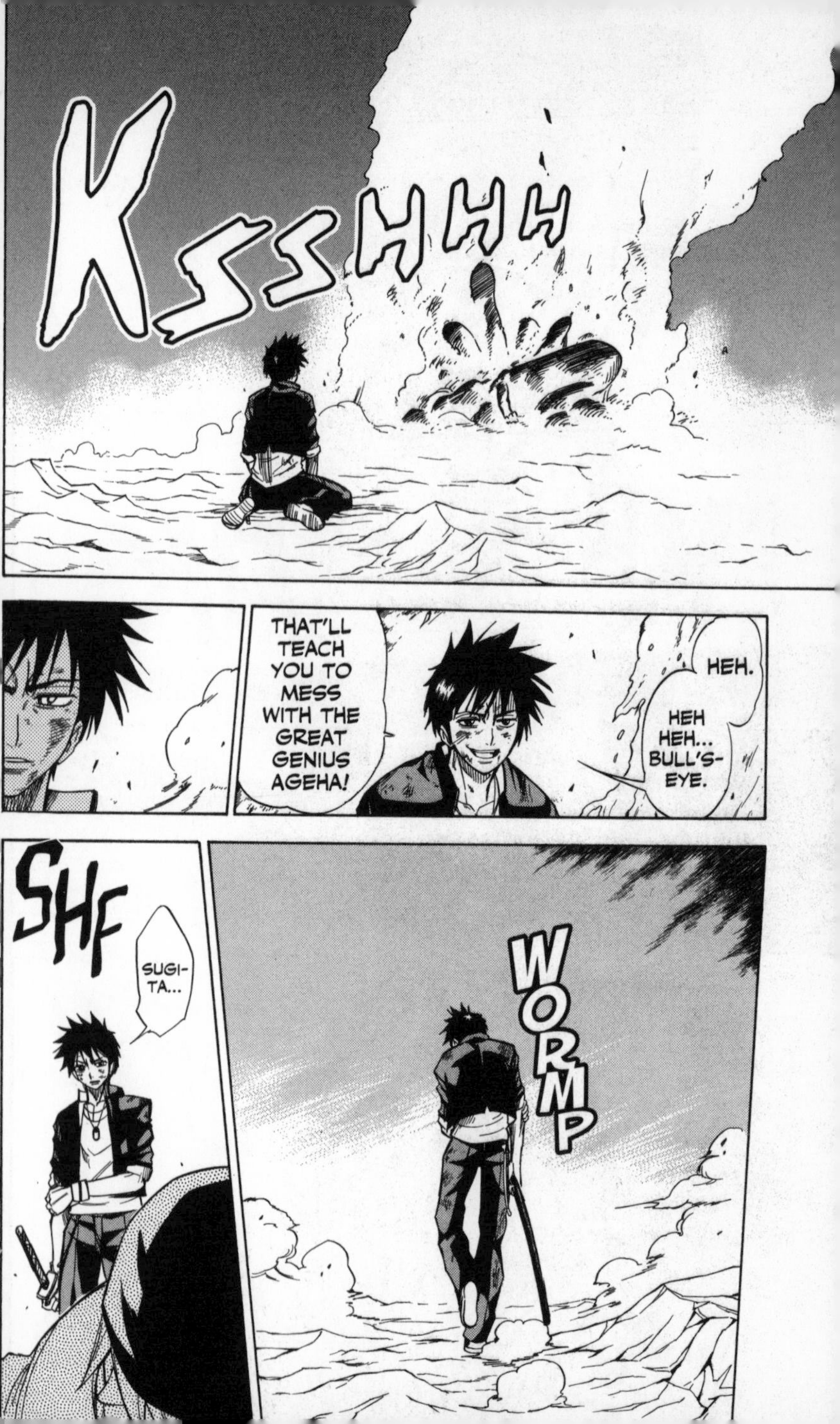
KSSHHH
HEH.
HEH HEH... BULL'S-EYE.
THAT'LL TEACH YOU TO MESS WITH THE GREAT GENIUS AGEHA!
WORMP
SHF
SUGI-TA...

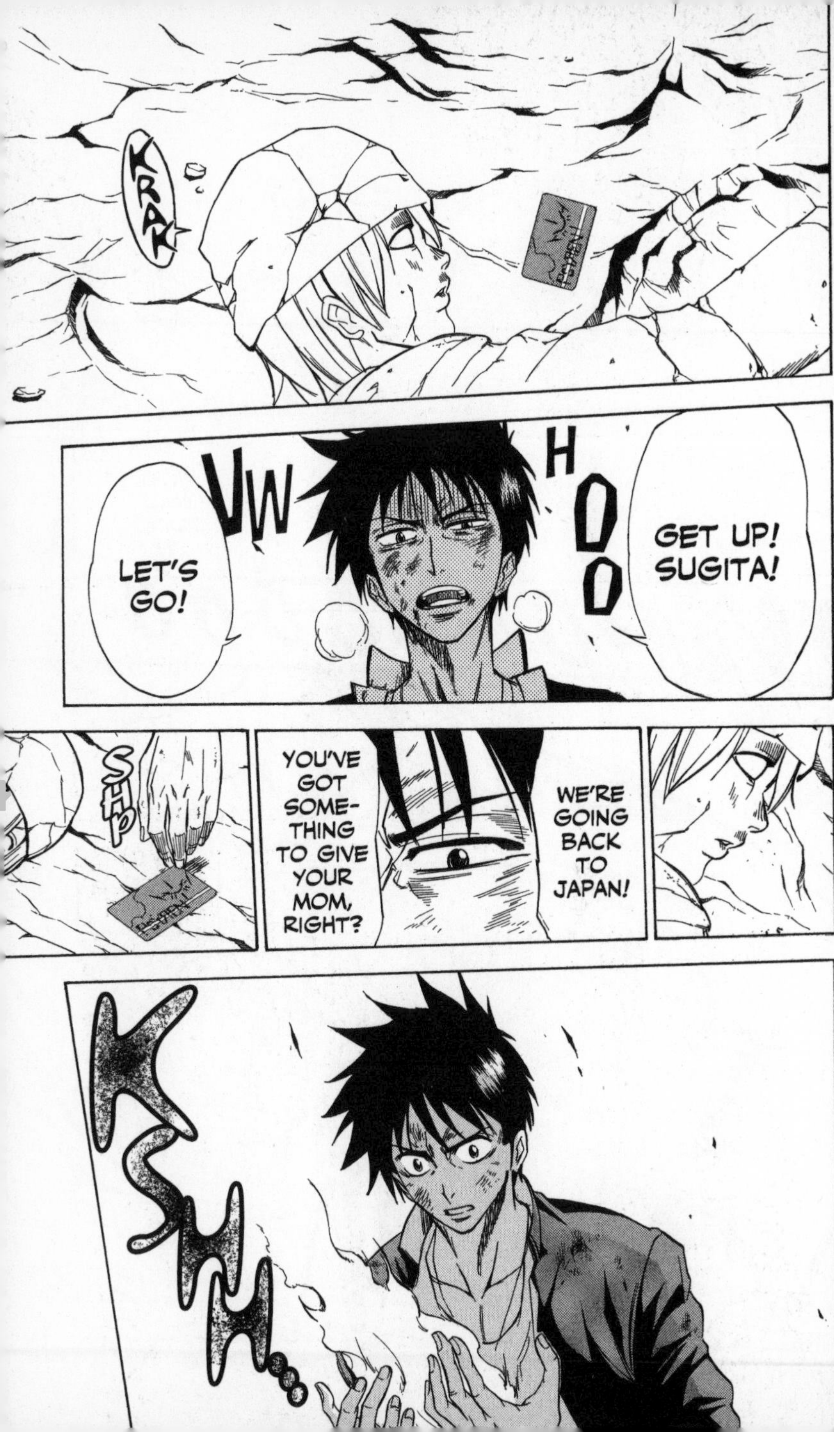
KRAK
GET UP! SUGITA!
LET'S GO!
WE'RE GOING BACK TO JAPAN!
YOU'VE GOT SOME-THING TO GIVE YOUR MOM, RIGHT?

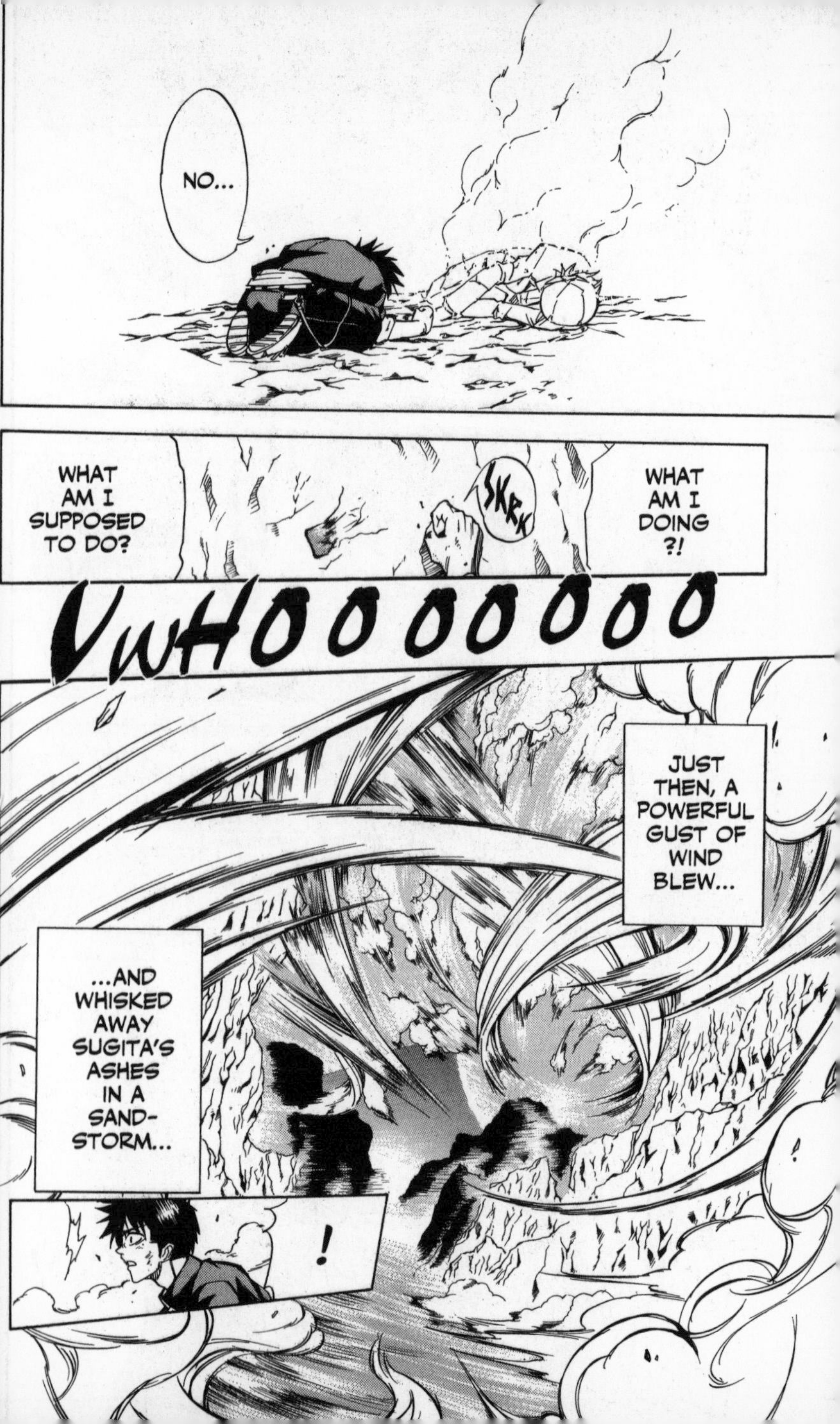
NO...
WHAT AM I DOING ?!
SKRK
WHAT AM I SUPPOSED TO DO?
VWHOOOOOOOO
JUST THEN, A POWERFUL GUST OF WIND BLEW...
...AND WHISKED AWAY SUGITA'S ASHES IN A SAND-STORM...
!

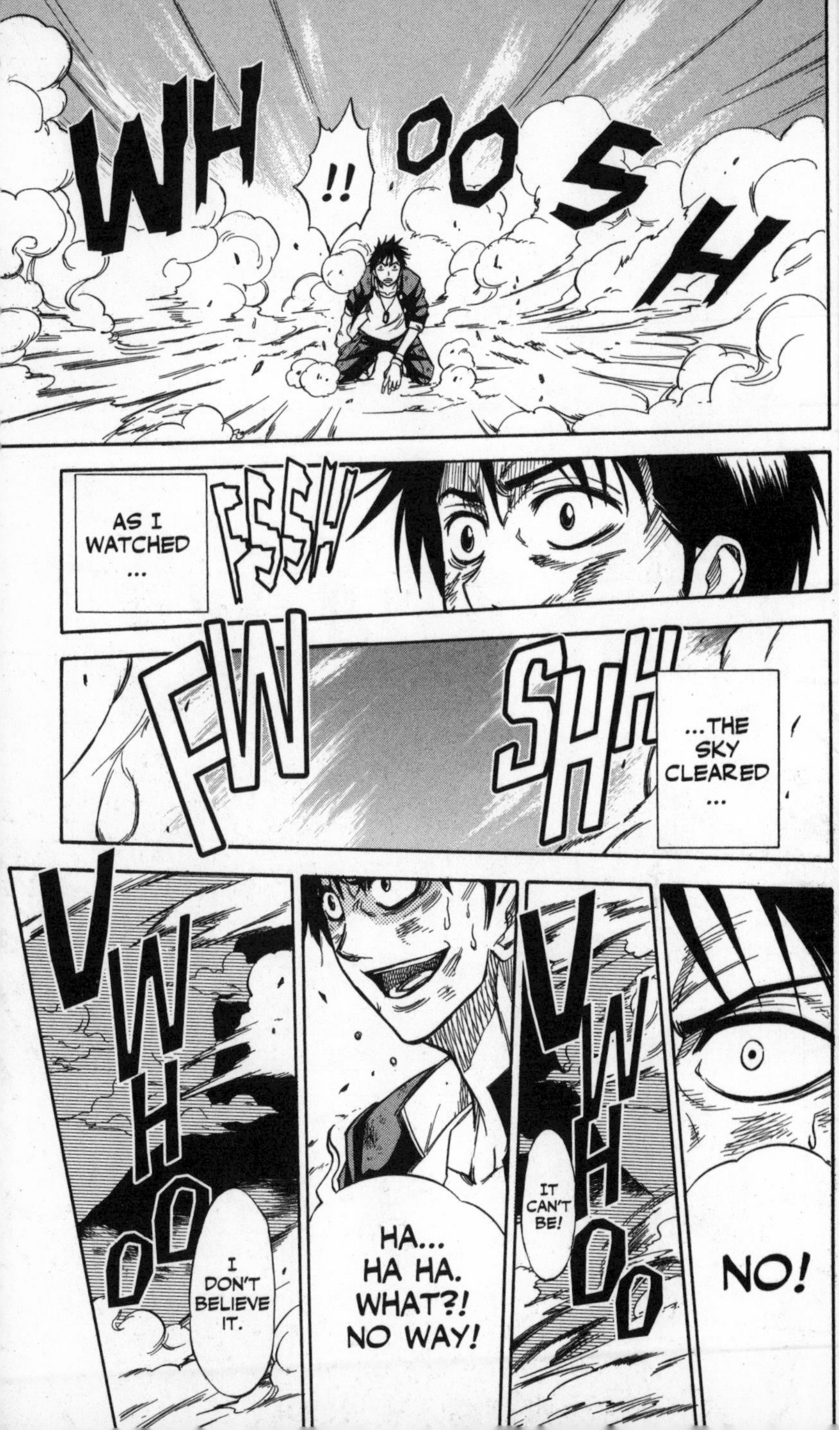
!!
WHOOSH
FSSH
AS I WATCHED ...
...THE SKY CLEARED ...
SHH
FW
NO!
VWHOO
IT CAN'T BE!
HA... HA HA. WHAT?! NO WAY!
VWHOO
I DON'T BELIEVE IT.

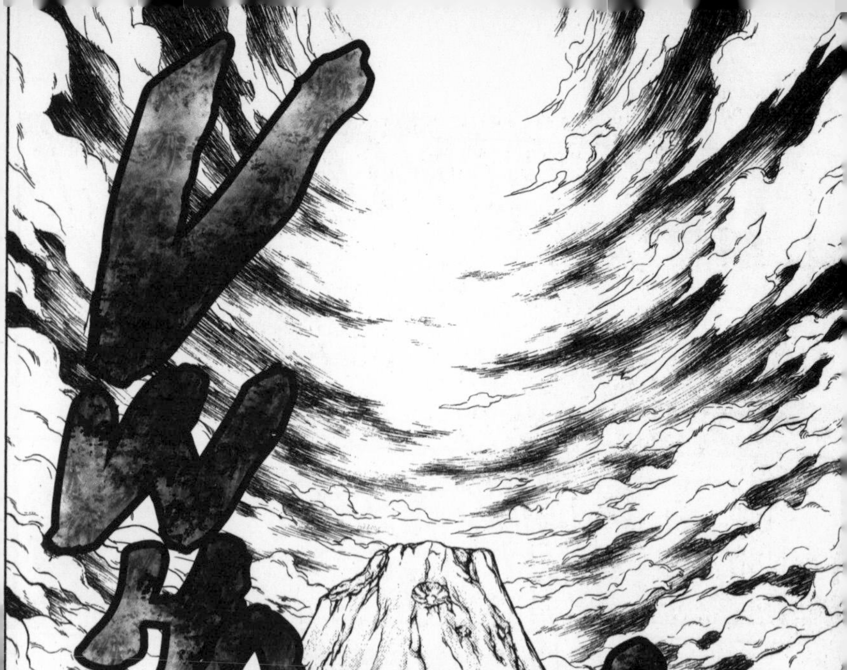
VWHOOM

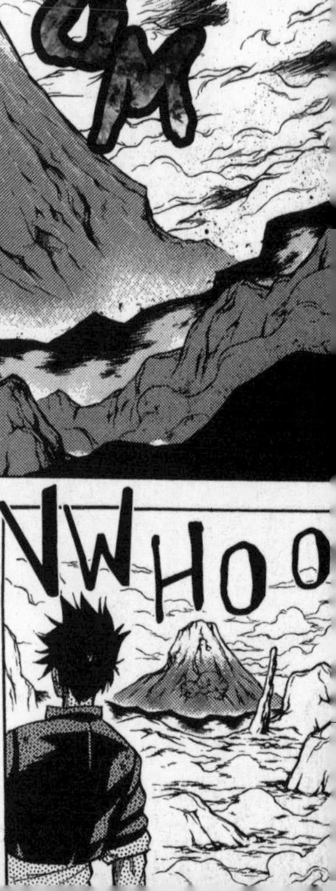
VWHOO

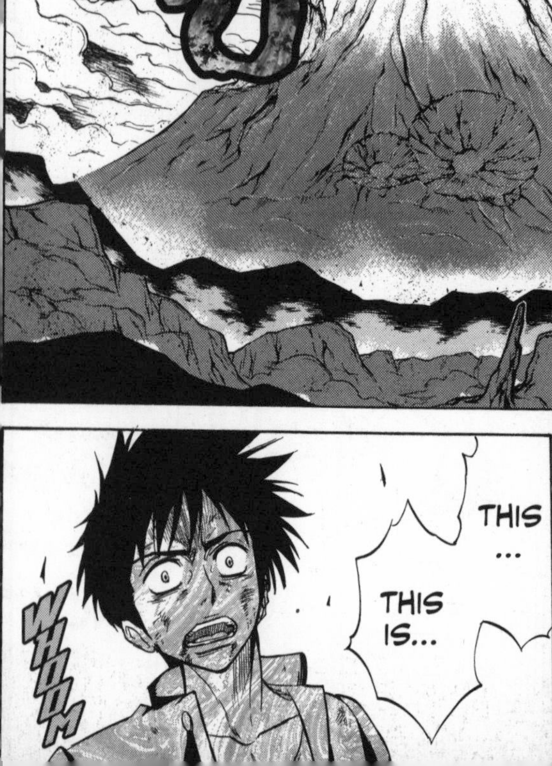
THIS ... THIS IS...
WHOOM

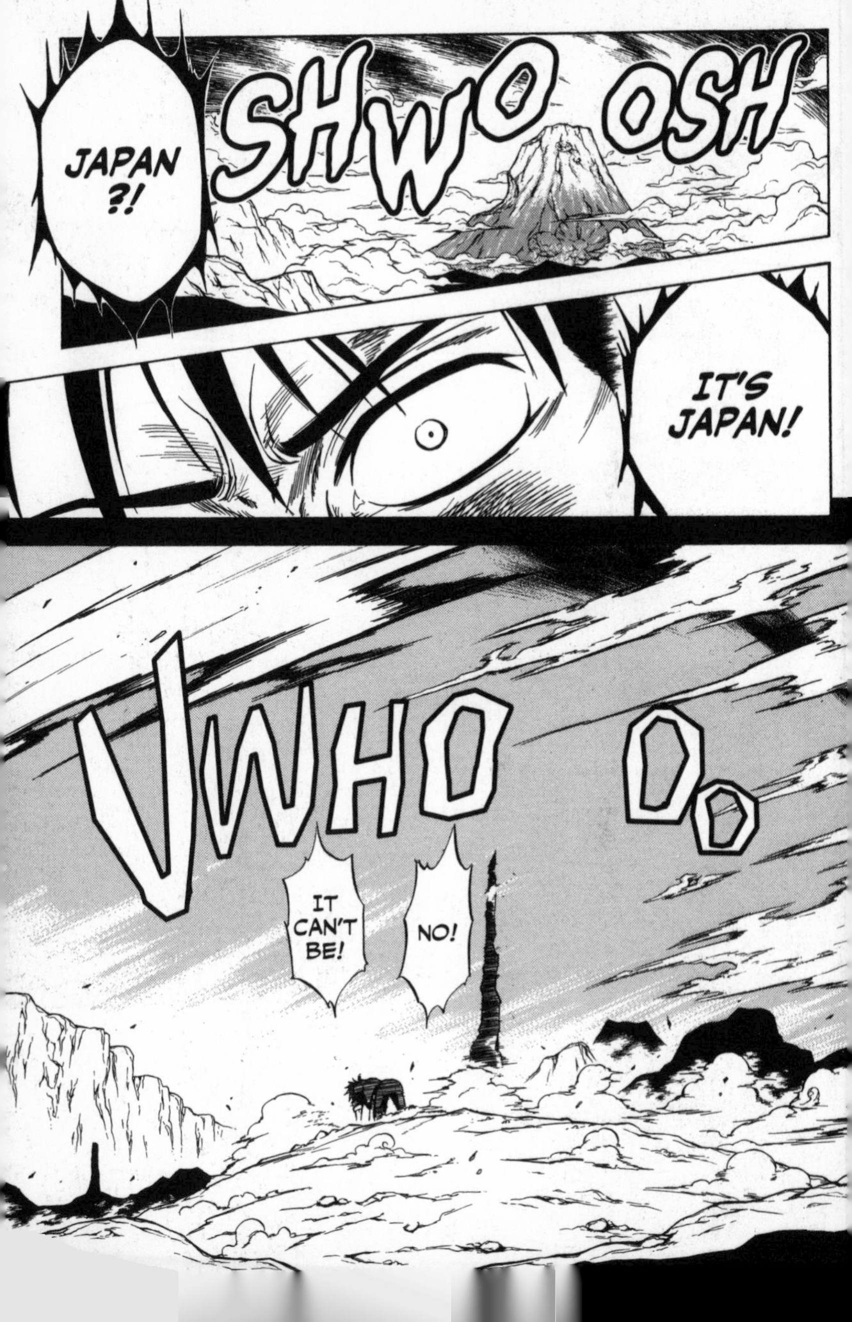
SHWO OSH
JAPAN ?!
IT'S JAPAN!
VWHO OO
NO!
IT CAN'T BE!

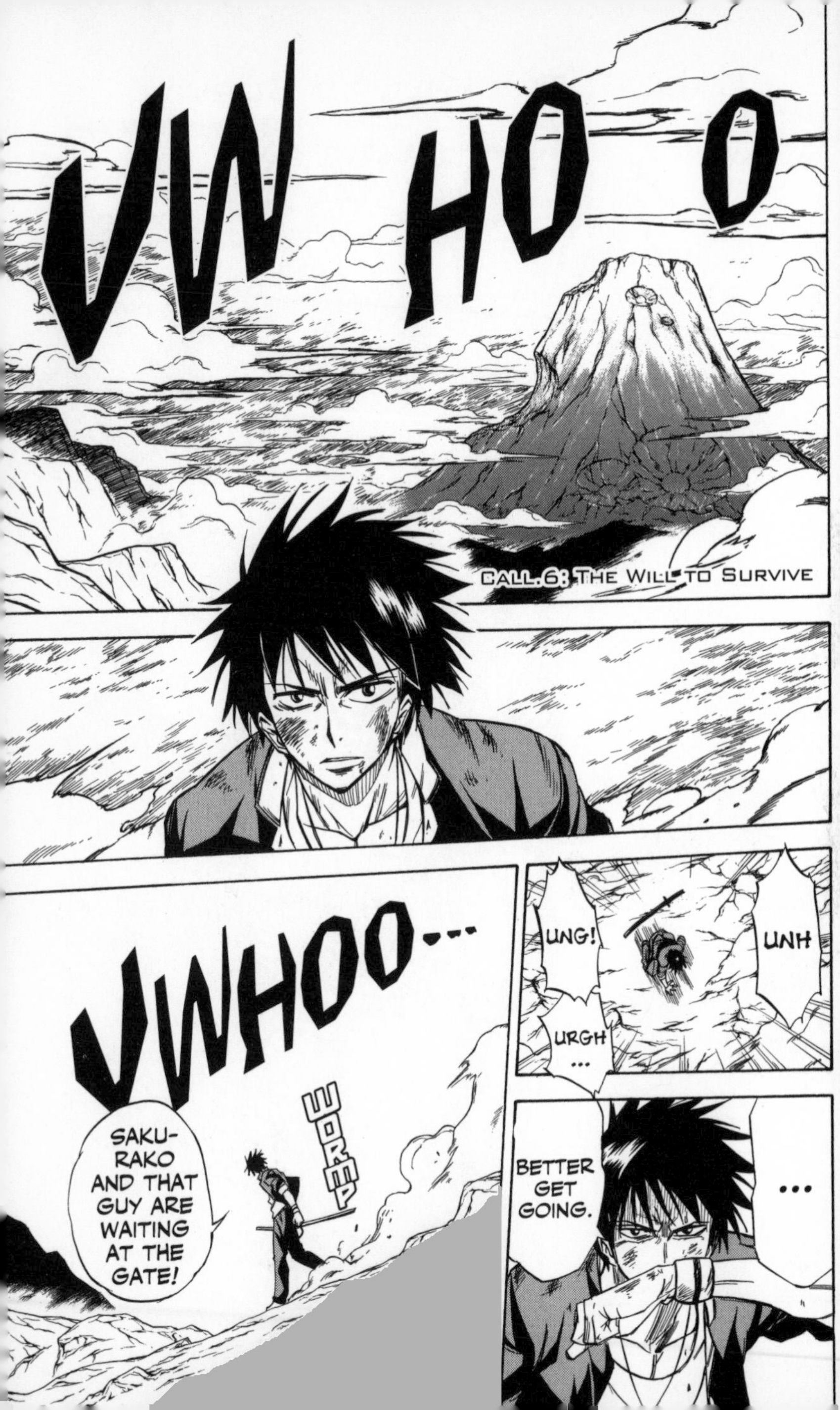
VWHOOO
CALL.6: THE WILL TO SURVIVE
UNH
UNG!
URGH...
...
BETTER GET GOING.
VWHOO...
WOMP
SAKU-RAKO AND THAT GUY ARE WAITING AT THE GATE!

# Call.6: The Will to Survive

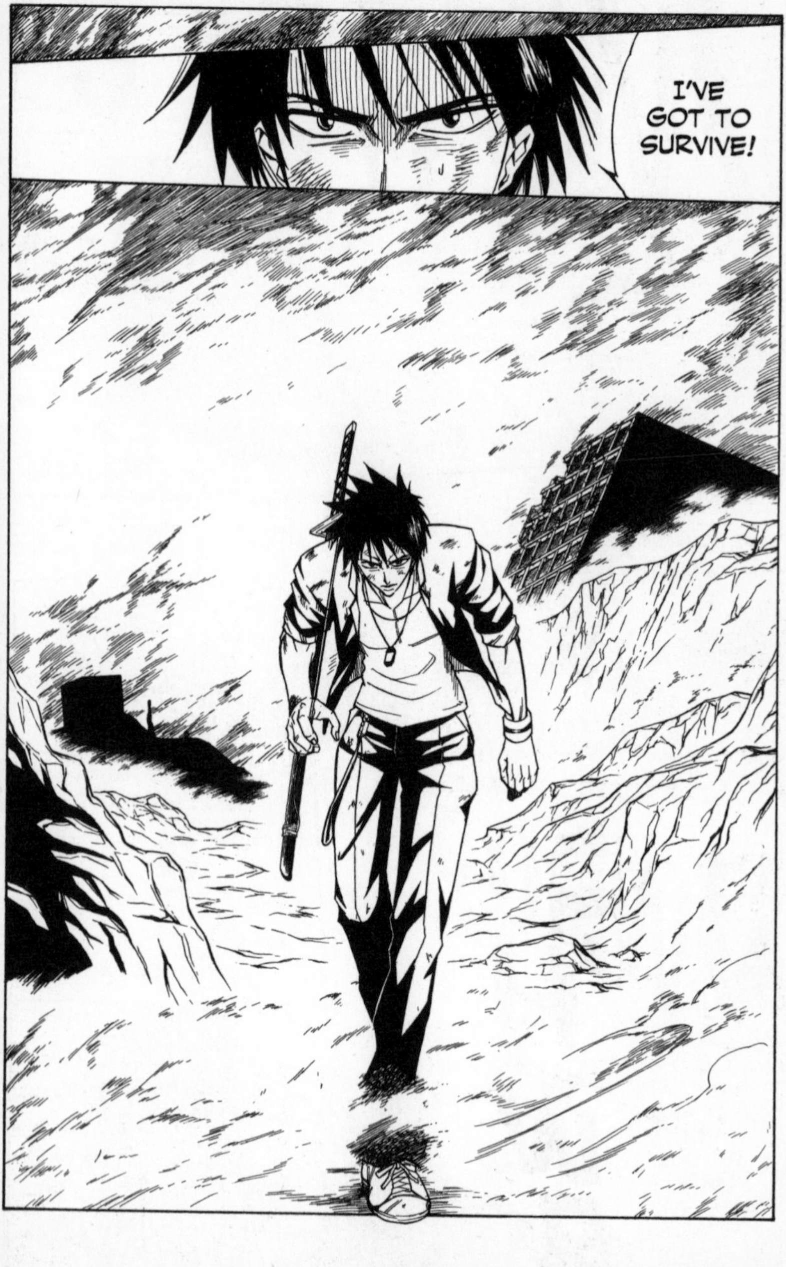
I'VE GOT TO SURVIVE!

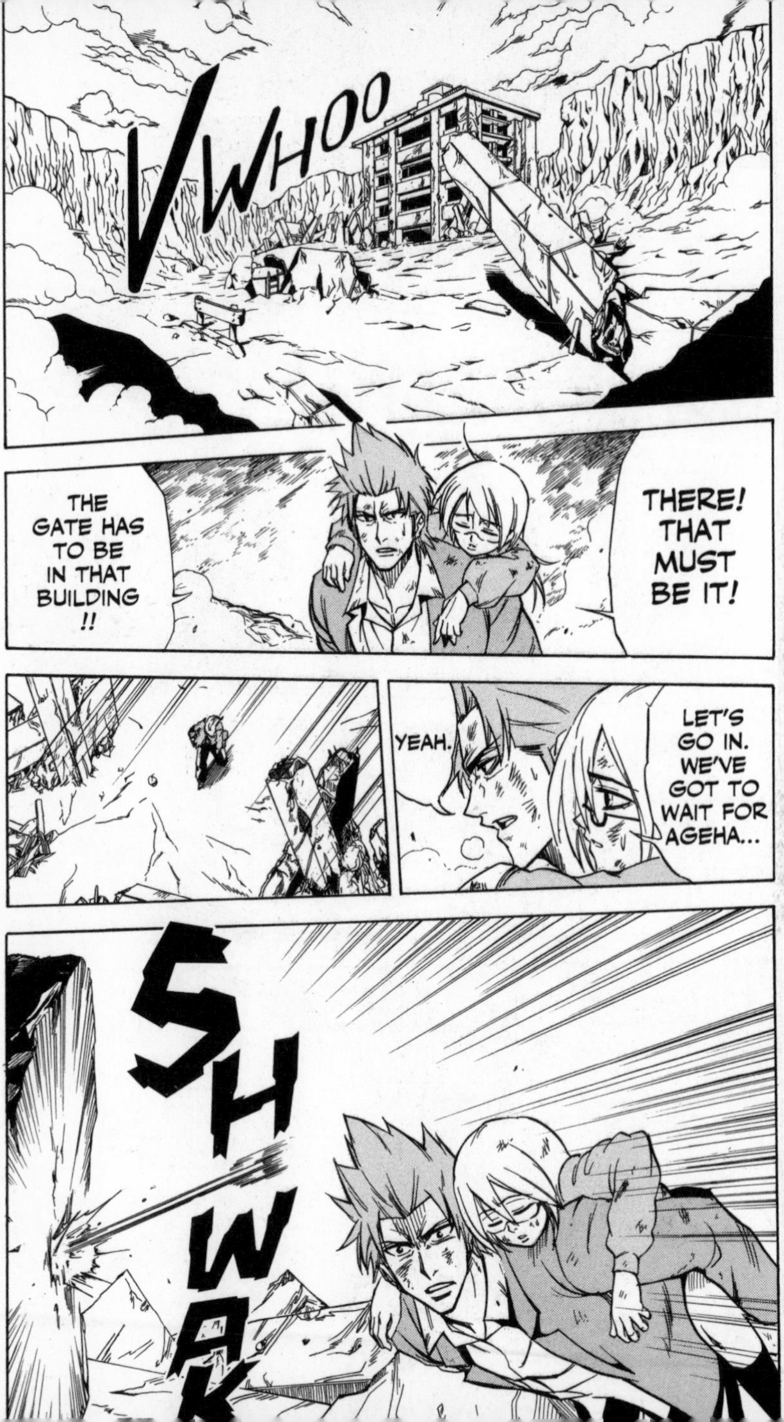
VWHOO
THERE! THAT MUST BE IT!
THE GATE HAS TO BE IN THAT BUILDING!!
LET'S GO IN. WE'VE GOT TO WAIT FOR AGEHA...
YEAH.
SHWAK

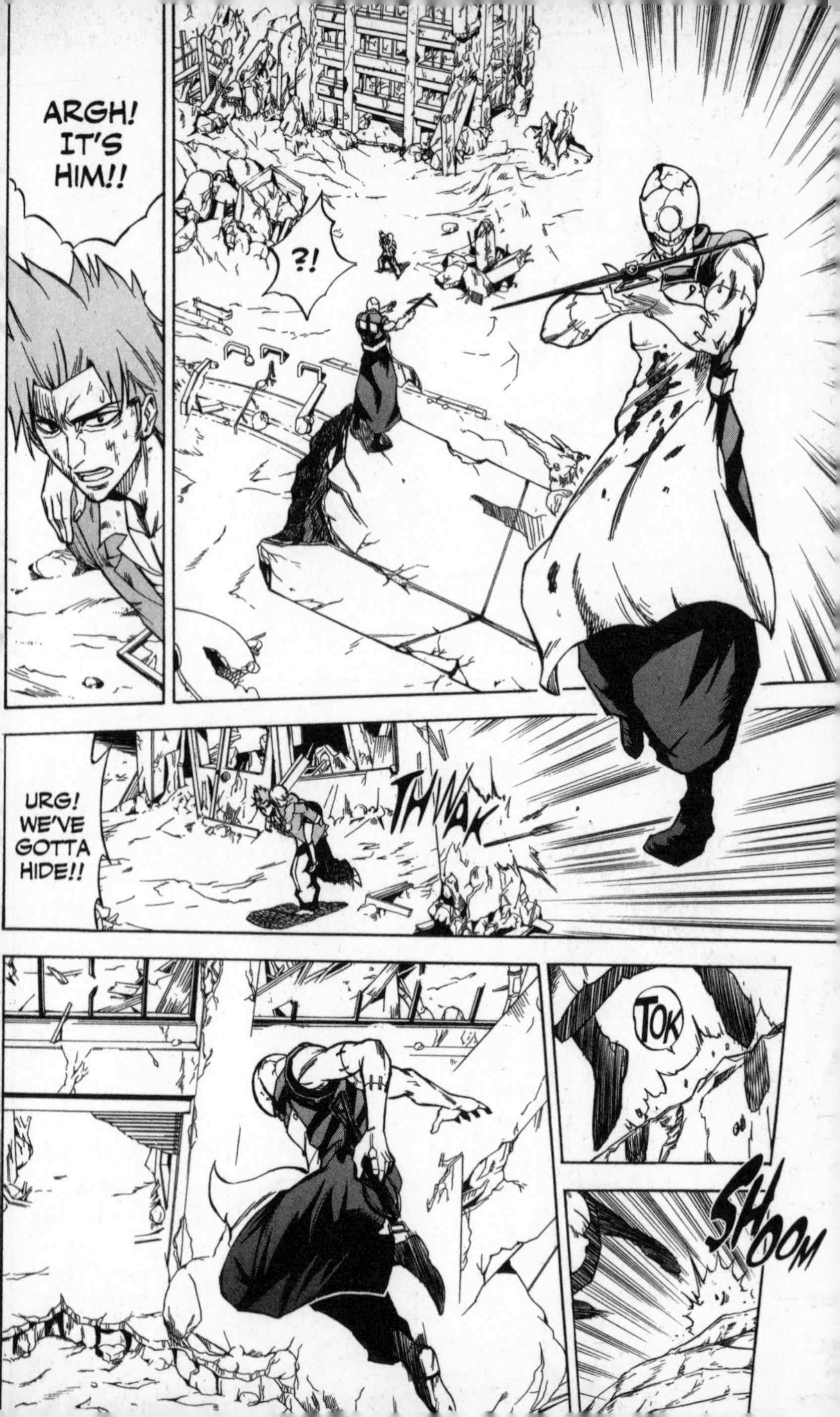

?!
ARGH! IT'S HIM!!
THWAK
URG! WE'VE GOTTA HIDE!!
TOK
SHOOM

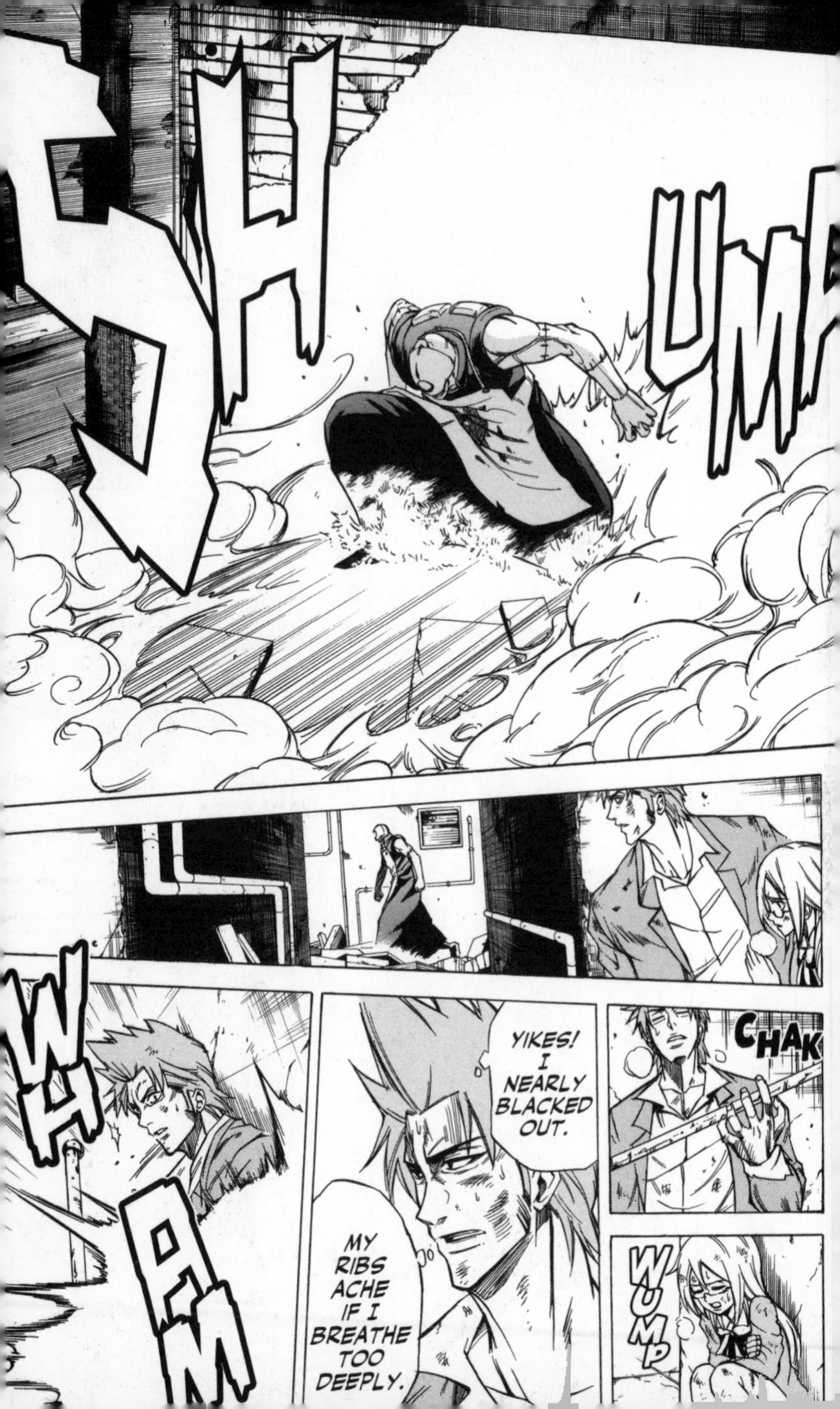
UMP
CHAK
WUMP
YIKES! I NEARLY BLACKED OUT.
MY RIBS ACHE IF I BREATHE TOO DEEPLY.
WHAM

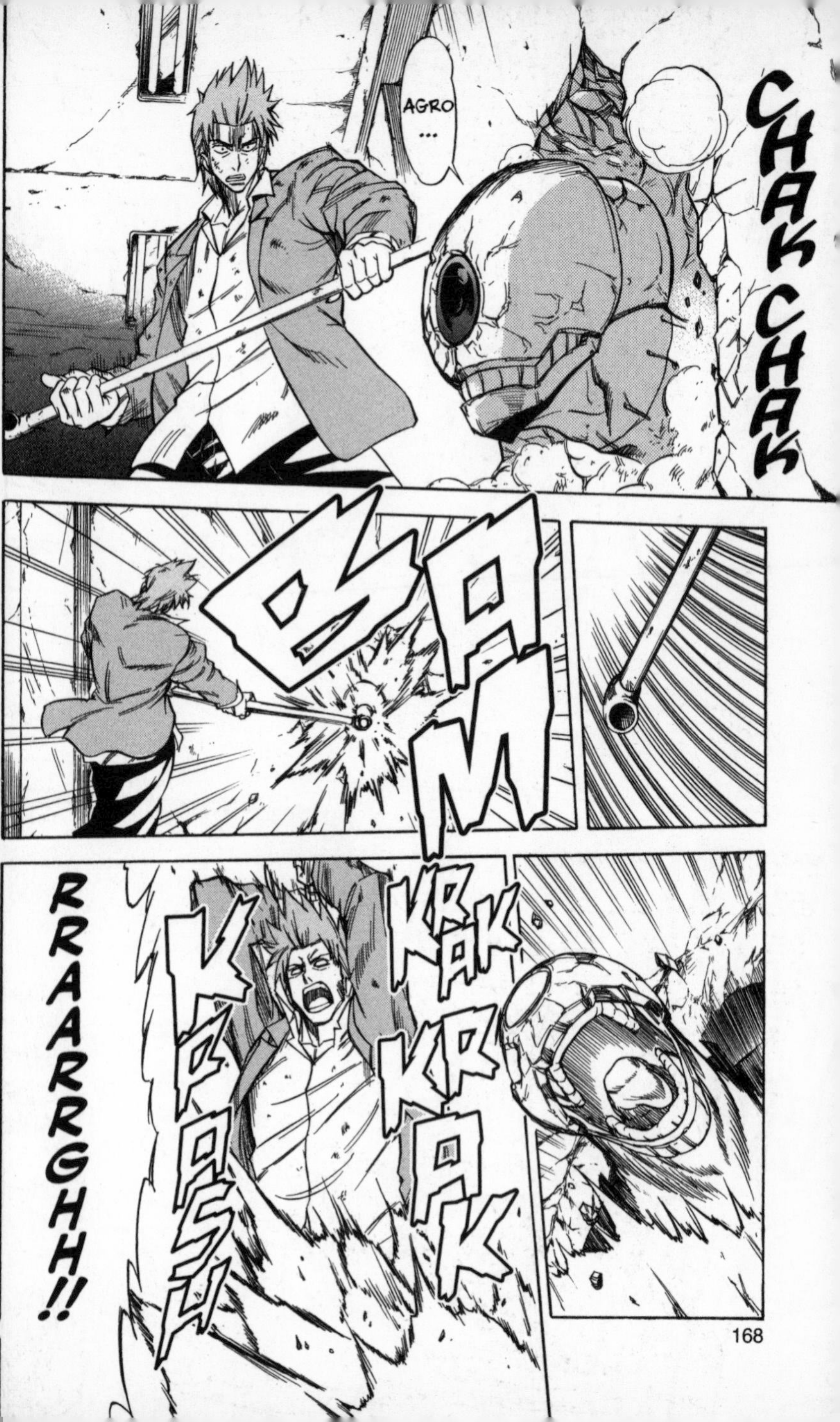
CHAK CHAK CHAK
AGRO ...
BAM
KRAK KRAK
VOOSH
RRAARRGHH!!

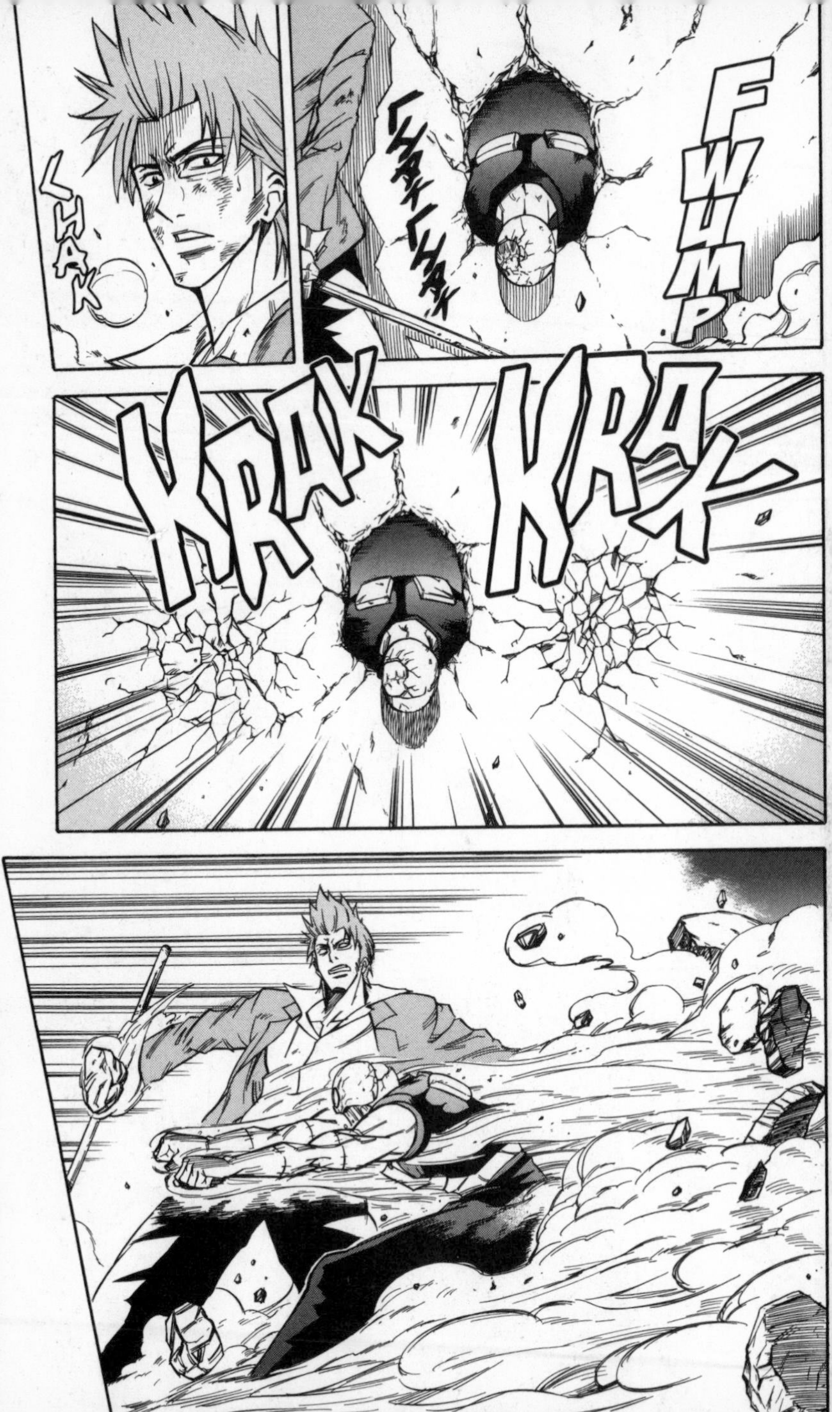
FWUMP
CHAK CHAK
CHAK
KRAK
KRAK

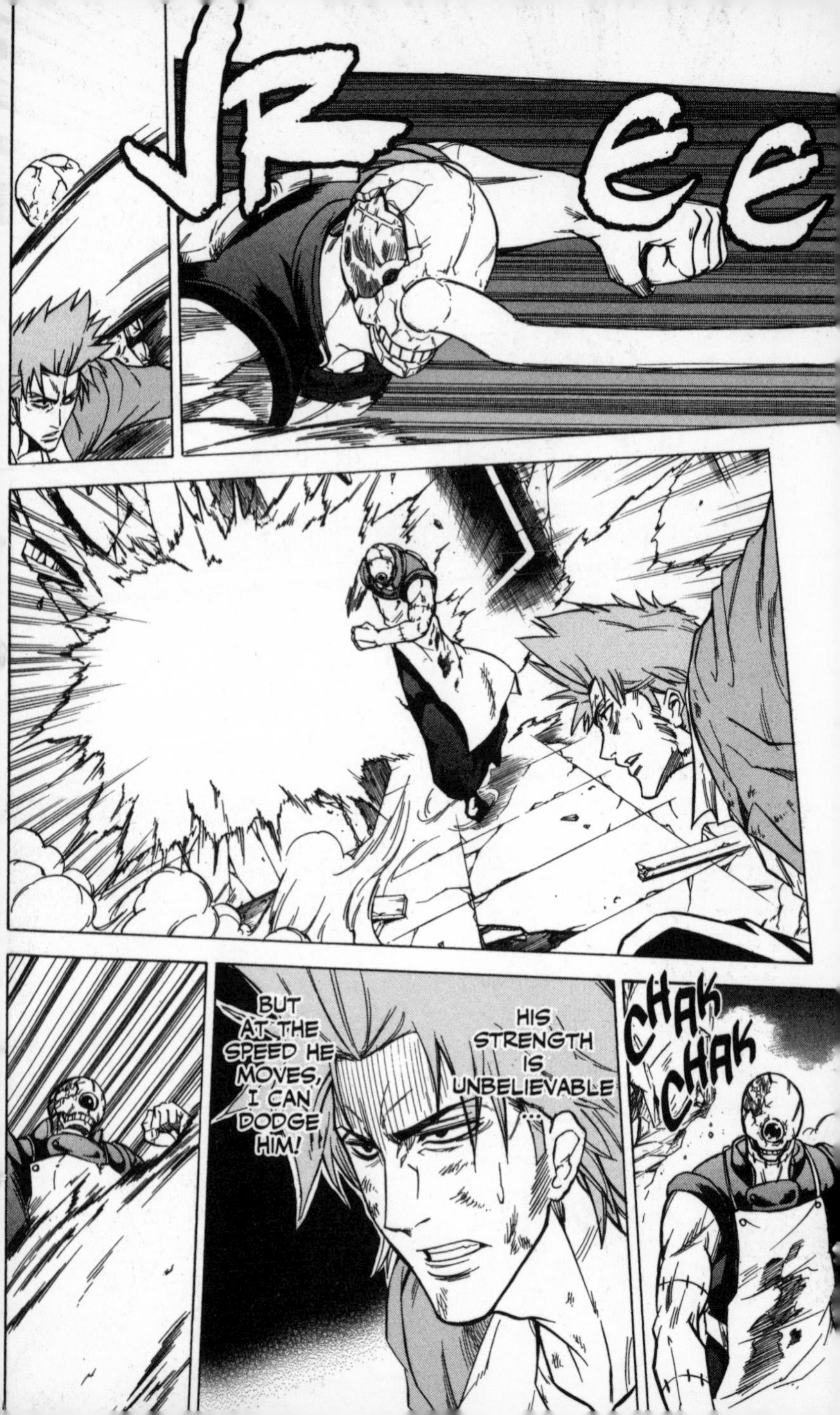
VRREE
CHAK CHAK
HIS STRENGTH IS UNBELIEVABLE...
BUT AT THE SPEED HE MOVES, I CAN DODGE HIM!

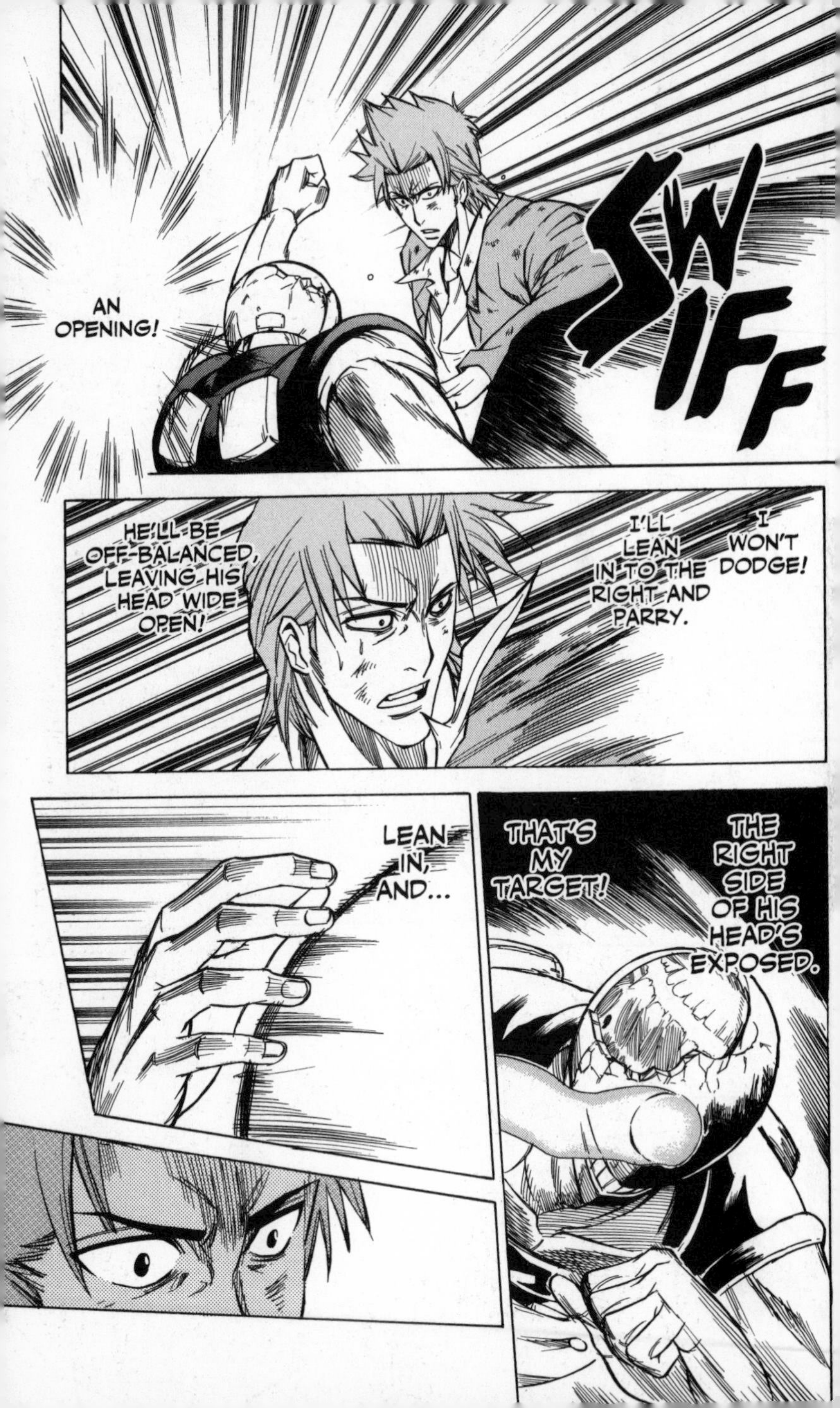
SWIFF
AN OPENING!
I WON'T DODGE!
I'LL LEAN IN TO THE RIGHT AND PARRY.
HE'LL BE OFF-BALANCED, LEAVING HIS HEAD WIDE OPEN!
THE RIGHT SIDE OF HIS HEAD'S EXPOSED.
THAT'S MY TARGET!
LEAN IN, AND...

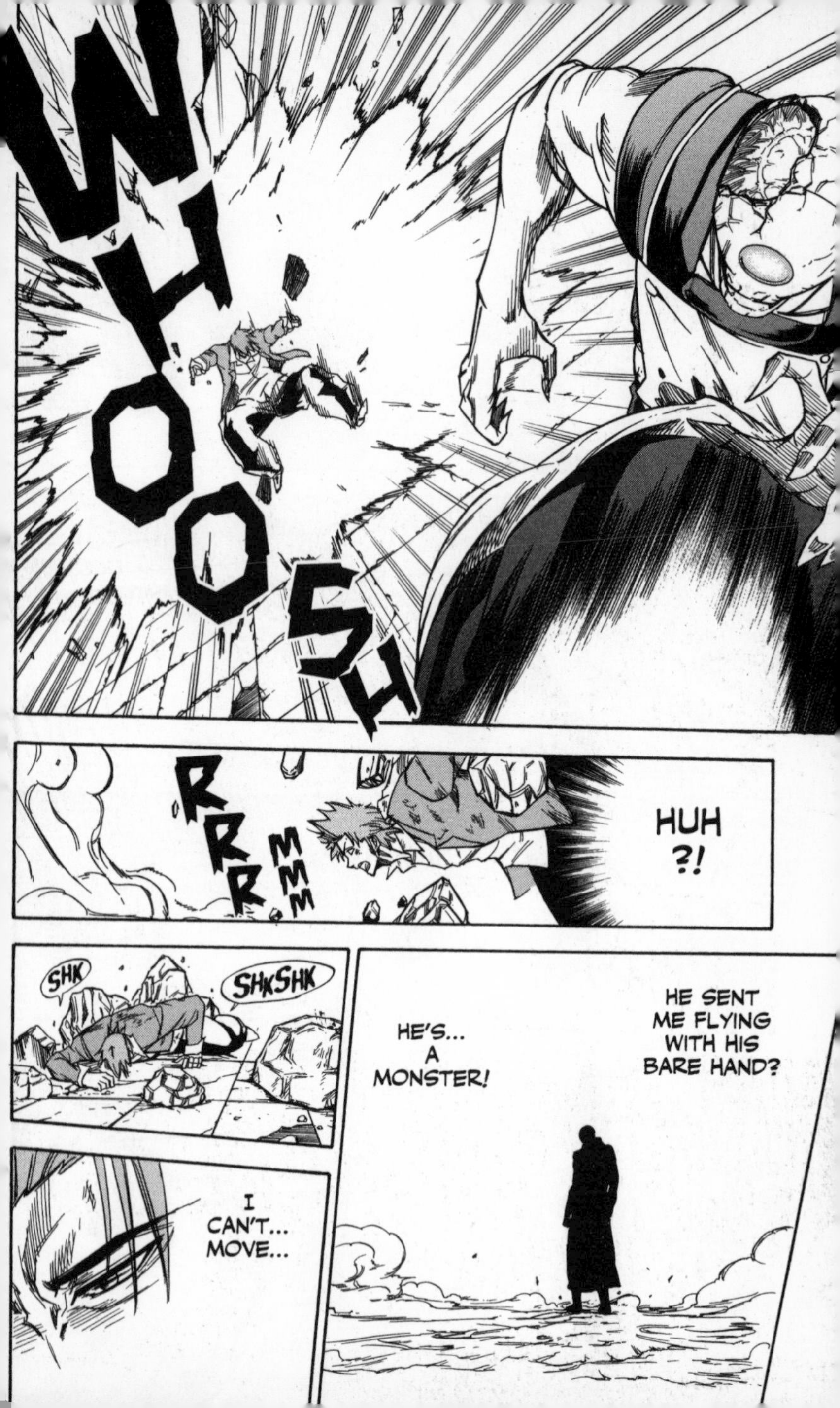
WHOOSH
HUH ?!
RRRMMM
HE SENT ME FLYING WITH HIS BARE HAND?
HE'S... A MONSTER!
SHKSHK
SHK
I CAN'T... MOVE...

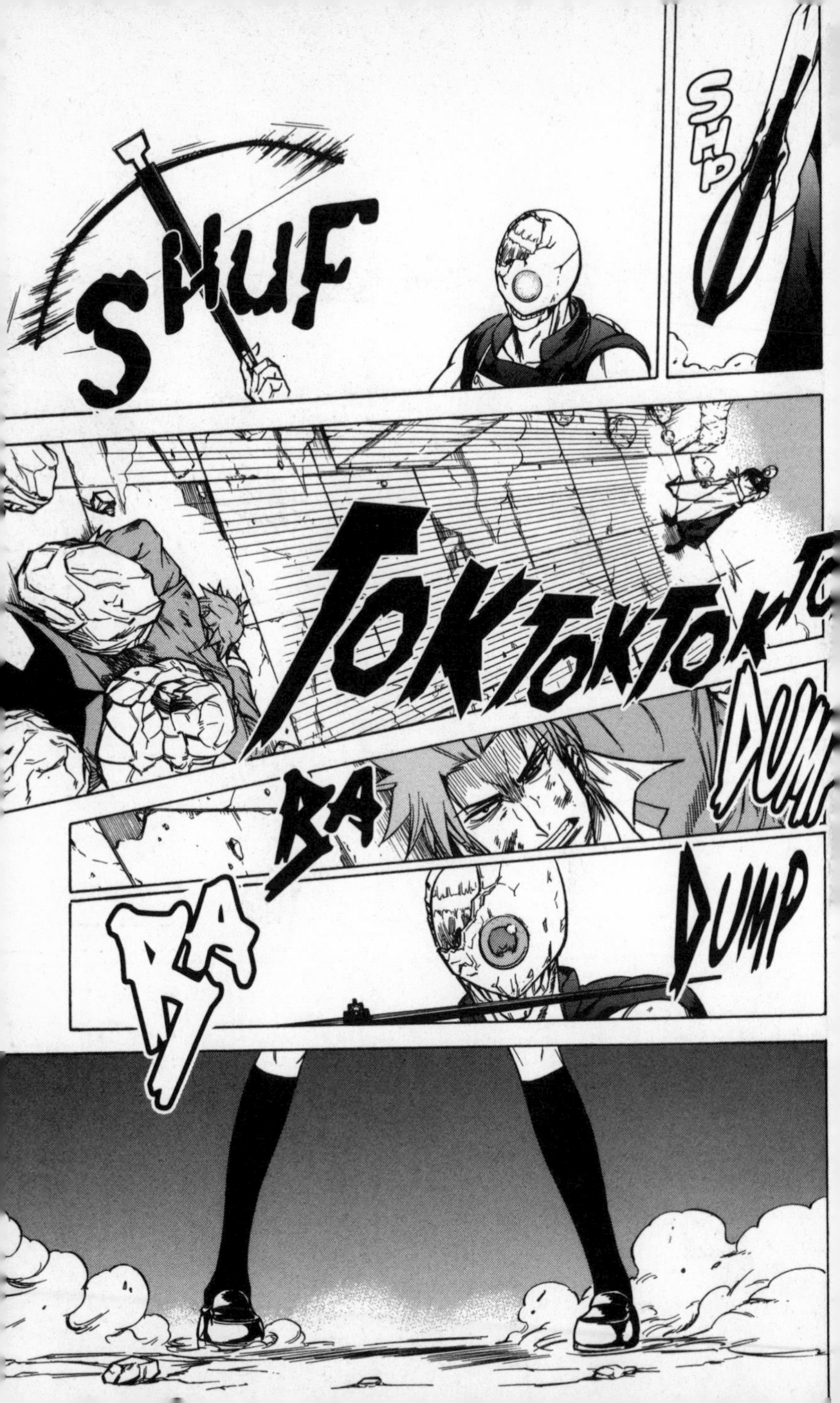
SHP
SHUF
TOKTOKTOKTO
DUM
BA
DUMP
BA

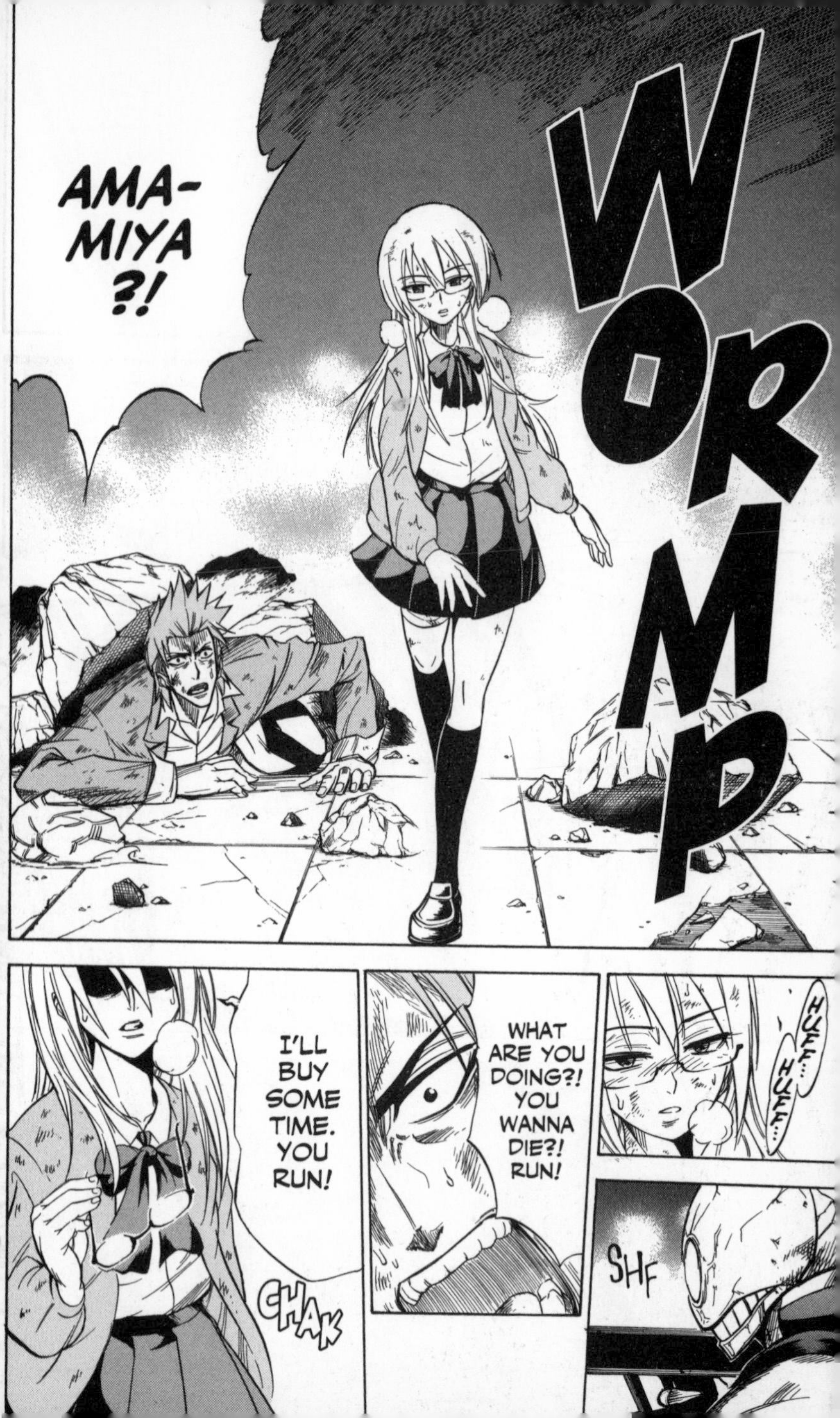
WOMP
AMA-MIYA?!
HUFF... HUFF...
SHF
WHAT ARE YOU DOING?! YOU WANNA DIE?! RUN!
I'LL BUY SOME TIME. YOU RUN!
CHAK

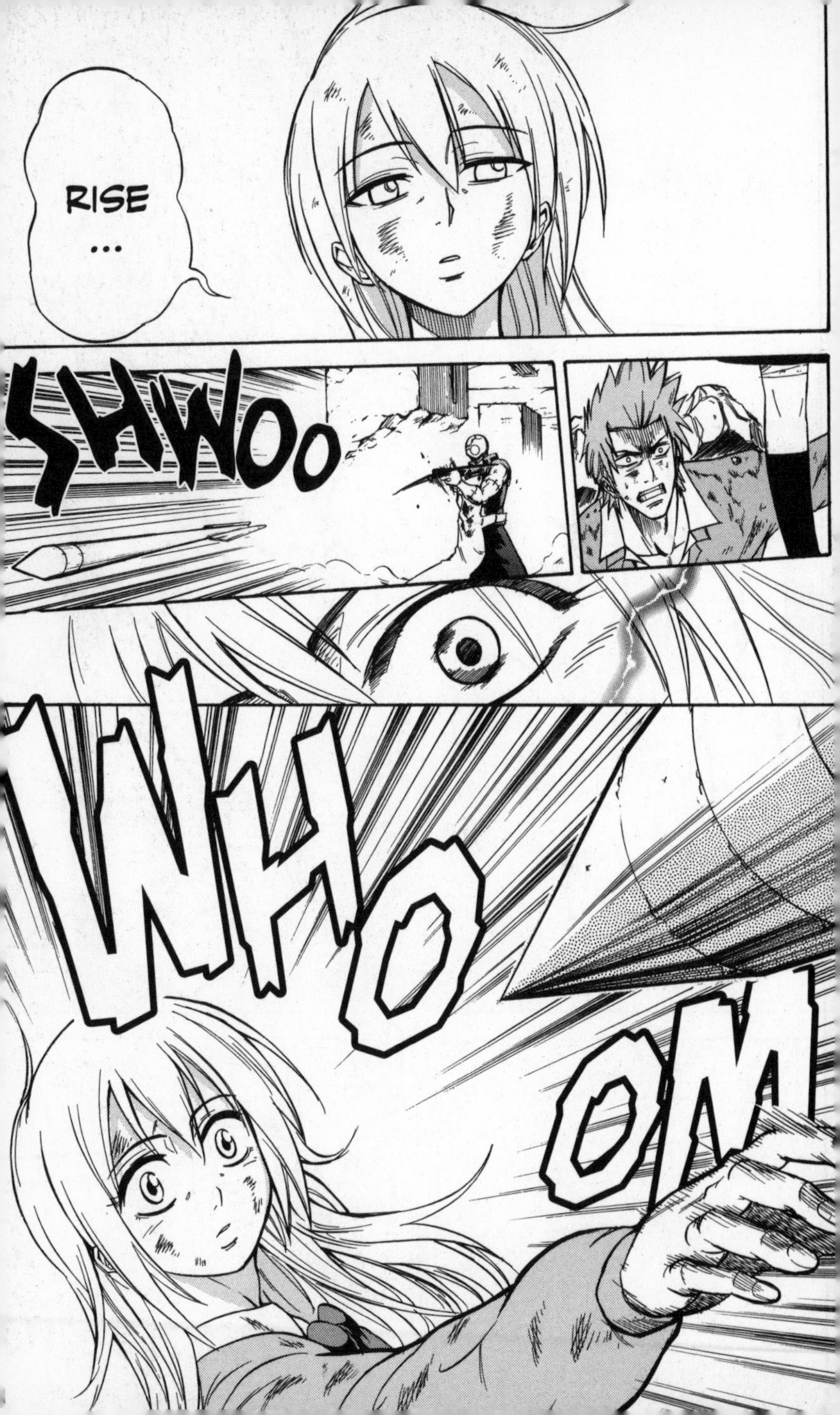
RISE
...
SHWOO
WHOOM

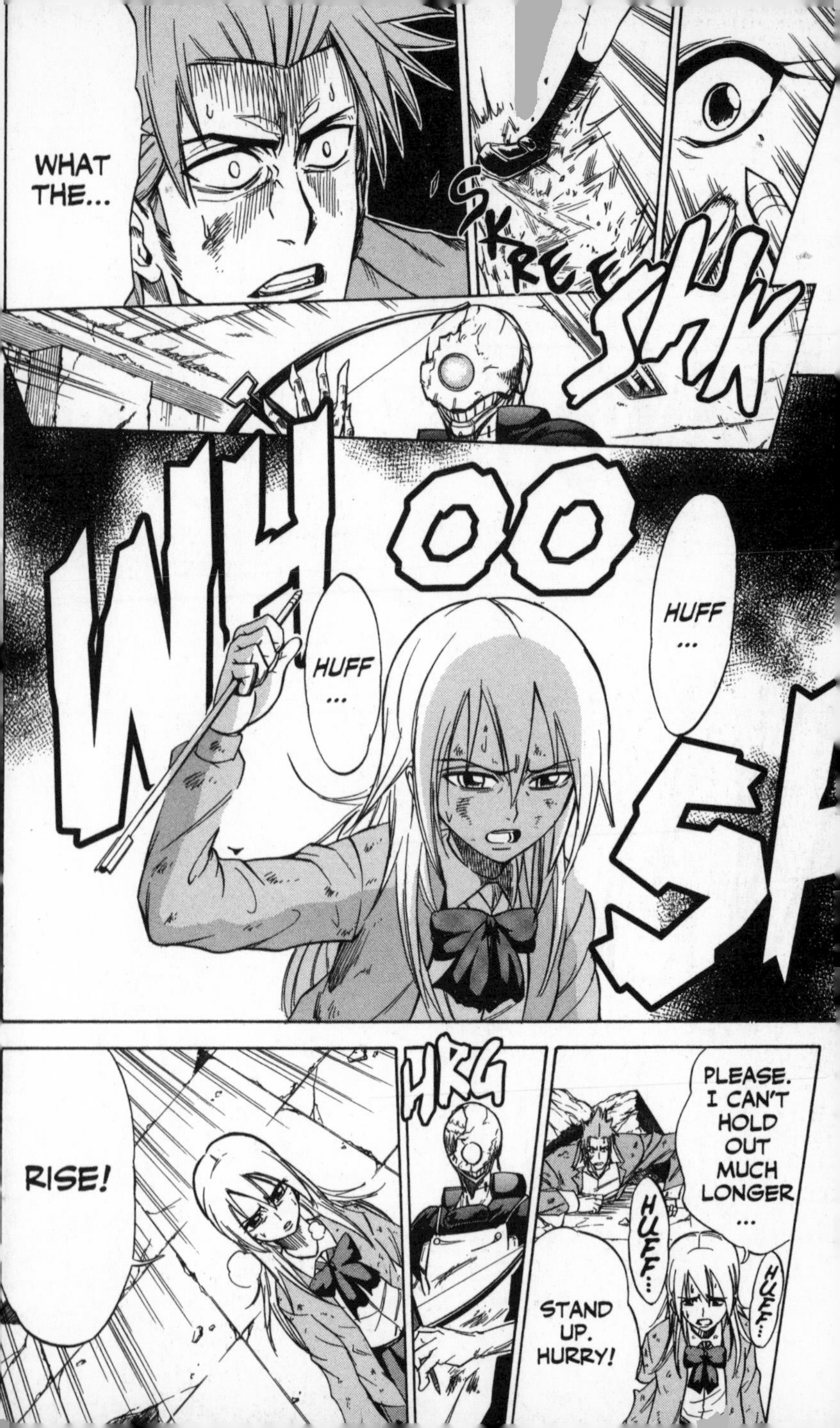
SKREEEEEEEEEEEEEEEEEEEEEEEEEEE SHK
WHAT THE...
WHOOSH
HUFF ...
HUFF ...
PLEASE. I CAN'T HOLD OUT MUCH LONGER ...
HUFF...
HUFF...
STAND UP. HURRY!
HRG
RISE!

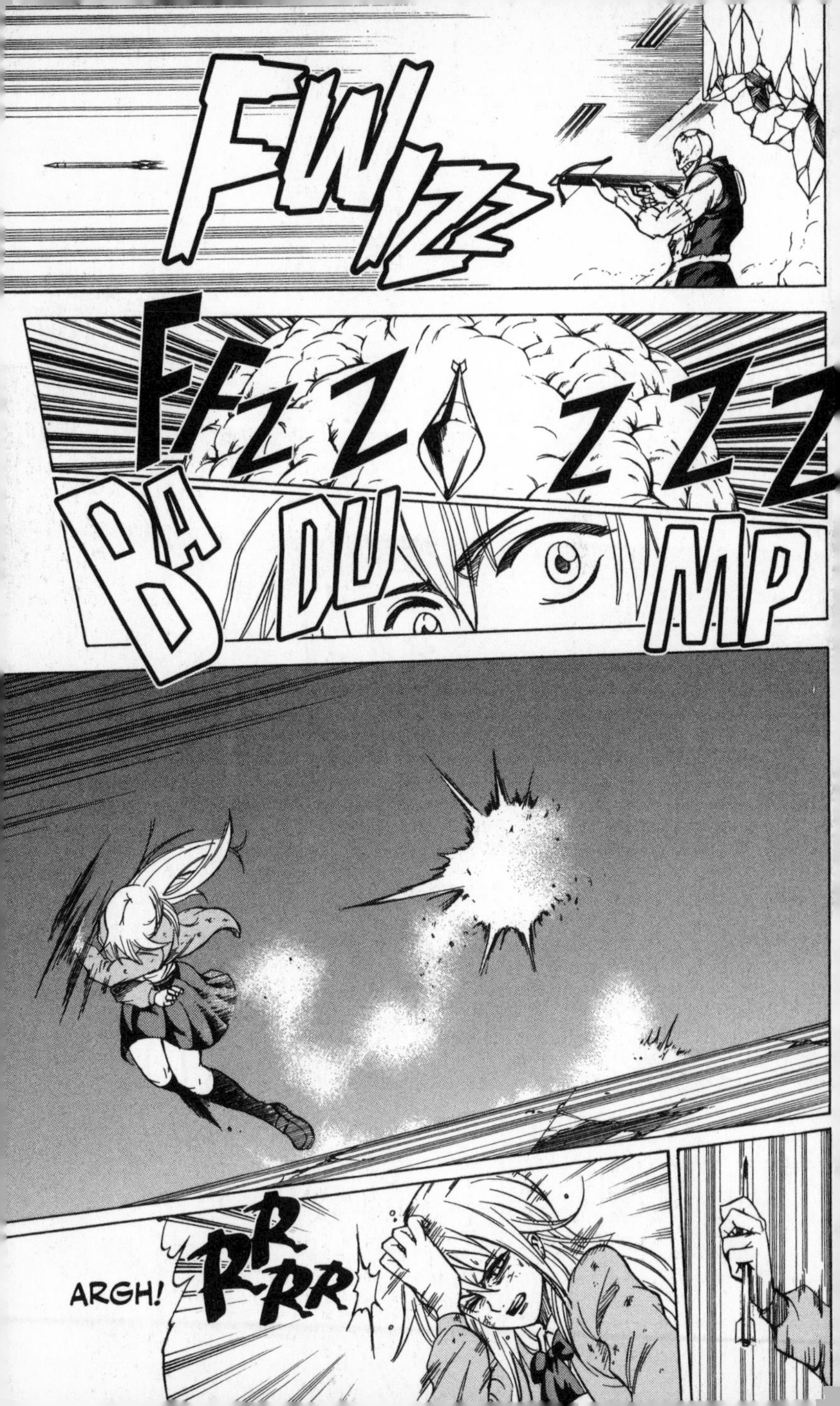
FWIZZ
FFZZZZZZ
BADUMP
RRRRR
ARGH!

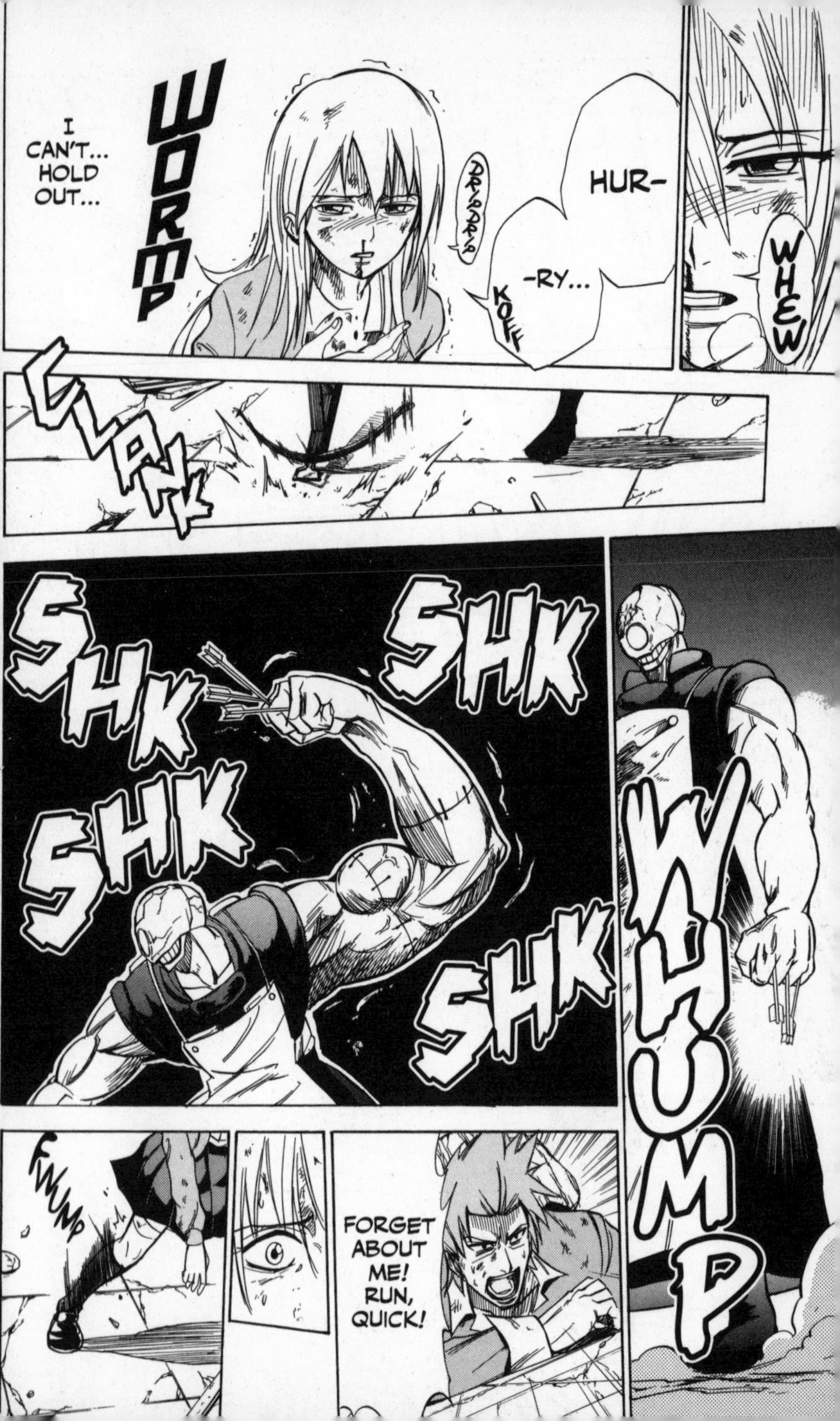
WHEW
HUR-
-RY...
KOFF
DRIPDRIP
WORMP
I CAN'T... HOLD OUT...
CLANK
WHUMP
SHK
SHK
SHK
SHK
FORGET ABOUT ME! RUN, QUICK!
FWUMP

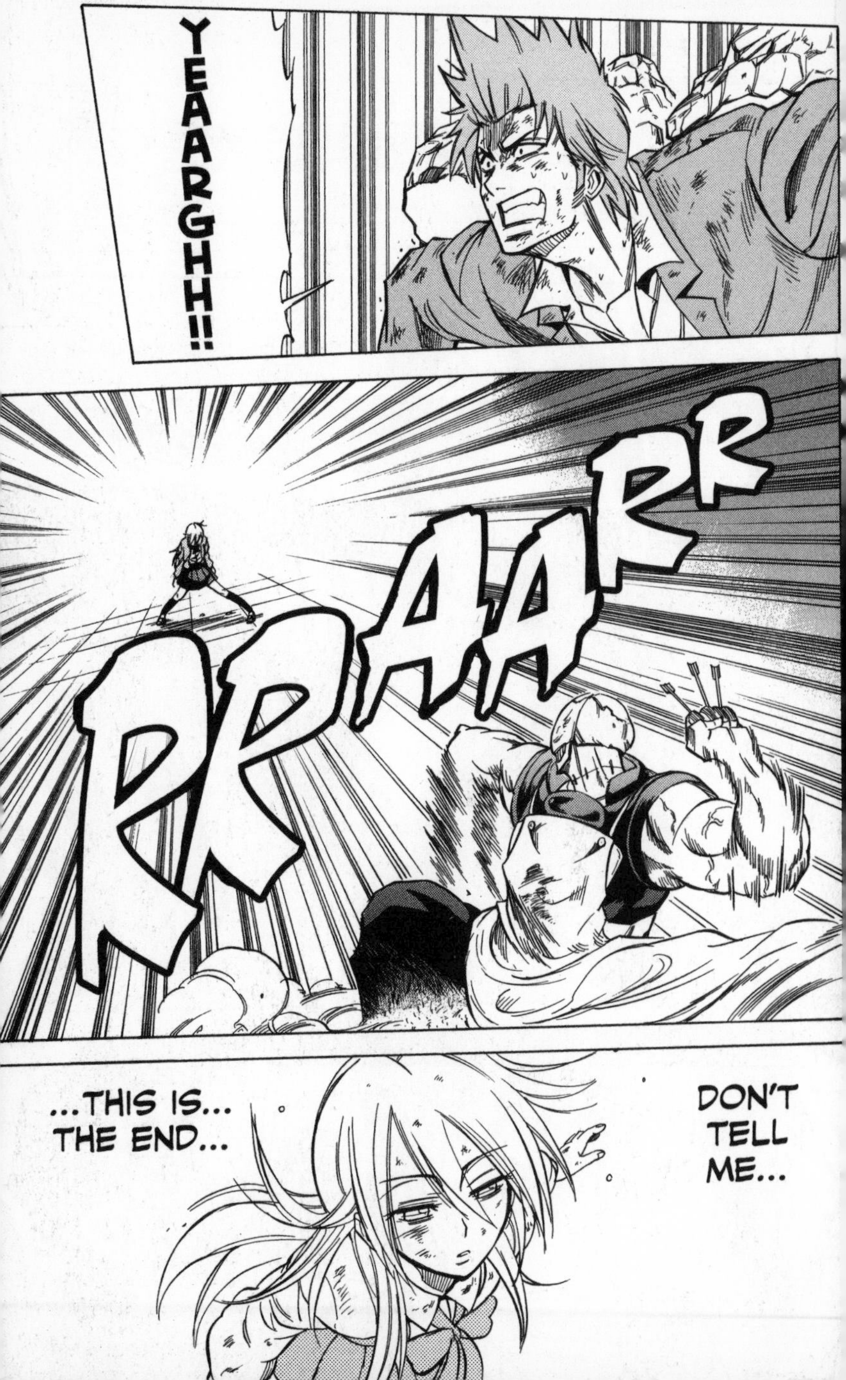
YEAARGHH!!
RRAARR
DON'T TELL ME...
...THIS IS... THE END...

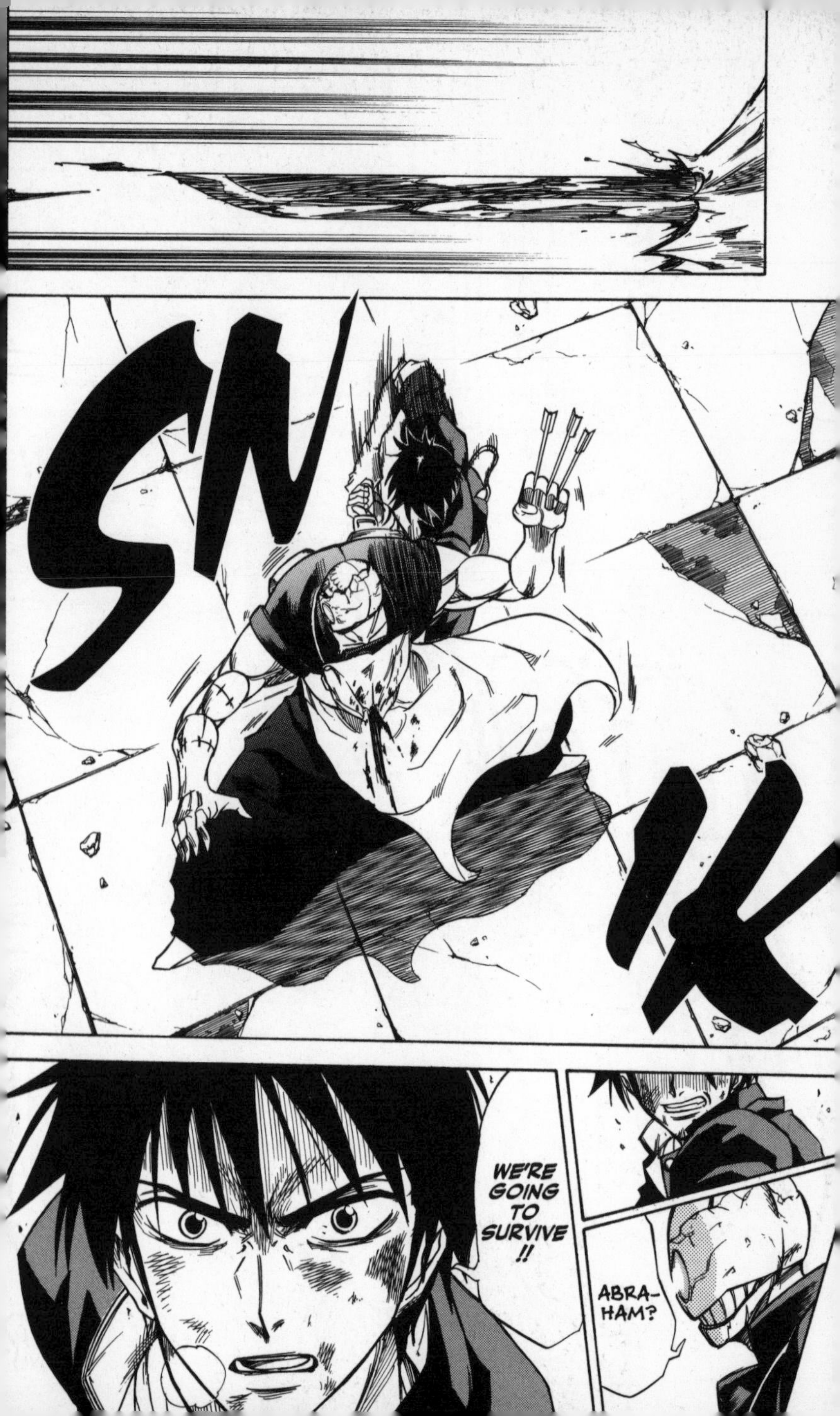
SNIK
WE'RE GOING TO SURVIVE !!
ABRA-HAM?

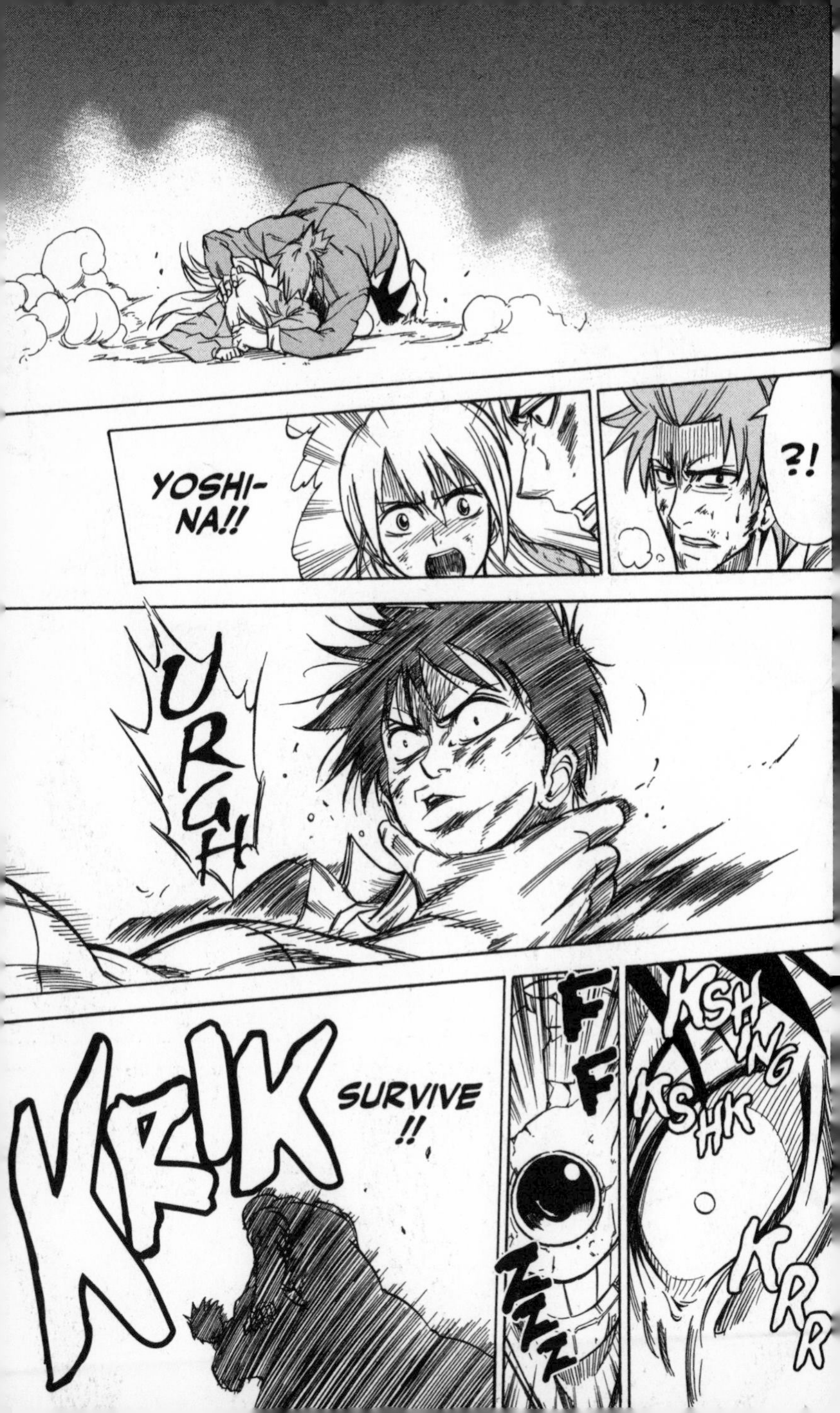
?!
YOSHI-
NA!!
URGH
FFF
KSHING
KSHK
KRR
ZZZ
SURVIVE
!!
KRIK

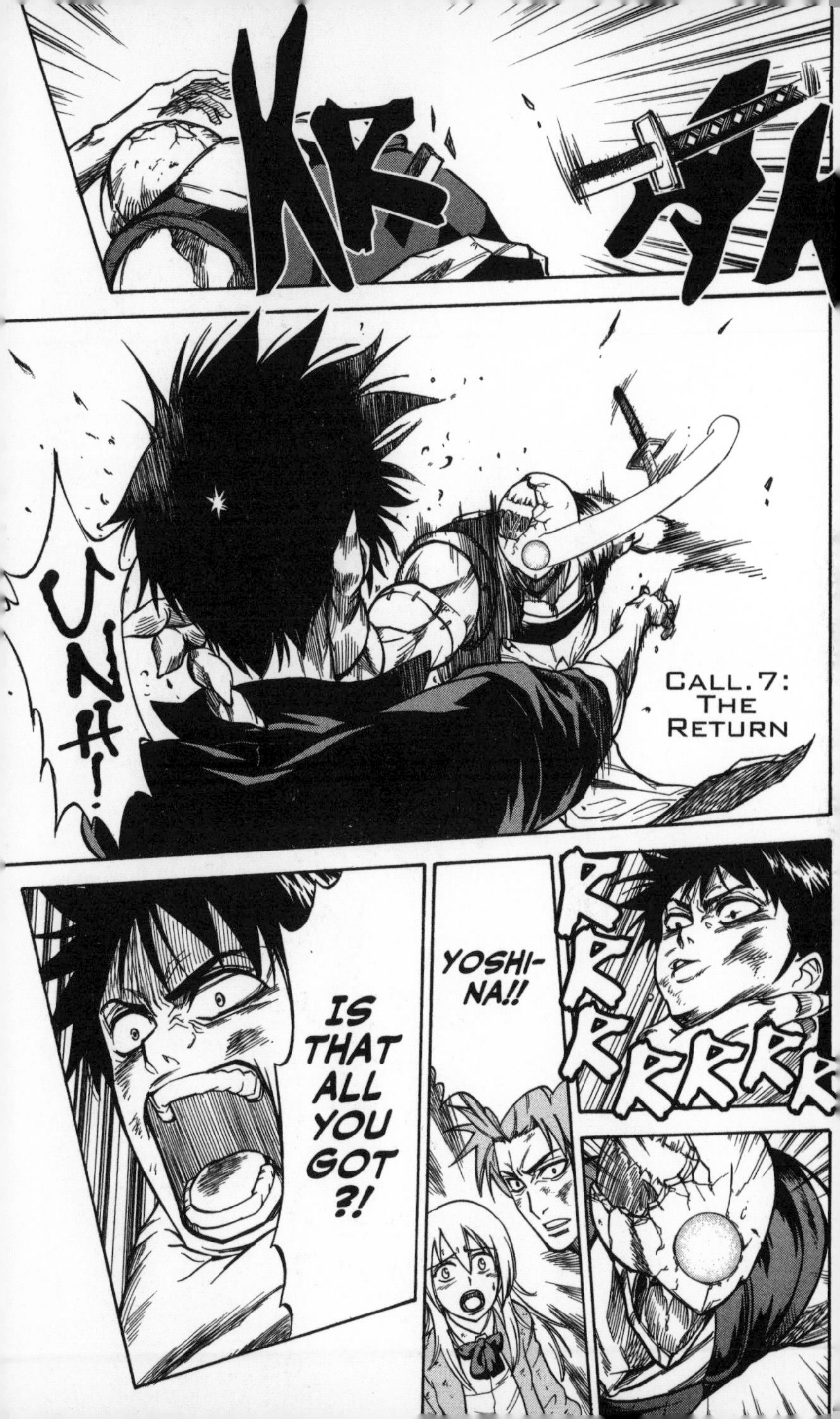

UNH!
Call. 7: The Return
YOSHI-NA!!
IS THAT ALL YOU GOT?!

# CALL. 7: THE RETURN

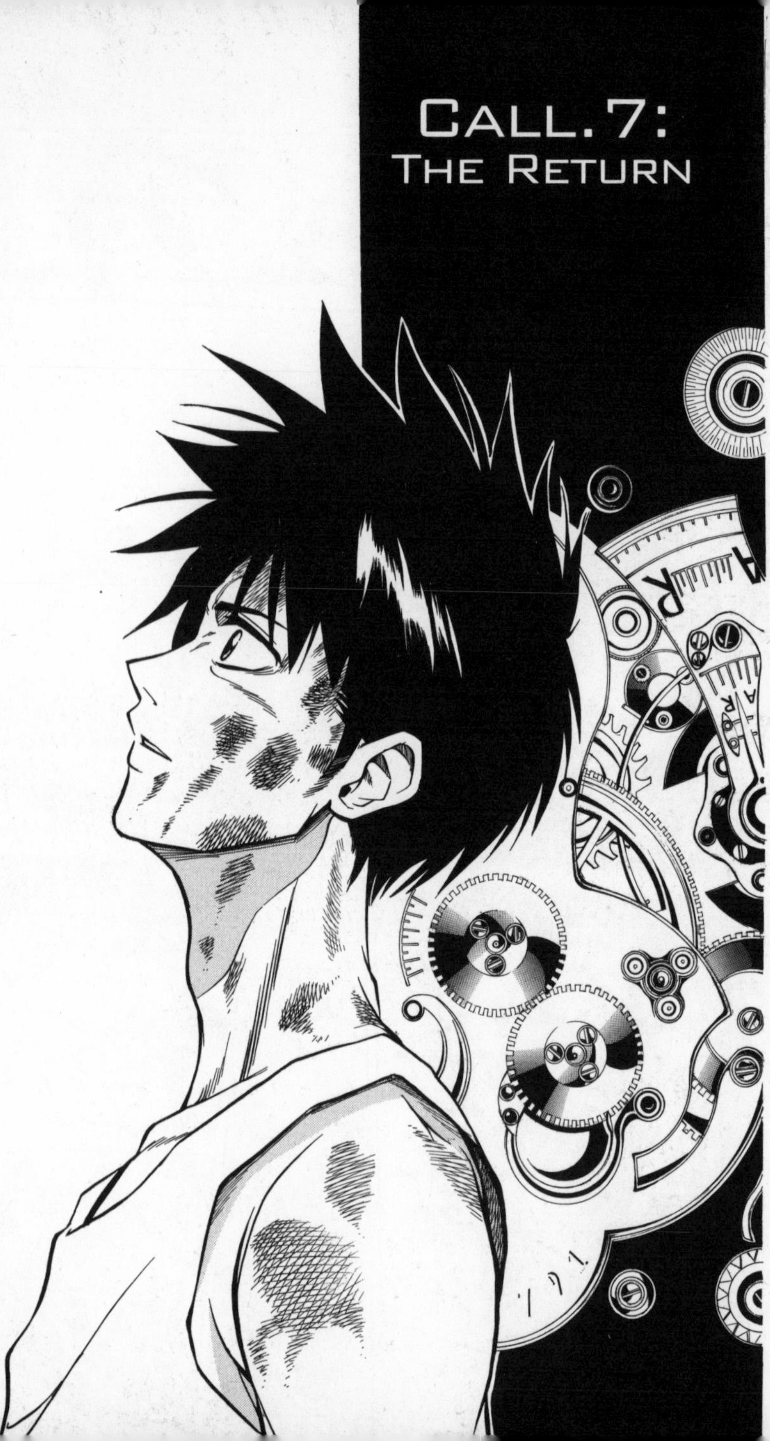

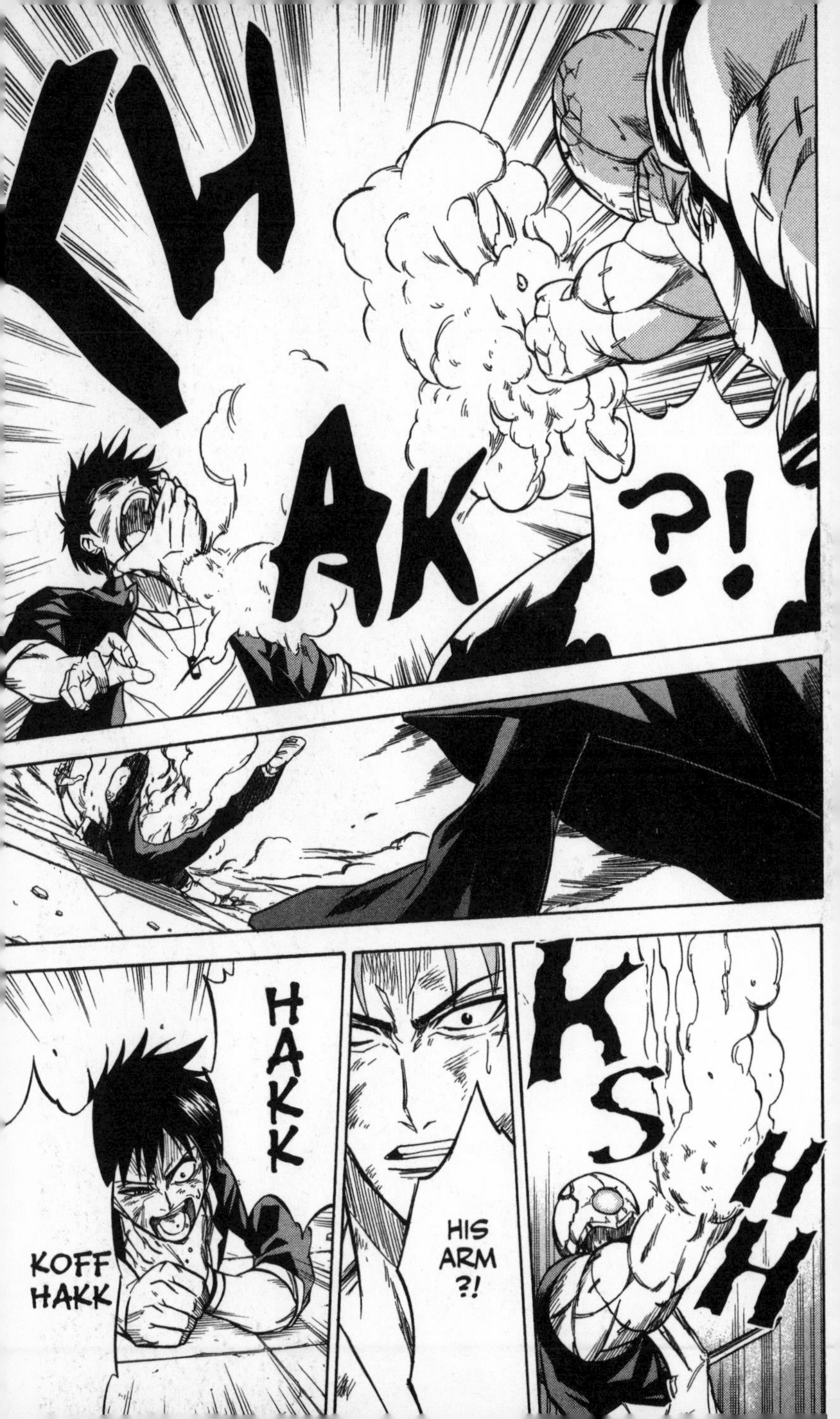
?!
WHAK
KSHH
HIS ARM ?!
HAKK
KOFF HAKK

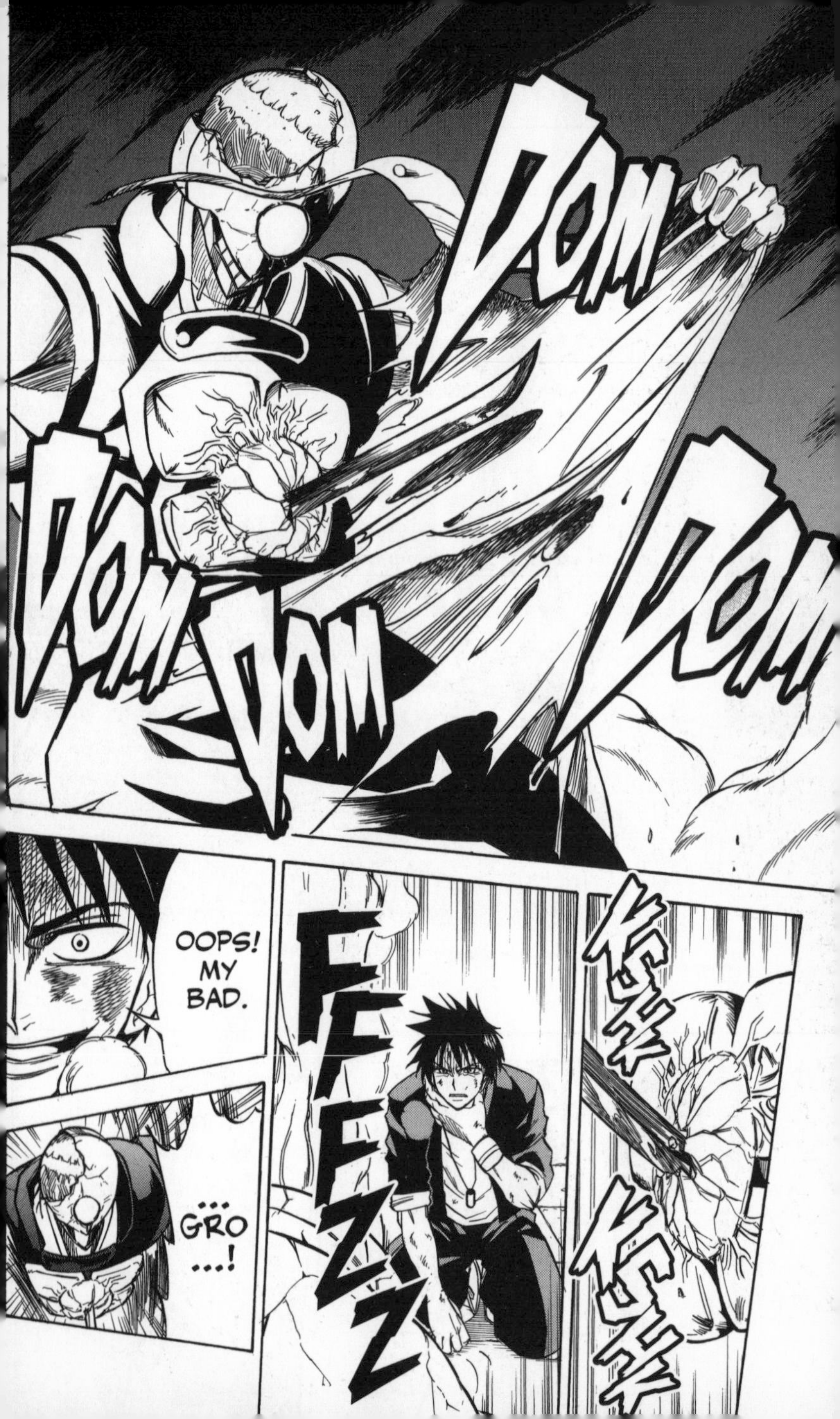
DOM
DOM
DOM
DOM
KSHK KSHK
FFEZZ
OOPS! MY BAD.
... GRO ...!

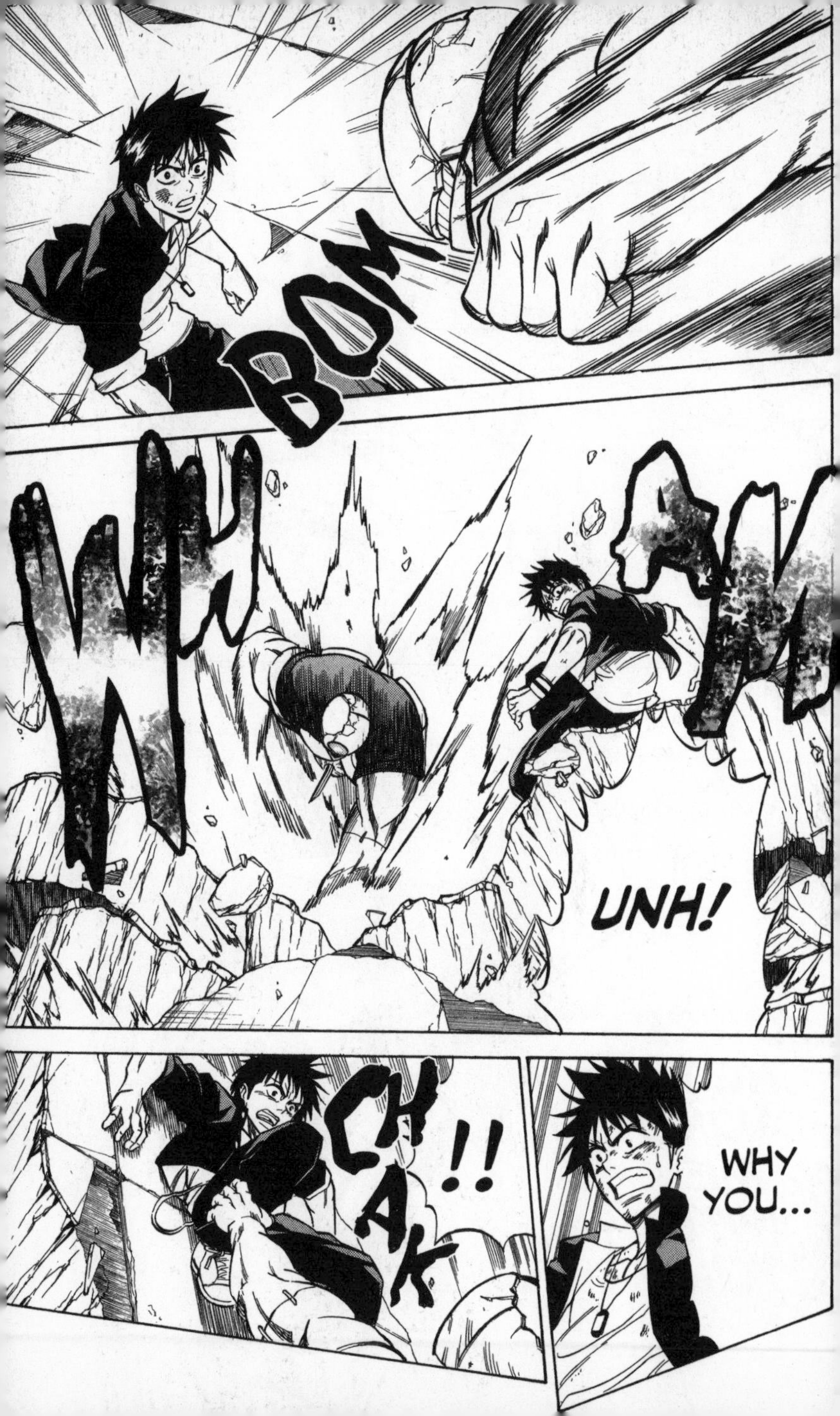
BOOM
WHAM
UNH!
WHY YOU...
CHAK!!

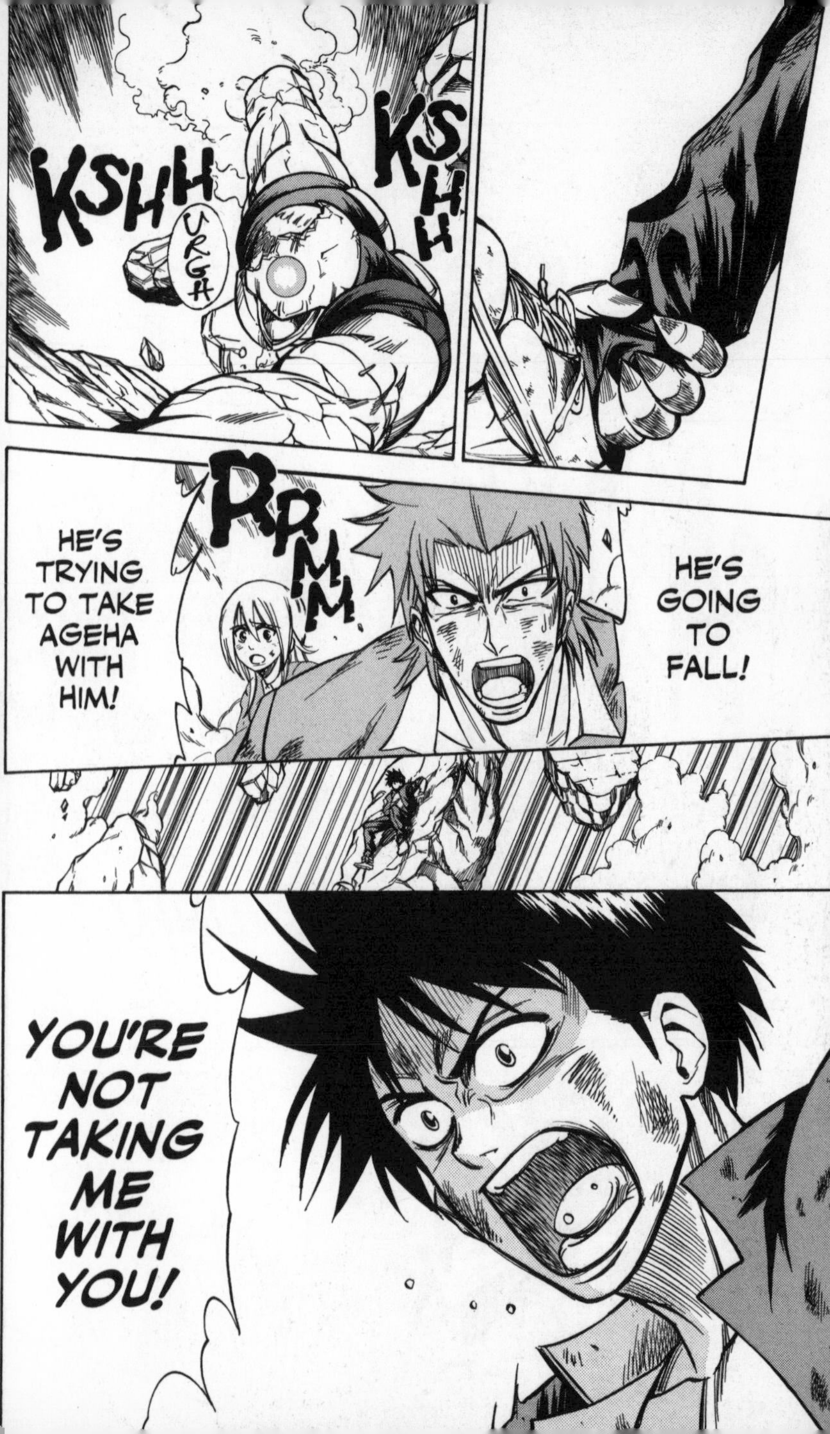
KSHH
KSHH
URGH
RRMM
HE'S GOING TO FALL!
HE'S TRYING TO TAKE AGEHA WITH HIM!
YOU'RE NOT TAKING ME WITH YOU!

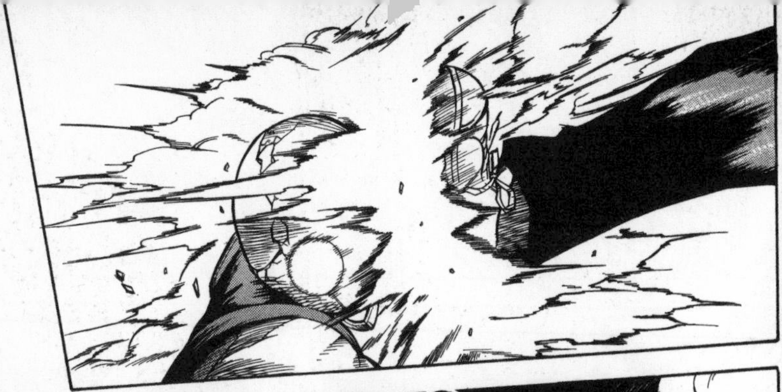

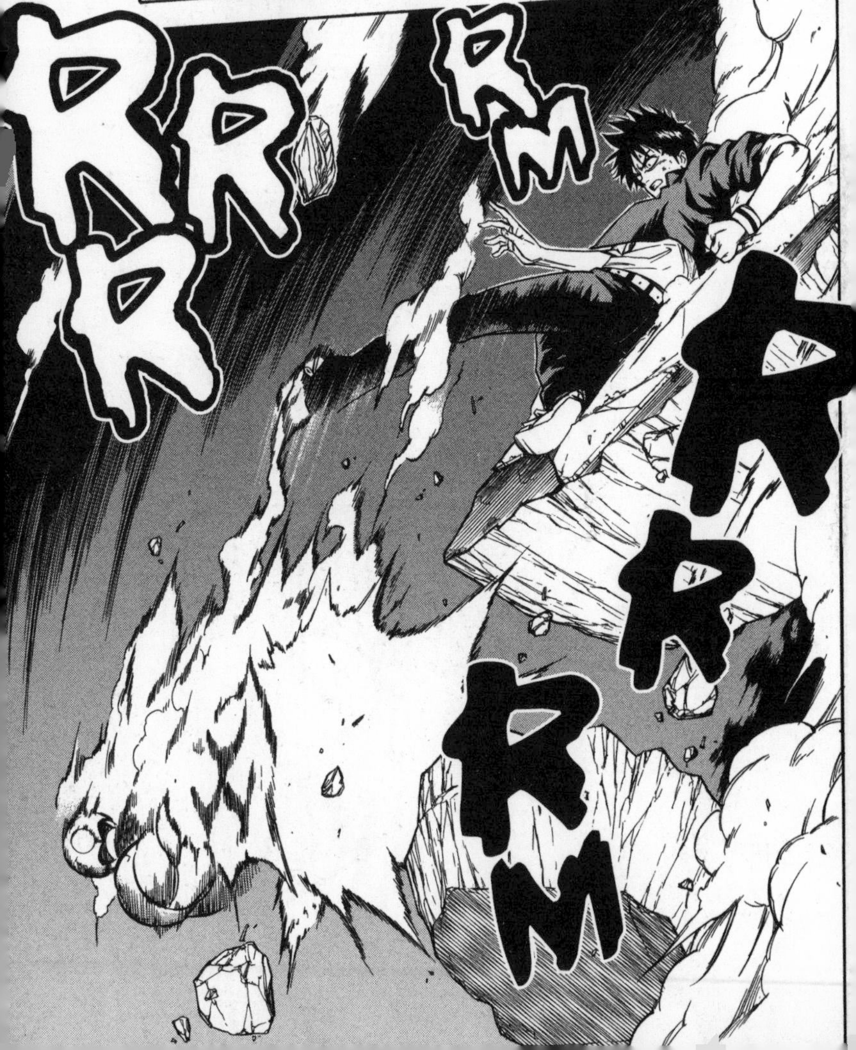
RM
RRR
RRRRM

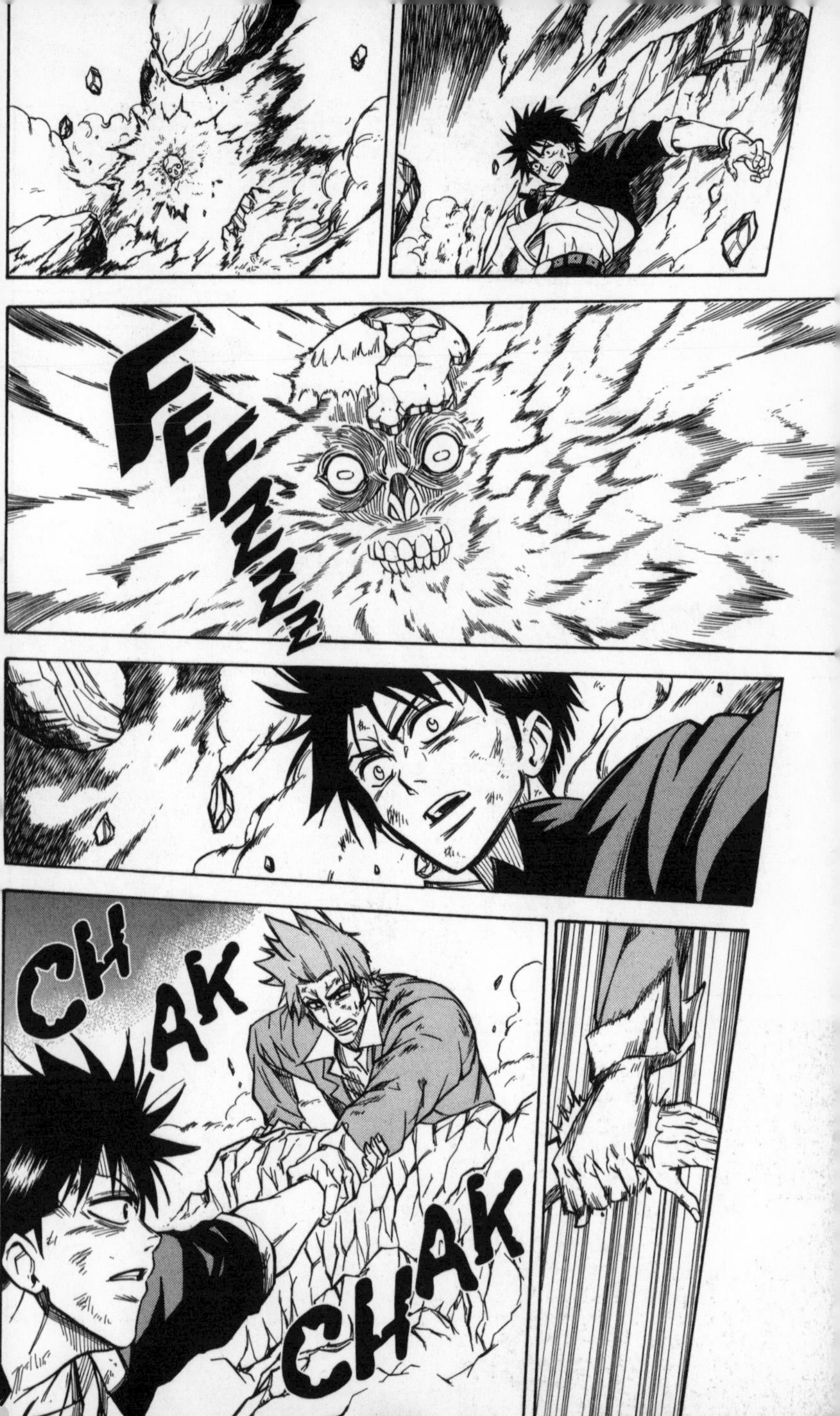
FFFZZZZZZ
CHAK
CHAK

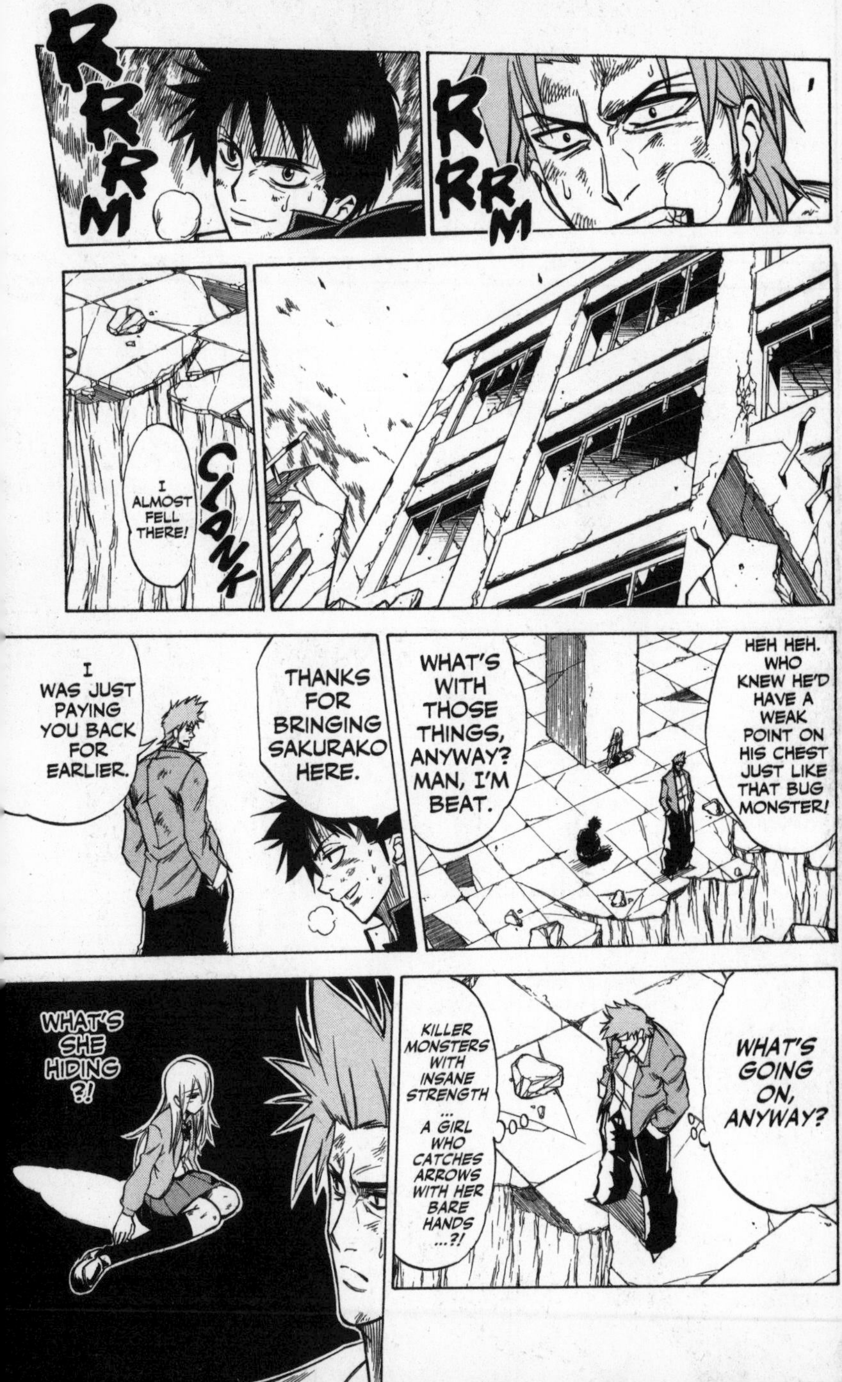
RRRM
RRRM
CLANK
I ALMOST FELL THERE!
HEH HEH. WHO KNEW HE'D HAVE A WEAK POINT ON HIS CHEST JUST LIKE THAT BUG MONSTER!
WHAT'S WITH THOSE THINGS, ANYWAY? MAN, I'M BEAT.
THANKS FOR BRINGING SAKURAKO HERE.
I WAS JUST PAYING YOU BACK FOR EARLIER.
WHAT'S GOING ON, ANYWAY?
KILLER MONSTERS WITH INSANE STRENGTH ... A GIRL WHO CATCHES ARROWS WITH HER BARE HANDS ...?!
WHAT'S SHE HIDING ?!

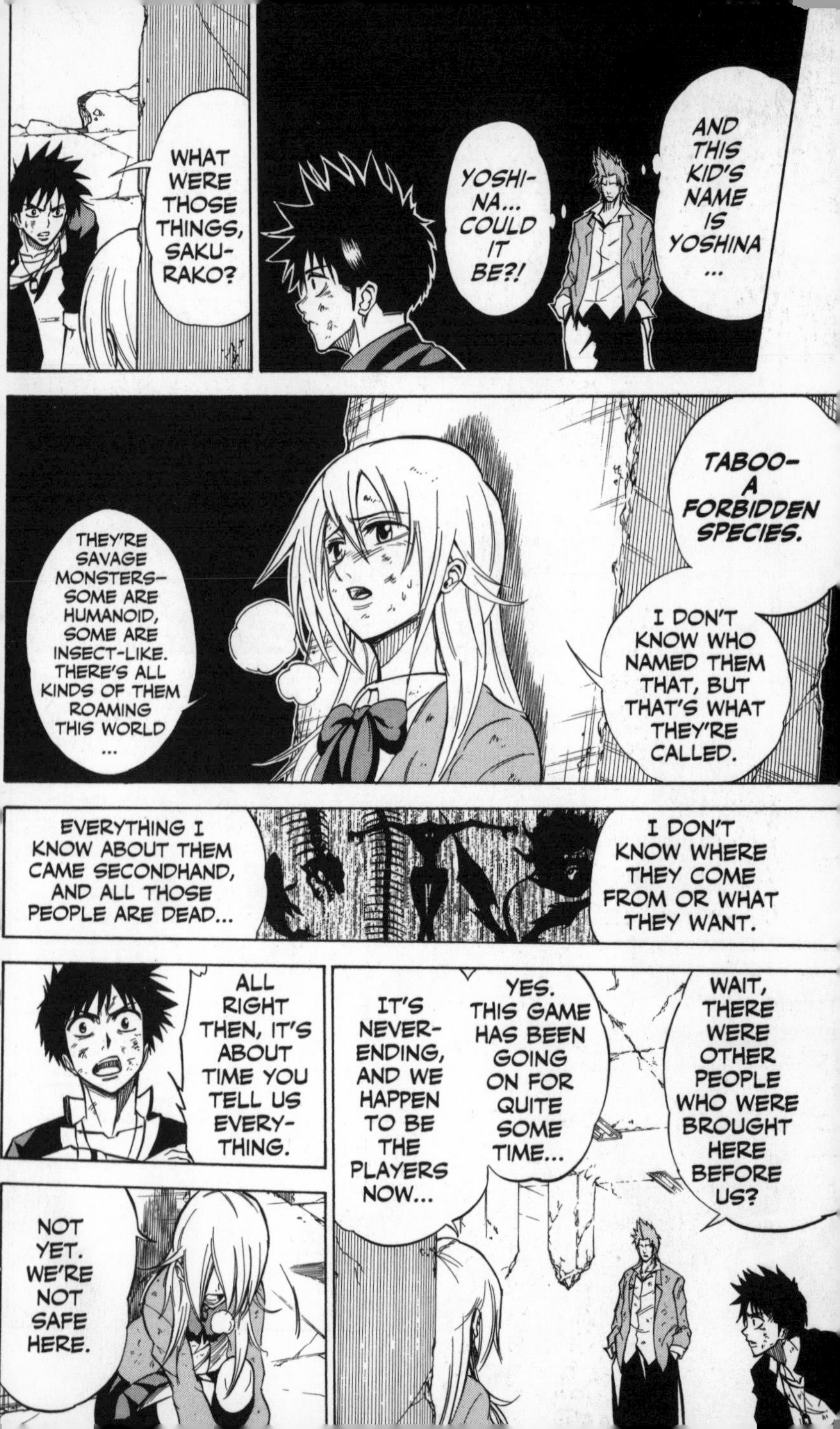
AND THIS KID'S NAME IS YOSHINA ...
YOSHI-NA... COULD IT BE?!
WHAT WERE THOSE THINGS, SAKU-RAKO?
TABOO— A FORBIDDEN SPECIES.
I DON'T KNOW WHO NAMED THEM THAT, BUT THAT'S WHAT THEY'RE CALLED.
THEY'RE SAVAGE MONSTERS— SOME ARE HUMANOID, SOME ARE INSECT-LIKE. THERE'S ALL KINDS OF THEM ROAMING THIS WORLD ...
I DON'T KNOW WHERE THEY COME FROM OR WHAT THEY WANT.
EVERYTHING I KNOW ABOUT THEM CAME SECONDHAND, AND ALL THOSE PEOPLE ARE DEAD...
WAIT, THERE WERE OTHER PEOPLE WHO WERE BROUGHT HERE BEFORE US?
YES. THIS GAME HAS BEEN GOING ON FOR QUITE SOME TIME...
IT'S NEVER-ENDING, AND WE HAPPEN TO BE THE PLAYERS NOW...
ALL RIGHT THEN, IT'S ABOUT TIME YOU TELL US EVERY-THING.
NOT YET. WE'RE NOT SAFE HERE.

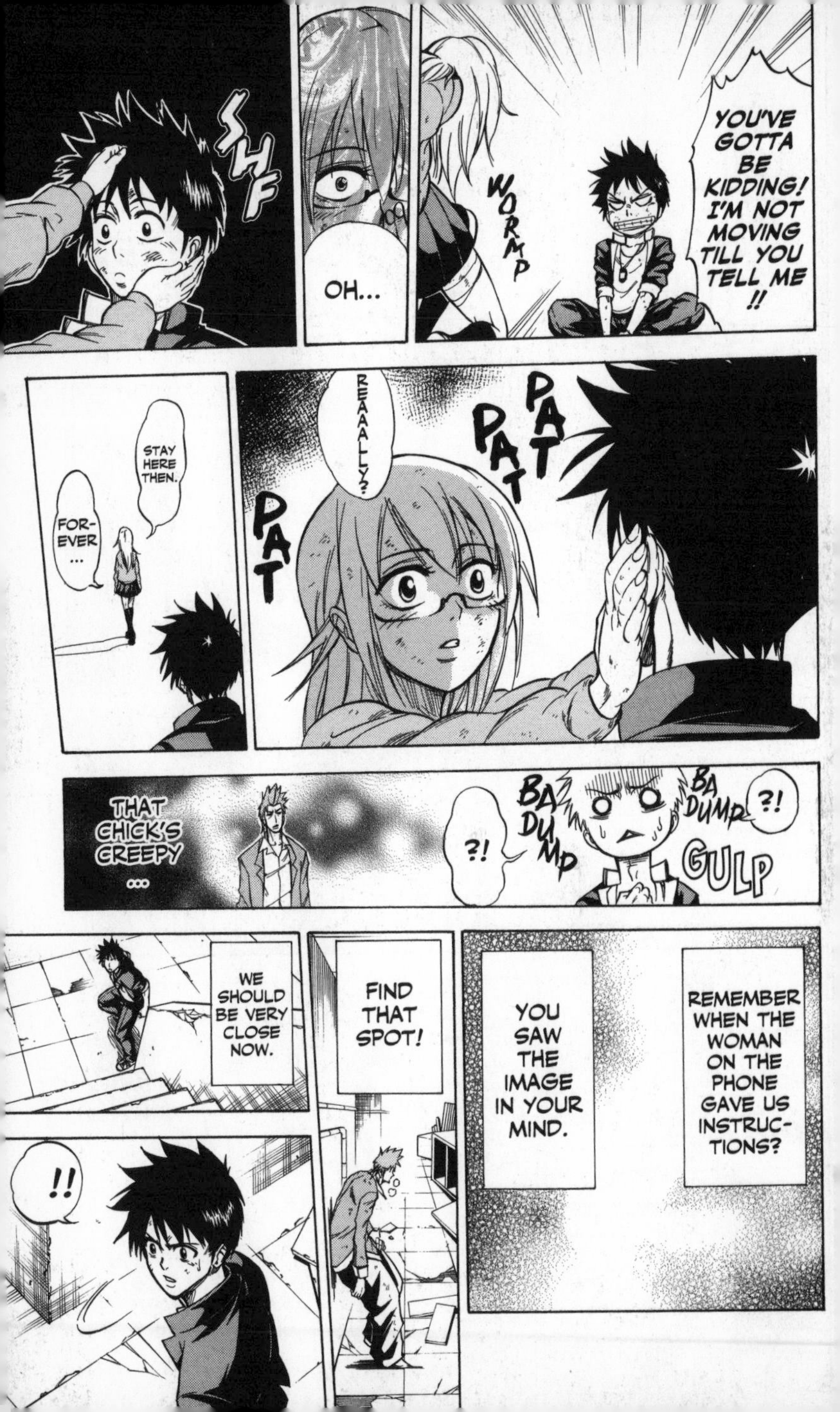
YOU'VE GOTTA BE KIDDING! I'M NOT MOVING TILL YOU TELL ME!!
WORMP
OH...
SHF
PAT PAT
PAT
REAAALLY?
STAY HERE THEN.
FOR-EVER...
?!
BA DUMP
GULP
BA DUMP
?!
THAT CHICK'S CREEPY...
REMEMBER WHEN THE WOMAN ON THE PHONE GAVE US INSTRUC-TIONS?
YOU SAW THE IMAGE IN YOUR MIND.
FIND THAT SPOT!
WE SHOULD BE VERY CLOSE NOW.
!!

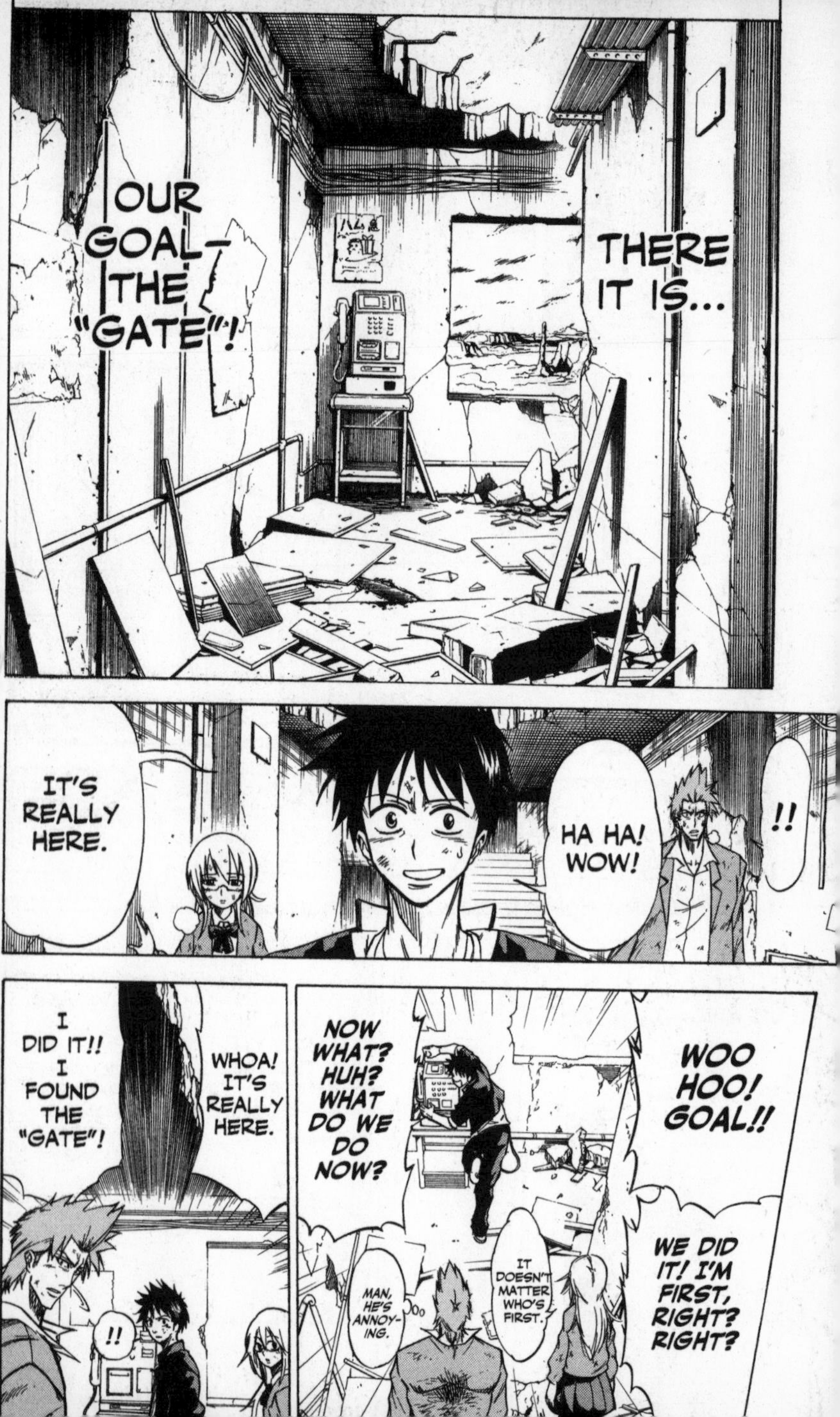
THERE IT IS...
OUR GOAL— THE "GATE"!
!!
HA HA! WOW!
IT'S REALLY HERE.
WOO HOO! GOAL!!
NOW WHAT? HUH? WHAT DO WE DO NOW?
WE DID IT! I'M FIRST, RIGHT? RIGHT?
IT DOESN'T MATTER WHO'S FIRST.
MAN, HE'S ANNOY-ING.
WHOA! IT'S REALLY HERE.
I DID IT!! I FOUND THE "GATE"!
!!

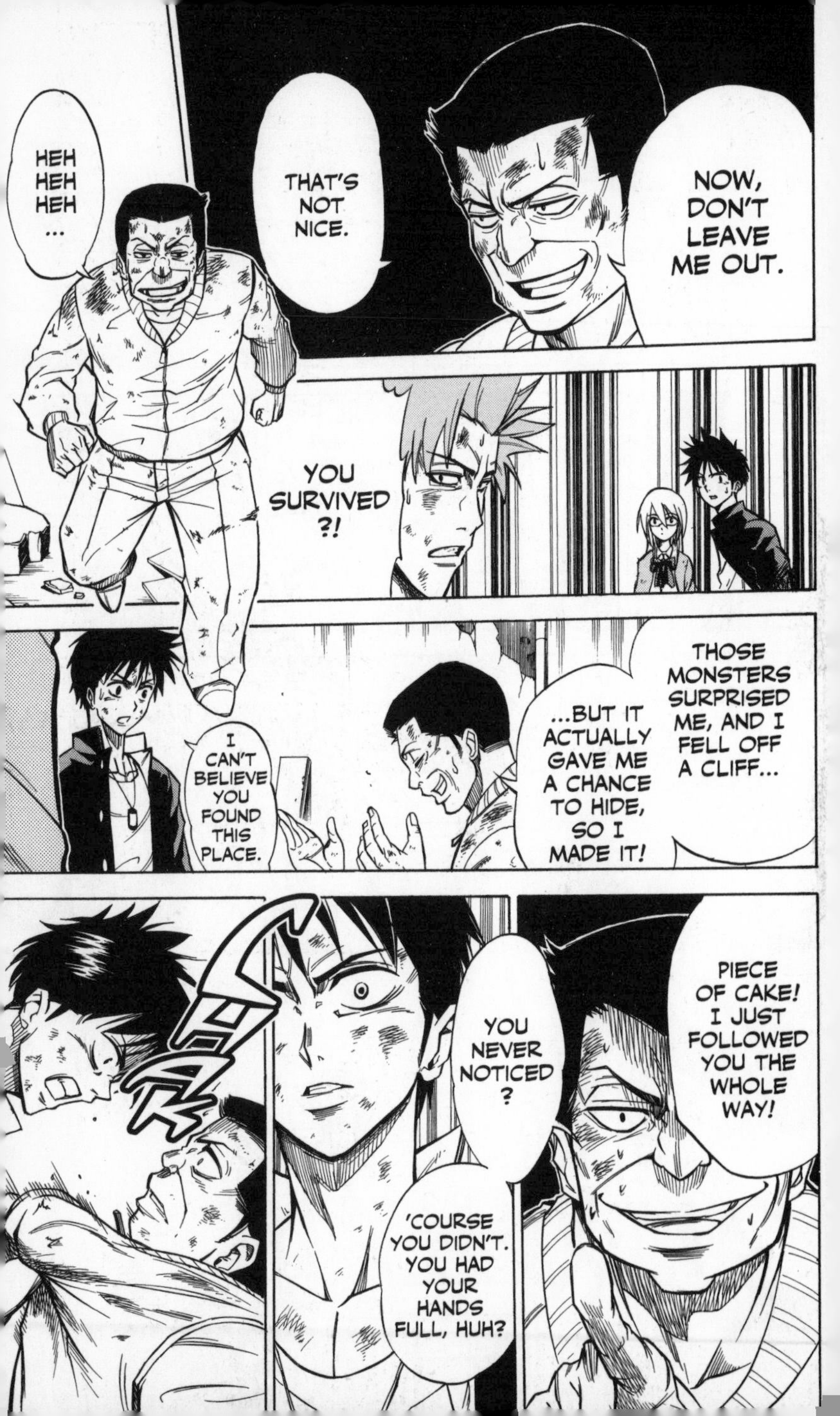
NOW, DON'T LEAVE ME OUT.
THAT'S NOT NICE.
HEH HEH HEH ...
YOU SURVIVED ?!
THOSE MONSTERS SURPRISED ME, AND I FELL OFF A CLIFF...
...BUT IT ACTUALLY GAVE ME A CHANCE TO HIDE, SO I MADE IT!
I CAN'T BELIEVE YOU FOUND THIS PLACE.
PIECE OF CAKE! I JUST FOLLOWED YOU THE WHOLE WAY!
YOU NEVER NOTICED ?
'COURSE YOU DIDN'T. YOU HAD YOUR HANDS FULL, HUH?

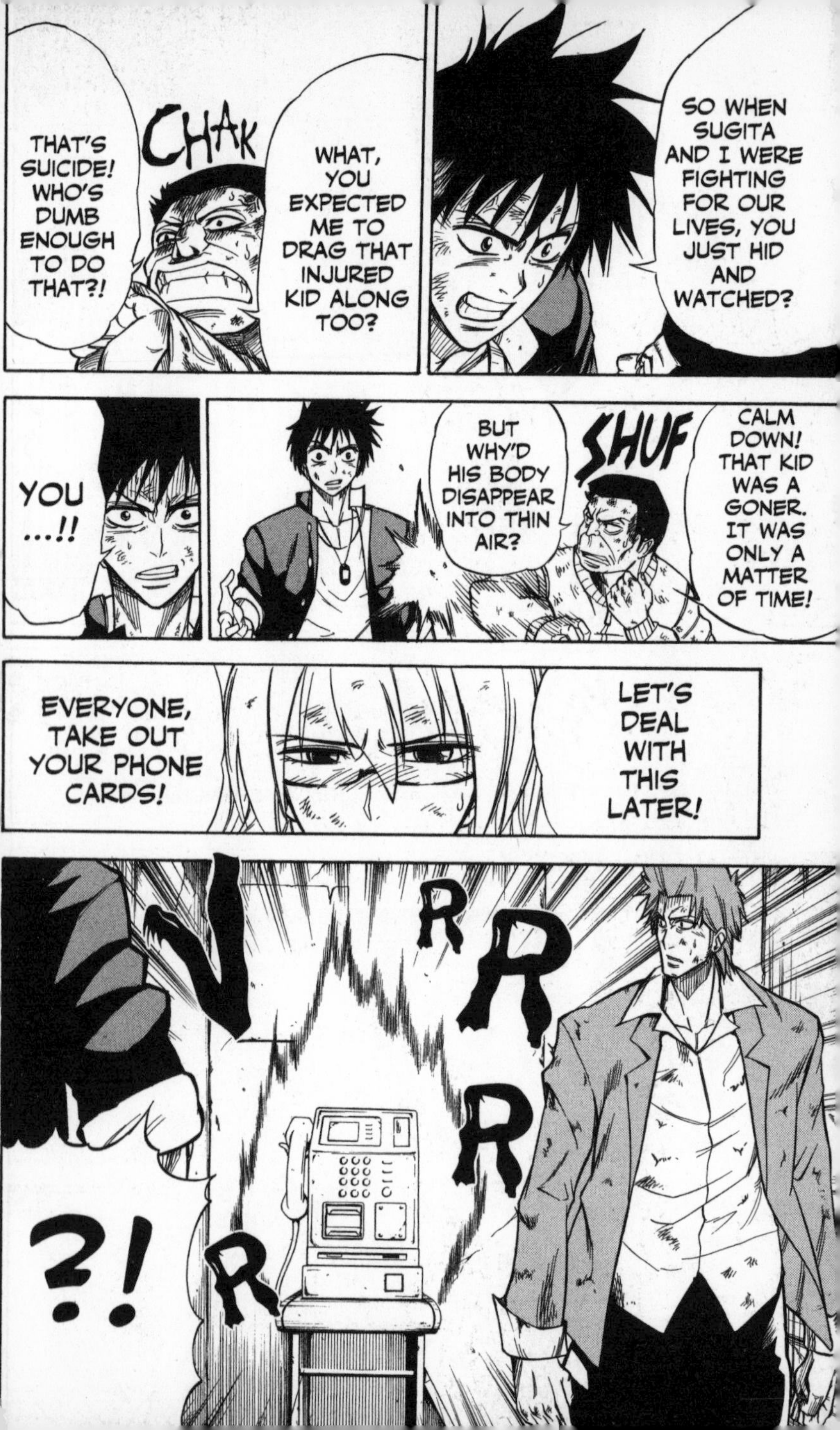
SO WHEN SUGITA AND I WERE FIGHTING FOR OUR LIVES, YOU JUST HID AND WATCHED?
WHAT, YOU EXPECTED ME TO DRAG THAT INJURED KID ALONG TOO?
CHAK
THAT'S SUICIDE! WHO'S DUMB ENOUGH TO DO THAT?!
CALM DOWN! THAT KID WAS A GONER. IT WAS ONLY A MATTER OF TIME!
SHUF
BUT WHY'D HIS BODY DISAPPEAR INTO THIN AIR?
YOU ...!!
LET'S DEAL WITH THIS LATER!
EVERYONE, TAKE OUT YOUR PHONE CARDS!
R
R
R
R
?!

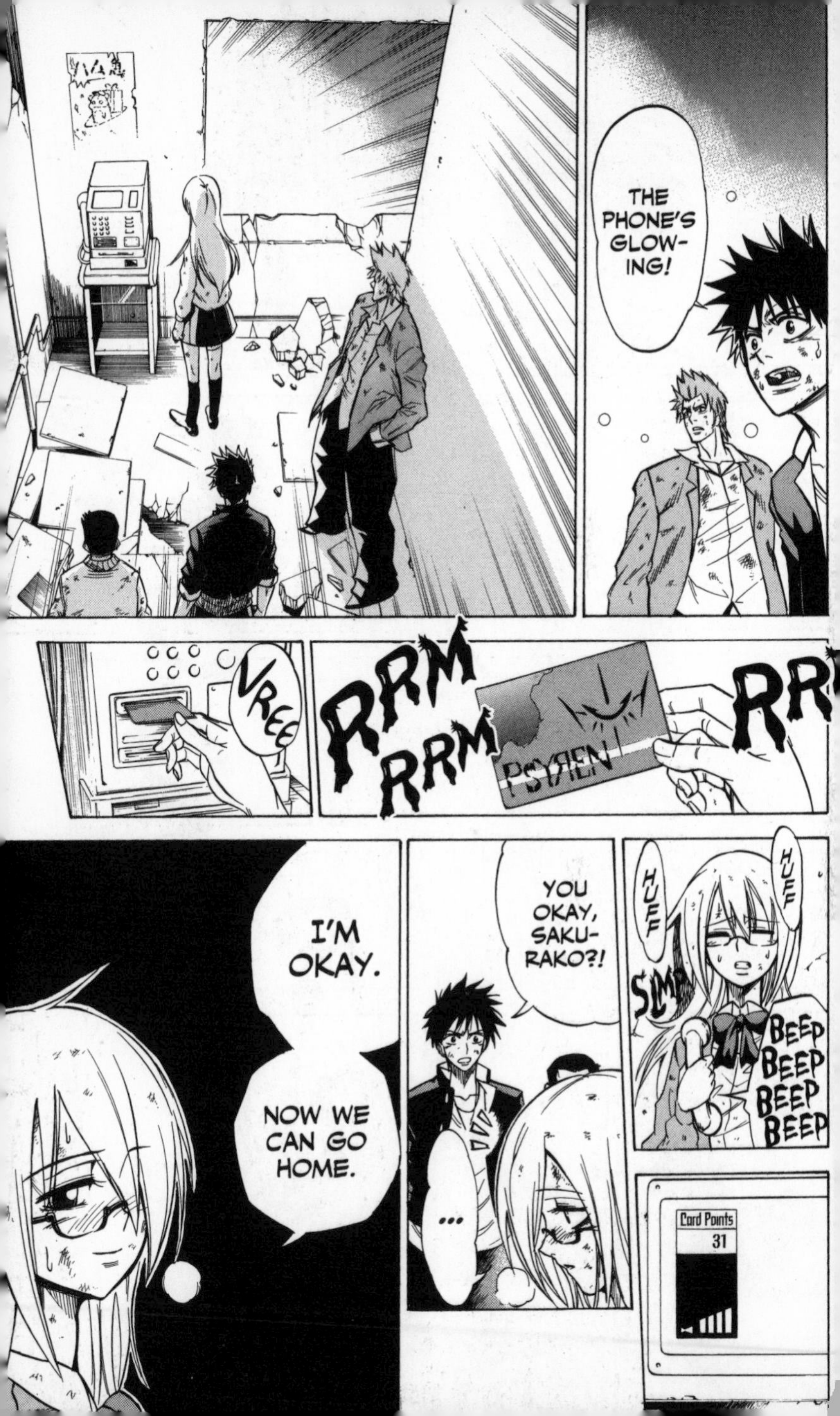

THE PHONE'S GLOW-ING!
RR
RRM RRM
PSYREN
VREE
HUFF
HUFF
SLMP
BEEP BEEP BEEP BEEP
Card Points
31
YOU OKAY, SAKU-RAKO?!
...
I'M OKAY.
NOW WE CAN GO HOME.

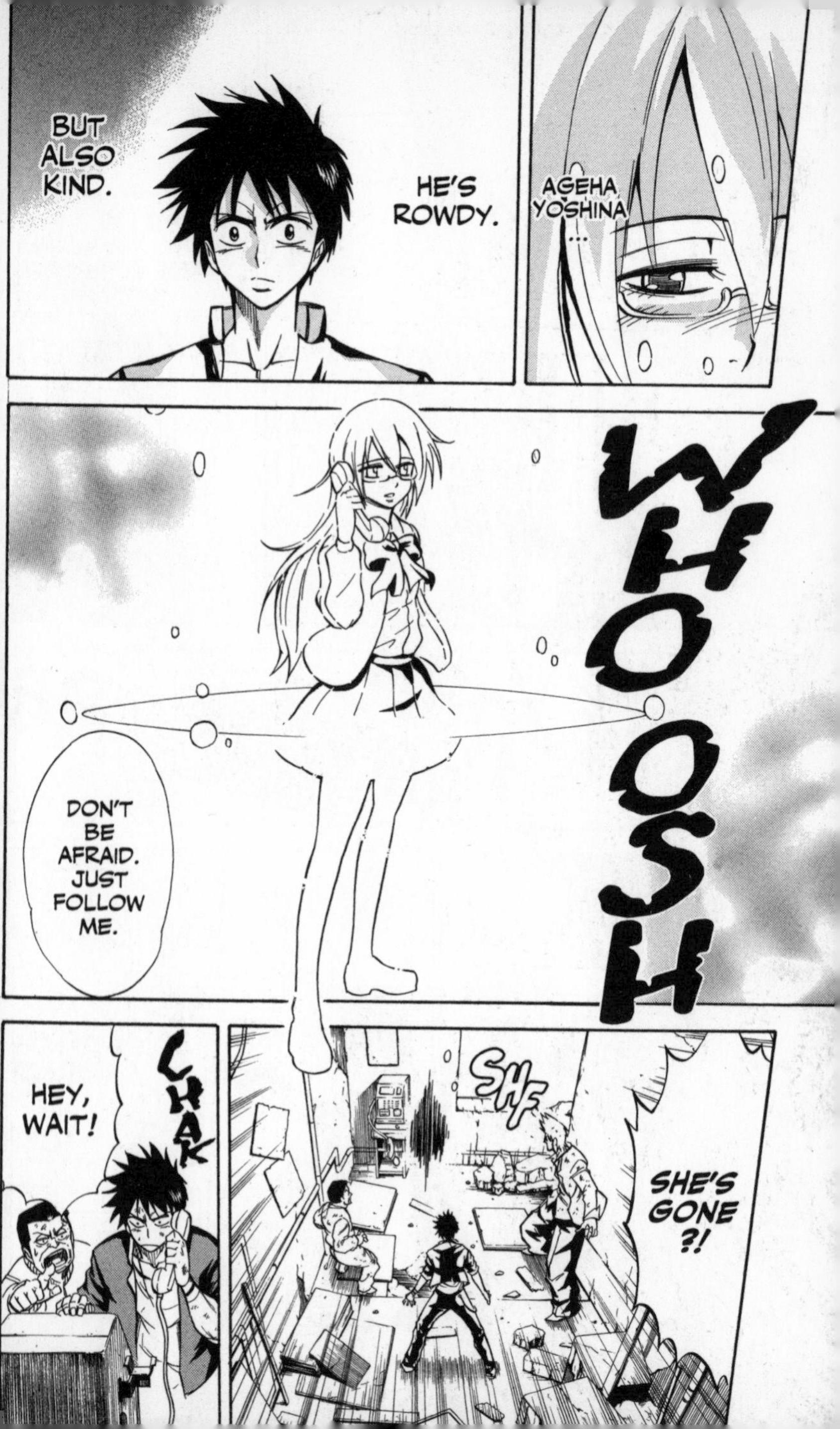
AGEHA YOSHINA ...
HE'S ROWDY.
BUT ALSO KIND.
WHOOSH
DON'T BE AFRAID. JUST FOLLOW ME.
SHF
SHE'S GONE ?!
CHAK
HEY, WAIT!

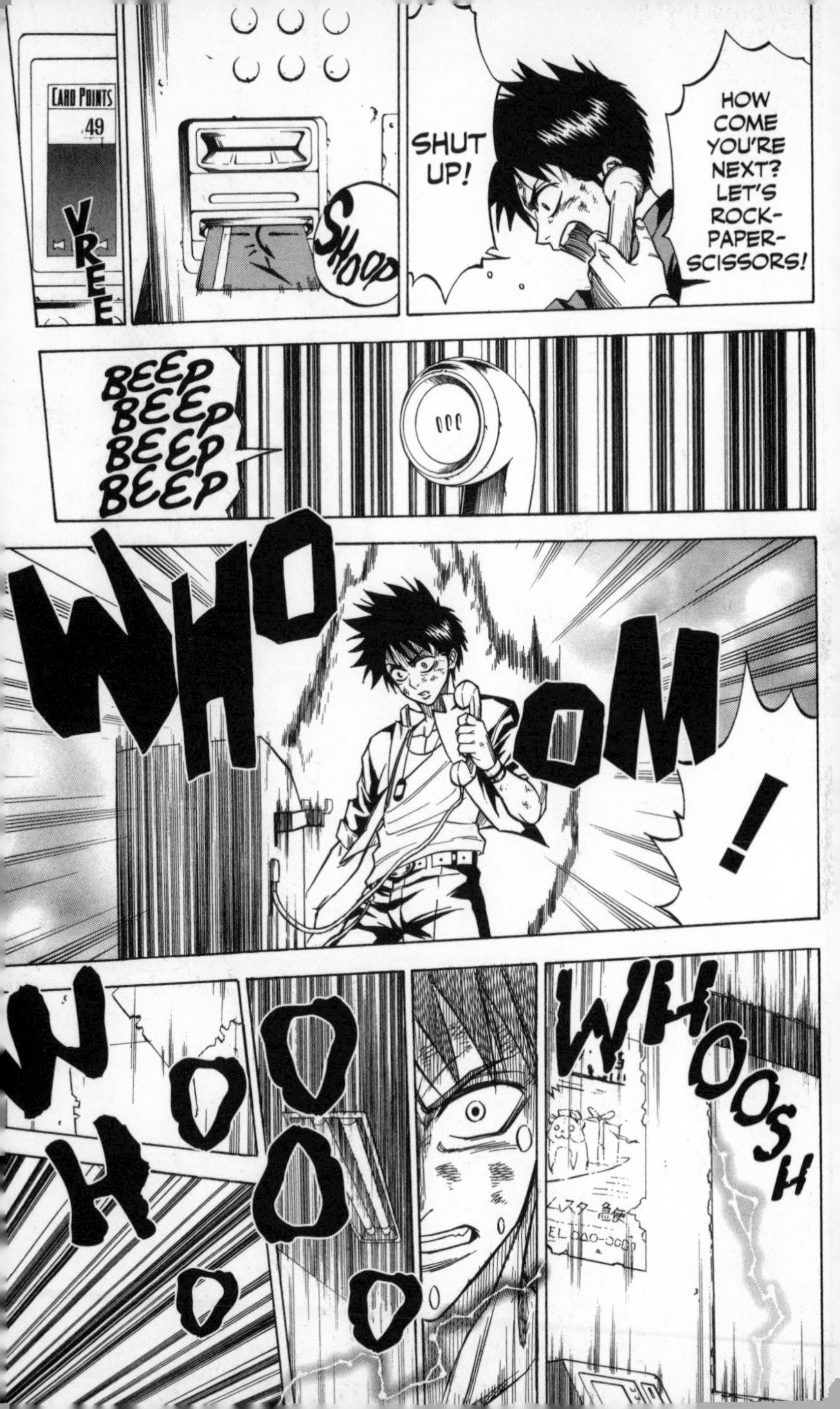
HOW COME YOU'RE NEXT? LET'S ROCK-PAPER-SCISSORS!
SHUT UP!
SHOOP
CARD POINTS
49
VREEE
BEEP BEEP BEEP BEEP
WHOOM!
WHOOSH
WHOOOOO

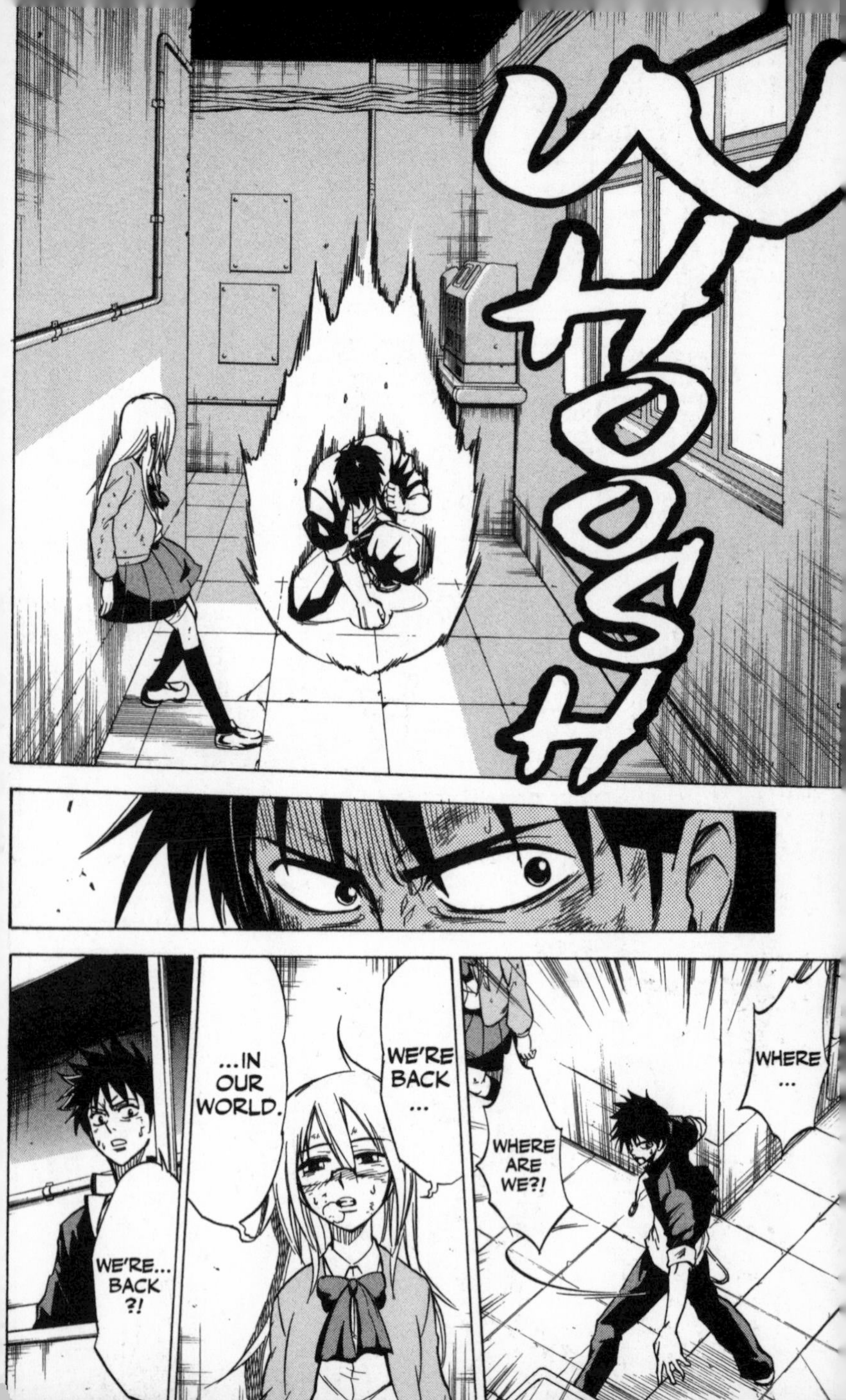
WHOOSH
WHERE...
WHERE ARE WE?!
WE'RE BACK...
...IN OUR WORLD.
WE'RE... BACK?!

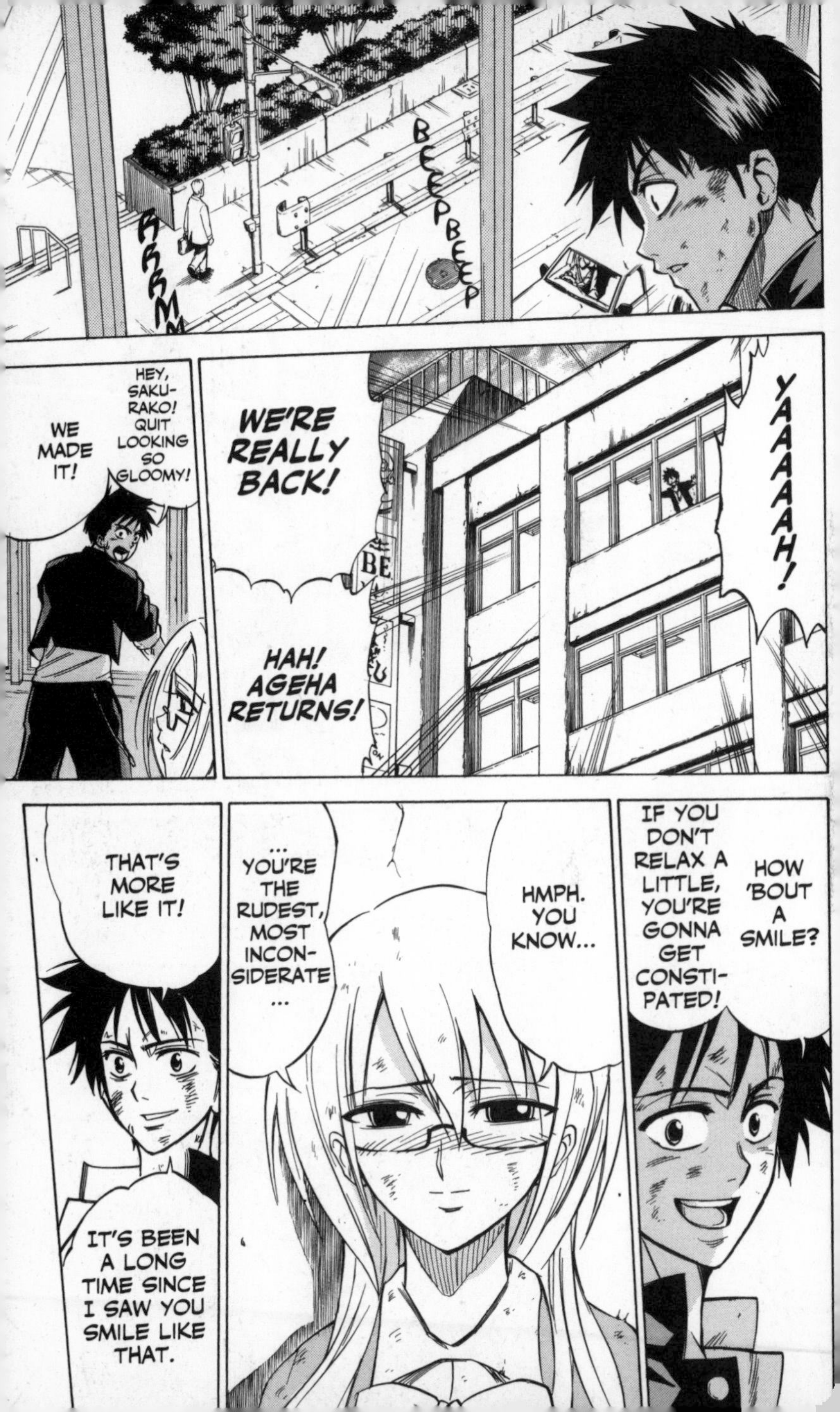
BEEPBEEP
RRRMM
YAAAAAH!
WE'RE REALLY BACK!
HAH! AGEHA RETURNS!
HEY, SAKU-RAKO! QUIT LOOKING SO GLOOMY!
WE MADE IT!
HOW 'BOUT A SMILE?
IF YOU DON'T RELAX A LITTLE, YOU'RE GONNA GET CONSTI-PATED!
HMPH. YOU KNOW...
... YOU'RE THE RUDEST, MOST INCON-SIDERATE ...
THAT'S MORE LIKE IT!
IT'S BEEN A LONG TIME SINCE I SAW YOU SMILE LIKE THAT.

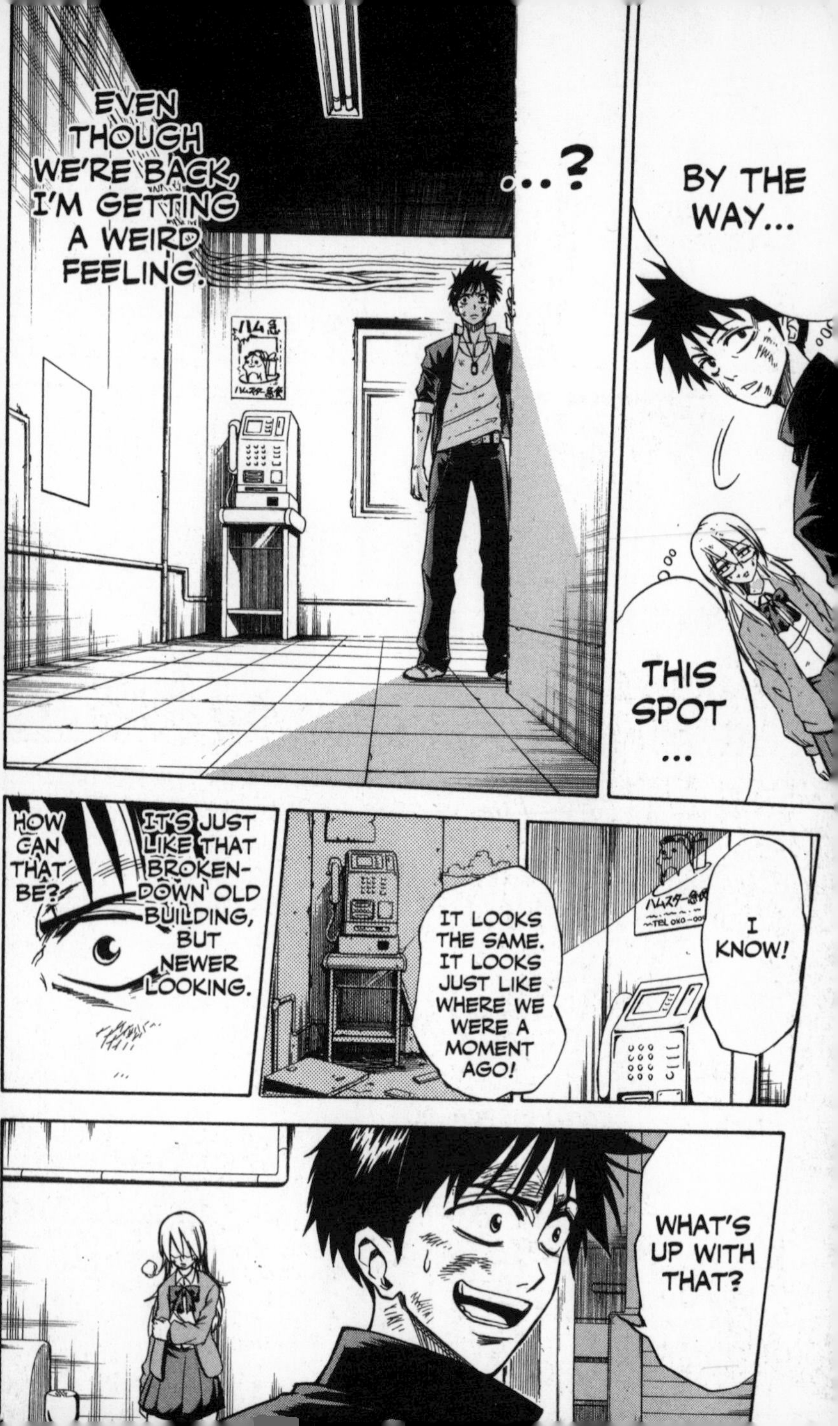
BY THE WAY...
THIS SPOT ...
...?
EVEN THOUGH WE'RE BACK, I'M GETTING A WEIRD FEELING.
I KNOW!
IT LOOKS THE SAME. IT LOOKS JUST LIKE WHERE WE WERE A MOMENT AGO!
IT'S JUST LIKE THAT BROKEN-DOWN OLD BUILDING, BUT NEWER LOOKING.
HOW CAN THAT BE?
WHAT'S UP WITH THAT?

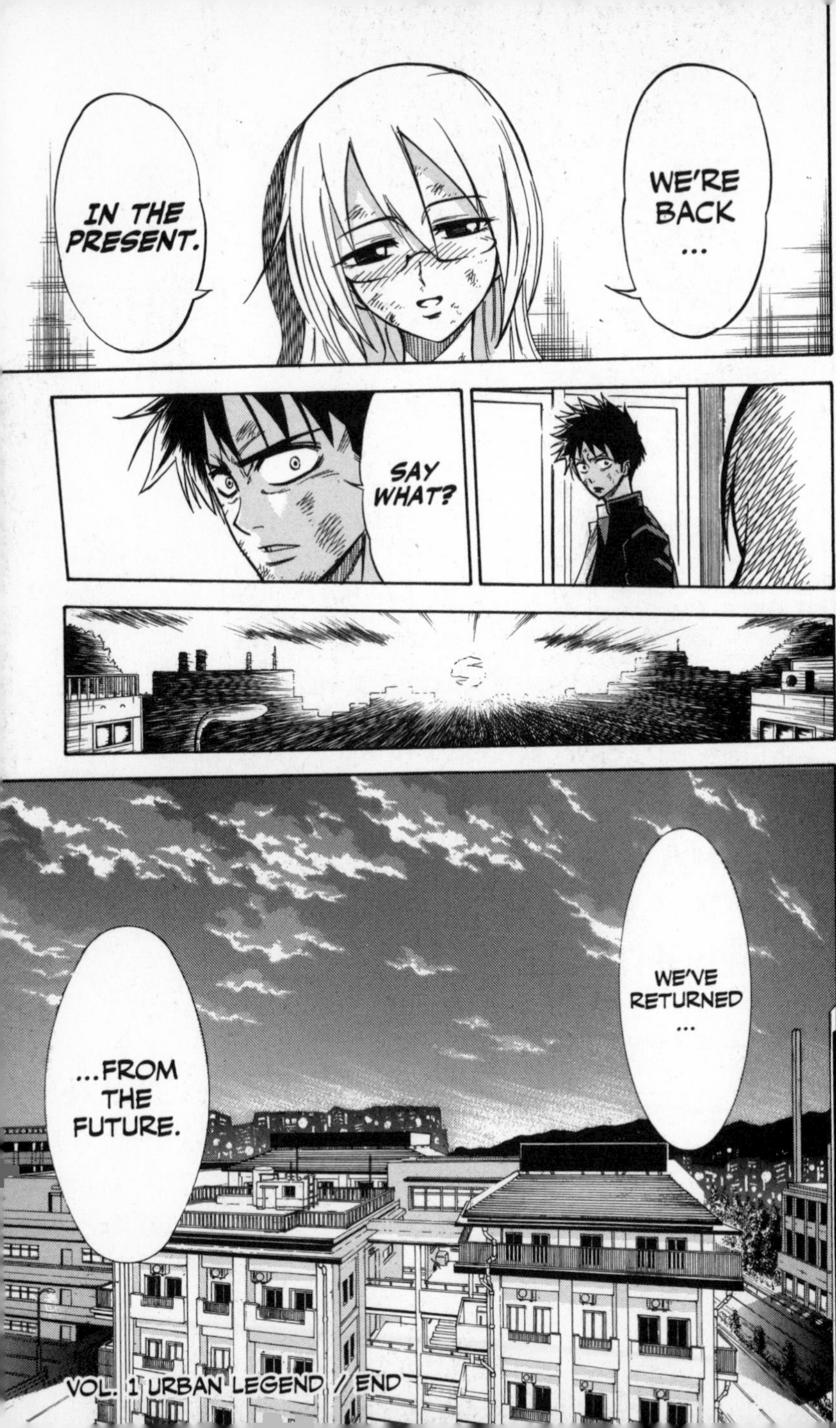
WE'RE BACK ...
IN THE PRESENT.
SAY WHAT?
WE'VE RETURNED ...
...FROM THE FUTURE.
VOL. 1 URBAN LEGEND / END

# Afterword

## VOLUME 1 IS OUT!

I WISH I COULD SHOUT IT AT THE
TOP OF MY LUNGS. AS YOU CAN TELL,
I'M PRETTY ECSTATIC RIGHT NOW AS
I WRITE THIS AFTERWORD.

IT'S BEEN ABOUT A YEAR SINCE I FINISHED MY
LAST PROJECT, *MIERU HITO*. I HAD SOME TIME TO
SPACE OUT AND PONDER WHAT I WANTED TO DO
DIFFERENTLY THIS TIME. THE RESULT IS *PSYREN*.
MY MOTTO FOR *PSYREN* IS, NO MATTER HOW ROUGH
IT GETS, I'M GOING TO HAVE FUN DRAWING THIS
MANGA. THAT'S THE LESSON I LEARNED LAST TIME.

WHEN I START COMPLAINING ABOUT HOW TIRED I AM,
I JUST FEEL WORSE. BUT IF I HOLD IT IN, I JUST TURN
INTO A BALL OF STRESS AND CAN'T EVEN HAVE
LIGHTHEARTED CONVERSATIONS WITH THE STAFF. MAN,
I'M WEAK! SO, THIS TIME, I'VE DECIDED JUST TO SHOUT...

## "HA HA HA!
## I'M WAAAAAY BEHIND!"
## [LAUGHTER]

...WHILE BURSTING OUT LAUGHING, THUS TOTALLY
CREEPING OUT THE STAFF.

THAT IS THE BEST METHOD.

I HOPE YOU WILL CONTINUE TO READ *PSYREN*.

TOSHIAKI IWASHIRO
APRIL 2008

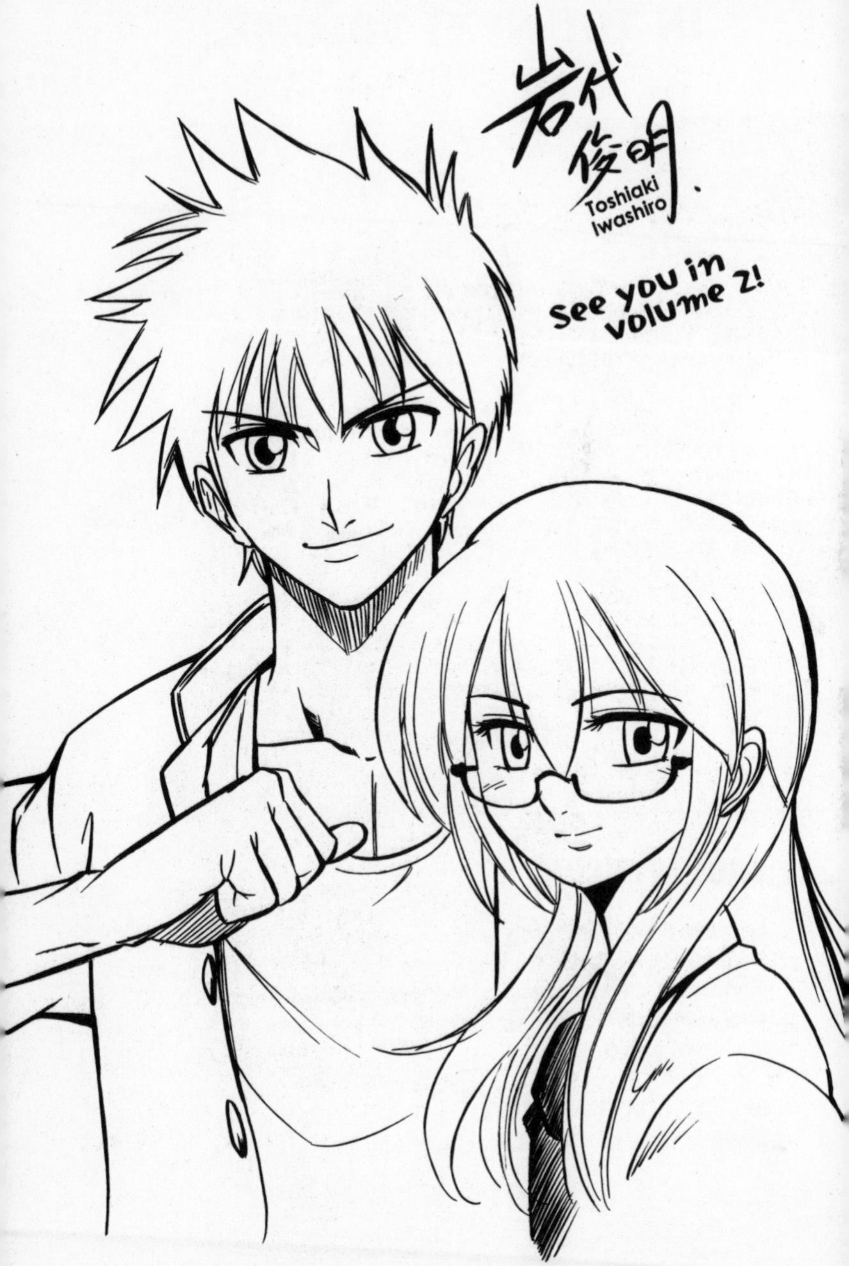
岩代俊明
Toshiaki Iwashiro
See you in volume 2!

# IN THE NEXT VOLUME...

## BABY UNIVERSE

After surviving his first trip to Psyren, Ageha suffers nosebleeds and a high fever, signifying the awakening of his psionic powers! Several days later, Sakurako summons Ageha telepathically to meet her PSI mentor, Matsuri Yagumo, who reveals to Ageha the terrifying rules of the Psyren game!

**Available JANUARY 2012!**
**Read it first in SHONEN JUMP magazine!**

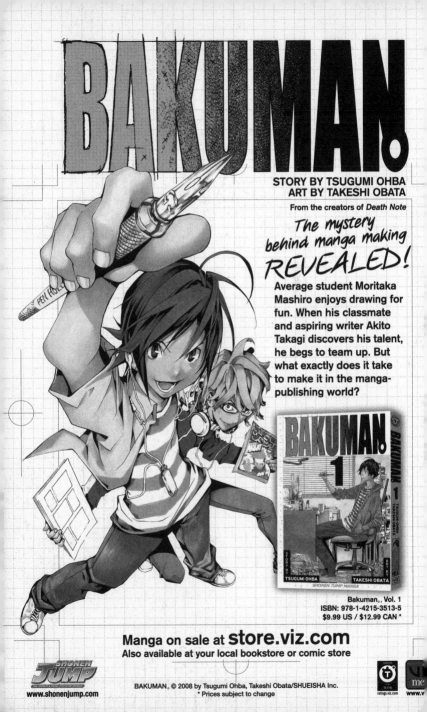

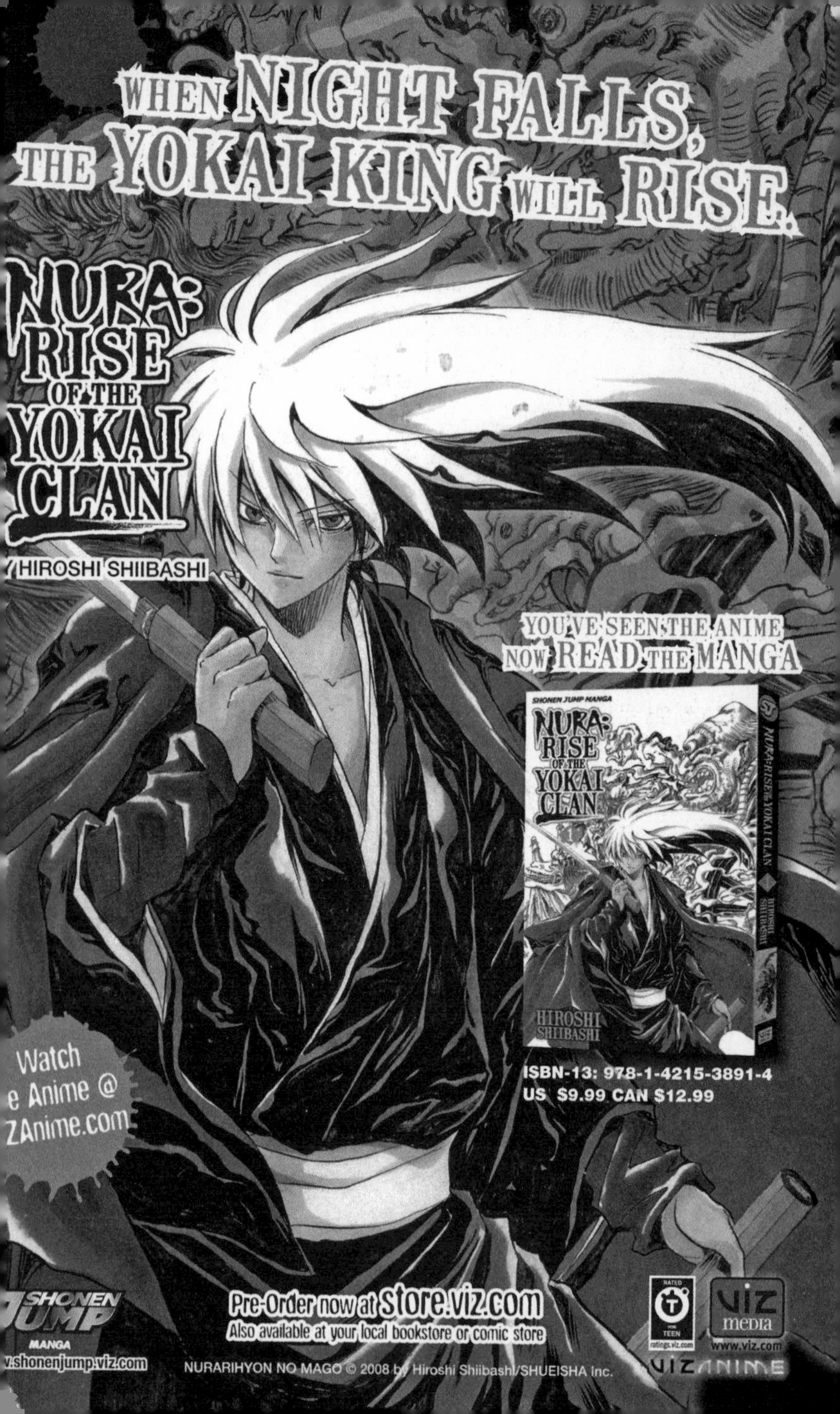

WHEN NIGHT FALLS, THE YOKAI KING WILL RISE.
NURA: RISE OF THE YOKAI CLAN
HIROSHI SHIIBASHI
YOU'VE SEEN THE ANIME NOW READ THE MANGA
SHONEN JUMP MANGA
NURA: RISE OF THE YOKAI CLAN
1
HIROSHI SHIIBASHI
ISBN-13: 978-1-4215-3891-4
US $9.99 CAN $12.99
Watch
e Anime @
ZAnime.com
SHONEN JUMP
MANGA
.shonenjump.viz.com
Pre-Order now at store.viz.com
Also available at your local bookstore or comic store
RATED
T
TEEN
ratings.viz.com
viz media
www.viz.com
NURARIHYON NO MAGO © 2008 by Hiroshi Shiibashi/SHUEISHA Inc.
VIZ ANIME